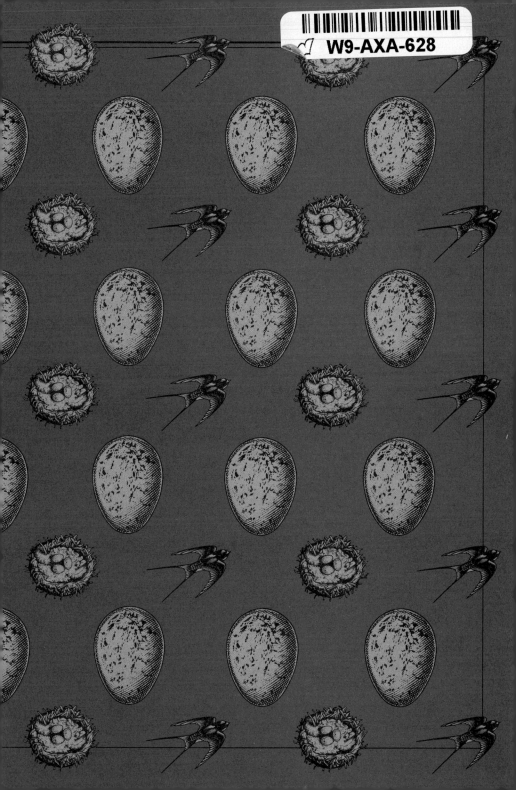

EYEWITNESS ● HANDBOOKS

BIRDS'
EGGS

EYEWITNESS ◉ HANDBOOKS

BIRDS' EGGS

MICHAEL WALTERS

Photography by
HARRY TAYLOR
(Natural History Museum, London)

Editorial Consultant
MARK ROBBINS
(Academy of Natural Sciences of Philadelphia)

DORLING KINDERSLEY
London • New York • Stuttgart

A DORLING KINDERSLEY BOOK

Publisher's Note
While every effort has been made to reproduce the exact tones and colors of
the individual eggs in this book, not even the most sophisticated technology
can consistently capture the subtleties of nature's art. We request the
reader's forbearance where these have proven elusive.

Project Editor Bella Pringle
Designers James Culver, Sharon Moore
Assistant Editor Lucinda Hawksley
Series Editor Jonathan Metcalf
Series Art Editor Spencer Holbrook
Production Controller Caroline Webber
U.S. Consultant Mark Robbins
U.S. Editor Charles A. Wills

First American Edition 1994
2 4 6 8 10 9 7 5 3 1

Published in the United States by Dorling Kindersley, Inc.,
95 Madison Avenue, New York 10016

Library of Congress Cataloging-in-Publication Data

Walters, Michael
Birds' eggs/by Michael Walters: photography by Harry Taylor.--1st American ed.
p. cm -- (Eyewitness handbooks)
Includes index.
ISBN 1-56458-178-0 (hardcover). -- ISBN 1-56458-175-6 (flexibinding)
1. Birds--Eggs. I. Title. II. Series.
QL675.W32 1994
598.233--dc20   92-53468 CIP

Computer page makeup by Adam Moore
Text film output by The Right Type, Great Britain
Reproduced by Colourscan, Singapore
Printed and bound by Kyodo Printing Co., Singapore

Note on Classification
The bird classification system employed in this handbook was based on
that used in Michael Walters, *The Complete Birds of the World* (David and
Charles, 1980). This in turn was based (with modifications) on J.L. Peters,
Checklist of Birds of the World (Harvard University Press, vols 1–6;
Museum of Comparative Zoology, vols 7–15; 1930–1986).

CONTENTS

AUTHOR'S INTRODUCTION

The hard shells of birds' eggs perform the vital function of protecting the developing embryo during incubation. They also provide clues to bird identification and the evolution of the species, but in addition they are beautiful objects in their own right, exhibiting a stunning array of colors, patterns, textures, and shapes.

B IRDS' EGGS HAVE BEEN admired for hundreds of years as objects of beauty. In the Middle Ages, eggshells were strung together and hung in decorative festoons. By the 18th century, eggs increasingly began to be prized as collectors' pieces and were displayed in cabinets to protect them from the sun's bleaching rays. These cabinets of eggs graced the drawing rooms of many nature-loving Victorians. Ostrich eggs were especially popular. Their thick shells could be carved to reveal layers of cream and ivory, then mounted in silver. In Imperial Russia, the jeweler Fabergé lined the inside of goose eggs with richly colored silk fabric and mounted these eggs in ostentatious jeweled stands.

EGGS IN PAINTING
In the 19th century, the popularity of birds' eggs and nests made them an attractive and profitable subject for still-life artists.

SCIENTIFIC STUDY

Naturalists began to collect eggs for scientific study in the 19th century, but surprisingly the eggs and nests of one third of the world's approximately 10,000 bird species have never been found or described. By studying eggs,

scientists have been able to uncover fascinating clues about the evolution of bird species and the relationships between bird families. And it was the study of birds' eggs that proved that the pervasive effects of pesticides such as DDT had reached crisis levels. Today, eggs are still the subject of scientific scrutiny, but those engaged in such study are more likely to work with a notebook and a camera than a collecting bag. Many countries have laws that prohibit collecting eggs or disturbing nesting birds, especially threatened or endangered species.

A UNIQUE DISPLAY

With the prohibition of egg collecting, the purpose of this book is to enable the reader to enjoy the beauty of eggs. No eggs were collected for this book; all the eggs shown here come from an existing museum collection. Many of the specimens are quite old and a few are the only surviving examples of the eggs of species that are now extinct. The eggs chosen for this book comprise the full range of colors, patterns, and shapes. If all members of a family lay nearly identical eggs, only one representative is shown. For those bird families whose eggs exhibit a wider range of colors, patterns, and shapes, we have tried to include a comprehensive selection. Where possible, we show the eggs of at least one species in each bird family. There are a few families for which no eggs are available to be photographed, because they have never been studied or because specimens are extremely rare. Wherever possible, descriptions of those eggs are included in the table on pp.20–25, which briefly outlines the appearance of the eggs of each bird family.

EGG COLOR

In a number of specimens, especially the blue and green, the color of the eggs is extremely subtle, and color photography is not always able to reproduce precisely the delicate shades of the original. All instances where the reproduced color deviates significantly from that of the original are indicated in the text. It is also important to remember that many of the eggs in museum collections have faded over time and would have been much brighter when newly laid. For example, the bright blue pigments of the Sparrowhawk's (see p.57) and the Goshawk's eggs (see p.59) disappears over a period of 20 years, leaving the shells white. In addition, a number of specimen eggs in collections that now have white shells once had a distinct and very beautiful pink flush when seen in the nest. In most cases this flush is not pigment but is due to the contents of the egg – the yolk and the embryo – showing through the shell and creating the impression of a pink hue. The lack of contents in these "blown" specimen eggs makes their shells appear lighter in color than fresh eggs. This should be taken into account when looking at the specimens.

EGGS IN PRINT
Few books on birds' eggs have ever been produced. These illustrative plates from different 19th-century publications show early attempts to represent the wide range of egg colors and patterns in print.

GREAT AUK
The flightless Great Auk, like the Dodo, became extinct in the early 19th century, and only about 75 of its eggs are known to have survived. Because of the rarity of these large eggs, they command exceptionally high prices at auctions.

OSTRICH EGG
These eggs were highly prized in the 19th century. They were often carved in cameo style and mounted in ornate silver settings.

Some species, such as the Ostrich (see p.26) and the strange Guira Cuckoo (see p.130), lay eggs that are distinctive and therefore easy to identify, but these are the exception rather than the rule. In many cases it is impossible to identify a bird's egg just by studying its color and shape. Many families, such as parrots, pigeons, bee-eaters, owls, and wood-peckers, lay pure white eggs that are indistinguishable from species to species except for their size. Furthermore, birds such as cuckoos, who lay their eggs in the nests of other birds, exhibit a wide range of egg color and pattern within each species. We have included information about each bird's breeding habits, nest site and nest structure, egg size, clutch size, and which parent bird incubates the egg (whether the male or female or both). The time required for incubation, and the bird's geographical range, during the breeding season and in winter, are also given within many of the species entries.

CONSERVATION

It is important to stress that this book is intended as a display case, not as a field guide. All the eggs shown on the following pages were photographed at London's Natural History Museum collection, and were not taken from birds' nests in the wild. Never disturb or harass nesting birds; your presence will prevent the parents from incubating their eggs, and your tracks may alert predators to a nest site they might otherwise have overlooked. If the disturbance is prolonged the birds may even abandon the nest, leaving it to the intruder so that they can breed again elsewhere. In Europe, the Osprey almost became extinct as a result of people disturbing nests and stealing eggs.

EDGE OF EXTINCTION

For many years the Osprey was endangered or extirpated in parts of its nearly worldwide range. Now protected by laws that enforce severe penalties for egg theft, the species has slowly begun to recover and is now no longer on the verge of extinction.

HOW THIS BOOK WORKS

THIS BOOK is divided into just two sections: non-passerines (all orders of birds except Passeriformes), which are shown on pp. 26–143; and then passerines (birds of the order Passeriformes, also known as the "perching birds") follow on pp.144–249. Within these sections, the eggs are arranged in family groups. Information relating to each species is shown in the color bands. The eggs are shown at actual size and distinctive features are highlighted by annotation. The sample page below shows how a typical species entry is organized.

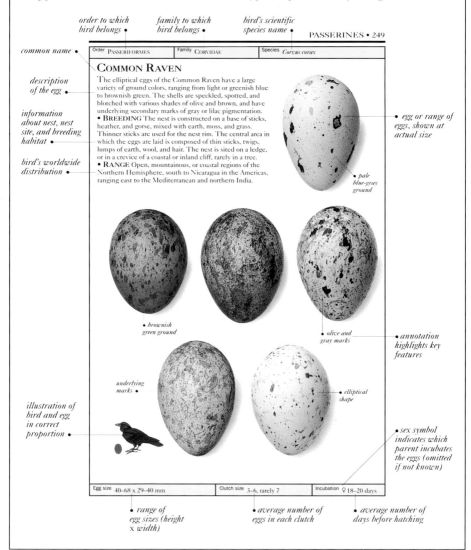

order to which bird belongs •

family to which bird belongs •

bird's scientific species name •

PASSERINES • 249

common name •

| Order PASSERIFORMES | Family CORVIDAE | Species *Corvus corax* |

COMMON RAVEN

description of the egg •

The elliptical eggs of the Common Raven have a large variety of ground colors, ranging from light or greenish blue to brownish green. The shells are speckled, spotted, and blotched with various shades of olive and brown, and have underlying secondary marks of gray or lilac pigmentation.

information about nest, nest site, and breeding habitat •

• BREEDING The nest is constructed on a base of sticks, heather, and gorse, mixed with earth, moss, and grass. Thinner sticks are used for the nest rim. The central area in which the eggs are laid is composed of thin sticks, twigs, lumps of earth, wool, and hair. The nest is sited on a ledge, or in a crevice of a coastal or inland cliff, rarely in a tree.

bird's worldwide distribution •

• RANGE Open, mountainous, or coastal regions of the Northern Hemisphere, south to Nicaragua in the Americas, ranging east to the Mediterranean and northern India.

• egg or range of eggs, shown at actual size

• pale blue-gray ground

• brownish green ground

• olive and gray marks

• annotation highlights key features

underlying marks •

• elliptical shape

illustration of bird and egg in correct proportion •

• sex symbol indicates which parent incubates the eggs (omitted if not known)

| Egg size 40–68 x 29–40 mm | Clutch size 3–6, rarely 7 | Incubation ♀ 18–20 days |

• range of egg sizes (height x width)

• average number of eggs in each clutch

• average number of days before hatching

WHAT IS AN EGG?

ALL ANIMALS can be described as being either viviparous, bearing live young, or oviparous, bearing young in the form of eggs. Most groups of animals include both viviparous and oviparous species, but all birds are oviparous. This has an obvious advantage for a flying creature because the female is not hampered by carrying heavy young.

By producing young inside eggs, she can void them from her body at a much earlier stage of development than a mammal can with its young.

INSIDE THE EGG

The main structures of an egg are the yolk, the albumen (or egg white), and the shell. The fertilized egg cell (from

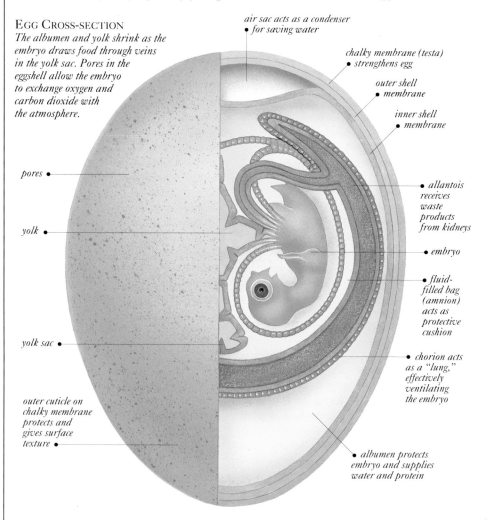

EGG CROSS-SECTION
The albumen and yolk shrink as the embryo draws food through veins in the yolk sac. Pores in the eggshell allow the embryo to exchange oxygen and carbon dioxide with the atmosphere.

air sac acts as a condenser for saving water

chalky membrane (testa) strengthens egg

outer shell membrane

inner shell membrane

pores

yolk

yolk sac

outer cuticle on chalky membrane protects and gives surface texture

allantois receives waste products from kidneys

embryo

fluid-filled bag (amnion) acts as protective cushion

chorion acts as a "lung," effectively ventilating the embryo

albumen protects embryo and supplies water and protein

OTHER EGG-LAYING CREATURES

Birds are not the only creatures that lay eggs. Amphibians lay simple jelly-covered eggs in water, but the embryo goes through a larval stage to complete its development. Reptiles lay plain white, soft- or hard-shelled eggs that are similar in structure to birds' eggs, in that they both contain a yolk. The eggs of turtles, lizards, and snakes are much softer than those of birds, because they have not developed a hard calcium shell. For this reason, these eggs are often buried in the sand for protection. Tortoises and crocodiles, however, lay eggs with a hard shell. These appear semitranslucent, in contrast to the opaque shells of birds'.

LIZARDS' EGGS

Lizards' eggs, unlike those of birds, are soft and leathery, though crocodiles and tortoises lay eggs with hard shells.

which the embryo forms) is part of the yolk and sits on its upper surface. The yolk is rich in fat and proteins, and provides the food required by the developing embryo. It is able to rotate to keep the embryo upright. As the egg cell moves down the oviduct (see diagram on p.15) it is coated in albumen for protection. The egg is then enclosed by a hard shell of calcium.

HARD SHELL

Eggshells are very tough and provide good protection from predators. The idea that all birds' eggs are delicate, fragile objects comes from our familiarity with the eggs of domestic chickens. The egg of a chicken has been selectively bred to produce larger and larger eggs. Thus the egg of a domesticated chicken is two or three times as large as the egg of its ancestor, the Red Junglefowl. The amount of shell material has not increased, however, so the same amount of shell material is stretched thinly over a much larger surface, making it thin and fragile.

The shell is covered by an outer cuticle which strengthens the shell and acts as a protective barrier against harmful bacteria. It is this cuticle that gives eggs their texture, whether smooth, glossy, chalky, or "soapy." But protecting the developing embryo is not the only function of the eggshell: through its pores it allows the passage of oxygen, carbon dioxide, and water vapor, thus permitting the chick to "breathe."

HOLE-NESTING BIRDS

Birds that nest in holes, like this kingfisher, often lay white eggs. This may help the birds to see their eggs more easily in the dark.

EGG SHAPE AND SIZE

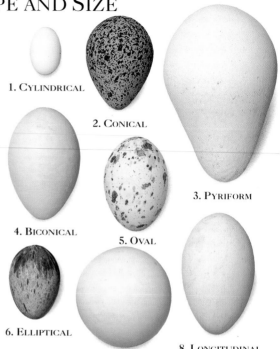

1. CYLINDRICAL

2. CONICAL

3. PYRIFORM

4. BICONICAL

5. OVAL

6. ELLIPTICAL

7. SPHERICAL

8. LONGITUDINAL

WHEN YOU LOOK closely at a group of eggs, it soon becomes clear that there is a great deal of variation in both shape and size, and that no two birds' eggs are exactly alike.

VARIATIONS IN SHAPE

It is incorrect to suppose that all eggs are "egg-shaped." They vary greatly, from the almost spherical eggs of owls and kingfishers to the cylindrical eggs of hummingbirds and some albatrosses. Never is there complete uniformity within a particular species. Also, egg shapes for a species or family can be expressed only in general terms, for even eggs in the same clutch may vary in shape. For example, the eggs laid by grebes are generally described as being biconical in shape, but in fact they may also be elliptical, cylindrical, or longitudinal. However, in cases where the shape of the egg is extremely important to the survival of the offspring, there is less variation. For example, the Common Murre (see p.121) lays elongated, pyriform eggs. This allows the eggs to roll around in circles rather than rolling off the precipitous cliff ledges on which they are laid.

LAPWING EGGS
These conical eggs can be packed closely together in the nest so that they all receive maximum warmth from the parent bird.

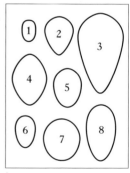

SHAPE CLASSIFICATION
There are several methods that are used to classify egg shapes. One of the simplest, shown above and on the right, recognizes the eight basic shapes. This method has been adopted for this book.

EGG SIZE

Like shape, egg size varies a great deal. The standard unit of measurement for bird egg dimensions, as used throughout this book, is the millimeter. Broadly speaking, the larger the bird, the larger the egg. Thus, the smallest birds, the hummingbirds, lay the smallest eggs, whereas the largest living bird, the Ostrich, lays the largest. The Ostrich egg, however, is one of the smallest eggs when compared with the bird's body size, whereas the hummingbird's egg is one of the largest. The egg of the Kiwi is the largest, relative to body size, of any living bird. Parasitic cuckoos, which make no nests of their own but lay their eggs in the nests of other birds, lay very small eggs for their size, because these eggs have evolved to match the size of the smaller host species. The extinct Elephant Bird of Madagascar laid a single egg measuring 340 x 245 mm, very much larger than that of the Ostrich (maximum 175 x 145 mm), even though the bird itself was not significantly larger.

Also, the eggs of altricial species, which hatch in a relatively un-developed state, generally weigh less than the eggs of precocial species, which mature further within the egg, though the mother birds may be of a similar size.

SURFACE QUALITIES

Another factor subject to great variation is the surface texture of an egg. Most species of birds lay eggs with smooth shells, but the surface can vary from dull to highly glossy. (No definite distinc-tion can be drawn between these though, because a large range of surface qualities occurs between these two types.) For example, the eggs of tinamous have shells that are exceptionally glossy, similar to glazed china; duck eggs have a greasy or "soapy" surface

texture; whereas some eggs laid by cormorants and grebes have a white chalky outer layer deposited over the actual shell. (The powdery outer layer of the eggs of flamingoes, however, is associated with a fatty deposit beneath the shell surface.)

OSTRICH EGG

RUFOUS HUMMINGBIRD EGGS

VARIATIONS IN SIZE
Egg sizes range from the minute eggs of the Rufous Hummingbird (left) to the huge Ostrich egg (above), the largest in the world.

EGG COLOR AND PATTERN

THE MANY COLOR COMBINATIONS and patterns found in the shells of birds' eggs, together with the large number of white eggs, has led ornithologists to propose many explanations for the variety. The eggs of reptiles, from which birds are descended, are always white and unmarked, and for this reason, bird species that lay plain white eggs are thought to be older and more primitive in evolutionary terms. However, a species may have gained and lost shell pigment several times over the millennia. Because white or pale blue eggs are usually laid by birds that nest in holes or covered nests, it is thought that pale-colored eggs enable the parent birds to see their eggs more clearly in a dark environment. Birds that cover their eggs with vegetation when leaving the nest site, such as ducks and grebes, or those birds that rarely leave their eggs unattended, such as owls, pigeons, and

white grebe's egg stained by • vegetation

NEST STAINS
Grebes lay white eggs, but when leaving the nest they cover the eggs with vegetation, which slowly decays, staining the chalky covering.

penguins, also lay white or plain eggs. They do not need color or patterned shells to conceal their eggs from potential enemies because they are hidden from view or fiercely guarded.

COLOR PIGMENTS
The pigments that color eggshells are related to the red blood pigment hemoglobin, and are of two kinds. One is a bluish green pigment derived from bile, and, when present, occurs throughout the shell structure. Depending on the strength of the pigment, the basic shell color may appear white or blue. The other pigment is in fact a group of tints that produces a range of colors, from yellow and pink to reddish buffs, browns, and black. These are often

OLIVE-GREEN

WHITE

ORANGE

BLUE-GRAY

RED

COLOR VARIATIONS
All shell colors are created by just two pigments. The color varies in strength according to whether it is on the surface or in deeper layers.

concentrated on the shell surface, and small quantities produce a buff- or yellow-colored egg. When red and blue pigments mix, a range of colors from violet to olive-green results.

Many strongly colored and patterned eggs tend to belong to birds like waders that nest in exposed sites on the ground. For these birds, egg color is necessary for camouflage. Furthermore, birds that nest in large colonies, such as guillemots, lay eggs with individual patterns, which may enable the parent birds to recognize them as their own.

SHELL MARKINGS

The size and shape of shell markings vary greatly. They may be irregular, round, or streaky, or, less often, vein- or hairlike. Some markings are added to the shell surface as the egg is laid, whereas others are formed in deeper layers. The latter are known as "underlying" or "secondary" marks. On white shells, these show through on the surface as gray or pink; on blue shells they appear mauve.

HOW COLOR IS ADDED

single ovum passes down oviduct •

ovum is coated in albumen •

• *shell membranes are added in isthmus*

pigmented egg is expelled •

egg moves into uterus to receive pigment •

EGG PIGMENTATION
The shell is formed in the isthmus and receives pigment when it enters the uterus.

CAMOUFLAGE
The beautiful eggs of the Ringed Plover (Charadrius hiaticula) closely resemble stones, and are thus well camouflaged on the pebbly shores where they breed. The eggs are laid in a scrape in an exposed site.

CAP OF COLOR

LARGE SPOTS

SPECKLES

STREAKS

EGG PATTERNS
Pigments produce a variety of patterns on shells. If pigment is added when the egg is stationary, spots result; if added when moving, streaks are produced.

SCRAWLS

BREEDING AND HATCHING

MOST BIRDS BREED in spring. The breeding season coincides with the time of year when food is plentiful, so there is a ready supply for the chicks. The availability of food influences the clutch size and the number of broods the parents rear in each breeding season. In parts of the Southern Hemisphere, such as central Australia, where rain and food supply vary greatly from year to year, birds may not breed at all when conditions are unfavorable.

THE BREEDING CYCLE

How do birds time their breeding cycle so that the food supply is at its peak when the young hatch? Most likely, they respond to changes in day length, breeding when days grow longer in the spring. In the tropics, however, day length changes little with the seasons. Thus, tropical birds are under less pressure to breed at a specific time, and many breed at any time of the year. Others breed at specific intervals. The tropical Sooty Tern, for example, breeds at nine-month intervals. The majority of non-passerines and larger passerines breed only once a year, because their long breeding cycles

THE DAILY CYCLE OF A BREEDING SPARROW

1. The female sparrow lays her fully formed egg in the early morning.

5. At dusk, the female returns to roost her egg.

BREAKING FREE OF THE SHELL
The time it takes for a chick to hatch, from the first chipping of the shell (below left) to the emergence of the chick (below far right), varies from half an hour in small birds to several hours in larger species. In some species, hatching is assisted by an "egg tooth" on the bill that is lost after birth. Parents may eat the discarded shell to absorb calcium, or carry it away to foil predators.

preclude a second brood. However, many smaller birds breed two or three times in each breeding season. The California Condor and Harpy Eagle, which have a nesting cycle of more than a year, can only breed in alternate years.

INCUBATION

The embryo must stay warm if it is to develop inside the egg. Because embryonic chicks do not produce enough metabolic heat during development to sustain themselves, the parent must supply warmth, which it usually does by sitting on the eggs. Most species of bird have a "brood patch," an area on the breast that loses most of its feathers and becomes suffused with blood vessels during the breeding season. If the egg or eggs are kept in contact with the brood patch, their temperature is raised to near body temperature. In hotter climates, parent birds may not need to spend so much time covering their eggs. The part played by the sexes in incubation differs from species to species, from equal sharing to incubation by one sex only. The amount of time spent sitting on the nest also varies.

HATCHING

"Precocial" chicks hatch at an advanced stage of development and are nearly or totally independent. "Altricial" chicks, on the other hand, are born blind, have little or no down, and are unable to walk or regulate body temperature. Altricial chicks require a long period of parental care before they can leave the nest. In precocial species, incubation begins after the last egg is laid. The chicks all hatch and leave the nest together. In many altricial species, incubation begins with the first egg, and the chicks hatch in sequence.

KING PENGUIN

The King Penguin roosts its eggs on its feet. The eggs are kept warm by heat from the feet and from an overlying flap of skin and feathers. During incubation, the parent remains standing upright.

2. The female leaves her nest in search of food.

3. The female must feed all day to build up protein to form the next egg.

4. Snail shells provide calcium for the eggshell.

NESTS

CONTRARY TO POPULAR BELIEF, birds do not live in nests. The nest is used only when caring for the eggs and nestlings. Not all birds build nests: many lay their eggs on the bare ground, or in the nests of other birds (either in old and disused nests, or by evicting their rightful owners). Some birds, such as the Fairy Tern, lay their eggs on the bare branches of trees. The "typical" birds' nest, a cup skillfully woven of twigs and leaves and snugly lined with soft materials, is actually the exception rather than the rule. This type of nest is constructed only by perching birds, and not even by all those species.

NEST BUILDING

In many cases, the materials used to build a nest are indiscriminately chosen, depending on what is available to the bird. Artificial materials such as string, bits of plastic, or nylon are often used. One nest of a House Sparrow was found to be made entirely from pieces of wire. Most large birds either construct an untidy, ugly heap of sticks, or plant stalks, or nest in a scrape on bare ground. Occasionally, the birds may choose to nest in an existing unlined hole in a tree. Empty nests, however, are difficult to identify, even though there are clues in the type of materials used, the structure, and chosen nest site. The only way to be certain of the species' identity is by observing the parent birds themselves, from a safe distance.

MUD

TWIGS

STICKS

CUP NEST
Simple passerine cup nests are built with materials such as twigs, leaves, grass, moss, or a combination of these, and lined with softer insulating material such as hair, feathers, or mud. The materials vary according to what is readily available.

PLATFORM NEST
Grebes, some ducks, and various other aquatic birds build platforms of vegetation floating on water. A heap of vegetation insulates the eggs and compensates for changing water levels.

THE PURPOSE OF NESTS

Some birds use nests primarily to incubate their eggs and keep them warm overnight when the temperature drops. By keeping their eggs warm, birds have been more successful than their reptilian predecessors at spreading out from the tropics into regions with cooler climates. Even in the extreme climate of Antarctica, the Emperor Penguin has adapted to survive and breed at sub-zero temperatures. The main advantage of incubation for all birds is that it reduces the time the egg needs to develop, so the eggs are vulnerable to predators for the minimum period of time. The nest structure also helps prevent eggs from rolling out of trees.

COMMUNAL NESTING

Some birds choose to breed in colonies. The small Sociable Weaver of Africa works in large groups to build a communal roof to protect the incubating eggs from sun, rain, and the eyes of predators. The Village Weaver (shown above) breeds during the rainy season, in colonies in isolated trees, often in or around villages. The bird's oval nest is made of strips of grass, reeds, sedges, and palm leaves. The pointed shape of the roof helps divert rain water off the nest and keeps it dry, while a short entrance spout protects the eggs from predators such as snakes, which are unable to enter. Each nest in the colony is fastened to the drooping end of a long branch. This keeps the eggs out of reach of other predators, who are unable to gain access to such a precarious position.

HOLE-NEST

Birds such as parrots, hornbills, woodpeckers, and bee-eaters choose to nest in holes, either in trees, rocks, the ground, or termite nests. In hole-nests the young are safer from attacks by mammals, and have a better chance of survival.

SCRAPE NEST

Many birds nest in a simple scrape in the ground, or in a depression formed by the sitting bird. Lining material may be added.

NEST TYPES

There is great variation in nest structure. A nest can be a simple mound, where eggs are buried in the ground and are incubated by the sun rather than by the parent birds sitting on the eggs. It can be a hole, where eggs are incubated in an enclosed cavity or burrow; an open nest, which may be a scrape, platform, cup, or bowl; or it can be a dome or a multi-chambered nest with an elaborately constructed roof.

BIRD FAMILIES

ALL THE WORLD'S BIRDS are classified in scientific orders which are made up of families, then smaller groupings called genera, and finally species. The main part of this book describes the eggs of individual species, but very often the eggs of birds from the same family share common features. In this section, the characteristic appearance of the eggs of each family, grouped by order, are described by shape, color, markings, and texture, as applicable.

STRUTHIONIFORMES *Ratites*
STRUTHIONIDAE *Ostriches* Almost spherical in shape; creamy porcelain-white ground color; shell pitted with visible pores.
RHEIDAE *Rheas* Longitudinal; white/yellowish ground color.
CASUARIIDAE *Cassowaries* Longitudinal in shape; green ground color; shell covered with series of raised pimples.
DROMAIIDAE *Emus* Longitudinal; dark green; turn black.
APTERYGIDAE *Kiwis* Longitudinal shape; white; unmarked.

RED-WINGED TINAMOU

TINAMIFORMES *Tinamous*
TINAMIDAE *Tinamous* Oval/spherical; blue/green/reddish/purple.

GREAT-CRESTED GREBE

SPHENISCIFORMES *Penguins*
SPHENISCIDAE *Penguins* Sharply pyriform in shape; plain white ground color; unmarked but usually nest-stained.

GAVIIFORMES *Divers*
GAVIIDAE *Loons* Elliptical; dark brown; black spots.

WANDERING ALBATROSS

PODICIPEDIFORMES *Grebes*
PODICIPEDIDAE *Grebes* Elliptical/longitudinal/biconical; white ground color when laid; stained to buffish brown in the nest.

PROCELLARIIFORMES *Tube-nosed Swimmers*
DIOMEDEIDAE *Albatrosses* Longitudinal/cylindrical in shape; white/stone ground color; pale flecks, nest-stained.
PROCELLARIIDAE *Petrels, Shearwaters* Elliptical/ longitudinal/pyriform/conical in shape; white ground color; unmarked.
HYDROBATIDAE *Storm-Petrels* Oval/elliptical; white with dots.
PELECANOIDAE *Diving-Petrels* Similar to Hydrobatidae.

PELECANIFORMES *Pelicans, Allies*
PHAETHONTIDAE *Tropicbirds* Oval/elliptical; white/pink/purplish gray; dark red/brown blotches or thick speckles.
PELECANIDAE *Pelicans* Elliptical in shape; white; nest-stained.
SULIDAE *Gannets, Boobies* Elliptical in shape; white/pale blue ground color; white chalky covering on surface of shell.
PHALACROCORACIDAE *Cormorants* Elliptical/longitudinal in shape; plain blue ground color; white chalky shell covering.
ANHINGIDAE *Darters* Elliptical/longitudinal in shape; pale blue ground color; no shell markings; white chalky surface cover.
FREGATIDAE *Frigatebirds* Elliptical shape; white; unmarked.

RED-BILLED TROPICBIRD

CICONIIFORMES *Storks, Herons, Ibises*
ARDEIDAE *Herons, Bitterns* Elliptical/biconical, often almost spherical; blue/white/olive (bright pea-green in one species).
COCHLEARIDAE *Boatbill* Elliptical/longitudinal; whitish/pale greenish blue ground color; sometimes with faint speckles.

GREAT BLUE HERON

SACRED IBIS

MUTE SWAN

RED KITE

RED JUNGLEFOWL

COMMON QUAIL

LIMPKIN

BALAENICIPITIDAE *Shoebill* Elliptical/longitudinal shape; white ground color; soon nest-stained; white chalky shell covering.
SCOPIDAE *Hammerhead* Elliptical in shape; white; nest-stained.
CICONIIDAE *Storks* Oval/elliptical/longitudinal, sometimes almost spherical in shape; plain white ground color; unmarked.
THRESKIORNITHIDAE *Ibises, Spoonbills* Oval/elliptical in shape. *Pseudibis* and *Threskiornis* genera: pale blue ground color. Buff-necked Ibis *(Theristicus)*: buff ground color; dark speckles. Madagascar Ibis *(Lophotibis)*: pure white eggs. *Eudocimus*: pale green eggs; brown blotches. *Plegadis*: blue, similar to a heron's. *Platalea*: similar to *Threskiornis*, white with brown speckles/spots.
PHOENICOPTERIDAE *Flamingoes* Longitudinal/weakly pyriform/biconical in shape; white ground color; chalky shell covering.

ANSERIFORMES *Waterfowl*
ANHIMIDAE *Screamers* Elliptical/longitudinal in shape; plain white/greenish ground color; no shell markings.
ANATIDAE *Ducks, Swans, Geese* Oval/elliptical/longitudinal (spherical in one species); white/creamy buff/bluish green ground.

FALCONIFORMES *Birds of Prey*
CATHARTIDAE *Cathartids (New World Vultures)* Oval/elliptical/longitudinal/pyriform; white; unmarked or blotched with brown.
SAGITTARIIDAE *Secretarybird* Oval/spherical; white; nest-stains.
ACCIPITRIDAE *Hawks, Eagles, True Vultures* Almost spherical/oval/elliptical; white/blue ground color; sometimes unmarked, but usually blotched/spotted/speckled with reddish brown.
PANDIONIDAE *Osprey* Oval in shape; white/creamy/pinkish ground color; blotched with brown and reddish purple.
FALCONIDAE *Falcons, Caracaras* Oval/elliptical; white/brown ground color; usually blotched, spotted, and speckled with brown.

GALLIFORMES *Game Birds*
MEGAPODIDAE *Megapodes* Longitudinal/cylindrical in shape; white/pinkish buff/light brownish ground color; unmarked.
CRACIDAE *Curassows, Guans* Elliptical/spherical; white.
TETRAONIDAE *Grouse* Oval/elliptical; white/buff ground color; unmarked or thickly spotted and speckled with brown or black.
PHASIANIDAE *Pheasants, Partridges, Quails* Oval/elliptical/conical/pyriform; white/buff/light brown in ground color; usually unmarked, but sometimes blotched/spotted/speckled in brown.
NUMIDIDAE *Guineafowls* Oval/conical in shape; white/buff ground color; in some species may be stippled or pitted.
MELEAGRIDAE *Turkeys* Elliptical/oval in shape; white/buffish ground color; spotted and dotted with brown shell markings.
OPISTHOCOMIDAE *Hoatzin* Oval; pink-white; red-brown marks.

GRUIFORMES *Cranes, Rails, Allies*
MESOENATIDAE *Mesites* Oval; white; marbled with gray.
TURNICIDAE *Hemipodes, Buttonquails* Elliptical/spherical in shape; white ground color; speckled with grayish brown.
PEDIONOMIDAE *Plains Wanderer* Strongly pyriform in shape; white ground color; spotted and speckled with blackish brown.
GRUIDAE *Cranes* Elliptical/longitudinal in shape; white/buffish/brown ground color; spotted/marbled with darker brown.
ARAMIDAE *Limpkin* Elliptical/longitudinal; buff; brown marbling.
PSOPHIIDAE *Trumpeters* Elliptical in shape; white ground color.

RALLIDAE *Rails* Oval/elliptical in shape; white/brownish buff ground color; stippled/spotted/blotched/marbled with varying dark shades, occasionally shells may be unmarked.
HELIORNITHIDAE *Finfoots* Almost spherical shape; white/pale pink ground color; sparsely spotted with gray and brown.
RHYNOCHETIDAE *Kagu* Oval in shape; pinkish buff ground color; streakily spotted with blackish brown pigmentation.
EURYPYGIDAE *Sunbittern* Oval; pinkish buff; brown blotches.
CARIAMIDAE *Cariamas* Oval/elliptical; white/pink; brown spots.
OTIDIDAE *Bustards* Spherical/oval in shape; plain ground color; handsomely marbled in varying shades of browns/greens/buffs.

GRAY-WINGED TRUMPETER

CHARADRIIFORMES *Waders*
JACANIDAE *Jacanas* Elliptical/conical in shape; rich, dark brown ground color; scrawls of black pigmentation; glossy texture. (One species has conical, brown, unmarked eggs.)
ROSTRATULIDAE *Painted Snipe* Elliptical; buff; black blotches.
HAEMATOPODIDAE *Oystercatchers* Oval/elliptical in shape; pale buff ground color; shell has bold black spots of pigmentation.
CHARADRIIDAE *Plovers* Elliptical/conical in shape; buff/olive/reddish ground color; variable brown/black blotches and spots.
SCOLOPACIDAE *Sandpipers, Snipe, Woodcocks* Elliptical/conical shape; white/buff/brown; variably marked in reds/browns/blacks.
RECURVIROSTRIDAE *Avocets, Stilts, Ibisbill* Elliptical/conical; buff ground color; spotted with black (*Stilts, Avocets*), gray with brown spots (*Ibisbill*); with chalky shell covering (*Banded Stilt*).
PHALAROPODIDAE *Phalaropes* Elliptical/conical shape; brown/buff ground color; blotches and spots of blackish pigmentation.
DROMADIDAE *Crab Plover* Elliptical shape; white ground color.
BURHINIDAE *Stone Curlews, Thicknees* Elliptical; white/pink/yellow-buff; black/brown blotches, speckles, spots, and streaks.
GLAREOLIDAE *Coursers, Pratincoles* Oval/elliptical; whitish/yellowish buff; blotched/marbled/speckled/spotted with brown.
THINOCORIDAE *Seedsnipe* Elliptical/pyriform in shape; white/gray ground color; marked with dots of black pigmentation.
CHIONIDIDAE *Sheathbills* Elliptical/longitudinal in shape; plain whitish ground color; blotches of dark gray pigmentation.
STERCORARIIDAE *Skuas, Jaegers* Oval/conical shape; brown/olive ground; spotted, blotched, and dotted with darker brown.
LARIDAE *Gulls, Terns* Oval/elliptical/conical; white/pink/blue/yellowish/green/buff/brown; brown/black/red spots and blotches.
RHYNCHOPIDAE *Skimmers* Elliptical in shape; white/pinkish/yellowish ground color; bold black/brown blotches and markings.
ALCIDAE *Auks* Oval/elliptical/longitudinal/pyriform; pure white (burrow-nesting species)/green/blue/buff/brown ground color; splashed/spotted/streaked/scribbled in buff, brown, and black.

KAGU

BLACK-BELLIED BUSTARD

JACANA

COMMON WOODCOCK

TWO-BANDED COURSER

COLUMBIFORMES *Pigeons, Allies*
PTEROCLIDAE *Sandgrouse* Elliptical/cylindrical in shape; pinkish/buff/olive; blotched and marbled with buff and brown.
COLUMBIDAE *Pigeons, Doves* Elliptical; white/yellowish cream .
RAPHIDAE *Dodos, Solitaires* Eggs unknown, probably white.

PSITTACIFORMES *Parrots*
PSITTACIDAE *Parrots* Elliptical/almost spherical in shape; plain white ground color; no shell markings.

SNOWY SHEATHBILL

ROSE-RINGED PARAKEET

GREAT SPOTTED CUCKOO

BARN OWL

JUNGLE NIGHTJAR

BLACK-HEADED TROGON

STRIATED MOUSEBIRD

RUFOUS-TAILED JACAMAR

BLUE-THROATED BARBET

RED-BILLED TOUCAN

CUCULIFORMES *Cuckoos*
MUSOPHAGIDAE *Turacos* Elliptical/spherical in shape; white ground color, sometimes with a greenish tinge; no shell markings.
CUCULIDAE *Cuckoos, Couas, Coucals* Elliptical in shape; almost every conceivable color and pattern known in bird eggs.

STRIGIFORMES *Owls*
TYTONIDAE *Barn Owls* Elliptical/spherical; white; unmarked.
STRIGIDAE *Typical Owls* Elliptical/spherical; white; unmarked.

CAPRIMULGIFORMES *Goatsuckers*
STEATORNITHIDAE *Oilbird* Elliptical/spherical; white; unmarked.
PODARGIDAE *Frogmouths* Elliptical in shape; white; unmarked.
NYCTIBIIDAE *Potoos* Elliptical; white ground color; gray spots.
AEGOTHELIDAE *Owlet-Nightjars* Elliptical; white; unmarked.
CAPRIMULGIDAE *Nightjars* Elliptical/cylindrical; gray/pink/buffish/white; often reddish, gray, or brown spots and marbling.

APODIFORMES *Swifts, Allies*
APODIDAE *Swifts* Elliptical/longitudinal shape; white; unmarked.
HEMIPROCNIDAE *Tree Swifts* Longitudinal; blue-gray; unmarked.
TROCHILIDAE *Hummingbirds* Longitudinal/cylindrical; white.

COLIIFORMES *Colies*
COLIIDAE *Colies/Mousebirds* Elliptical/almost spherical in shape; white ground color; sometimes streaked with brown.

TROGONIFORMES *Trogons*
TROGONIDAE *Trogons* Almost spherical in shape; white/pinkish/blue/creamy buff ground color; no shell markings.

CORACIIFORMES *Rollers, Kingfishers, Allies*
ALCEDINIDAE *Kingfishers* Spherical shape; white ground color.
TODIDAE *Todies* Spherical shape; white ground color; unmarked.
MOMOTIDAE *Motmots* Spherical; white ground color; unmarked.
MEROPIDAE *Bee-Eaters* Spherical shape; white; unmarked.
CORACIIDAE *Rollers* Elliptical/spherical shape; white; unmarked.
BRACHYPTERACIIDAE *Ground-Rollers* Elliptical/spherical; white.
LEPTOSOMATIDAE *Cuckoo-Roller* Eggs unknown.
UPUPIDAE *Hoopoes* Elliptical/longitudinal in shape; pale blue/buff/gray/brown ground color; no shell markings.
PHOENICULIDAE *Wood-Hoopoes* Elliptical/longitudinal in shape; ground color varies from medium to dark blue; unmarked.
BUCEROTIDAE *Hornbills* Elliptical/spherical; white/buff/grayish.

PICIFORMES *Picarian Birds*
GALBULIDAE *Jacamars* Almost spherical shape; white; unmarked.
BUCCONIDAE *Puffbirds* Almost spherical shape; white; unmarked.
CAPITONIDAE *Barbets* Elliptical/almost spherical in shape; white.
INDICATORIDAE *Honeyguides* Elliptical shape; white; unmarked.
RAMPHASTIDAE *Toucans* Elliptical/almost spherical; white.
PICIDAE *Woodpeckers* Elliptical/spherical; white; unmarked.

PASSERIFORMES *Passerines*
EURYLAIMIDAE *Broadbills* Elliptical in shape; white/pink-buff ground color; unmarked or spotted thickly with brown.
DENDROCOLAPTIDAE *Woodcreepers* Elliptical/cylindrical in shape; white ground color tinged with green; no shell markings.
FURNARIIDAE *Ovenbirds* Elliptical; white/blue; unmarked.

FORMICARIIDAE *Antbirds* Elliptical/spherical; white/blue ground color; unmarked or blotched/stippled with purple markings.
CONOPOPHAGIDAE *Antpipits, Gnateaters* Elliptical in shape; plain buff ground color; shell markings of dark pigmentation.
RHINOCRYPTIDAE *Tapaculos* Elliptical/spherical; white ground.
COTINGIDAE *Cotingas* White/green/buff; black blotches or spots.
PIPRIDAE *Manakins* Oval/elliptical; white/buff; dark spots/streaks.
TYRANNIDAE *Tyrant Flycatchers* Elliptical; white/buff/reddish ground color; unmarked or red/brown/black shell markings.
OXYRUNCIDAE *Sharpbill* Eggs unknown.
PHYTOTOMIDAE *Plantcutters* Oval/elliptical in shape; blue/brownish green ground color; brown spots of pigmentation.
PITTIDAE *Pittas* Elliptical/spherical; white/buff; dark spots.
ACANTHISITTIDAE *New Zealand Wrens* Elliptical; white ground.
PHILEPITTIDAE *Asities* Elliptical shape; white ground color.
MENURIDAE *Lyrebirds* Oval/elliptical; dark gray; black markings.
ATRICHORNITHIDAE *Scrub-birds* Oval in shape; white/pinkish ground color; shell markings of red/lavender pigmentation.
ALAUDIDAE *Larks* White or pink ground color; brown speckles.
HIRUNDINIDAE *Swallows* Elliptical/longitudinal shape; white ground color; unmarked or with reddish brown spots.
MOTACILLIDAE *Wagtails, Pipits* Oval/elliptical shape; white/red-brown ground color; variably speckled with brown and red.
CAMPEPHAGIDAE *Cuckoo-Shrikes, Minivets* Oval/elliptical; white/green ground; reddish brown blotches, spots, speckles.
PYCNONOTIDAE *Bulbuls* Oval/elliptical shape; white/pinkish ground color; blotched/streaked/spotted with reddish purple.
IRENIDAE *Leafbirds* Oval/elliptical; white/pink; brown streaks.
LANIIDAE *Shrikes* White/pink/blue ground; brown spots and dots.
VANGIDAE *Vangas* Pink/blue ground; brown spots and dots.
BOMBYCILLIDAE *Waxwings, Silky Flycatchers, Hypocolius* Blue-gray ground; black spots (faint in *Hypocolius*).
DULIDAE *Palm Chat* White; gray spots form wreath at larger end.
CINCLIDAE *Dippers* Oval/elliptical shape; white ground color.
TROGLODYTIDAE *Wrens* White ground color; thick reddish dots.
MIMIDAE *Thrashers, Mockingbirds* White/blue; brown speckles.
PRUNELLIDAE *Accentors* Oval/elliptical; pale blue ground color.
TURDIDAE *Thrushes* Oval/elliptical in shape; white/pink/blue; unmarked/brown speckles or spots which may obscure ground.
TIMALIIDAE *Babblers* Oval/elliptical in shape; white/pink/blue ground color; unmarked/brown spots which may obscure ground.
CHAMAEIDAE *Wrentit* Elliptical shape; pale blue ground color.
PARADOXORNITHIDAE *Parrotbills* Oval/elliptical; white/pink/blue; unmarked, or brown speckles which may obscure ground.
PICATHARTIDAE *Picathartes* Elliptical; white; brown blotches.
POLIOPTILIDAE *Gnatcatchers* White/pale blue; brown freckles.
SYLVIIDAE *Old-world Warblers* Oval/elliptical in shape; white/pinkish/greenish/blue in ground color; brown spots on shell.
LAMPROLIDAE *Silktail* Elliptical; pale pink; dark pink spots.
REGULIDAE *Kinglets* White/pink; brown speckles and spots.
MALURIDAE *Australian Wrens* Oval/elliptical; white/pink ground; varying shades of brown spots and speckles may obscure ground.
EPHTHIANURIDAE *Australian Chats* White/pink; brown spots.
ACANTHIZIDAE *Australian Warblers* Oval/elliptical; white/pink ground color; brown spots and speckles may obscure ground.

RUFOUS GNATEATER

ANDEAN TAPACULO

ORANGE COCK-OF-THE-ROCK

WOODLARK

SKYLARK

COMMON DIPPER

CACTUS WREN

ROCK WREN

MISTLE THRUSH

SHORT-TAILED WREN BABBLER

GARDEN WARBLER

SILKTAIL

SPOTTED
FLYCATCHER

THICK-BILLED FLOWERPECKER

OLIVE SUNBIRD

NORTHERN CARDINAL

BLACK-WHISKERED VIREO

YELLOW-
THROATED
ROCK-SPARROW

BLACK-
NAPED
ORIOLE

CAPE CROW

MUSCICAPIDAE *Old-world Flycatchers* Oval/elliptical shape; white/pink/blue; brown spots which may obscure ground color.
TURNAGRIDAE *New Zealand Thrush* Oval; white; blackish dots.
AEGITHALIDAE *Long-tailed Titmice* White; red-brown dots.
REMIZIDAE *Penduline Tits* Oval/elliptical shape; white/pale blue ground color; unmarked shell or with reddish brown speckles.
PARIDAE *Titmice, Chickadees* Oval/elliptical; white; brown spots.
HYPOSITTIDAE *Coral-billed Nuthatch* Eggs unknown.
DAPHONOSITTIDAE *Sittellas* Blue-gray ground color; black dots.
TICHODROMADIDAE *Wallcreeper* White; very sparse speckles.
SITTIDAE *Nuthatches* White; reddish brown spots and speckles.
CERTHIIDAE *Treecreepers* Oval/elliptical; reddish brown speckles.
SALPORNITHIDAE *Spotted Creeper* Bluish gray; brown spots.
RHABDORNITHIDAE *Philippine Creepers* Eggs unknown.
CLIMACTERIDAE *Australian Creepers* Oval/elliptical in shape; white or pinkish ground color; reddish brown spots on shell.
DICAEIDAE *Flowerpeckers* Oval/elliptical in shape; white or pinkish ground color; unmarked or speckled with reddish brown.
NECTARINIIDAE *Sunbirds, Spiderhunters* Oval/elliptical; white/pink/blue; unmarked, or brown speckles obscure ground color.
ZOSTEROPIDAE *White-eyes* Elliptical; pale blue sometimes white.
MELIPHAGIDAE *Honeyeaters, Sugarbirds, Promerops* Oval/elliptical; white/pink/blue; unmarked, or with brown speckles.
EMBERIZIDAE *Buntings, American Sparrows* White/pink/blue ground color; unmarked/brown spots which may obscure ground.
CARDINALIDAE *Cardinal Grosbeaks* Oval/elliptical shape; white/pink/blue ground color; brown speckles may obscure ground.
THRAUPIDAE *Tanagers* White/pink/blue; unmarked or speckled.
VIREONIDAE *Peppershrikes, Shrike-Vireos, True Vireos* Oval/elliptical in shape; white ground color; black spots and speckles.
PARULIDAE *Parulid Warblers* Oval/elliptical; white/pink/blue ground color; unmarked/brown speckles may obscure ground.
DREPANIDIDAE *Hawaiian Honeycreepers* Oval/elliptical in shape; plain whitish ground color; grayish brown speckles.
ICTERIDAE *Icterids* Oval/elliptical in shape; plain white/pink/blue ground color; unmarked or with brown speckles.
FRINGILLIDAE *Finches* Oval/elliptical; white/pink/blue ground color; unmarked/dense brown spots which may obscure ground.
ESTRILDIDAE *Waxbills* Oval to elliptical; white ground color.
PLOCEIDAE *Weavers, Widowbirds, Sparrows* White or pale blue; unmarked or spotted with a range of colors according to species.
STURNIDAE *Starlings* Blue; unmarked/reddish brown spots.
ORIOLIDAE *Orioles* White/pink/yellow ground color; black spots.
DICRURIDAE *Drongos* White/pink/yellow; spotted with black.
CALLAEIDAE *Kokako, Saddleback* Plain gray; dark blotches.
GRALLINIDAE *Magpie Larks* White/pink/blue; brown spots.
ARTAMIDAE *Woodswallows* White/buff; gray-brown blotches.
CRACTICIDAE *Bellmagpies, Butcherbirds, Currawongs* Brown/blue/green ground color; reddish brown scrawls and blotches.
PTILONORHYNCHIDAE *Bowerbirds* Oval/elliptical in shape; creamy/buffy white; unmarked, or brown scrawls and spots.
PARADISAEIDAE *Birds of Paradise* Elliptical/longitudinal; white/yellowish/pink ground color; distinctive brown streaks.
CORVIDAE *Crows* Oval/elliptical; white/pink/green/blue ground color; unmarked or brown spots/speckles may obscure ground.

NON-PASSERINES

Order STRUTHIONIFORMES	Family STRUTHIONIDAE	Species *Struthio camelus*

OSTRICH

The eggs of the Ostrich are cream in color with distinctive pitted surfaces. The eggshell is usually smooth and porcelainlike in texture. In relation to the size of the bird, the eggs are small.

• **BREEDING** The nest is situated in sand and is simply a shallow depression surrounded by a low wall of excavated sand. The male is polygamous and mates with several females who lay their eggs in a communal nest.

• **RANGE** Ostriches inhabit desert regions, dry savannah, and scrub. They are now confined to Africa south of the Sahara. In the past, they inhabited much of Asia and the Arabian peninsula.

almost spherical
• *shape*

• *visible pitted pores*

Egg size 127–175 x 111–145 mm	Clutch size 15–20	Incubation ♂ 35–42 days

Order STRUTHIONIFORMES	Family RHEIDAE	Species *Rhea americana*

GREATER RHEA

The two species of rhea, the Greater Rhea and Darwin's Rhea, lay eggs that are impossible to distinguish from each other's. The shell color of the Greater Rhea's eggs has been described as ranging from yellowish green to pale or dark olive-buff when newly laid, fading to parchment-white or light ocher in museum collections. The eggs are remarkably smooth in texture and have a distinct oval shape.

• **BREEDING** A communal nest is constructed in open country. It is simply a scrape made in the ground and lined with a small amount of dry grass. The male is polygamous, collecting a harem of five or six females that lay in the communal nest. Approximately 60–80 eggs may be laid by the harem of females at any one time, 130 being the record number of eggs.

• **RANGE** The birds travel in flocks across open country through eastern South America, from eastern Brazil, through Paraguay to northern Argentina.

• **REMARK** Both species of rhea superficially resemble ostriches and are sometimes called South American Ostriches. However, they are much smaller in size, and their eggs are different in color and in shape.

smooth, unmarked shell •————

parchment-white ground

Egg size 126–152 x 82–102 mm	Clutch size 10–12	Incubation ♂ 42 days

Order STRUTHIONIFORMES	Family CASUARIIDAE	Species *Casuarius casuarius*

SOUTHERN CASSOWARY

The eggs of all three species of cassowary are pea-green in color. This comparatively vivid shade of green is most unusual among birds. However, if the eggs are left exposed for a long time they can lose their color. They are usually elliptical in shape and have a glossy surface which can be finely granulated or rougher in texture.

• **BREEDING** The nest is a shallow platform located on the forest floor, usually in scrub that is difficult to penetrate. It is built using sticks, leaves, and vegetable debris, or blades of grass and fern fronds. The eggs are incubated by the male bird.

• **RANGE** Dense tropical rain forest throughout western, southern, and eastern New Guinea, the Aru Islands, and also Queensland in Australia.

• **REMARK** Cassowaries are powerful birds and can be aggressive.

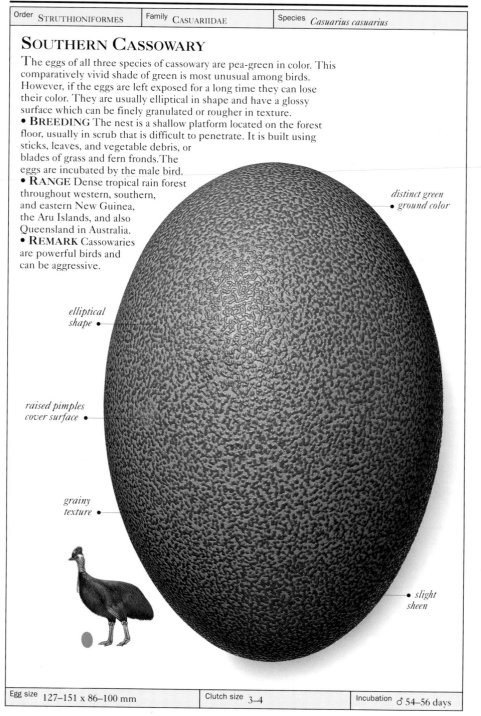

distinct green ground color

elliptical shape

raised pimples cover surface

grainy texture

slight sheen

Egg size 127–151 x 86–100 mm	Clutch size 3–4	Incubation ♂ 54–56 days

Order STRUTHIONIFORMES	Family DROMAIIDAE	Species *Dromaius novaehollandiae*

AUSTRALIAN EMU

The eggs of the Australian Emu appear similar to those of a cassowary but are in fact a deeper olive-green. They soon darken to an inky blue or black in collections. In the wild, however, the eggs fade from green to almost white on exposure to the sun. This color change is unique among birds and the reason for it is unknown. The eggs are oval in shape with a rough surface similar to cassowaries' eggs (opposite).

• BREEDING The nest is situated on the ground in grassland, woodland, scrub, forest, or heath. It consists of a platform of sticks, grass, leaves, and bark, with a shallow, irregular, unlined depression in the middle for the eggs to sit in. The oval eggs tend to roll out of the nest and are rolled back in by the male, who sits on the nest incubating the eggs and gathering up vegetation.

• RANGE Although closely related to the cassowaries, the Emu favors woodland, open plains, and desert throughout Australia, but it is also found in coastal areas.

• REMARK Its range has greatly contracted over the years. Only a single species of emu is extant, but several other now-extinct species occurred on Tasmania and offshore islands.

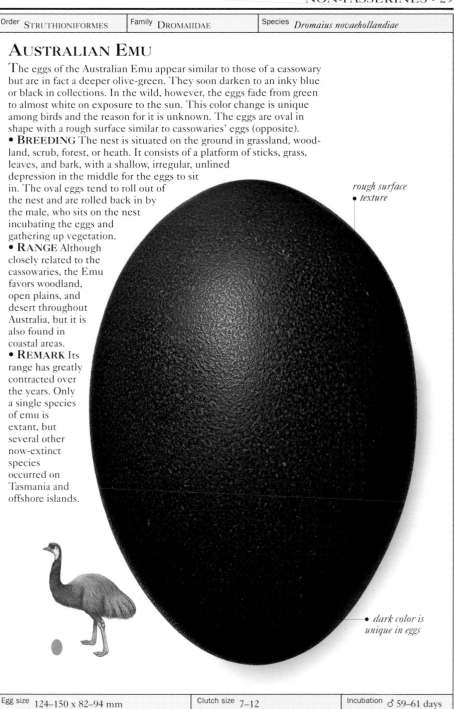

rough surface
• *texture*

• *dark color is unique in eggs*

Egg size 124–150 x 82–94 mm	Clutch size 7–12	Incubation ♂ 59–61 days

Order STRUTHIONIFORMES	Family APTERYGIDAE	Species *Apteryx australis*

BROWN KIWI

The single oval egg of the Brown Kiwi is chalky white in ground color, occasionally tinged with green, and has a smooth texture. Like those of the other two species of kiwi, the egg is relatively large, being almost a quarter of the size of the female's body.

• **BREEDING** The Brown Kiwi's breeding habits are secretive. The nest is an underground chamber at the end of a burrow, which is excavated by the parent birds months before use so that all traces of freshly dug soil disappear, and moss and ferns have time to grow up and conceal the entrance. The chamber is lined with a thin layer of vegetable material such as dry fern fronds, and more may be added by the male kiwi during incubation.

These burrows are well hidden in steep, hilly country, between tree roots or in a cavity under a tree stump. Nests can also be in steep banks within thick, damp forests, or occasionally under dense layers of fern fronds. A hollow log may be used when more usual nest sites are not available.

• **RANGE** In subtropical to temperate forests and shrublands, but wetter sites are favored over dry. Occurs in New Zealand; on North Island, South Island, and Stewart Island.

• **REMARK** The two other kiwi species are also from New Zealand but are restricted in range.

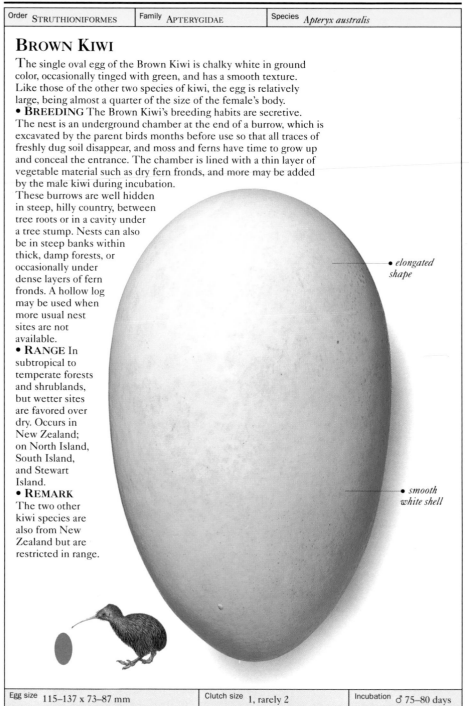

• *elongated shape*

• *smooth white shell*

Egg size 115–137 x 73–87 mm	Clutch size 1, rarely 2	Incubation ♂ 75–80 days

Order TINAMIFORMES	Family TINAMIDAE	Species *Tinamus tao*

GRAY TINAMOU

The eggs of all five species of the genus *Tinamus* are similar in color, and are described variously as greenish or sky-blue. However, in museum collections they fade to cobalt-blue.

• **BREEDING** The Gray Tinamou, like its close relative the Great Tinamou, probably lays its eggs on bare earth, sheltered by the roots of a medium-sized tree.

• **RANGE** Tropical and subtropical forests of much of northern South America, prefers damp undergrowth.

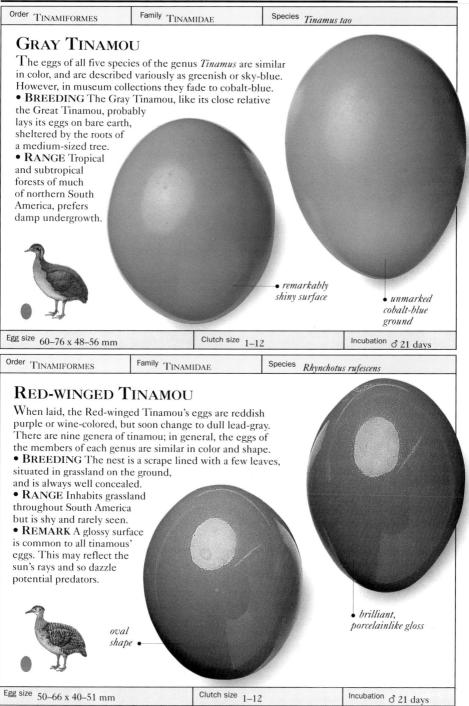

• *remarkably shiny surface*

• *unmarked cobalt-blue ground*

Egg size 60–76 x 48–56 mm	Clutch size 1–12	Incubation ♂ 21 days

Order TINAMIFORMES	Family TINAMIDAE	Species *Rhynchotus rufescens*

RED-WINGED TINAMOU

When laid, the Red-winged Tinamou's eggs are reddish purple or wine-colored, but soon change to dull lead-gray. There are nine genera of tinamou; in general, the eggs of the members of each genus are similar in color and shape.

• **BREEDING** The nest is a scrape lined with a few leaves, situated in grassland on the ground, and is always well concealed.

• **RANGE** Inhabits grassland throughout South America but is shy and rarely seen.

• **REMARK** A glossy surface is common to all tinamous' eggs. This may reflect the sun's rays and so dazzle potential predators.

oval shape •

• *brilliant, porcelainlike gloss*

Egg size 50–66 x 40–51 mm	Clutch size 1–12	Incubation ♂ 21 days

Order TINAMIFORMES	Family TINAMIDAE	Species *Eudromia elegans*

ELEGANT TINAMOU

The Elegant Tinamou's eggs are bright grass-green in ground color, sometimes yellow or tinged with a hint of blue. Like all tinamous' eggs, they are smooth and glossy. Eggs of the genus *Tinamotis* are similar.
• **BREEDING** The nest is crudely constructed and consists of a slight hollow in the ground, partly bare of vegetation and often under the lee of a low hillock of earth in grasslands, arid hills, and barren flats, but favors thorny bushes that provide cover.
• **RANGE** Through Chile and Argentina, north to southeastern Bolivia.

glossy shell •

• *grass-green ground color*

Egg size 50–60 x 35–41 mm	Clutch size 1–12	Incubation ♂ 21 days

Order TINAMIFORMES	Family TINAMIDAE	Species *Crypturellus cinnamomeus*

RUFESCENT TINAMOU

The eggs of the Rufescent Tinamou are light purplish red when laid, but in collections this color fades to pale brownish pink.
• **BREEDING** In the few recorded examples of nest sites, such as the one found in El Salvador in 1925, the nest was simply a scratched-out hollow in which no nest material was used.
• **RANGE** Wooded country in Mexico through Central America to Costa Rica. It is also found in coffee plantations. Rarely is more than one individual encountered at a time.

highly glossy • *surface*

• *brownish pink ground*

Egg size 41–48 x 36–42 mm	Clutch size 1–12	Incubation ♂ 21 days

Order SPHENISCIFORMES	Family SPHENISCIDAE	Species *Aptenodytes patagonica*

KING PENGUIN

All penguin eggs are white or greenish white when laid, but soon become soiled in the breeding colony by mud and dirt. The eggs of the King Penguin are distinctively pear-shaped, while those of smaller species are more rounded.
• **BREEDING** King Penguins breed on islands in large colonies. Birds gather together on gently sloping beaches or at the mouths of valleys where they are protected from biting winds. Both the King and its close relative the Emperor Penguin incubate a single egg on their feet, protected by a flap of skin and feathers. Other species of penguin make nests on the ground or in holes.
• **RANGE** Found in subantarctic seas, coming ashore to island sites to breed.

• *eggs soon become soiled by mud and dirt*

• *eggs of King Penguin are pear shaped*

Egg size 90–115 x 66–82 mm	Clutch size 1	Incubation ♂♀ 53–57 days

Order GAVIIFORMES	Family GAVIIDAE	Species *Gavia immer*

COMMON LOON

The Common Loon lays eggs with a dark olive-brown ground color, patterned with bold, blackish brown spots. This coloration is in contrast to most of the other lower orders of birds, which tend to lay white eggs. The shell is glossy with a grainy texture. The dark pigmentation may have evolved as the result of a need for the eggs to be cryptic, as the birds nest in isolation, often in exposed situations. The other three species of loons have eggs with pigmentation similar to this, which are distinguishable only by size.
• **BREEDING** The nest is situated on the ground beside rivers and lakes. Exposed, raised sites within easy reach of the water are favored. The nest is simply a slight, hollow scrape lined with a small amount of plant material, though in reed beds a large nesting mound is made.
• **RANGE** The Common Loon occurs throughout North America and the North Atlantic Ocean.

grainy but glossy surface

dark olive-brown ground

Egg size 84–101 x 54–62 mm	Clutch size 2, rarely 1 or 3	Incubation ♂♀ 29 days

Order PODICIPEDIFORMES	Family PODICIPEDIDAE	Species *Podiceps cristatus*

GREAT CRESTED GREBE

When laid, the eggs of all grebes are white with a smooth, chalky surface. They are soon stained brown by the rotting vegetation in the nest, which the bird uses to cover the eggs. As the grebe's eggs are never normally left exposed, there is probably no need for them to have evolved pigmentation.
• **BREEDING** The nest is concealed among reeds or built on a platform of plant material. It consists of a bare, hollow scrape lined with vegetation.
• **RANGE** Large bodies of fresh water, including lakes, rivers, and ponds. Some rare species of grebes may be confined to a single lake. This species occurs in much of the Old World, from Europe to New Zealand.

chalky white layer

shell stained brown by rotting vegetation

Egg size 46–62 x 33–39 mm	Clutch size 1–9, usually 4	Incubation ♂♀ 27–29 days

Order PROCELLARIIFORMES	Family DIOMEDEIDAE	Species *Diomedea exulans*

WANDERING ALBATROSS

The Wandering Albatross, like other albatrosses, has white eggs, though usually with buff or light brown speckles and clouding, most often at the larger end. It is a member of the tube-nosed swimmers, a group consisting of a total of four families. The albatrosses and fulmars are the only members that nest in the open, but the fact that they still have almost white eggs suggests that, like their relatives, albatrosses formerly nested in holes. In addition, some species of the four families also lay eggs with light speckling. This suggests that before nesting in holes, they all bred in the open and had pigmented eggs. Thus the albatrosses have done an evolutionary figure-8, going from open- to hole-nesting and back again.
• **BREEDING** Come ashore to islands to breed in colonies. The cone-shaped nest is built on bare ground using grass, twigs, moss, and soil.
• **RANGE** Occurs across oceans throughout the Southern Hemisphere.

reddish flecks
• *are usual*

• *smooth, matte shell*

Egg size 119–145 x 78–85 mm	Clutch size 1	Incubation ♂♀ 68–79 days

Order PROCELLARIIFORMES	Family PROCELLARIIDAE	Species *Bulweria bulwerii*

BULWER'S PETREL

The eggs laid by all members of the family Procellariidae, including the Bulwer's Petrel, are white and nonglossy, making them difficult to distinguish from one another.
• **BREEDING** Bulwer's Petrels are hole-nesting, the nest being situated among fallen rocks at the base of sea cliffs. Feathers and bones may be scraped together to line the nest, but usually no lining material is used.
• **RANGE** Pelagic out of the breeding season. Occurs widely over the Atlantic and Pacific Oceans, north and south of the equator.

matte white shell •

Egg size 39–46 x 28–33 mm	Clutch size 1	Incubation ♂♀ 44–47 days

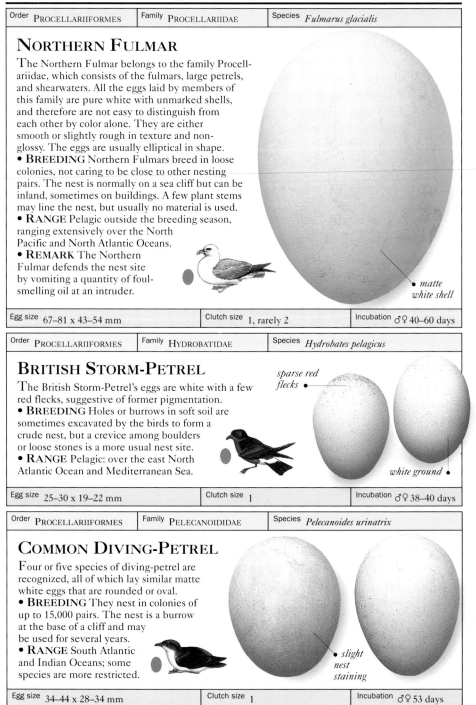

Order PROCELLARIIFORMES	Family PROCELLARIIDAE	Species *Fulmarus glacialis*

NORTHERN FULMAR

The Northern Fulmar belongs to the family Procellariidae, which consists of the fulmars, large petrels, and shearwaters. All the eggs laid by members of this family are pure white with unmarked shells, and therefore are not easy to distinguish from each other by color alone. They are either smooth or slightly rough in texture and non-glossy. The eggs are usually elliptical in shape.
• **BREEDING** Northern Fulmars breed in loose colonies, not caring to be close to other nesting pairs. The nest is normally on a sea cliff but can be inland, sometimes on buildings. A few plant stems may line the nest, but usually no material is used.
• **RANGE** Pelagic outside the breeding season, ranging extensively over the North Pacific and North Atlantic Oceans.
• **REMARK** The Northern Fulmar defends the nest site by vomiting a quantity of foul-smelling oil at an intruder.

matte white shell

Egg size 67–81 x 43–54 mm	Clutch size 1, rarely 2	Incubation ♂♀ 40–60 days

Order PROCELLARIIFORMES	Family HYDROBATIDAE	Species *Hydrobates pelagicus*

BRITISH STORM-PETREL

sparse red flecks

The British Storm-Petrel's eggs are white with a few red flecks, suggestive of former pigmentation.
• **BREEDING** Holes or burrows in soft soil are sometimes excavated by the birds to form a crude nest, but a crevice among boulders or loose stones is a more usual nest site.
• **RANGE** Pelagic: over the east North Atlantic Ocean and Mediterranean Sea.

white ground

Egg size 25–30 x 19–22 mm	Clutch size 1	Incubation ♂♀ 38–40 days

Order PROCELLARIIFORMES	Family PELECANOIDIDAE	Species *Pelecanoides urinatrix*

COMMON DIVING-PETREL

Four or five species of diving-petrel are recognized, all of which lay similar matte white eggs that are rounded or oval.
• **BREEDING** They nest in colonies of up to 15,000 pairs. The nest is a burrow at the base of a cliff and may be used for several years.
• **RANGE** South Atlantic and Indian Oceans; some species are more restricted.

slight nest staining

Egg size 34–44 x 28–34 mm	Clutch size 1	Incubation ♂♀ 53 days

Order PELECANIFORMES	Family PHAETHONTIDAE	Species *Phaethon aethereus*

RED-BILLED TROPICBIRD

The pale eggs of all three species of tropic-bird are blotched and stained with dark pinkish purple markings. Tropicbirds are the most aberrant members of the order Pelecaniformes, and their eggs suggest an independent family origin.
• **BREEDING** The Red-billed Tropicbird nests on flat islets, ledges, under shrubs, or in crevices. The nest is a simple scrape that is surrounded by stones, shells, twigs, and leaves.
• **RANGE** Pelagic, ranging over the Indian and Pacific Oceans.

• *dark purple blotches*

Egg size 51–64 x 36–48 mm	Clutch size 1	Incubation ♂♀ 40–42 days

Order PELECANIFORMES	Family PELECANIDAE	Species *Pelecanus onocrotalus*

GREAT WHITE PELICAN

• *nest stains*

The pelicans and their allies consist of six families of birds. With the exception of the tropicbirds, all members of these families lay eggs with a white or pale blue ground color, overlaid by a chalky white, amorphous layer. This outer layer tends to become scratched or stained whilst in the nest during incubation.
• **BREEDING** The Great White Pelican breeds near large stretches of water on low sandbanks or islands, or on offshore islets. All species of pelican breed in large colonies, and the nests, situated on the ground or in trees, are densely crowded together. The nest itself is usually a mere unlined scrape excavated in the ground, but occasionally it can be constructed of a large heap of reeds lined with feathers.
• **RANGE** The colonies of Great White Pelicans inhabit large bodies of water such as lakes, river deltas, and brackish or saline lagoons, estuaries, or coastal waters. The chosen nesting areas are distributed throughout southeast Europe, Asia, and Africa.

• *white ground obscured*

Egg size 80–104 x 52–64 mm	Clutch size 2, rarely 3–5	Incubation ♂♀ 29–30 days

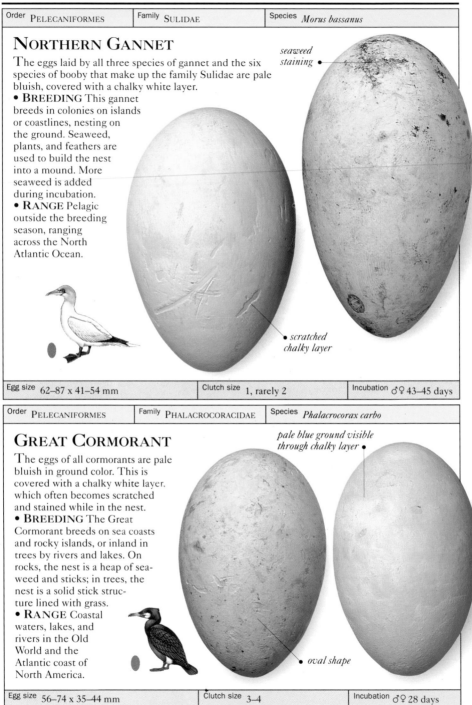

Order PELECANIFORMES	Family SULIDAE	Species *Morus bassanus*

NORTHERN GANNET

The eggs laid by all three species of gannet and the six species of booby that make up the family Sulidae are pale bluish, covered with a chalky white layer.
• **BREEDING** This gannet breeds in colonies on islands or coastlines, nesting on the ground. Seaweed, plants, and feathers are used to build the nest into a mound. More seaweed is added during incubation.
• **RANGE** Pelagic outside the breeding season, ranging across the North Atlantic Ocean.

seaweed staining •

• *scratched chalky layer*

Egg size 62–87 x 41–54 mm	Clutch size 1, rarely 2	Incubation ♂♀ 43–45 days

Order PELECANIFORMES	Family PHALACROCORACIDAE	Species *Phalacrocorax carbo*

GREAT CORMORANT

The eggs of all cormorants are pale bluish in ground color. This is covered with a chalky white layer. which often becomes scratched and stained while in the nest.
• **BREEDING** The Great Cormorant breeds on sea coasts and rocky islands, or inland in trees by rivers and lakes. On rocks, the nest is a heap of seaweed and sticks; in trees, the nest is a solid stick structure lined with grass.
• **RANGE** Coastal waters, lakes, and rivers in the Old World and the Atlantic coast of North America.

pale blue ground visible through chalky layer •

• *oval shape*

Egg size 56–74 x 35–44 mm	Clutch size 3–4	Incubation ♂♀ 28 days

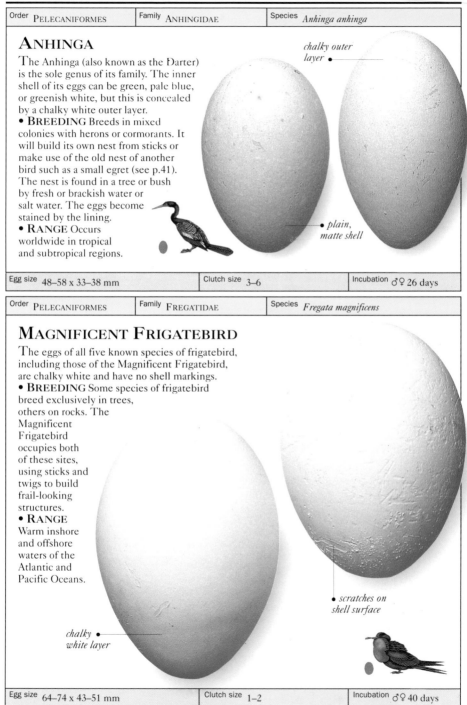

Order PELECANIFORMES	Family ANHINGIDAE	Species Anhinga anhinga

ANHINGA

The Anhinga (also known as the Darter) is the sole genus of its family. The inner shell of its eggs can be green, pale blue, or greenish white, but this is concealed by a chalky white outer layer.
• **BREEDING** Breeds in mixed colonies with herons or cormorants. It will build its own nest from sticks or make use of the old nest of another bird such as a small egret (see p.41). The nest is found in a tree or bush by fresh or brackish water or salt water. The eggs become stained by the lining.
• **RANGE** Occurs worldwide in tropical and subtropical regions.

chalky outer layer

plain, matte shell

Egg size 48–58 x 33–38 mm	Clutch size 3–6	Incubation ♂♀ 26 days

Order PELECANIFORMES	Family FREGATIDAE	Species Fregata magnificens

MAGNIFICENT FRIGATEBIRD

The eggs of all five known species of frigatebird, including those of the Magnificent Frigatebird, are chalky white and have no shell markings.
• **BREEDING** Some species of frigatebird breed exclusively in trees, others on rocks. The Magnificent Frigatebird occupies both of these sites, using sticks and twigs to build frail-looking structures.
• **RANGE** Warm inshore and offshore waters of the Atlantic and Pacific Oceans.

scratches on shell surface

chalky white layer

Egg size 64–74 x 43–51 mm	Clutch size 1–2	Incubation ♂♀ 40 days

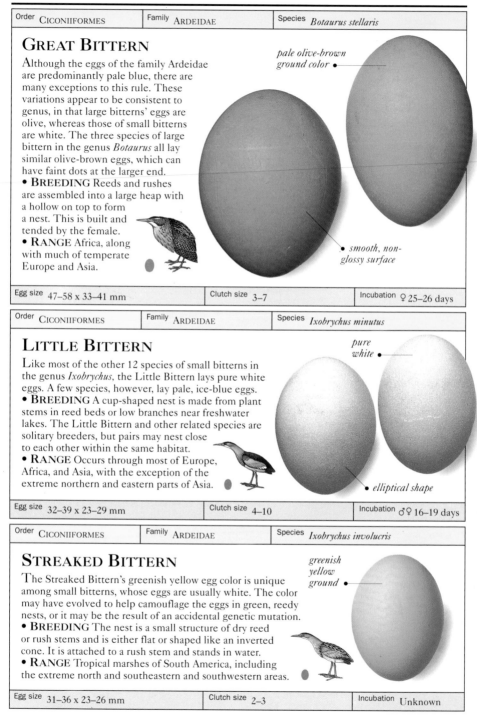

Order CICONIIFORMES	Family ARDEIDAE	Species *Botaurus stellaris*

GREAT BITTERN

Although the eggs of the family Ardeidae are predominantly pale blue, there are many exceptions to this rule. These variations appear to be consistent to genus, in that large bitterns' eggs are olive, whereas those of small bitterns are white. The three species of large bittern in the genus *Botaurus* all lay similar olive-brown eggs, which can have faint dots at the larger end.
• **BREEDING** Reeds and rushes are assembled into a large heap with a hollow on top to form a nest. This is built and tended by the female.
• **RANGE** Africa, along with much of temperate Europe and Asia.

pale olive-brown ground color •

• *smooth, non-glossy surface*

Egg size 47–58 x 33–41 mm	Clutch size 3–7	Incubation ♀ 25–26 days

Order CICONIIFORMES	Family ARDEIDAE	Species *Ixobrychus minutus*

LITTLE BITTERN

Like most of the other 12 species of small bitterns in the genus *Ixobrychus*, the Little Bittern lays pure white eggs. A few species, however, lay pale, ice-blue eggs.
• **BREEDING** A cup-shaped nest is made from plant stems in reed beds or low branches near freshwater lakes. The Little Bittern and other related species are solitary breeders, but pairs may nest close to each other within the same habitat.
• **RANGE** Occurs through most of Europe, Africa, and Asia, with the exception of the extreme northern and eastern parts of Asia.

pure white •

• *elliptical shape*

Egg size 32–39 x 23–29 mm	Clutch size 4–10	Incubation ♂♀ 16–19 days

Order CICONIIFORMES	Family ARDEIDAE	Species *Ixobrychus involucris*

STREAKED BITTERN

The Streaked Bittern's greenish yellow egg color is unique among small bitterns, whose eggs are usually white. The color may have evolved to help camouflage the eggs in green, reedy nests, or it may be the result of an accidental genetic mutation.
• **BREEDING** The nest is a small structure of dry reed or rush stems and is either flat or shaped like an inverted cone. It is attached to a rush stem and stands in water.
• **RANGE** Tropical marshes of South America, including the extreme north and southeastern and southwestern areas.

greenish yellow ground •

Egg size 31–36 x 23–26 mm	Clutch size 2–3	Incubation Unknown

Order CICONIIFORMES	Family ARDEIDAE	Species *Bubulcus ibis*

CATTLE EGRET

The eggs of the Cattle Egret are larger and paler than the Squacco and Pond Herons', (genus *Ardeola*) with which it is often linked. These differences suggest they are not closely related.
• **BREEDING** The nest is a shallow structure of twigs and reeds. Nesting is usually synchronized within the colony.
• **RANGE** The Iberian peninsula, Africa, and Asia.

pale ground

Egg size 40–53 x 30–36 mm	Clutch size 1–3 or 3–6	Incubation ♂♀ 21–25 days

Order CICONIIFORMES	Family ARDEIDAE	Species *Ardeola ralloides*

SQUACCO HERON

Like the other species of the genus *Ardeola*, the Squacco Heron lays greenish blue eggs.
• **BREEDING** Breeds in freshwater reeds, trees, and bushes. The nest structure is determined by available materials.
• **RANGE** Southern Europe, the Middle East, Africa, and Madagascar, where it is displacing the Madagascar Squacco Heron.

pale blue ground

Egg size 35–42 x 27–31 mm	Clutch size 2–4	Incubation ♂♀ 22–24 days

Order CICONIIFORMES	Family ARDEIDAE	Species *Ardea herodias*

GREAT BLUE HERON

The seven families usually placed in the order Ciconiiformes are a rather loose assortment, and their eggs differ greatly. The Great Blue Heron's greenish blue eggs are typical of those of the genus *Ardea*, all members of which lay darker blue eggs than those of the other blue-egged genera in the family Ardeidae. However, the eggs fade in museum collections.
• **BREEDING** A tree is the usual nest site, but mangrove bushes may be used in the south of the range. The nest is a large, flat platform of sticks, lined with leaves, grass, fine twigs, and other plant material. At first the nests are rather flimsy structures, but because they are used year after year, the nest material accumulates and they gradually increase in size.
• **RANGE** River and lake edges, and wetlands in North and Central America.

faded gray-blue ground

Egg size 47–71 x 35–50 mm	Clutch size 3–7	Incubation ♂♀ 28 days

| Order CICONIIFORMES | Family COCHLEARIDAE | Species *Cochlearius cochlearius* |

BOAT-BILLED HERON

The Boat-billed Heron is an aberrant heron. Its eggs are pale bluish white (difficult to capture photographically), and may have light brown dots at one end or be unmarked.
• **BREEDING** The nest is a small structure of sticks in a tree overhanging water. The breeding season varies, and depends on rain and food.
• **RANGE** Marshland from Mexico south to Peru and Brazil.

slight nest staining

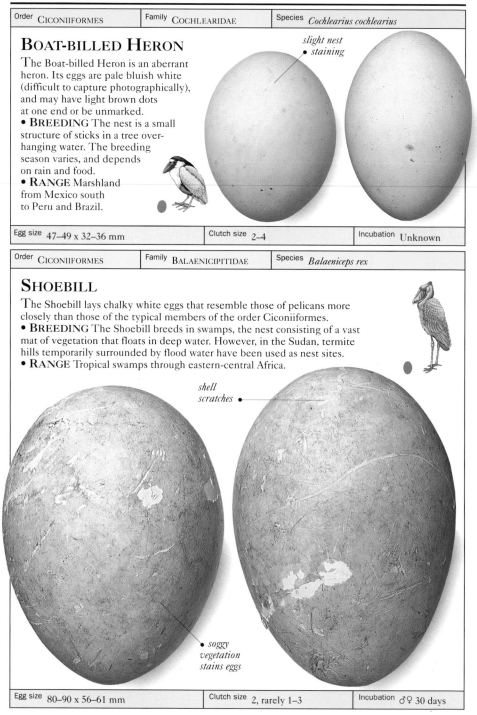

| Egg size 47–49 x 32–36 mm | Clutch size 2–4 | Incubation Unknown |

| Order CICONIIFORMES | Family BALAENICIPITIDAE | Species *Balaeniceps rex* |

SHOEBILL

The Shoebill lays chalky white eggs that resemble those of pelicans more closely than those of the typical members of the order Ciconiiformes.
• **BREEDING** The Shoebill breeds in swamps, the nest consisting of a vast mat of vegetation that floats in deep water. However, in the Sudan, termite hills temporarily surrounded by flood water have been used as nest sites.
• **RANGE** Tropical swamps through eastern-central Africa.

shell scratches

soggy vegetation stains eggs

| Egg size 80–90 x 56–61 mm | Clutch size 2, rarely 1–3 | Incubation ♂♀ 30 days |

| Order CICONIIFORMES | Family SCOPIDAE | Species *Scopus umbretta* |

HAMMERHEAD

The eggs of the Hammerhead, the only species in its family, are white when first laid but become discolored by mud.
• **BREEDING** The nest is a gigantic construction of sticks, reeds, grass, and stems, and has been known to weigh as much as 110 lb (50 kg). It is usually built in a large tree overhanging the water's edge. Pairs are territorial and often build up to three large nests within their territory, but usually only one of these is occupied.
• **RANGE** Occurs in aquatic habitats, but only in Africa south of the Sahara.

• nest stains

• smooth, matte surface

| Egg size 41–48 x 30–36 mm | Clutch size 3–6 | Incubation ♂♀ 30 days |

| Order CICONIIFORMES | Family CICONIIDAE | Species *Ciconia ciconia* |

WHITE STORK

Like all members of its family, the White Stork lays white, sometimes slightly glossy eggs.
• **BREEDING** Nests near humans, often on roofs. The nests are made of sticks, grass, and earth and lined with vegetation and feathers.
• **RANGE** Throughout Europe and western Asia, wintering in Africa.

• pure white eggs

• oval shape

| Egg size 65–81 x 46–56 mm | Clutch size 1–7 | Incubation ♂♀ 29–31 days |

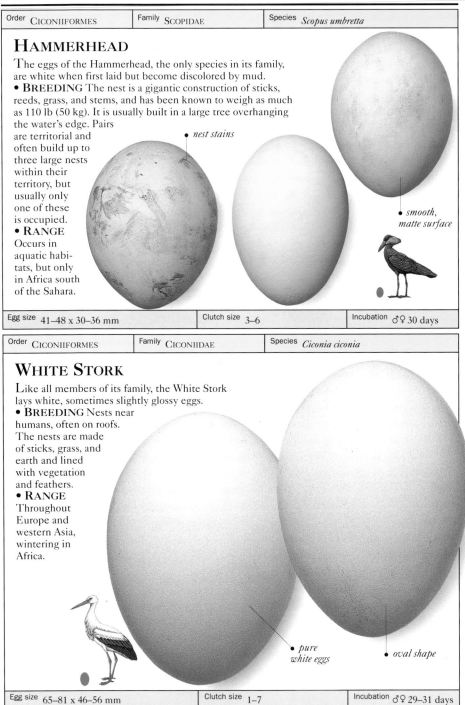

| Order CICONIIFORMES | Family THRESKIORNITHIDAE | Species *Eudocimus ruber* |

SCARLET IBIS

The two species that make up the genus *Eudocimus*, the Scarlet Ibis and the White Ibis, lay similar pale greenish white eggs with variable brown shell markings.
• **BREEDING** The Scarlet Ibis constructs a loose platform of sticks. The nest is usually in trees, mangroves, or bushes, near river mouths or close by lagoons.
• **RANGE** In mangrove swamps, coastal mudflats, and river estuaries over much of tropical South America.

cap of brown spots

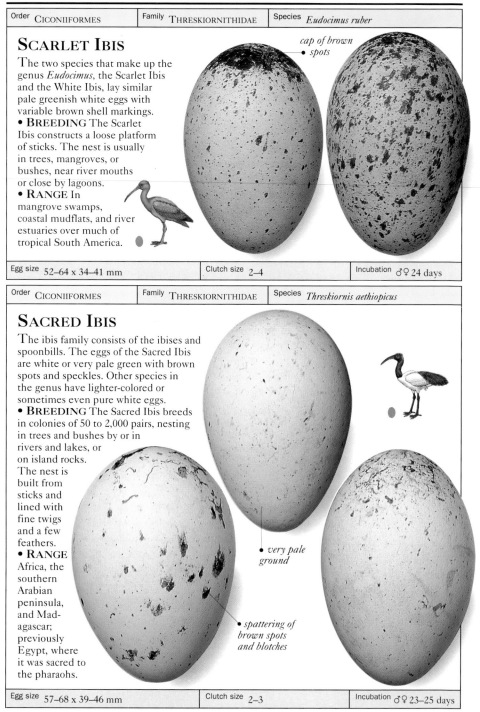

| Egg size 52–64 x 34–41 mm | Clutch size 2–4 | Incubation ♂♀ 24 days |

| Order CICONIIFORMES | Family THRESKIORNITHIDAE | Species *Threskiornis aethiopicus* |

SACRED IBIS

The ibis family consists of the ibises and spoonbills. The eggs of the Sacred Ibis are white or very pale green with brown spots and speckles. Other species in the genus have lighter-colored or sometimes even pure white eggs.
• **BREEDING** The Sacred Ibis breeds in colonies of 50 to 2,000 pairs, nesting in trees and bushes by or in rivers and lakes, or on island rocks. The nest is built from sticks and lined with fine twigs and a few feathers.
• **RANGE** Africa, the southern Arabian peninsula, and Madagascar; previously Egypt, where it was sacred to the pharaohs.

very pale ground

spattering of brown spots and blotches

| Egg size 57–68 x 39–46 mm | Clutch size 2–3 | Incubation ♂♀ 23–25 days |

Order CICONIIFORMES	Family THRESKIORNITHIDAE	Species *Geronticus eremita*

WALDRAPP

The eggs of the Waldrapp are similar to those of the Sacred Ibis (opposite), being white or pale blue, and blotched or speckled with brown.
• **BREEDING** The Waldrapp builds a loose platform of twigs lined with grass and stems. It breeds in colonies of from 3 to 40 pairs in dry, arid areas.
• **RANGE** North Africa east to Iraq; formerly widespread.

sparse brown marks •

Egg size 60–69 x 42–46 mm	Clutch size 2–3	Incubation ♂♀ 24–25

Order CICONIIFORMES	Family THRESKIORNITHIDAE	Species *Hagedashia hagedash*

HADADA IBIS

The Hadada Ibis's eggs are buff, olive, or light green, and thickly blotched with brown. The Hadada Ibis is often merged with the ibises in the genus *Bostrychia*, but the difference in the appearance of their eggs leaves this association open to doubt.
• **BREEDING** A basket-shaped nest is built in a tree.
• **RANGE** Occurs widely over Africa south of the Sahara.

• *pale buff ground*

• *heavy brown blotching*

Egg size 58–68 x 38–44 mm	Clutch size 2–3, rarely 4	Incubation ♂♀ 25–30 days

Order CICONIIFORMES	Family THRESKIORNITHIDAE	Species *Plegadis falcinellus*

GLOSSY IBIS

The three species of the genus *Plegadis* have very deep gray-blue eggs quite different from those of any other ibis; in fact they are more like a heron's. The eggs of the three species are indistinguishable.
• **BREEDING** This ibis breeds in the company of several other waterbirds, usually in freshwater marshes and swamps. It uses twigs or reeds to construct its nest.
• **RANGE** Eurasia, Indonesia, Australia, Africa, Madagascar, and the Caribbean.

• faded gray-blue ground

Egg size 46–58 x 32–40 mm	Clutch size 3–4, rarely 6	Incubation ♂♀ 21 days

Order CICONIIFORMES	Family THRESKIORNITHIDAE	Species *Ajaia ajaja*

ROSEATE SPOONBILL

The five white species of spoonbills lay eggs that have a pale ground color similar to that of the Sacred Ibis's eggs (see p.44); the Roseate Spoonbill's eggs are richer in color, however, streaked with golden brown marks.
• **BREEDING** The Roseate Spoonbill lays its eggs in mangroves or trees located in or near water. The nest is a bulky edifice made of sticks and twigs.
• **RANGE** The Caribbean islands, Florida and Texas, to South America.

• smooth, non-glossy surface

• golden brown marks create marbled effect

Egg size 59–71 x 41–46 mm	Clutch size 2–5	Incubation ♂♀ 23–24 days

Order PHOENICOPTERIFORMES	Family PHOENICOPTERIDAE	Species *Phoenicopterus ruber*

GREATER FLAMINGO

All species of flamingo lay pale greenish white eggs. These are oval and have a soft, chalky white outer layer covering the green tinge which easily becomes discolored by mud in the nest during the incubation period.
• BREEDING The nest stands in shallow water on the edge of lakes or lagoons or around islands. It is a pedestallike mound built from mud, that dries to form a hard structure. Flamingoes breed together in huge colonies of birds.
• RANGE The Greater Flamingo frequents watercourses in the Mediterranean, Africa to western Asia, the Caribbean, and the Galapagos Islands. The Lesser Flamingo is found in Africa; the remaining species only in South America.

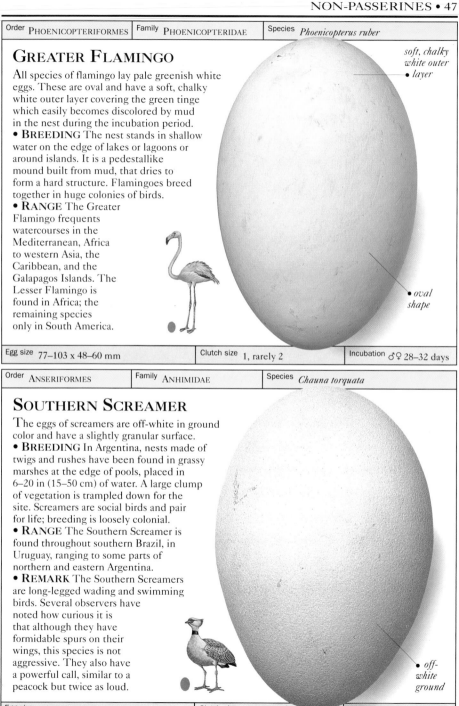

soft, chalky white outer layer

oval shape

Egg size 77–103 x 48–60 mm	Clutch size 1, rarely 2	Incubation ♂♀ 28–32 days

Order ANSERIFORMES	Family ANHIMIDAE	Species *Chauna torquata*

SOUTHERN SCREAMER

The eggs of screamers are off-white in ground color and have a slightly granular surface.
• BREEDING In Argentina, nests made of twigs and rushes have been found in grassy marshes at the edge of pools, placed in 6–20 in (15–50 cm) of water. A large clump of vegetation is trampled down for the site. Screamers are social birds and pair for life; breeding is loosely colonial.
• RANGE The Southern Screamer is found throughout southern Brazil, in Uruguay, ranging to some parts of northern and eastern Argentina.
• REMARK The Southern Screamers are long-legged wading and swimming birds. Several observers have noted how curious it is that although they have formidable spurs on their wings, this species is not aggressive. They also have a powerful call, similar to a peacock but twice as loud.

off-white ground

Egg size 80–91 x 55–61 mm	Clutch size 2–6	Incubation ♂♀ 42–44 days

Order ANSERIFORMES	Family ANATIDAE	Species *Cygnus olor*

MUTE SWAN

The Mute Swan's eggs are usually blue-gray in color, but can be almost white, though the pale ground often becomes stained in the nest during incubation. Other species of swans lay eggs that are creamy white.

• **BREEDING** The nest is built from a huge heap of reed stems, waterweed roots, sticks, rushes, and other vegetable matter. It is roughly cone-shaped, and the inner cup is often lined with down. The nest is built at the water's edge, either on land or small islands. Pairs of swans nest solitarily, though semi-domestic pairs may nest colonially.

• **RANGE** The Mute Swan inhabits Europe and Central Asia, ranging further south in winter.

• **REMARK** In Britain, from the 13th to 18th centuries all swans were royal property. Mute Swans have been introduced in parks in the United States and have become well established in the wild.

• *elliptical shape*

Egg size 100–122 x 70–80 mm	Clutch size 4–7, rarely up to 12	Incubation ♀ 35–38 days

Order ANSERIFORMES	Family ANATIDAE	Species *Anas platyrhynchos*

MALLARD

The smooth eggs of the Mallard can be buffish green, pale green or pale blue, bluish green, or creamy white in ground color, and have no markings.
• **BREEDING** A hollow nest, built and tended by the female, is lined with grass, leaves, and feathers.
• **RANGE** This species is found in both temperate and subtropical regions across the Northern Hemisphere.

creamy ground

Egg size 50–65 x 37–45 mm	Clutch size 10–12	Incubation ♀ 22–28 days

Order ANSERIFORMES	Family ANATIDAE	Species *Somateria mollissima*

COMMON EIDER

The Common Eider is a more northern species than the Mallard. Its eggs are usually darker in color, varying from dark green through olive to pale gray, blue, or buff. The eggs are smooth and glossy.
• **BREEDING** The nest is a hollow filled with seaweed or other vegetation, lined with eiderdown. Duck eggs are similar, so identification is made by the color of the down in the nest. The site is on an island or may be on the mainland.
• **RANGE** Seacoasts and inshore waters. It breeds over the northern regions of the Northern Hemisphere and winters south, to the latitude of the Mediterranean and the Gulf of St. Lawrence.

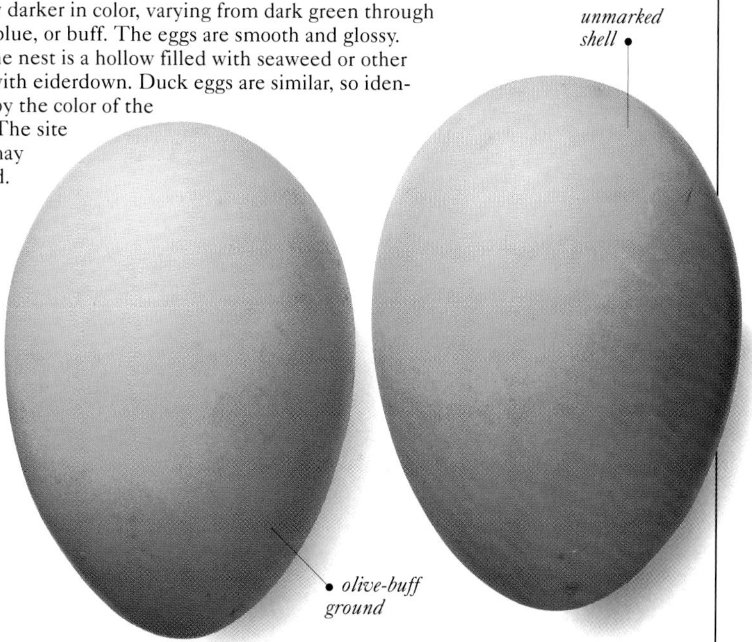

unmarked shell

olive-buff ground

Egg size 63–89 x 43–56 mm	Clutch size 4–6, rarely 3–10	Incubation ♀ 27–28 days

Order ANSERIFORMES	Family ANATIDAE	Species *Rhodonessa caryophyllacea*

PINK-HEADED DUCK

spherical shape •

The buff-white, spherical eggs of the Pink-headed Duck do not resemble those of any other duck, which suggests that it is a very old species, a relic of a once widespread group. It is now believed to be extinct.
• **BREEDING** It nested in tufts of long grass in swampland. The nest was built from vegetation growing nearby. Only one or two nests were ever found, for the birds were solitary and secretive.
• **RANGE** The Pink-headed Duck inhabited the eastern part of the Indian Subcontinent, especially around the Ganges River delta and its surrounding swampland.

Egg size 43–47 x 40–44 mm	Clutch size 5–10	Incubation 23–25 days

Order ANSERIFORMES	Family ANATIDAE	Species *Anser anser*

GRAYLAG GOOSE

creamy white ground •

All the eggs laid by the family Anatidae are greenish, creamy, or white, but provide no clues to the relationships between species. Nest identification is based on the type of down used in the nest, rather than on eggs.
• **BREEDING** Breeds on islands in lakes and rivers or in marshes, swamps, and moorlands. The nest is a scrape lined with vegetation and down.
• **RANGE** Occurs throughout Europe and Asia.

• *slightly granular texture*

Egg size 76–99 x 52–62 mm	Clutch size 4–7, rarely up to 8	Incubation ♀ 27–28 days

Order FALCONIFORMES	Family CATHARTIDAE	Species *Vultur gryphus*

ANDEAN CONDOR

The single white egg of the Andean Condor is smooth, nonglossy, and elliptical in shape.

• **BREEDING** This condor is a solitary nester, choosing to nest on a cliff ledge in a covered site, or occasionally in a cave. No material is used to line the nest, the egg being laid instead among sand or other sediment on the ledge or cave floor. The Andean Condor breeds infrequently, only every second year. This is generally assumed to be due to the fact that it is a long-lived bird with few, if any, enemies, and that its habitat can support only a small population. The slow breeding cycle has proved disastrous for the Andean Condor's close relative, the Californian Condor, which was forced close to extinction as a direct result of human invasion of its homeland.

• *smooth, nonglossy surface*

• **RANGE** Occurs throughout the Andean mountain chain in South America, often at high altitudes, but can be found down to sea level in the southernmost parts of the range.

• **REMARK** The Cathartidae, or New World Vultures, are placed in the order Falconiformes for convenience, although there is evidence to suggest that they may have been descended from storks.

white egg distinguishes condors from smaller cathartid vultures

Egg size 106–126 x 65–72 mm	Clutch size 1	Incubation ♂♀ 54–58 days

Order FALCONIFORMES	Family CATHARTIDAE	Species *Coragyps atratus*

BLACK VULTURE

• *brown blotches*

The Black Vulture's eggs are pale gray-green blotched and spotted with brown and chocolate, and not unlike the eggs of some ibises. This helps to support the theory that the Cathartidae are closely related to the Ciconiiformes.

• **BREEDING** The Black Vulture lays its eggs on bare stone, either on a low cliff ledge, or on a rock shelf in a shallow cave.

• **RANGE** Occurs in the United States, Mexico, and throughout Central and South America.

Egg size 63–90 x 43–56 mm	Clutch size 2	Incubation ♂♀ 32–39 days

Order FALCONIFORMES	Family CATHARTIDAE	Species *Cathartes aura*

TURKEY VULTURE

The eggs are dull white or cream and handsomely marked with spots and blotches of brown.

cream coloration, with brown spots and blotches •

• **BREEDING** No nest is made; the eggs are simply laid on bare rock on a ledge in a shallow cave, or on a low cliff.

• **RANGE** Occurs in both tropical and temperate plains, deserts, and forests of America, from southern Canada south to Tierra del Fuego.

• **REMARK** In the southern regions of the United States, the Turkey Vulture is popularly called the Buzzard.

Egg size 62–83 x 43–50 mm	Clutch size 2	Incubation ♂♀ 38–41 days

Order FALCONIFORMES	Family CATHARTIDAE	Species *Sarcorhamphus papa*

KING VULTURE

The King Vulture is really a type of condor, and, unlike the Black Vulture and Turkey Vulture, the eggs of this group are plain white or off-white in ground color. The genus *Sarcorhamphus* is made up of one extant species, several fossils, and the Painted Vulture of the southern United States. The latter looked similar to the King Vulture, but became extinct in the 18th century.
• BREEDING The King Vulture has been successfully bred in captivity, but very little is known about its natural breeding habits as only one nest has ever been found in the wild. This nest was a hollow stump in rain forest.
• RANGE Lowland rain forest (where it is the most numerous and often the only vulture present). It also occurs, though less commonly, in savannah, and open areas in Central and South America, ranging from Mexico south to Argentina.

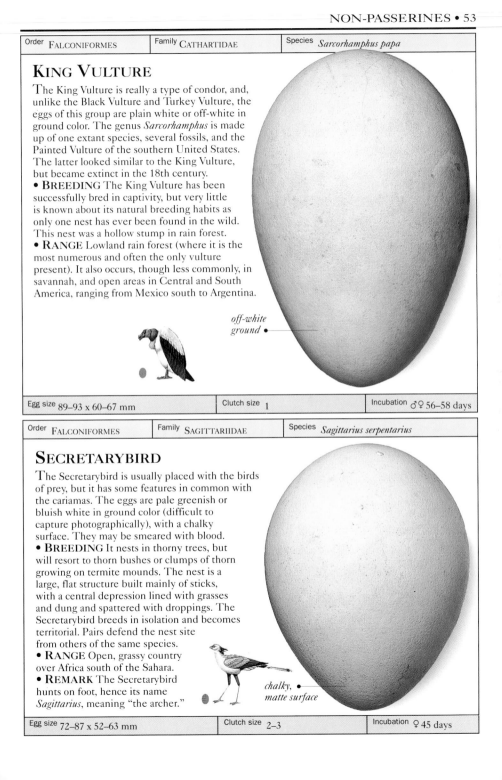

off-white ground •

Egg size 89–93 x 60–67 mm	Clutch size 1	Incubation ♂♀ 56–58 days

Order FALCONIFORMES	Family SAGITTARIIDAE	Species *Sagittarius serpentarius*

SECRETARYBIRD

The Secretarybird is usually placed with the birds of prey, but it has some features in common with the cariamas. The eggs are pale greenish or bluish white in ground color (difficult to capture photographically), with a chalky surface. They may be smeared with blood.
• BREEDING It nests in thorny trees, but will resort to thorn bushes or clumps of thorn growing on termite mounds. The nest is a large, flat structure built mainly of sticks, with a central depression lined with grasses and dung and spattered with droppings. The Secretarybird breeds in isolation and becomes territorial. Pairs defend the nest site from others of the same species.
• RANGE Open, grassy country over Africa south of the Sahara.
• REMARK The Secretarybird hunts on foot, hence its name *Sagittarius*, meaning "the archer."

chalky, matte surface •

Egg size 72–87 x 52–63 mm	Clutch size 2–3	Incubation ♀ 45 days

Order FALCONIFORMES	Family ACCIPITRIDAE	Species *Torgos tracheliotus*

LAPPET-FACED VULTURE

The single egg of the Lappet-faced Vulture is
dull white in ground color and spotted and
blotched with brown pigmentation.
• **BREEDING** The nest is a huge, flat
structure on top of a flat-topped thorny
tree, usually an acacia. Where no trees
exist, the species will build on crags.
The nest is constructed of sticks,
lined with fur (often camel hair),
bits of dung, and blades of grass.
Sometimes the Lappet-faced
Vulture will use an old nest
of the Secretarybird (see p.53).
• **RANGE** Inhabits both bush
and desert through the drier
parts of Africa, from the northwest Sahara to Eritrea and south
to the Cape Province of South
Africa. In most parts of Africa it is
a solitary bird, but in Somalia and
southwest Africa, it has often been
seen in flocks of up to 100 birds.

• *dull white
ground*

• **REMARK** Other than the seven
typical species placed in the genus
Gyps, vultures tend to be distinctly
different from one another, and the
remaining seven species are placed
in monotypic genera. The Lappet-
faced Vulture can be recognized by
the remarkable folds, or lappets, of
skin that hang down from its neck.

• *mud stains
from nest*

Egg size 83–101 x 65–74 mm	Clutch size 1	Incubation ♂♀ 53 days

Order FALCONIFORMES	Family ACCIPITRIDAE	Species *Gyps fulvus*

GRIFFON VULTURE

The single white egg of the Griffon Vulture is
lightly flecked with brown markings. It is oval
in shape, smooth in texture, and nonglossy.
• **BREEDING** The nest is a simple flattish
structure of sticks. When built on a cliff, it is
a very flimsy construction, consisting of just
a few twigs and grass. The Griffon Vulture
also breeds in huge nests in trees, but
these structures are usually the old nests
of other species. It has a tendency to
breed mainly in colonies but can
sometimes be found in solitary pairs.
• **RANGE** Inhabits only mountainous
country from southern Europe and North
Africa east through to the Himalayas.
• **REMARK** The Griffon Vulture
is a member of the family
Accipitridae, which includes   *white eggs soon*
eagles, hawks, buzzards,   *become flecked*
harriers, kites, and   *with nest stains* •
true vultures. All
family members,
including the Griffon
Vulture, have slow
reproductive rates.

Egg size 82–106 x 64–75 mm	Clutch size 1	Incubation ♂♀ 52 days

Order FALCONIFORMES	Family ACCIPITRIDAE	Species *Neophron percnopterus*

EGYPTIAN VULTURE

The Egyptian Vulture is a small species of vulture.
Its eggs have a buff, reddish, or dirty white ground
color. They are sometimes unmarked but more
often clouded and blotched with dark brown or
reddish purple spots. The variable markings
may be sparse or dense; occasionally they are
so dense that they obscure the ground color.
• **BREEDING** The Egyptian Vulture roosts
on crags, either singly or in pairs, both in open
country and in the neighborhood of towns. The
nest is situated in a small crevice or cavity in a
rocky outcrop, or more rarely on a building. It is
a slight structure made of sticks, and lined with
rags, fur, skin, and other rubbish. It is often so
thickly plastered with droppings
as to be obscured.   *dense, dark*
• **RANGE** Southern   *brown markings* •
Europe, Africa,
the Middle East,
and India.

Egg size 57–76 x 41–56 mm	Clutch size 1–3	Incubation ♂♀ 42 days

Order FALCONIFORMES	Family ACCIPITRIDAE	Species *Aegypius monachus*

CINEREOUS VULTURE

The Cinereous Vulture lays a single egg, which can have either white or pale buff ground coloration. It is densely marked with purplish and reddish brown. The shell texture is coarse and tends to have a pitted or corrugated surface.
• **BREEDING** The Cinereous Vulture builds huge nests in tree tops using sticks. It lines the nest with leafy branches, bark, and skin. The nest is reused each year, and more material is added, making the old nest gradually bigger.
• **RANGE** The Mediterranean, and across Asia to the Urals, the Himalayas, China, and Japan.
• **REMARK** The eggs of birds in the family Accipitridae are bewilderingly variable, and egg color is not a good index to relationships in this family. However, it is fairly consistent among members of the same genus or subfamily.

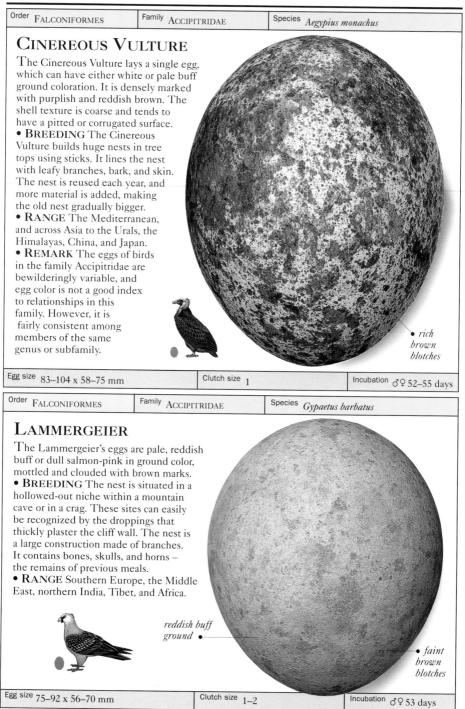

• *rich brown blotches*

Egg size 83–104 x 58–75 mm	Clutch size 1	Incubation ♂♀ 52–55 days

Order FALCONIFORMES	Family ACCIPITRIDAE	Species *Gypaetus barbatus*

LAMMERGEIER

The Lammergeier's eggs are pale, reddish buff or dull salmon-pink in ground color, mottled and clouded with brown marks.
• **BREEDING** The nest is situated in a hollowed-out niche within a mountain cave or in a crag. These sites can easily be recognized by the droppings that thickly plaster the cliff wall. The nest is a large construction made of branches. It contains bones, skulls, and horns – the remains of previous meals.
• **RANGE** Southern Europe, the Middle East, northern India, Tibet, and Africa.

reddish buff ground •

• *faint brown blotches*

Egg size 75–92 x 56–70 mm	Clutch size 1–2	Incubation ♂♀ 53 days

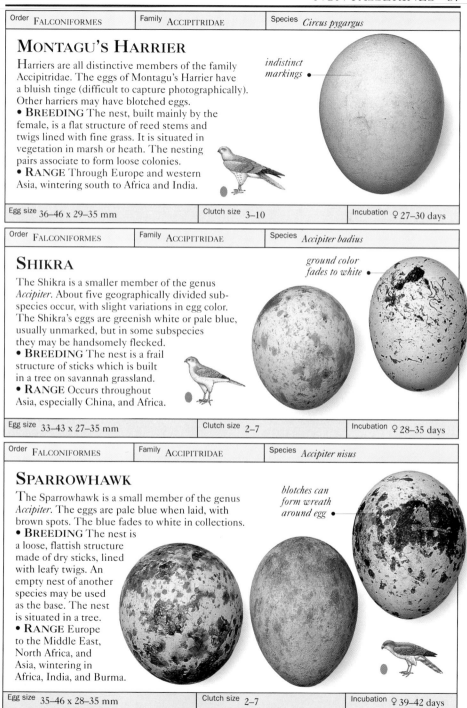

| Order FALCONIFORMES | Family ACCIPITRIDAE | Species *Circus pygargus* |

MONTAGU'S HARRIER

Harriers are all distinctive members of the family
Accipitridae. The eggs of Montagu's Harrier have
a bluish tinge (difficult to capture photographically).
Other harriers may have blotched eggs.

indistinct markings •

• **BREEDING** The nest, built mainly by the
female, is a flat structure of reed stems and
twigs lined with fine grass. It is situated in
vegetation in marsh or heath. The nesting
pairs associate to form loose colonies.
• **RANGE** Through Europe and western
Asia, wintering south to Africa and India.

| Egg size 36–46 x 29–35 mm | Clutch size 3–10 | Incubation ♀ 27–30 days |

| Order FALCONIFORMES | Family ACCIPITRIDAE | Species *Accipiter badius* |

SHIKRA

ground color fades to white •

The Shikra is a smaller member of the genus
Accipiter. About five geographically divided subspecies occur, with slight variations in egg color.
The Shikra's eggs are greenish white or pale blue,
usually unmarked, but in some subspecies
they may be handsomely flecked.
• **BREEDING** The nest is a frail
structure of sticks which is built
in a tree on savannah grassland.
• **RANGE** Occurs throughout
Asia, especially China, and Africa.

| Egg size 33–43 x 27–35 mm | Clutch size 2–7 | Incubation ♀ 28–35 days |

| Order FALCONIFORMES | Family ACCIPITRIDAE | Species *Accipiter nisus* |

SPARROWHAWK

The Sparrowhawk is a small member of the genus
Accipiter. The eggs are pale blue when laid, with
brown spots. The blue fades to white in collections.

blotches can form wreath around egg •

• **BREEDING** The nest is
a loose, flattish structure
made of dry sticks, lined
with leafy twigs. An
empty nest of another
species may be used
as the base. The nest
is situated in a tree.
• **RANGE** Europe
to the Middle East,
North Africa, and
Asia, wintering in
Africa, India, and Burma.

| Egg size 35–46 x 28–35 mm | Clutch size 2–7 | Incubation ♀ 39–42 days |

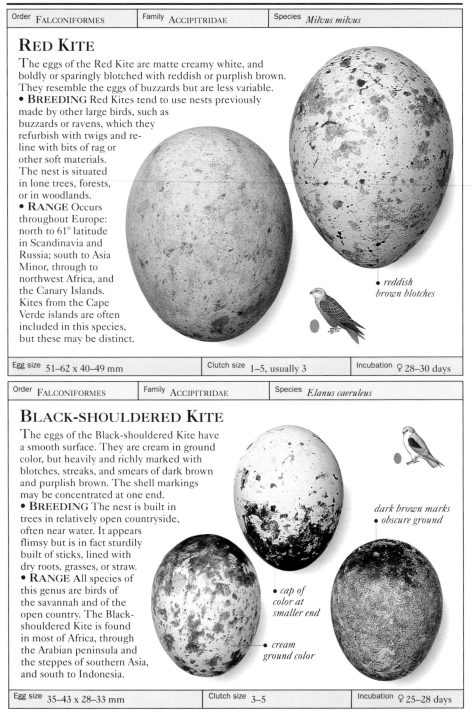

Order FALCONIFORMES	Family ACCIPITRIDAE	Species *Milvus milvus*

RED KITE

The eggs of the Red Kite are matte creamy white, and boldly or sparingly blotched with reddish or purplish brown. They resemble the eggs of buzzards but are less variable.

• **BREEDING** Red Kites tend to use nests previously made by other large birds, such as buzzards or ravens, which they refurbish with twigs and re-line with bits of rag or other soft materials. The nest is situated in lone trees, forests, or in woodlands.

• **RANGE** Occurs throughout Europe: north to 61° latitude in Scandinavia and Russia; south to Asia Minor, through to northwest Africa, and the Canary Islands. Kites from the Cape Verde islands are often included in this species, but these may be distinct.

• *reddish brown blotches*

Egg size 51–62 x 40–49 mm	Clutch size 1–5, usually 3	Incubation ♀ 28–30 days

Order FALCONIFORMES	Family ACCIPITRIDAE	Species *Elanus caeruleus*

BLACK-SHOULDERED KITE

The eggs of the Black-shouldered Kite have a smooth surface. They are cream in ground color, but heavily and richly marked with blotches, streaks, and smears of dark brown and purplish brown. The shell markings may be concentrated at one end.

• **BREEDING** The nest is built in trees in relatively open countryside, often near water. It appears flimsy but is in fact sturdily built of sticks, lined with dry roots, grasses, or straw.

• **RANGE** All species of this genus are birds of the savannah and of the open country. The Black-shouldered Kite is found in most of Africa, through the Arabian peninsula and the steppes of southern Asia, and south to Indonesia.

dark brown marks
• *obscure ground*

• *cap of color at smaller end*

• *cream ground color*

Egg size 35–43 x 28–33 mm	Clutch size 3–5	Incubation ♀ 25–28 days

| Order FALCONIFORMES | Family ACCIPITRIDAE | Species *Accipiter gentilis* |

NORTHERN GOSHAWK

• *nest stains*

The rough-textured eggs of the
Northern Goshawk are a pale
blue in ground color, but this
often fades to white in
museum collections.
• **BREEDING** The
Northern Goshawk's
nest is situated in single
trees, and in forests. It
is a large, untidy struc-
ture built mainly of
twigs and it is re-
furbished annually
by the same parents.
• **RANGE** Occurs in
much of the temperate
Northern Hemisphere,
north to the timber line.

| Egg size 51–65 x 40–50 mm | Clutch size 1–5 | Incubation ♀ 36–38 days |

| Order FALCONIFORMES | Family ACCIPITRIDAE | Species *Circaetus gallicus* |

SHORT-TOED EAGLE

The Short-toed Eagle lays a single smooth white egg.
It is the most widespread of the four species of harrier-
eagles, or snake-eagles, in the genus *Circaetus*.
• **BREEDING** The nest is a small, hollowed-out
structure of thin
twigs, lined
with leaves.

*stains
from
nest* •

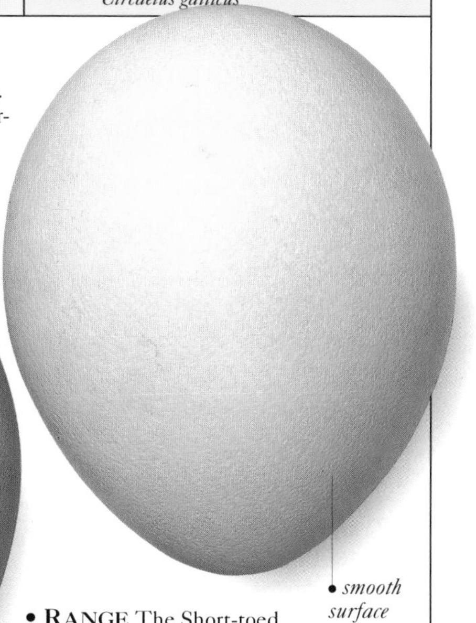

• **RANGE** The Short-toed
Eagle occurs throughout
southern Europe, Africa, and
also east to India and Mongolia.
In winter the species can be found
further south to Indonesia.

• *smooth
surface*

| Egg size 66–83 x 52–63 mm | Clutch size 1 | Incubation ♀ 47 days |

Order FALCONIFORMES	Family ACCIPITRIDAE	Species *Pernis apivorus*

HONEY BUZZARD

The eggs of the Honey Buzzard are white or buff, clouded, spotted, or speckled with rich reddish brown. These dense markings often obscure the ground.
• **BREEDING** The nest is built of sticks and twigs and located in a tree. The old nest of another species may be used as a base.
• **RANGE** Europe, Asia from China to Japan, and India. Western birds migrate south to Africa in winter.

reddish brown marks over ground

slightly glossy shell

Egg size 46–58 x 38–44 mm	Clutch size 1–3	Incubation ♂♀ 30–35 days

Order FALCONIFORMES	Family ACCIPITRIDAE	Species *Spilornis cheela*

CRESTED SERPENT EAGLE

The single egg of the Crested Serpent Eagle varies greatly in color, but is usually matte white, reddish white, or buff in ground color. Reddish brown smears and blotches may be sparsely or thickly distributed over the entire eggshell or may form a cap at one end.
• **BREEDING** The relatively small nest is built solely of sticks and is located in wooded areas.
• **RANGE** Widespread in both forests and woodland, from India to south China, Southeast Asia, and Indonesia.

reddish brown spots and blotches

Egg size 58–77 x 47–58 mm	Clutch size 1	Incubation ♀ 35 days

Order FALCONIFORMES	Family ACCIPITRIDAE	Species *Buteo lagopus*

ROUGH-LEGGED HAWK

The eggs of the Rough-legged Hawk are off-white in ground color, heavily smudged and streaked with brown. Occasionally the brown markings are sparsely distributed or even absent.
• **BREEDING** The Rough-legged Hawk builds a small nest of twigs on rocky outcrops, in tundra and in moorland landscapes.
• **RANGE** Cold areas of the Northern Hemisphere, wintering in southern Europe, North America, and Asia.

• *pale ground*

• *brown smudges*

Egg size 50–64 x 40–48 mm	Clutch size 3–4, rarely 7	Incubation ♀ 28–31 days

Order FALCONIFORMES	Family ACCIPITRIDAE	Species *Haliaeetus leucocephalus*

BALD EAGLE

The Bald Eagle's eggs are pure matte white, but they are often discolored in the nest during the comparatively long incubation period. They are very different from the eggs of the Golden Eagle (see p.62) and other species in the genus *Aquila*.
• **BREEDING** The nest is a large structure, built of sticks and lined with softer material such as pine needles. It is sited in tall trees or cliffs in remote forests and mountains, especially at or very near the coastline.
• **RANGE** North America from the Aleutian Islands, Alaska, and northern Canada, south to Florida and northern Mexico.
• **REMARK** The Bald Eagle is a member of the genus *Haliaeetus*, commonly known as the sea eagles. They are primarily associated with salt water, and fish are an important part of their diet.

• *matte white ground*

Egg size 58–84 x 47–63 mm	Clutch size 1–3	Incubation ♂♀ 31–46 days

Order FALCONIFORMES	Family ACCIPITRIDAE	Species *Haliastur indus*

BRAHMINY KITE

The eggs of the Brahminy Kite are matte white, and sparsely blotched and freckled with reddish or yellowish brown.
• **BREEDING** The nest is built of sticks in trees or on the ground. It is lined with seaweed, leaves, wool, and other debris.
• **RANGE** India and Sri Lanka, southern China, the Solomon Islands, and Australia.

cap of color

dark brown markings

Egg size 45–57 x 36–46 mm	Clutch size 1–4	Incubation ♀ 26–27 days

Order FALCONIFORMES	Family ACCIPITRIDAE	Species *Aquila chrysaetos*

GOLDEN EAGLE

The eggs of the Golden Eagle are typically matte white in ground color, blotched and spotted with various shades of brown, and red-brown. These marks are often rich and dense, though sometimes only sparse.
• **BREEDING** The Golden Eagle nests on crags or in trees amid mountains and remote heathlands. One pair may have several nests, used in rotation. Site permitting, the nest can be a huge structure of sticks; elsewhere it is a simple scrape.
• **RANGE** In much of the Northern Hemisphere, south to North Africa, the Arabian peninsula, the Himalayas, and Mexico.

matte white ground

sprinkling of chocolate-brown marks

blurred gray-brown marks

Egg size 67–88 x 51–66 mm	Clutch size 1–3, usually 2	Incubation ♀ 43–45 days

Order FALCONIFORMES	Family ACCIPITRIDAE	Species *Polyboroides typus*

GYMNOGENE

The eggs of the Gymnogene are buff or cream in ground color, richly blotched and spotted with reddish brown and chocolate.
• **BREEDING** The Gymnogene's nest is built of sticks and copiously lined with green leaves. It is usually placed in the fork of a tree in open forest, woodland, or savannah.
• **RANGE** Occurs throughout Africa south of the Sahara.

• *ground obscured by blotches*

Egg size 50–62 x 39–46 mm	Clutch size 1–3	Incubation ♂♀ 36 days

Order FALCONIFORMES	Family PANDIONIDAE	Species *Pandion haliaetus*

OSPREY

The Osprey's slightly glossy eggs are creamy white, boldly and handsomely marked with dark red and reddish brown blotches.
• **BREEDING** The Osprey uses sticks to construct a very large, round nest, which is then lined with grass. The nest is located high in the branches of a tree, which is situated in woodland or moorland, always close to lakes, rivers, or the coast.
• **RANGE** Worldwide in woodland and moorland habitats, although less common in the Southern Hemisphere.

• *oval shape*

• *creamy white ground*

Egg size 50–69 x 40–52 mm	Clutch size 2–4, usually 3	Incubation ♂♀ 32–38 days

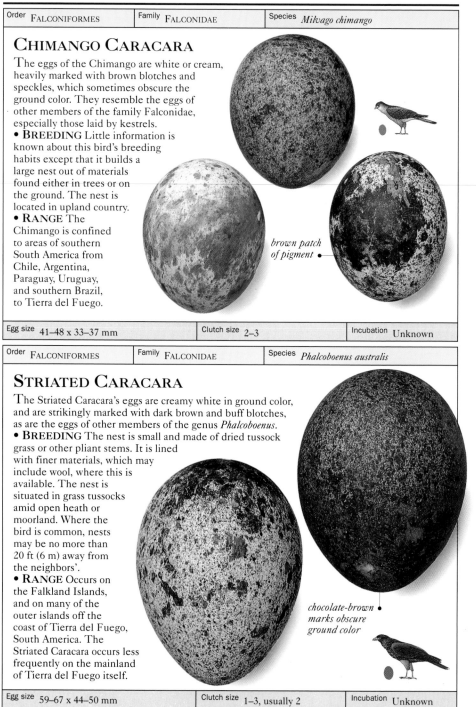

| Order FALCONIFORMES | Family FALCONIDAE | Species *Milvago chimango* |

CHIMANGO CARACARA

The eggs of the Chimango are white or cream, heavily marked with brown blotches and speckles, which sometimes obscure the ground color. They resemble the eggs of other members of the family Falconidae, especially those laid by kestrels.
• **BREEDING** Little information is known about this bird's breeding habits except that it builds a large nest out of materials found either in trees or on the ground. The nest is located in upland country.
• **RANGE** The Chimango is confined to areas of southern South America from Chile, Argentina, Paraguay, Uruguay, and southern Brazil, to Tierra del Fuego.

brown patch of pigment •

| Egg size 41–48 x 33–37 mm | Clutch size 2–3 | Incubation Unknown |

| Order FALCONIFORMES | Family FALCONIDAE | Species *Phalcoboenus australis* |

STRIATED CARACARA

The Striated Caracara's eggs are creamy white in ground color, and are strikingly marked with dark brown and buff blotches, as are the eggs of other members of the genus *Phalcoboenus*.
• **BREEDING** The nest is small and made of dried tussock grass or other pliant stems. It is lined with finer materials, which may include wool, where this is available. The nest is situated in grass tussocks amid open heath or moorland. Where the bird is common, nests may be no more than 20 ft (6 m) away from the neighbors'.
• **RANGE** Occurs on the Falkland Islands, and on many of the outer islands off the coast of Tierra del Fuego, South America. The Striated Caracara occurs less frequently on the mainland of Tierra del Fuego itself.

chocolate-brown • *marks obscure ground color*

| Egg size 59–67 x 44–50 mm | Clutch size 1–3, usually 2 | Incubation Unknown |

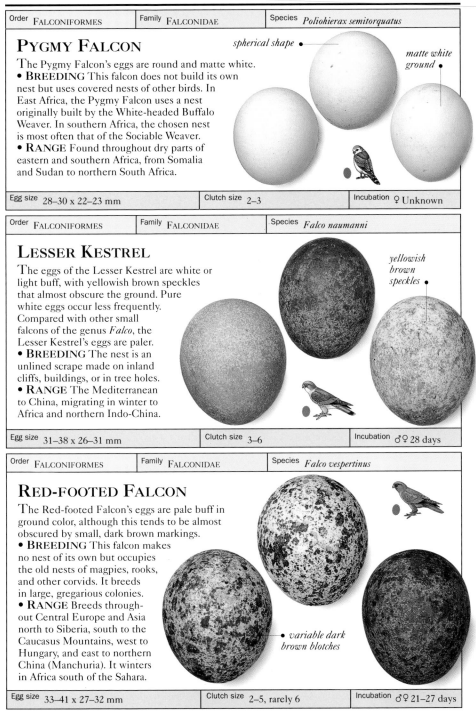

Order FALCONIFORMES	Family FALCONIDAE	Species *Poliohierax semitorquatus*

PYGMY FALCON

spherical shape •

matte white ground •

The Pygmy Falcon's eggs are round and matte white.
• **BREEDING** This falcon does not build its own
nest but uses covered nests of other birds. In
East Africa, the Pygmy Falcon uses a nest
originally built by the White-headed Buffalo
Weaver. In southern Africa, the chosen nest
is most often that of the Sociable Weaver.
• **RANGE** Found throughout dry parts of
eastern and southern Africa, from Somalia
and Sudan to northern South Africa.

Egg size 28–30 x 22–23 mm	Clutch size 2–3	Incubation ♀ Unknown

Order FALCONIFORMES	Family FALCONIDAE	Species *Falco naumanni*

LESSER KESTREL

yellowish brown speckles •

The eggs of the Lesser Kestrel are white or
light buff, with yellowish brown speckles
that almost obscure the ground. Pure
white eggs occur less frequently.
Compared with other small
falcons of the genus *Falco*, the
Lesser Kestrel's eggs are paler.
• **BREEDING** The nest is an
unlined scrape made on inland
cliffs, buildings, or in tree holes.
• **RANGE** The Mediterranean
to China, migrating in winter to
Africa and northern Indo-China.

Egg size 31–38 x 26–31 mm	Clutch size 3–6	Incubation ♂♀ 28 days

Order FALCONIFORMES	Family FALCONIDAE	Species *Falco vespertinus*

RED-FOOTED FALCON

The Red-footed Falcon's eggs are pale buff in
ground color, although this tends to be almost
obscured by small, dark brown markings.
• **BREEDING** This falcon makes
no nest of its own but occupies
the old nests of magpies, rooks,
and other corvids. It breeds
in large, gregarious colonies.
• **RANGE** Breeds throughout Central Europe and Asia
north to Siberia, south to the
Caucasus Mountains, west to
Hungary, and east to northern
China (Manchuria). It winters
in Africa south of the Sahara.

• *variable dark brown blotches*

Egg size 33–41 x 27–32 mm	Clutch size 2–5, rarely 6	Incubation ♂♀ 21–27 days

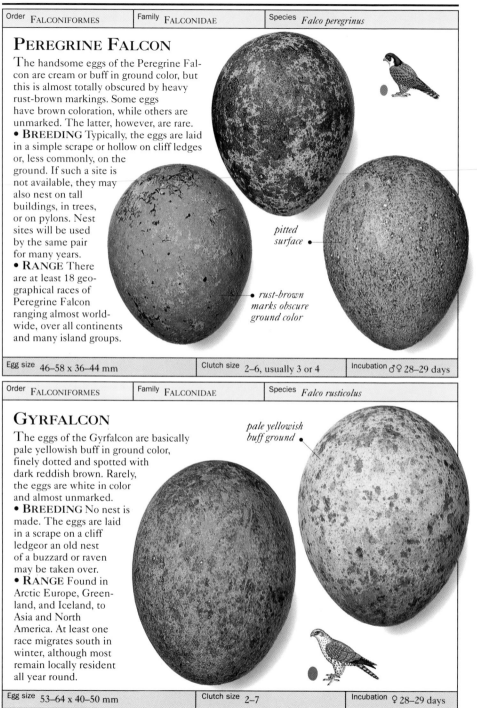

Order FALCONIFORMES	Family FALCONIDAE	Species *Falco peregrinus*

PEREGRINE FALCON

The handsome eggs of the Peregrine Falcon are cream or buff in ground color, but this is almost totally obscured by heavy rust-brown markings. Some eggs have brown coloration, while others are unmarked. The latter, however, are rare.

• **BREEDING** Typically, the eggs are laid in a simple scrape or hollow on cliff ledges or, less commonly, on the ground. If such a site is not available, they may also nest on tall buildings, in trees, or on pylons. Nest sites will be used by the same pair for many years.

• **RANGE** There are at least 18 geographical races of Peregrine Falcon ranging almost worldwide, over all continents and many island groups.

pitted surface

rust-brown marks obscure ground color

Egg size 46–58 x 36–44 mm	Clutch size 2–6, usually 3 or 4	Incubation ♂♀ 28–29 days

Order FALCONIFORMES	Family FALCONIDAE	Species *Falco rusticolus*

GYRFALCON

The eggs of the Gyrfalcon are basically pale yellowish buff in ground color, finely dotted and spotted with dark reddish brown. Rarely, the eggs are white in color and almost unmarked.

• **BREEDING** No nest is made. The eggs are laid in a scrape on a cliff ledgeor an old nest of a buzzard or raven may be taken over.

• **RANGE** Found in Arctic Europe, Greenland, and Iceland, to Asia and North America. At least one race migrates south in winter, although most remain locally resident all year round.

pale yellowish buff ground

Egg size 53–64 x 40–50 mm	Clutch size 2–7	Incubation ♀ 28–29 days

Order FALCONIFORMES	Family FALCONIDAE	Species *Polyborus cheriway*

CHERIWAY CARACARA

The eggs of the Cheriway Caracara are white, pink, or buff in ground color and are thickly blotched with reddish brown markings.
• **BREEDING** The nest is an untidy structure built solely of sticks. It is usually unlined, though it may sometimes be lined with dry dung and other debris, such as bones or skin. It is situated in a tree, usually in open countryside.
• **RANGE** Southern United States and Cuba, south to Peru and the Guianas in South America.

dense, reddish brown mottling

pinkish buff ground

Egg size 58–60 x 45–46 mm	Clutch size 2–4	Incubation ♂♀ 28 days

Order GALLIFORMES	Family MEGAPODIDAE	Species *Megapodius freycinet*

COMMON SCRUB FOWL

The large eggs of the Common Scrub Fowl have white shells covered in a yellow or pinkish brown outer layer.
• **BREEDING** The nest is a carefully collected mound composed of decaying leafy vegetation. The heat generated as the moldy vegetation rots incubates the buried eggs. The male parent attends the nest, controlling the temperature by opening up or closing part of the mound. The nest is located on the ground, amid forest or dry scrubland.
• **RANGE** From the Nicobar Islands (west of Thailand), through Indonesia, to Australia and the New Hebrides.

oval shape

underlying white layer shows through pink-brown outer layer

Egg size 70–93 x 40–57 mm	Clutch size Unknown	Incubation ♂ 56–63 days

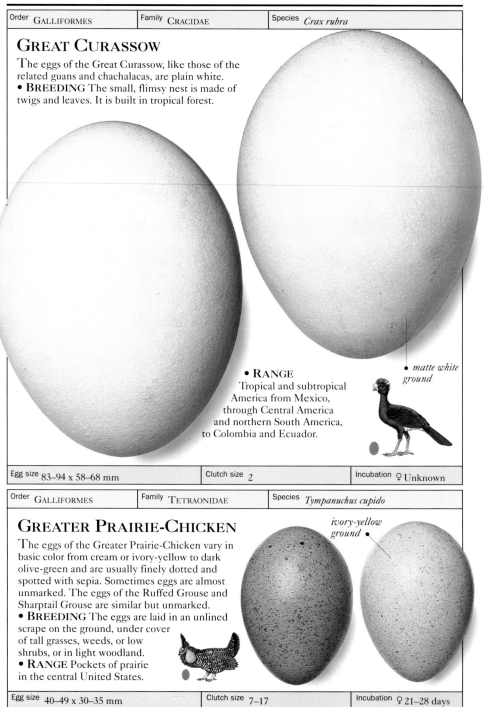

| Order GALLIFORMES | Family CRACIDAE | Species *Crax rubra* |

GREAT CURASSOW

The eggs of the Great Curassow, like those of the related guans and chachalacas, are plain white.
• **BREEDING** The small, flimsy nest is made of twigs and leaves. It is built in tropical forest.

• **RANGE**
Tropical and subtropical America from Mexico, through Central America and northern South America, to Colombia and Ecuador.

• *matte white ground*

| Egg size 83–94 x 58–68 mm | Clutch size 2 | Incubation ♀ Unknown |

| Order GALLIFORMES | Family TETRAONIDAE | Species *Tympanuchus cupido* |

GREATER PRAIRIE-CHICKEN

ivory-yellow ground •

The eggs of the Greater Prairie-Chicken vary in basic color from cream or ivory-yellow to dark olive-green and are usually finely dotted and spotted with sepia. Sometimes eggs are almost unmarked. The eggs of the Ruffed Grouse and Sharptail Grouse are similar but unmarked.
• **BREEDING** The eggs are laid in an unlined scrape on the ground, under cover of tall grasses, weeds, or low shrubs, or in light woodland.
• **RANGE** Pockets of prairie in the central United States.

| Egg size 40–49 x 30–35 mm | Clutch size 7–17 | Incubation ♀ 21–28 days |

Order GALLIFORMES	Family TETRAONIDAE	Species *Tetrao urogallus*

CAPERCAILLIE

Grouse lay several types of eggs that are usually alike within the genus. The eggs of the Capercaillie are pale yellow in ground color and spotted and blotched with brown, like those of the Black Grouse.
• **BREEDING** The Capercaillie nests in a shallow scrape in the ground under thick cover, often at the base of a tree.
• **RANGE** Northern Europe to the Pyrenees, the Alps, Cantabrians, Balkans, and southern Urals; also west to Siberia and south to Mongolia.

• *yellowish ground*

• *scattered brown spots*

Egg size 50–62 x 39–43 mm	Clutch size 4–15, usually 5–8	Incubation ♀ 26–29 days

Order GALLIFORMES	Family TETRAONIDAE	Species *Centrocercus urophasianus*

SAGE GROUSE

The Sage Grouse's eggs are yellow, green, or olive-brown in ground color, evenly marked with dots and spots of dark brown. They are similar to but larger and paler than the Spruce Grouse's eggs (see p.70).
• **BREEDING** The nest site is under the shelter of a sagebrush bush, where the eggs are laid in a small depression. The nest may be lined with leaves or small twigs.
• **RANGE** Confined to the sagebrush plains of western North America, ranging from Washington, Idaho, Montana, and North Dakota south to California, Nevada, Utah, Colorado, and Wyoming.

• *regular dark brown spots*

• *yellowish tan ground*

Egg size 51–59 x 35–40 mm	Clutch size 7–17, usually 8	Incubation ♀ 22 days

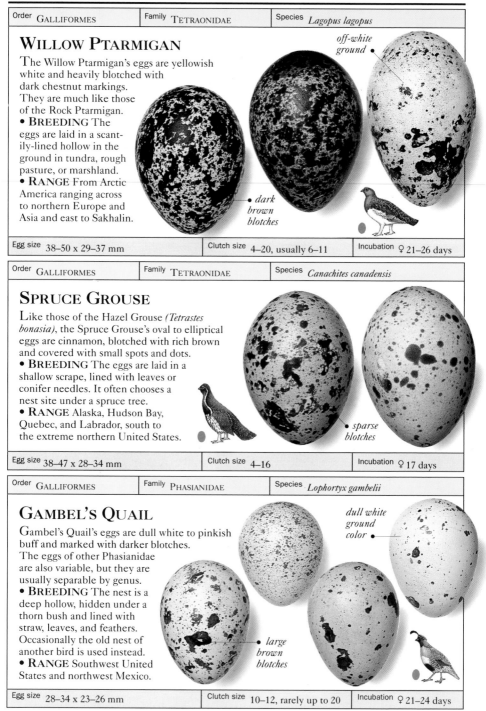

Order GALLIFORMES	Family TETRAONIDAE	Species *Lagopus lagopus*

WILLOW PTARMIGAN

The Willow Ptarmigan's eggs are yellowish white and heavily blotched with dark chestnut markings. They are much like those of the Rock Ptarmigan.
• BREEDING The eggs are laid in a scantily-lined hollow in the ground in tundra, rough pasture, or marshland.
• RANGE From Arctic America ranging across to northern Europe and Asia and east to Sakhalin.

off-white ground

dark brown blotches

Egg size 38–50 x 29–37 mm	Clutch size 4–20, usually 6–11	Incubation ♀ 21–26 days

Order GALLIFORMES	Family TETRAONIDAE	Species *Canachites canadensis*

SPRUCE GROUSE

Like those of the Hazel Grouse *(Tetrastes bonasia)*, the Spruce Grouse's oval to elliptical eggs are cinnamon, blotched with rich brown and covered with small spots and dots.
• BREEDING The eggs are laid in a shallow scrape, lined with leaves or conifer needles. It often chooses a nest site under a spruce tree.
• RANGE Alaska, Hudson Bay, Quebec, and Labrador, south to the extreme northern United States.

sparse blotches

Egg size 38–47 x 28–34 mm	Clutch size 4–16	Incubation ♀ 17 days

Order GALLIFORMES	Family PHASIANIDAE	Species *Lophortyx gambelii*

GAMBEL'S QUAIL

Gambel's Quail's eggs are dull white to pinkish buff and marked with darker blotches. The eggs of other Phasianidae are also variable, but they are usually separable by genus.
• BREEDING The nest is a deep hollow, hidden under a thorn bush and lined with straw, leaves, and feathers. Occasionally the old nest of another bird is used instead.
• RANGE Southwest United States and northwest Mexico.

dull white ground color

large brown blotches

Egg size 28–34 x 23–26 mm	Clutch size 10–12, rarely up to 20	Incubation ♀ 21–24 days

| Order GALLIFORMES | Family PHASIANIDAE | Species *Colinus virginianus* |

NORTHERN BOBWHITE

conical shape •

The eggs of the Northern Bobwhite are white or occasionally buffish and have no marks.
• **BREEDING** The Northern Bobwhite lays its eggs in a shallow scrape, carefully concealed in long grass or under bushes, in abandoned fields or amid pine trees.
• **RANGE** Eastern United States and eastern and southern Mexico. Scattered populations occur in Central America and the western United States; feral populations are also found in other parts of the world.

| Egg size 26–33 x 21–26 mm | Clutch size 7–20 | Incubation ♂♀ 23–24 days |

| Order GALLIFORMES | Family PHASIANIDAE | Species *Ammoperdix griseogularis* |

SEE-SEE PARTRIDGE

• *smooth ivory ground*

The eggs of the See-see Partridge are creamy or ivory-white, and unmarked.
• **BREEDING** The See-see Part-ridge lays its eggs in a scrape usually in the shelter of coarse grass, or by a boulder in arid, stony landscapes.
• **RANGE** Semidesert and stony areas ranging from southeastern Turkey through Iraq and Iran, east to Pakistan and north to southeastern Uzbekistan and western Tadzhikistan.

| Egg size 32–38 x 23–28 mm | Clutch size 6–9, sometimes 5–16 | Incubation ♀ 21 days |

| Order GALLIFORMES | Family PHASIANIDAE | Species *Alectoris graeca* |

ROCK PARTRIDGE

The Rock Partridge's eggs are yellowish cream to pale buff in ground color, lightly to heavily speckled with reddish brown. They are similar to the eggs of the six other species in the genus *Alectoris*.
• **BREEDING** It nests in a scrape on a stony hill or mountain, lined with the minimum of vegetation, and usually sheltered by a shrub or rock.
• **RANGE** Mountainous regions of Europe from France, Austria, and Italy to Sicily, Greece, and Bulgaria.

cream ground •

• *light stippling*

| Egg size 36–43 x 28–32 mm | Clutch size 8–14, rarely 6–21 | Incubation ♀ 24–26 days |

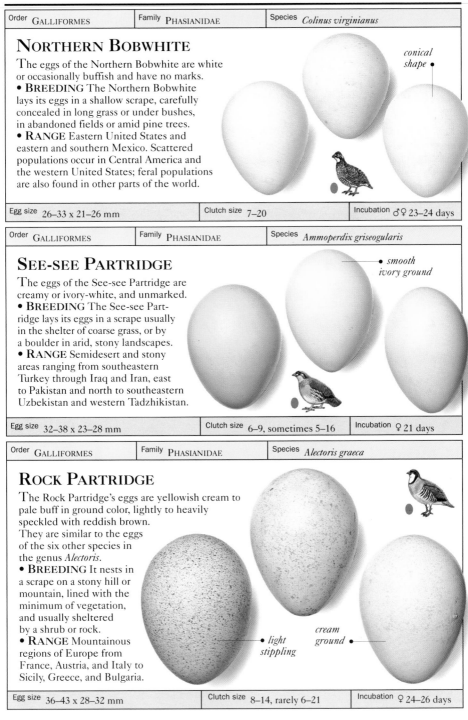

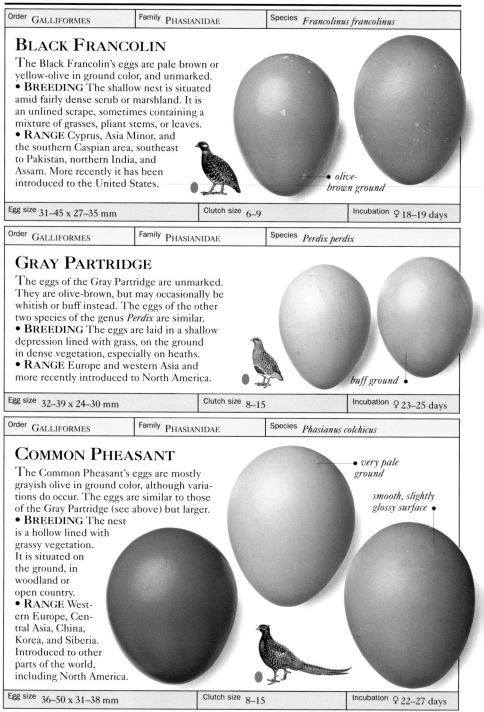

| Order GALLIFORMES | Family PHASIANIDAE | Species *Francolinus francolinus* |

BLACK FRANCOLIN

The Black Francolin's eggs are pale brown or yellow-olive in ground color, and unmarked.
• **BREEDING** The shallow nest is situated amid fairly dense scrub or marshland. It is an unlined scrape, sometimes containing a mixture of grasses, pliant stems, or leaves.
• **RANGE** Cyprus, Asia Minor, and the southern Caspian area, southeast to Pakistan, northern India, and Assam. More recently it has been introduced to the United States.

olive-brown ground

| Egg size 31–45 x 27–35 mm | Clutch size 6–9 | Incubation ♀ 18–19 days |

| Order GALLIFORMES | Family PHASIANIDAE | Species *Perdix perdix* |

GRAY PARTRIDGE

The eggs of the Gray Partridge are unmarked. They are olive-brown, but may occasionally be whitish or buff instead. The eggs of the other two species of the genus *Perdix* are similar.
• **BREEDING** The eggs are laid in a shallow depression lined with grass, on the ground in dense vegetation, especially on heaths.
• **RANGE** Europe and western Asia and more recently introduced to North America.

buff ground

| Egg size 32–39 x 24–30 mm | Clutch size 8–15 | Incubation ♀ 23–25 days |

| Order GALLIFORMES | Family PHASIANIDAE | Species *Phasianus colchicus* |

COMMON PHEASANT

The Common Pheasant's eggs are mostly grayish olive in ground color, although variations do occur. The eggs are similar to those of the Gray Partridge (see above) but larger.
• **BREEDING** The nest is a hollow lined with grassy vegetation. It is situated on the ground, in woodland or open country.
• **RANGE** Western Europe, Central Asia, China, Korea, and Siberia. Introduced to other parts of the world, including North America.

very pale ground

smooth, slightly glossy surface

| Egg size 36–50 x 31–38 mm | Clutch size 8–15 | Incubation ♀ 22–27 days |

Order GALLIFORMES	Family PHASIANIDAE	Species *Gallus gallus*

RED JUNGLEFOWL

The Red Junglefowl, the ancestor of the domestic farm hen, lays white, creamy, or brownish pink eggs.
• **BREEDING** The eggs are laid in a scrape lined with soft vegetation. The nest is found in a variety of locations, mostly on the ground but occasionally on secure ledges off the ground, or amid a clump of bamboo or under a bush.
• **RANGE** From the Himalayas and eastern India through most of Southeast Asia; now there are also widespread feral populations in Indonesia and the western Pacific islands.
• **REMARK** That the birds carry the genes in their cells to produce color and speckling on the eggs is strongly suggested by the fact that domestic hens may produce brown or speckled eggs. The larger size (and greater fragility) of the eggs of farm hens is the result of selective breeding over centuries. It would seem that although the contents of the eggs have increased in volume, the actual quantity of shell material per egg has not altered significantly, so the shells are much thinner.

speckled shell •

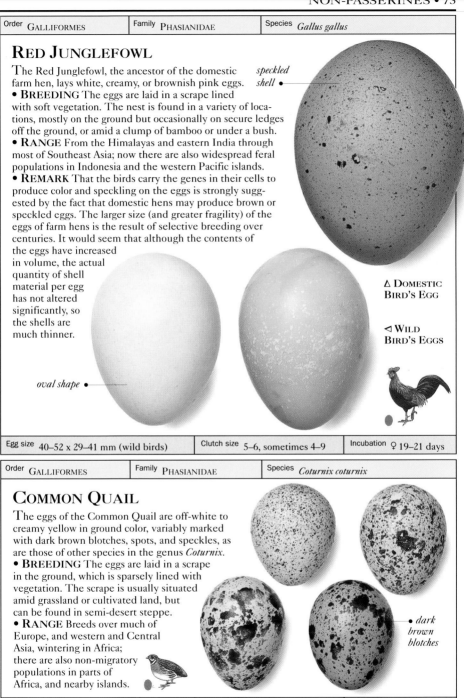

△ DOMESTIC BIRD'S EGG

◁ WILD BIRD'S EGGS

oval shape •

Egg size 40–52 x 29–41 mm (wild birds)	Clutch size 5–6, sometimes 4–9	Incubation ♀ 19–21 days

Order GALLIFORMES	Family PHASIANIDAE	Species *Coturnix coturnix*

COMMON QUAIL

The eggs of the Common Quail are off-white to creamy yellow in ground color, variably marked with dark brown blotches, spots, and speckles, as are those of other species in the genus *Coturnix*.
• **BREEDING** The eggs are laid in a scrape in the ground, which is sparsely lined with vegetation. The scrape is usually situated amid grassland or cultivated land, but can be found in semi-desert steppe.
• **RANGE** Breeds over much of Europe, and western and Central Asia, wintering in Africa; there are also non-migratory populations in parts of Africa, and nearby islands.

• *dark brown blotches*

Egg size 25–33 x 20–25 mm	Clutch size 6–18	Incubation ♀ 16–21 days

Order GALLIFORMES	Family PHASIANIDAE	Species *Synoicus australis*

BROWN QUAIL

The Brown Quail's eggs are pale yellowish white to pale yellowish green, often speckled with greenish brown. The genus *Synoicus* is sometimes merged with *Coturnix* but the eggs of the two are very different. Recent DNA studies support the view that the genus *Synoicus* is monotypic.
• **BREEDING** Few examples of the Brown Quail's nest have ever been found, but it is probably a simple scrape lined with grasses in dry, open grassland.
• **RANGE** Australia, New Guinea, and the Lesser Sunda Islands; also introduced into New Zealand.

• *red-brown spots*

Egg size 26–33 x 21–25 mm	Clutch size 10–18	Incubation 18 days

Order GALLIFORMES	Family PHASIANIDAE	Species *Excalfactoria chinensis*

PAINTED QUAIL

• *oval shape*

The Painted Quail's eggs are light yellowish or greenish brown to olive-brown, speckled all over with dark brown or black. These distinctive eggs highlight the difference between this species and the genus *Coturnix*, in which it is often included. The eggs of the two species of *Excalfactoria*, however, are similar.
• **BREEDING** The nest is a mere scrape, located among swamp, marshland vegetation, or tall grasses.
• **RANGE** India, southeast China, Indonesia, north and east Australia.

• *olive-brown ground*

Egg size 22–28 x 17–21 mm	Clutch size 4–8	Incubation ♀ c. 16 days

Order GALLIFORMES	Family PHASIANIDAE	Species *Perdicula asiatica*

JUNGLE BUSH-QUAIL

• *smooth, creamy white ground*

The Jungle Bush-Quail's eggs are creamy white in ground color. They are indistinguishable from the eggs of the other three species of bush-quail resident in the Indian Subcontinent.
• **BREEDING** The nest is a shallow scrape, lined with grass and often concealed by being sited at the base of a grass tussock. It is located on the ground in dry scrub, scrub jungle, or semidesert.
• **RANGE** Indian Subcontinent and Sri Lanka.

• *elliptical shape*

Egg size 24–28 x 18–22 mm	Clutch size 4–8	Incubation ♀ 16–18 days

Order GALLIFORMES	Family PHASIANIDAE	Species *Tetraogallus tibetanus*

TIBETAN SNOWCOCK

The eggs of the Tibetan Snowcock are pale yellowish stone to reddish buff with scattered reddish brown speckles and blotches. The Tibetan Snowcock is a typical member of the genus *Tetraogallus*. The eggs of the other four snowcock species are similar.
• **BREEDING** The Tibetan Snowcock lays its eggs in a natural or scraped hollow, that is lined with dried leaves and grasses. The nest is concealed among stones and boulders, or sited under the shelter of a small rock, amid mountain scrub and alpine meadows.
• **RANGE** Occurs from the Pamir and Himalayan ranges east to Tibet, to northwestern Szechwan and northeastern India.

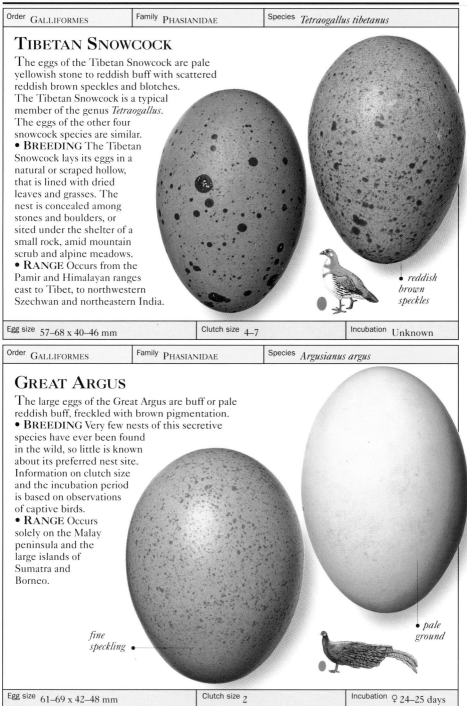

• *reddish brown speckles*

Egg size 57–68 x 40–46 mm	Clutch size 4–7	Incubation Unknown

Order GALLIFORMES	Family PHASIANIDAE	Species *Argusianus argus*

GREAT ARGUS

The large eggs of the Great Argus are buff or pale reddish buff, freckled with brown pigmentation.
• **BREEDING** Very few nests of this secretive species have ever been found in the wild, so little is known about its preferred nest site. Information on clutch size and the incubation period is based on observations of captive birds.
• **RANGE** Occurs solely on the Malay peninsula and the large islands of Sumatra and Borneo.

fine speckling •

• *pale ground*

Egg size 61–69 x 42–48 mm	Clutch size 2	Incubation ♀ 24–25 days

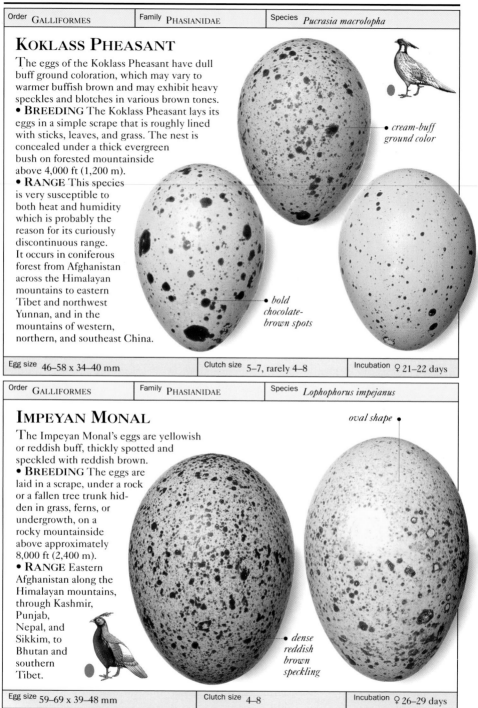

| Order GALLIFORMES | Family PHASIANIDAE | Species *Pucrasia macrolopha* |

KOKLASS PHEASANT

The eggs of the Koklass Pheasant have dull buff ground coloration, which may vary to warmer buffish brown and may exhibit heavy speckles and blotches in various brown tones.
• **BREEDING** The Koklass Pheasant lays its eggs in a simple scrape that is roughly lined with sticks, leaves, and grass. The nest is concealed under a thick evergreen bush on forested mountainside above 4,000 ft (1,200 m).
• **RANGE** This species is very susceptible to both heat and humidity which is probably the reason for its curiously discontinuous range. It occurs in coniferous forest from Afghanistan across the Himalayan mountains to eastern Tibet and northwest Yunnan, and in the mountains of western, northern, and southeast China.

• *cream-buff ground color*

• *bold chocolate-brown spots*

| Egg size 46–58 x 34–40 mm | Clutch size 5–7, rarely 4–8 | Incubation ♀ 21–22 days |

| Order GALLIFORMES | Family PHASIANIDAE | Species *Lophophorus impejanus* |

IMPEYAN MONAL

oval shape •

The Impeyan Monal's eggs are yellowish or reddish buff, thickly spotted and speckled with reddish brown.
• **BREEDING** The eggs are laid in a scrape, under a rock or a fallen tree trunk hidden in grass, ferns, or undergrowth, on a rocky mountainside above approximately 8,000 ft (2,400 m).
• **RANGE** Eastern Afghanistan along the Himalayan mountains, through Kashmir, Punjab, Nepal, and Sikkim, to Bhutan and southern Tibet.

• *dense reddish brown speckling*

| Egg size 59–69 x 39–48 mm | Clutch size 4–8 | Incubation ♀ 26–29 days |

Order GALLIFORMES	Family NUMIDIDAE	Species *Acryllium vulturinum*

VULTURINE GUINEAFOWL

The eggs of all guineafowl, including those of the
Vulturine Guineafowl, are creamy white or pale
brown, either with or without marks. The
eggshells have a slightly pitted surface.
• BREEDING No nest is made.
The eggs are laid in a simple
scrape on the ground concealed
among thick grass or scrub.
• RANGE The range of the
Vulturine Guineafowl is very
small; it is confined to an area
of Africa that spans
from northeastern
Uganda, south
Ethiopia, Somalia,
Kenya, and
northern Tanzania.

• *fine stippling*

• *pitted surface*

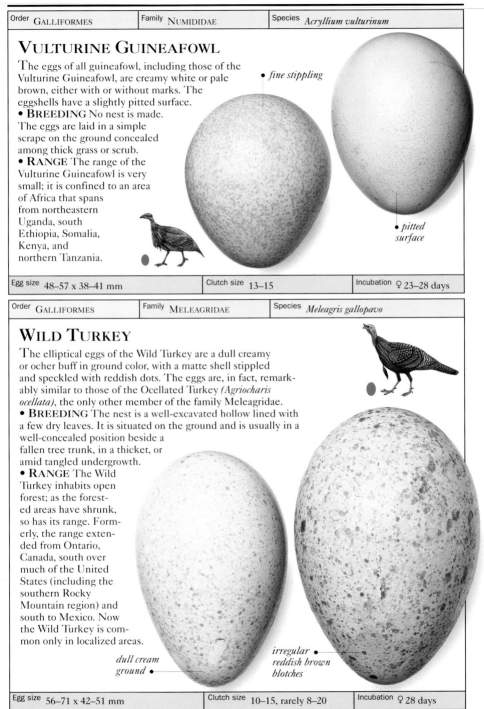

Egg size 48–57 x 38–41 mm	Clutch size 13–15	Incubation ♀ 23–28 days

Order GALLIFORMES	Family MELEAGRIDAE	Species *Meleagris gallopavo*

WILD TURKEY

The elliptical eggs of the Wild Turkey are a dull creamy
or ocher buff in ground color, with a matte shell stippled
and speckled with reddish dots. The eggs are, in fact, remarkably similar to those of the Ocellated Turkey *(Agriocharis
ocellata)*, the only other member of the family Meleagridae.
• BREEDING The nest is a well-excavated hollow lined with
a few dry leaves. It is situated on the ground and is usually in a
well-concealed position beside a
fallen tree trunk, in a thicket, or
amid tangled undergrowth.
• RANGE The Wild
Turkey inhabits open
forest; as the forest-
ed areas have shrunk,
so has its range. Form-
erly, the range exten-
ded from Ontario,
Canada, south over
much of the United
States (including the
southern Rocky
Mountain region) and
south to Mexico. Now
the Wild Turkey is com-
mon only in localized areas.

*dull cream
ground* •

irregular •
*reddish brown
blotches*

Egg size 56–71 x 42–51 mm	Clutch size 10–15, rarely 8–20	Incubation ♀ 28 days

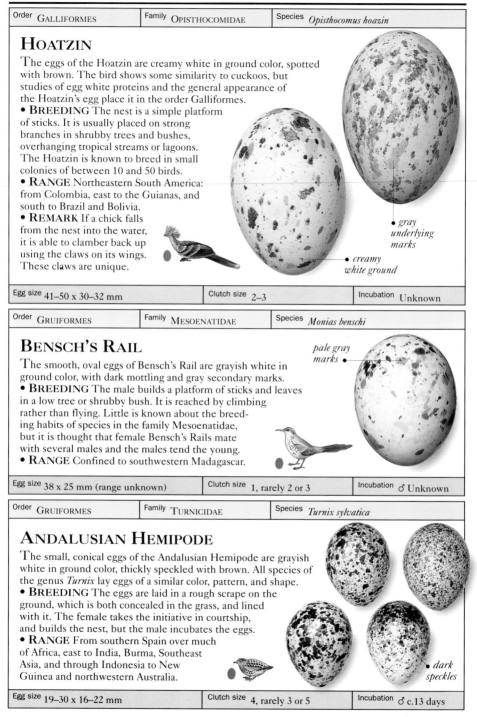

Order GALLIFORMES	Family OPISTHOCOMIDAE	Species *Opisthocomus hoazin*

HOATZIN

The eggs of the Hoatzin are creamy white in ground color, spotted with brown. The bird shows some similarity to cuckoos, but studies of egg white proteins and the general appearance of the Hoatzin's egg place it in the order Galliformes.
• **BREEDING** The nest is a simple platform of sticks. It is usually placed on strong branches in shrubby trees and bushes, overhanging tropical streams or lagoons. The Hoatzin is known to breed in small colonies of between 10 and 50 birds.
• **RANGE** Northeastern South America: from Colombia, east to the Guianas, and south to Brazil and Bolivia.
• **REMARK** If a chick falls from the nest into the water, it is able to clamber back up using the claws on its wings. These claws are unique.

• *gray underlying marks*

• *creamy white ground*

Egg size 41–50 x 30–32 mm	Clutch size 2–3	Incubation Unknown

Order GRUIFORMES	Family MESOENATIDAE	Species *Monias benschi*

BENSCH'S RAIL

pale gray marks •

The smooth, oval eggs of Bensch's Rail are grayish white in ground color, with dark mottling and gray secondary marks.
• **BREEDING** The male builds a platform of sticks and leaves in a low tree or shrubby bush. It is reached by climbing rather than flying. Little is known about the breeding habits of species in the family Mesoenatidae, but it is thought that female Bensch's Rails mate with several males and the males tend the young.
• **RANGE** Confined to southwestern Madagascar.

Egg size 38 x 25 mm (range unknown)	Clutch size 1, rarely 2 or 3	Incubation ♂ Unknown

Order GRUIFORMES	Family TURNICIDAE	Species *Turnix sylvatica*

ANDALUSIAN HEMIPODE

The small, conical eggs of the Andalusian Hemipode are grayish white in ground color, thickly speckled with brown. All species of the genus *Turnix* lay eggs of a similar color, pattern, and shape.
• **BREEDING** The eggs are laid in a rough scrape on the ground, which is both concealed in the grass, and lined with it. The female takes the initiative in courtship, and builds the nest, but the male incubates the eggs.
• **RANGE** From southern Spain over much of Africa, east to India, Burma, Southeast Asia, and through Indonesia to New Guinea and northwestern Australia.

• *dark speckles*

Egg size 19–30 x 16–22 mm	Clutch size 4, rarely 3 or 5	Incubation ♂ c.13 days

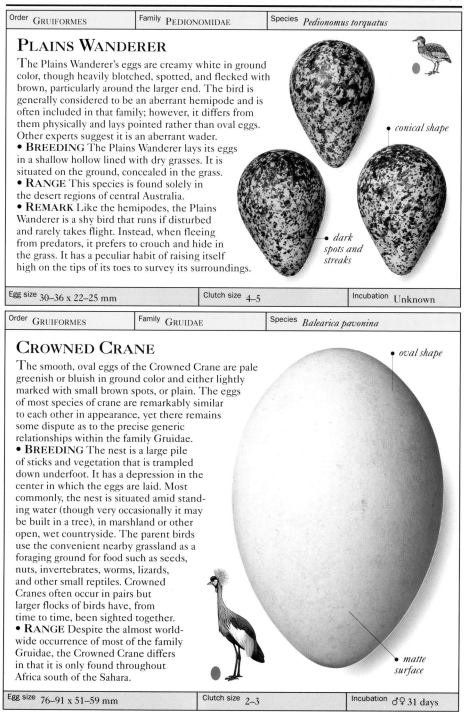

Order GRUIFORMES	Family PEDIONOMIDAE	Species *Pedionomus torquatus*

PLAINS WANDERER

The Plains Wanderer's eggs are creamy white in ground color, though heavily blotched, spotted, and flecked with brown, particularly around the larger end. The bird is generally considered to be an aberrant hemipode and is often included in that family; however, it differs from them physically and lays pointed rather than oval eggs. Other experts suggest it is an aberrant wader.
• **BREEDING** The Plains Wanderer lays its eggs in a shallow hollow lined with dry grasses. It is situated on the ground, concealed in the grass.
• **RANGE** This species is found solely in the desert regions of central Australia.
• **REMARK** Like the hemipodes, the Plains Wanderer is a shy bird that runs if disturbed and rarely takes flight. Instead, when fleeing from predators, it prefers to crouch and hide in the grass. It has a peculiar habit of raising itself high on the tips of its toes to survey its surroundings.

• *conical shape*

• *dark spots and streaks*

Egg size 30–36 x 22–25 mm	Clutch size 4–5	Incubation Unknown

Order GRUIFORMES	Family GRUIDAE	Species *Balearica pavonina*

CROWNED CRANE

• *oval shape*

The smooth, oval eggs of the Crowned Crane are pale greenish or bluish in ground color and either lightly marked with small brown spots, or plain. The eggs of most species of crane are remarkably similar to each other in appearance, yet there remains some dispute as to the precise generic relationships within the family Gruidae.
• **BREEDING** The nest is a large pile of sticks and vegetation that is trampled down underfoot. It has a depression in the center in which the eggs are laid. Most commonly, the nest is situated amid standing water (though very occasionally it may be built in a tree), in marshland or other open, wet countryside. The parent birds use the convenient nearby grassland as a foraging ground for food such as seeds, nuts, invertebrates, worms, lizards, and other small reptiles. Crowned Cranes often occur in pairs but larger flocks of birds have, from time to time, been sighted together.
• **RANGE** Despite the almost worldwide occurrence of most of the family Gruidae, the Crowned Crane differs in that it is only found throughout Africa south of the Sahara.

• *matte surface*

Egg size 76–91 x 51–59 mm	Clutch size 2–3	Incubation ♂♀ 31 days

Order GRUIFORMES	Family GRUIDAE	Species *Grus grus*

COMMON CRANE

The eggs of the Common Crane are grayish olive-green to olive-brown in ground color, and handsomely marbled. All cranes' eggs are very large and are elliptical in shape.

• **BREEDING** The nest is a large structure of sticks built above the water level, either at the edge of or within water. Most often it is situated in marshes or other similar areas of wetland (such as the tundra). The same nest site is used year after year by the same pair.

Territories are normally very large, although the size of each is determined by the richness of the habitat, in particular the amount of food the territory provides.

• **RANGE** Occurs in Scandinavia south to Germany and the Balkans. Some local breeding populations reside in Spain and Italy. It winters from the Mediterranean and northern Africa to southern India and Southeast Asia.

• *olive ground*

Egg size 88–110 x 57–66 mm	Clutch size 1–3	Incubation ♂♀ 28–30 days

| Order GRUIFORMES | Family GRUIDAE | Species *Grus antigone* |

SARUS CRANE

The massive oval eggs of the Sarus Crane are pinkish or greenish white, blotched and spotted with brown. This egg coloration is paler than that of most cranes. The eggs fade to white in museum collections.
• **BREEDING** The nest is a pile of sticks and other vegetation, built up out of the water. Its usual location is in a shallow part of a marsh. Some nests are used year after year. Sarus Cranes pair for life; the devotion exhibited by these birds is legendary throughout India.

• **RANGE** India, to Assam, Burma, Thailand, and southern Vietnam. It has recently colonized north Australia and is extending its range there.

oval shape •

| Egg size 85–114 x 55–70 mm | Clutch size 2 | Incubation ♂♀ 28–34 days |

Order GRUIFORMES	Family ARAMIDAE	Species *Aramus guarauna*

LIMPKIN

The eggs laid by the Limpkin are buff in color, and are blotched and spotted with brown marks. They are similar in appearance to cranes' eggs but smaller. The blotches on the eggs of both the Limpkin and cranes tend to be more blurred than those on the eggs of rails.

• **BREEDING** The nest is simply a loose, bulky pile of leaves, twigs, and moss. It is situated over or close to water in marshes or swamps, sometimes in low trees or bushes. However, the nest may also be sited in sawgrass, where it includes stems of living plants within the structure.

• **RANGE** Locally over the warmer regions of the southeastern United States, the Greater Antilles, Central and South America.

blurred brown blotches

Egg size 55–64 x 41–47 mm	Clutch size 4–8, usually 6	Incubation ♂♀ Unknown

Order GRUIFORMES	Family PSOPHIIDAE	Species *Psophia crepitans*

GRAY-WINGED TRUMPETER

The eggs laid by the Gray-winged Trumpeter in captivity (South American Indians commonly keep them as pets) are white; however, eggs with a pale greenish hue have also been reported. The other two species of trumpeter lay similar-colored eggs.

• **BREEDING** Conflicting reports exist of where this bird nests. Some authorities claim that it nests on the ground; others describe a stick nest in among tree branches; and yet others refer to a nest in a tree hole, incubated by the male.

• **RANGE** In South America, north from the Amazon Basin, including eastern regions of Venezuela, Colombia, and Ecuador.

eggs of captive birds are white

Egg size 50–55 x 37–42 mm	Clutch size 6–10	Incubation Unknown

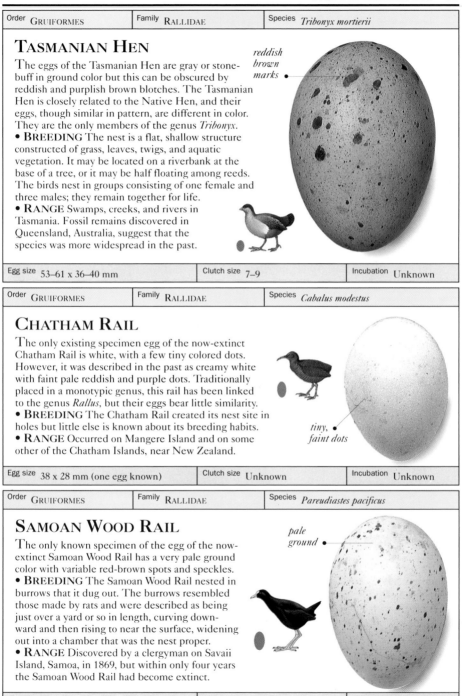

| Order GRUIFORMES | Family RALLIDAE | Species *Tribonyx mortierii* |

TASMANIAN HEN

The eggs of the Tasmanian Hen are gray or stone-buff in ground color but this can be obscured by reddish and purplish brown blotches. The Tasmanian Hen is closely related to the Native Hen, and their eggs, though similar in pattern, are different in color. They are the only members of the genus *Tribonyx*.
• BREEDING The nest is a flat, shallow structure constructed of grass, leaves, twigs, and aquatic vegetation. It may be located on a riverbank at the base of a tree, or it may be half floating among reeds. The birds nest in groups consisting of one female and three males; they remain together for life.
• RANGE Swamps, creeks, and rivers in Tasmania. Fossil remains discovered in Queensland, Australia, suggest that the species was more widespread in the past.

reddish brown marks •

| Egg size 53–61 x 36–40 mm | Clutch size 7–9 | Incubation Unknown |

| Order GRUIFORMES | Family RALLIDAE | Species *Cabalus modestus* |

CHATHAM RAIL

The only existing specimen egg of the now-extinct Chatham Rail is white, with a few tiny colored dots. However, it was described in the past as creamy white with faint pale reddish and purple dots. Traditionally placed in a monotypic genus, this rail has been linked to the genus *Rallus*, but their eggs bear little similarity.
• BREEDING The Chatham Rail created its nest site in holes but little else is known about its breeding habits.
• RANGE Occurred on Mangere Island and on some other of the Chatham Islands, near New Zealand.

tiny, faint dots •

| Egg size 38 x 28 mm (one egg known) | Clutch size Unknown | Incubation Unknown |

| Order GRUIFORMES | Family RALLIDAE | Species *Pareudiastes pacificus* |

SAMOAN WOOD RAIL

The only known specimen of the egg of the now-extinct Samoan Wood Rail has a very pale ground color with variable red-brown spots and speckles.
• BREEDING The Samoan Wood Rail nested in burrows that it dug out. The burrows resembled those made by rats and were described as being just over a yard or so in length, curving down-ward and then rising to near the surface, widening out into a chamber that was the nest proper.
• RANGE Discovered by a clergyman on Savaii Island, Samoa, in 1869, but within only four years the Samoan Wood Rail had become extinct.

pale ground •

| Egg size 45 x 31 mm (one egg known) | Clutch size Unknown | Incubation Unknown |

| Order GRUIFORMES | Family RALLIDAE | Species *Atlantisia rogersi* |

INACCESSIBLE RAIL

buff tinge

The eggs of the Inaccessible Rail are grayish milk-white in ground color, tinged with buff and lightly spotted with dark brown-red, with underlying lavender dots.
• BREEDING A grass structure with a matted roof is woven by the birds to form a nest. These tiny rails breed together in island colonies amid tussocks of spartina grass.
• RANGE Exclusive to a pillar of rock known as Inaccessible Island, within the Tristan de Cunha group in the South Atlantic Ocean.

| Egg size 31–34 x 21–24 mm | Clutch size 2 | Incubation Unknown |

| Order GRUIFORMES | Family RALLIDAE | Species *Rallina canningi* |

ANDAMAN BANDED CRAKE

smooth white ground

The Andaman Banded Crake's eggs are plain white, as are the eggs of other members of the genus *Rallina*; but some authorities claim that the Andaman Banded Crake's eggs have a more pronounced shiny yellowish white surface.
• BREEDING The nest is made of grasses and leaves. It is situated on or near the ground in tangled undergrowth or at the base of a tree; it can be close to water.
• RANGE Confined to the Andaman Islands in the northern Indian Ocean, although its range within the archipelago has never been mapped.

| Egg size 37–43 x 29–32 mm | Clutch size Unknown | Incubation ♂♀ Unknown |

| Order GRUIFORMES | Family RALLIDAE | Species *Gallinula chloropus* |

COMMON MOORHEN

The eggs of the Common Moorhen (or Florida Gallinule) are whitish gray, buff, or greenish, blotched with reddish brown and pale ash-gray.
• BREEDING The Moorhen breeds on or near still or slow-running waters. The cup-shaped nest is built of dead reeds, and is sited among aquatic plants.
• RANGE Occurs in tropical, subtropical, and temperate areas, except Australasia and the South Pacific islands.

reddish brown spots and blotches

buff ground color

| Egg size 37–51 x 27–34 mm | Clutch size 4–26, usually 5–11 | Incubation ♂♀ 19–22 days |

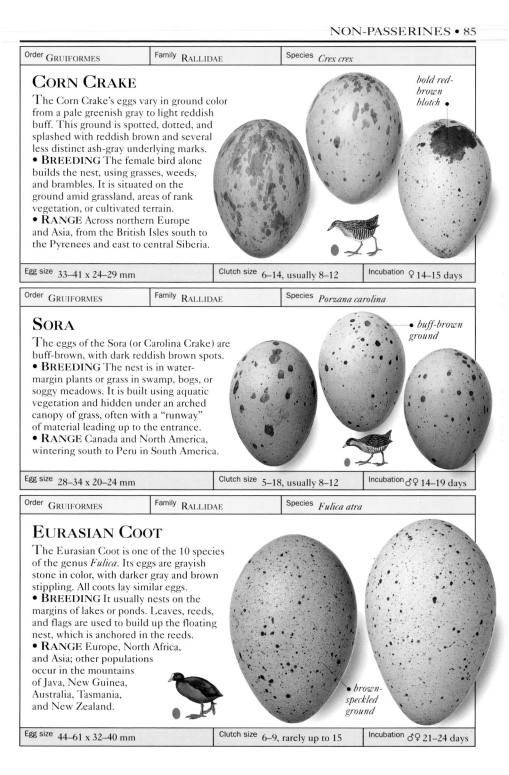

| Order GRUIFORMES | Family RALLIDAE | Species *Crex crex* |

CORN CRAKE

The Corn Crake's eggs vary in ground color from a pale greenish gray to light reddish buff. This ground is spotted, dotted, and splashed with reddish brown and several less distinct ash-gray underlying marks.
• **BREEDING** The female bird alone builds the nest, using grasses, weeds, and brambles. It is situated on the ground amid grassland, areas of rank vegetation, or cultivated terrain.
• **RANGE** Across northern Europe and Asia, from the British Isles south to the Pyrenees and east to central Siberia.

bold red-brown blotch

| Egg size 33–41 x 24–29 mm | Clutch size 6–14, usually 8–12 | Incubation ♀ 14–15 days |

| Order GRUIFORMES | Family RALLIDAE | Species *Porzana carolina* |

SORA

The eggs of the Sora (or Carolina Crake) are buff-brown, with dark reddish brown spots.
• **BREEDING** The nest is in water-margin plants or grass in swamp, bogs, or soggy meadows. It is built using aquatic vegetation and hidden under an arched canopy of grass, often with a "runway" of material leading up to the entrance.
• **RANGE** Canada and North America, wintering south to Peru in South America.

buff-brown ground

| Egg size 28–34 x 20–24 mm | Clutch size 5–18, usually 8–12 | Incubation ♂♀ 14–19 days |

| Order GRUIFORMES | Family RALLIDAE | Species *Fulica atra* |

EURASIAN COOT

The Eurasian Coot is one of the 10 species of the genus *Fulica*. Its eggs are grayish stone in color, with darker gray and brown stippling. All coots lay similar eggs.
• **BREEDING** It usually nests on the margins of lakes or ponds. Leaves, reeds, and flags are used to build up the floating nest, which is anchored in the reeds.
• **RANGE** Europe, North Africa, and Asia; other populations occur in the mountains of Java, New Guinea, Australia, Tasmania, and New Zealand.

brown-speckled ground

| Egg size 44–61 x 32–40 mm | Clutch size 6–9, rarely up to 15 | Incubation ♂♀ 21–24 days |

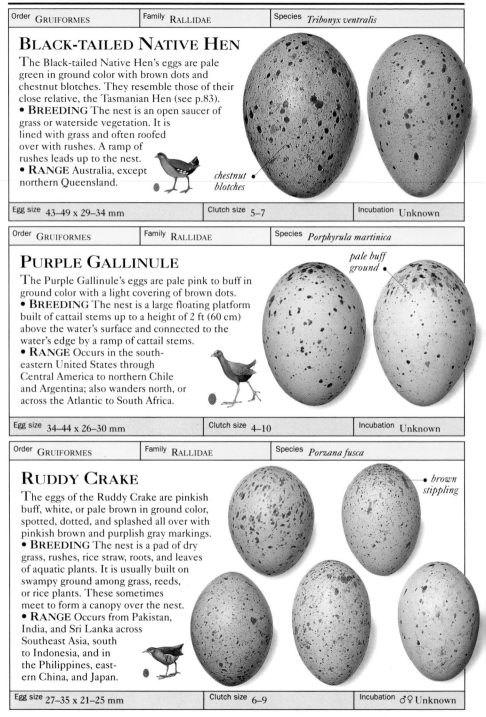

| Order GRUIFORMES | Family RALLIDAE | Species *Tribonyx ventralis* |

BLACK-TAILED NATIVE HEN

The Black-tailed Native Hen's eggs are pale green in ground color with brown dots and chestnut blotches. They resemble those of their close relative, the Tasmanian Hen (see p.83).
• **BREEDING** The nest is an open saucer of grass or waterside vegetation. It is lined with grass and often roofed over with rushes. A ramp of rushes leads up to the nest.
• **RANGE** Australia, except northern Queensland.

chestnut blotches

| Egg size 43–49 x 29–34 mm | Clutch size 5–7 | Incubation Unknown |

| Order GRUIFORMES | Family RALLIDAE | Species *Porphyrula martinica* |

PURPLE GALLINULE

pale buff ground

The Purple Gallinule's eggs are pale pink to buff in ground color with a light covering of brown dots.
• **BREEDING** The nest is a large floating platform built of cattail stems up to a height of 2 ft (60 cm) above the water's surface and connected to the water's edge by a ramp of cattail stems.
• **RANGE** Occurs in the southeastern United States through Central America to northern Chile and Argentina; also wanders north, or across the Atlantic to South Africa.

| Egg size 34–44 x 26–30 mm | Clutch size 4–10 | Incubation Unknown |

| Order GRUIFORMES | Family RALLIDAE | Species *Porzana fusca* |

RUDDY CRAKE

brown stippling

The eggs of the Ruddy Crake are pinkish buff, white, or pale brown in ground color, spotted, dotted, and splashed all over with pinkish brown and purplish gray markings.
• **BREEDING** The nest is a pad of dry grass, rushes, rice straw, roots, and leaves of aquatic plants. It is usually built on swampy ground among grass, reeds, or rice plants. These sometimes meet to form a canopy over the nest.
• **RANGE** Occurs from Pakistan, India, and Sri Lanka across Southeast Asia, south to Indonesia, and in the Philippines, eastern China, and Japan.

| Egg size 27–35 x 21–25 mm | Clutch size 6–9 | Incubation ♂♀ Unknown |

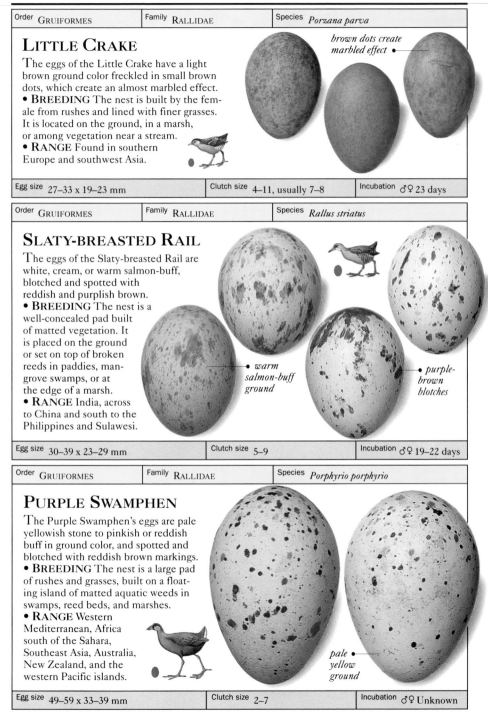

Order GRUIFORMES	Family RALLIDAE	Species *Porzana parva*

LITTLE CRAKE

The eggs of the Little Crake have a light brown ground color freckled in small brown dots, which create an almost marbled effect.
• **BREEDING** The nest is built by the female from rushes and lined with finer grasses. It is located on the ground, in a marsh, or among vegetation near a stream.
• **RANGE** Found in southern Europe and southwest Asia.

brown dots create marbled effect •

Egg size 27–33 x 19–23 mm	Clutch size 4–11, usually 7–8	Incubation ♂♀ 23 days

Order GRUIFORMES	Family RALLIDAE	Species *Rallus striatus*

SLATY-BREASTED RAIL

The eggs of the Slaty-breasted Rail are white, cream, or warm salmon-buff, blotched and spotted with reddish and purplish brown.
• **BREEDING** The nest is a well-concealed pad built of matted vegetation. It is placed on the ground or set on top of broken reeds in paddies, mangrove swamps, or at the edge of a marsh.
• **RANGE** India, across to China and south to the Philippines and Sulawesi.

• *warm salmon-buff ground*

• *purple-brown blotches*

Egg size 30–39 x 23–29 mm	Clutch size 5–9	Incubation ♂♀ 19–22 days

Order GRUIFORMES	Family RALLIDAE	Species *Porphyrio porphyrio*

PURPLE SWAMPHEN

The Purple Swamphen's eggs are pale yellowish stone to pinkish or reddish buff in ground color, and spotted and blotched with reddish brown markings.
• **BREEDING** The nest is a large pad of rushes and grasses, built on a floating island of matted aquatic weeds in swamps, reed beds, and marshes.
• **RANGE** Western Mediterranean, Africa south of the Sahara, Southeast Asia, Australia, New Zealand, and the western Pacific islands.

pale • *yellow ground*

Egg size 49–59 x 33–39 mm	Clutch size 2–7	Incubation ♂♀ Unknown

Order GRUIFORMES	Family RALLIDAE	Species *Aramides ypecaha*

GIANT WOOD-RAIL

The eggs of the Giant Wood-Rail are usually white in ground color but may be tinted pale yellow, green, pink, or orange, blotched, spotted, and dotted with dark red-brown.
• **BREEDING** The nest is built of grasses and weed stems. It is located in a small shrub or in broken-down vegetation in marshland, above ground level.
• **RANGE** Reed beds and along marshy borders of rivers in South America: eastern Brazil, Paraguay, Uruguay, and eastern Argentina.

reddish brown markings •

• *orange-tinted ground*

Egg size 51–63 x 35–40 mm	Clutch size 5	Incubation Unknown

Order GRUIFORMES	Family HELIORNITHIDAE	Species *Heliopais personata*

ASIAN FINFOOT

The eggs of the Asian Finfoot, like those of some species of bustard, are basically cream-colored but tinged with faint green or pink, with small blotches of reddish and blackish brown and underlying lavender-gray markings.
• **BREEDING** The nest is a circular pad of twigs with a depression in the center. It is usually sited on a branch of a partly submerged tree amid dense jungle swamp.
• **RANGE** Marsh and water, from Bangladesh southeast through the Malay peninsula. Winters south to Sumatra and Java. The two other species of finfoot inhabit tropical Africa and tropical America respectively.

secondary lavender marks •

• *almost spherical shape*

Egg size 46–56 x 40–46 mm	Clutch size 5–6	Incubation ♂♀ Unknown

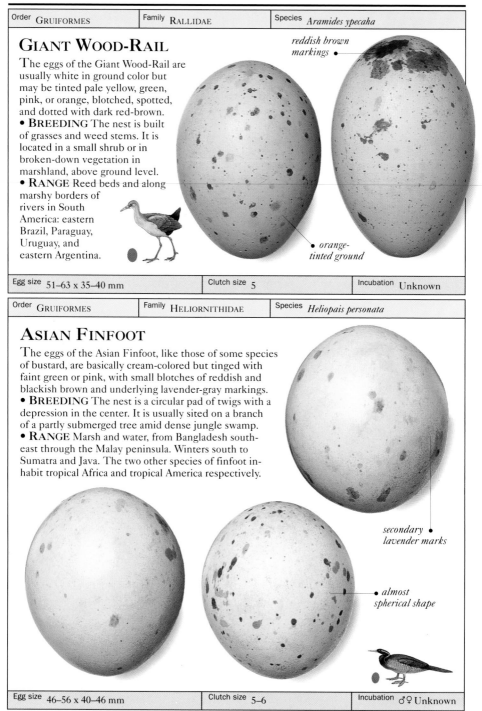

| Order GRUIFORMES | Family RHYNOCHETIDAE | Species *Rhynochetus jubata* |

KAGU

The eggs of the Kagu – a mysterious and almost flightless bird that is the only member of its family and is now verging on extinction – are creamy or pinkish buff, spotted and streaked with purplish brown and gray markings.
• **BREEDING** A nest has never been discovered in the wild; captive Kagus are known to build a nest of leaves and twigs on the ground.
• **RANGE** The Kagu is now limited in range to the mountain forests of New Caledonia in the southwest Pacific.
• **REMARK** It is an aberrant member of the Gruiformes, with no close relatives.

brown • and gray marks

creamy buff ground •

| Egg size 59–64 x 43–48 mm | Clutch size 1 | Incubation ♂♀ 36 days |

| Order GRUIFORMES | Family EURYPYGIDAE | Species *Eurypyga helias* |

SUNBITTERN

The eggs of the Sunbittern are pinkish buff in ground color, with a spattering of dark brown, chestnut, and gray blotches and spots, especially at the larger end.
• **BREEDING** The bulky, domed nest has a side entrance and is built of leaves, stems, mosses, and other local vegetation. The nest is sited in a tree, usually near a stream.
• **RANGE** Forests from Guatemala to northern South America south to central Bolivia, southern Peru, and the Matto Grosso, Brazil.

• pinkish buff ground color

chestnut blotches • at larger end

| Egg size 41–46 x 33–36 mm | Clutch size 2 | Incubation Unknown |

| Order GRUIFORMES | Family CARIAMIDAE | Species *Cariama cristata* |

RED-LEGGED SERIEMA

The Red-legged Seriema's eggs are whitish or pinkish buff with bold red-brown marks, but the ground often fades to off-white during incubation. Some eggs resemble those of the Sunbittern (see p.89) but are larger.
• **BREEDING** It nests on the ground, building a bulky construction of twigs and vegetation.
• **RANGE** Semi-desert country or open savannah from Brazil to Bolivia, Paraguay, and Argentina.

whitish ground •

| Egg size 56–68 x 45–50 mm | Clutch size 2 | Incubation ♂♀ 25–26 days |

| Order GRUIFORMES | Family OTIDIDAE | Species *Otis tetrax* |

LITTLE BUSTARD

The eggs of the Little Bustard vary from light greenish olive to dark olive-brown or occasionally pale blue, with darker streaks and smears.
• **BREEDING** The eggs are laid in a simple scrape on the ground in open countryside. The nest site is usually sheltered by vegetation.
• **RANGE** The western population occurs in west France to North Africa; eastern populations breed in eastern Europe and western Asia.

• *light olive-green ground*

• *glossy surface*

| Egg size 46–57 x 35–41 mm | Clutch size 3–5 | Incubation ♀ 20–21 days |

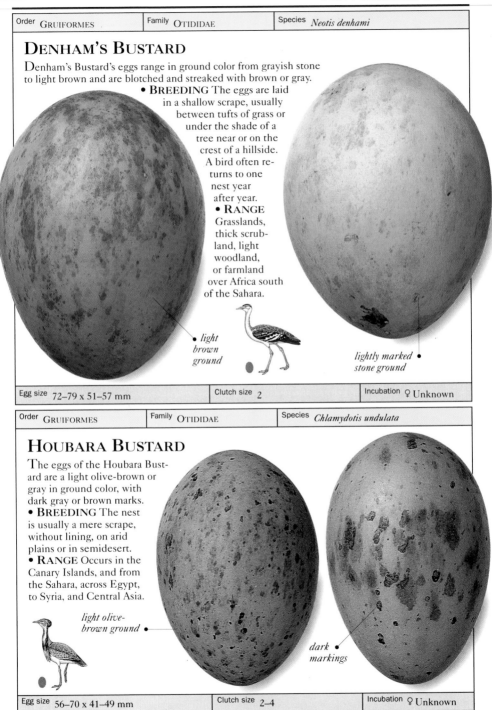

| Order GRUIFORMES | Family OTIDIDAE | Species *Neotis denhami* |

DENHAM'S BUSTARD

Denham's Bustard's eggs range in ground color from grayish stone to light brown and are blotched and streaked with brown or gray.
• **BREEDING** The eggs are laid in a shallow scrape, usually between tufts of grass or under the shade of a tree near or on the crest of a hillside. A bird often returns to one nest year after year.
• **RANGE** Grasslands, thick scrubland, light woodland, or farmland over Africa south of the Sahara.

light brown ground

lightly marked stone ground

| Egg size 72–79 x 51–57 mm | Clutch size 2 | Incubation ♀ Unknown |

| Order GRUIFORMES | Family OTIDIDAE | Species *Chlamydotis undulata* |

HOUBARA BUSTARD

The eggs of the Houbara Bustard are a light olive-brown or gray in ground color, with dark gray or brown marks.
• **BREEDING** The nest is usually a mere scrape, without lining, on arid plains or in semidesert.
• **RANGE** Occurs in the Canary Islands, and from the Sahara, across Egypt, to Syria, and Central Asia.

light olive-brown ground

dark markings

| Egg size 56–70 x 41–49 mm | Clutch size 2–4 | Incubation ♀ Unknown |

Order GRUIFORMES	Family OTIDIDAE	Species *Eupodotis ruficrista*

RED-CRESTED BUSTARD

The eggs of the Red-crested Bustard are cream to olive-buff in ground color. The glossy shells are handsomely blotched and streaked with reddish brown and gray.
• **BREEDING** This is a very secretive bird that has been little studied, but it is known that the nest is a scrape on the ground, generally in the shade or cover of a large plant or bush, amid arid or semi-arid savannah, scrubland, or light woodland.
• **RANGE** Widely separated populations occur through Africa: from Senegal and Gambia locally through the Sahel belt to northern Nigeria; from Somalia to Ethiopia, Kenya, and northern Tanzania; ranging to southern Africa: Angola, Botswana, Zambia, Zimbabwe, and Mozambique.

• spherical shape

• glossy surface

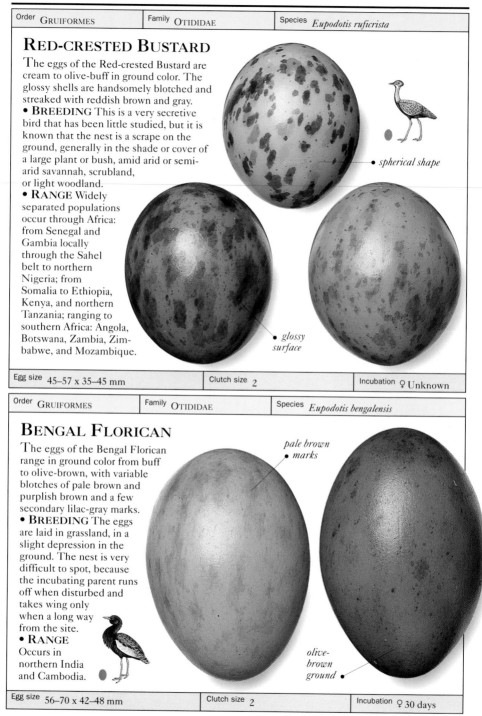

Egg size 45–57 x 35–45 mm	Clutch size 2	Incubation ♀ Unknown

Order GRUIFORMES	Family OTIDIDAE	Species *Eupodotis bengalensis*

BENGAL FLORICAN

The eggs of the Bengal Florican range in ground color from buff to olive-brown, with variable blotches of pale brown and purplish brown and a few secondary lilac-gray marks.
• **BREEDING** The eggs are laid in grassland, in a slight depression in the ground. The nest is very difficult to spot, because the incubating parent runs off when disturbed and takes wing only when a long way from the site.
• **RANGE** Occurs in northern India and Cambodia.

pale brown • marks

olive-brown ground •

Egg size 56–70 x 42–48 mm	Clutch size 2	Incubation ♀ 30 days

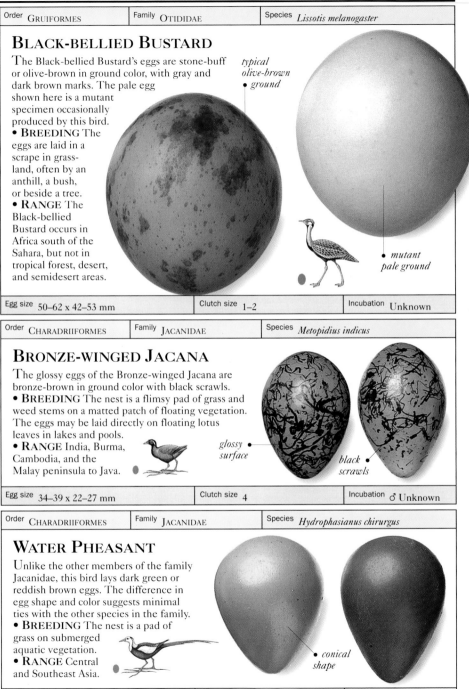

| Order GRUIFORMES | Family OTIDIDAE | Species *Lissotis melanogaster* |

BLACK-BELLIED BUSTARD

The Black-bellied Bustard's eggs are stone-buff or olive-brown in ground color, with gray and dark brown marks. The pale egg shown here is a mutant specimen occasionally produced by this bird.
• **BREEDING** The eggs are laid in a scrape in grassland, often by an anthill, a bush, or beside a tree.
• **RANGE** The Black-bellied Bustard occurs in Africa south of the Sahara, but not in tropical forest, desert, and semidesert areas.

typical olive-brown
• *ground*

• *mutant pale ground*

| Egg size 50–62 x 42–53 mm | Clutch size 1–2 | Incubation Unknown |

| Order CHARADRIIFORMES | Family JACANIDAE | Species *Metopidius indicus* |

BRONZE-WINGED JACANA

The glossy eggs of the Bronze-winged Jacana are bronze-brown in ground color with black scrawls.
• **BREEDING** The nest is a flimsy pad of grass and weed stems on a matted patch of floating vegetation. The eggs may be laid directly on floating lotus leaves in lakes and pools.
• **RANGE** India, Burma, Cambodia, and the Malay peninsula to Java.

glossy • *surface*

black • *scrawls*

| Egg size 34–39 x 22–27 mm | Clutch size 4 | Incubation ♂ Unknown |

| Order CHARADRIIFORMES | Family JACANIDAE | Species *Hydrophasianus chirurgus* |

WATER PHEASANT

Unlike the other members of the family Jacanidae, this bird lays dark green or reddish brown eggs. The difference in egg shape and color suggests minimal ties with the other species in the family.
• **BREEDING** The nest is a pad of grass on submerged aquatic vegetation.
• **RANGE** Central and Southeast Asia.

• *conical shape*

| Egg size 34–41 x 26–29 mm | Clutch size 4 | Incubation ♂ 26 days |

Order CHARADRIIFORMES	Family ROSTRATULIDAE	Species *Rostratula benghalensis*

PAINTED SNIPE

The eggs of the Painted Snipe are yellowish, greenish, or grayish stone, boldly blotched with blackish brown.
• **BREEDING** The male constructs a pad of grasses or rushes with a central depression, located either on the ground or floating amid reedy marshes and grass tussocks in wetlands or paddy fields. The female mates with several males.
• **RANGE** Africa south of the Sahara, Turkey, Asia, India, China, Japan, the Malay peninsula, and Australia.

• *bold, blackish brown marks*

• *slight sheen*

Egg size 32–39 x 23–28 mm	Clutch size 3–4	Incubation ♂ Unknown

Order CHARADRIIFORMES	Family HAEMATOPODIDAE	Species *Haematopus ostralegus*

EURASIAN OYSTERCATCHER

The Eurasian Oystercatcher's eggs are yellowish stone to clay-buff in ground color, spotted, and streaked with brown and black. About nine species are known, but their eggs are not distinguishable.
• **BREEDING** The eggs are laid in a shallow depression usually lined with stones or shells, although sometimes no nesting material at all is used. The nest is in a gravel bed among rocks, in sand dunes or grassy banks.
• **RANGE** Occurs on the coasts of America, across northern and western Europe, eastern Asia, Japan, and south to Australia. This species is the most wide-ranging member of the family Haematopodidae.

yellowish stone
• *ground*

• *clay-buff ground*

• *brown scrawls*

Egg size 49–70 x 35–49 mm	Clutch size 2–4	Incubation ♂♀ 24–27 days

| Order CHARADRIIFORMES | Family CHARADRIIDAE | Species *Vanellus vanellus* |

NORTHERN LAPWING

The Northern Lapwing's eggs are stone, olive, or brown in ground color, and are blotched or heavily spotted with black.
• **BREEDING** The nest is a muddy hollow lined with grass stalks which make it bulky. It can be sited on the ground, or on a raised site in grass or on moors.
• **RANGE** Northern and western Europe, northern Siberia, Turkestan, and China.

dense blotches

pale ground

| Egg size 39–53 x 30–36 mm | Clutch size 3–5 | Incubation ♂♀ 24–25 days |

| Order CHARADRIIFORMES | Family CHARADRIIDAE | Species *Pluvialis apricaria* |

GREATER GOLDEN PLOVER

cap of color

The eggs of the Greater Golden Plover are grayish buff or yellowish stone, and boldly blotched with brownish black and some sienna-brown markings.
• **BREEDING** The eggs are laid in a depression in the ground amid upland moors, rough pasture, or tundra. There is often a scanty lining of twigs, though sometimes the nest is a more substantial construction.
• **RANGE** The Greater Golden Plover occurs in Iceland, northern Europe, and Siberia, but migrates south in winter.

smooth, matte surface

| Egg size 48–55 x 33–38 mm | Clutch size 3–4 | Incubation ♂♀ 27–28 days |

| Order CHARADRIIFORMES | Family CHARADRIIDAE | Species *Charadrius hiaticula* |

RINGED PLOVER

The eggs of the Ringed Plover are yellowish stone with black spots. They can also be very heavily blotched or plain white.
• **BREEDING** The nest is a shell-lined hollow on shores and estuaries, or in the tundra.
• **RANGE** Southern Canada, Mediterranean Europe, and east to northern Siberia.

fine spots

| Egg size 30–39 x 23–28 mm | Clutch size 3–5 | Incubation ♂♀ 23–25 days |

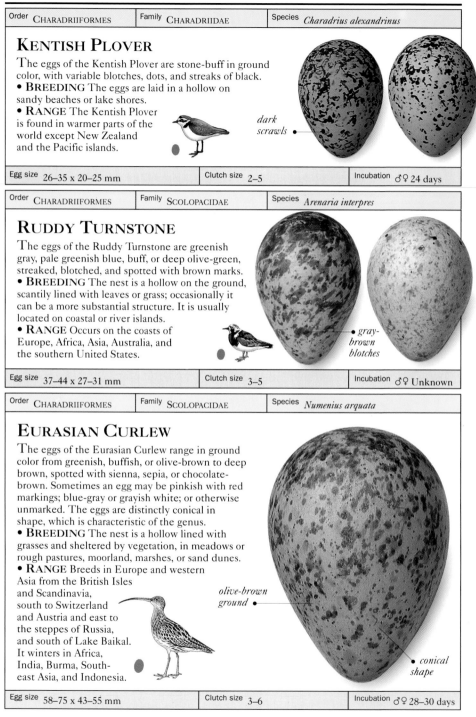

Order CHARADRIIFORMES	Family CHARADRIIDAE	Species *Charadrius alexandrinus*

KENTISH PLOVER

The eggs of the Kentish Plover are stone-buff in ground color, with variable blotches, dots, and streaks of black.
• **BREEDING** The eggs are laid in a hollow on sandy beaches or lake shores.
• **RANGE** The Kentish Plover is found in warmer parts of the world except New Zealand and the Pacific islands.

dark scrawls •

Egg size 26–35 x 20–25 mm	Clutch size 2–5	Incubation ♂♀ 24 days

Order CHARADRIIFORMES	Family SCOLOPACIDAE	Species *Arenaria interpres*

RUDDY TURNSTONE

The eggs of the Ruddy Turnstone are greenish gray, pale greenish blue, buff, or deep olive-green, streaked, blotched, and spotted with brown marks.
• **BREEDING** The nest is a hollow on the ground, scantily lined with leaves or grass; occasionally it can be a more substantial structure. It is usually located on coastal or river islands.
• **RANGE** Occurs on the coasts of Europe, Africa, Asia, Australia, and the southern United States.

• *gray-brown blotches*

Egg size 37–44 x 27–31 mm	Clutch size 3–5	Incubation ♂♀ Unknown

Order CHARADRIIFORMES	Family SCOLOPACIDAE	Species *Numenius arquata*

EURASIAN CURLEW

The eggs of the Eurasian Curlew range in ground color from greenish, buffish, or olive-brown to deep brown, spotted with sienna, sepia, or chocolate-brown. Sometimes an egg may be pinkish with red markings; blue-gray or grayish white; or otherwise unmarked. The eggs are distinctly conical in shape, which is characteristic of the genus.
• **BREEDING** The nest is a hollow lined with grasses and sheltered by vegetation, in meadows or rough pastures, moorland, marshes, or sand dunes.
• **RANGE** Breeds in Europe and western Asia from the British Isles and Scandinavia, south to Switzerland and Austria and east to the steppes of Russia, and south of Lake Baikal. It winters in Africa, India, Burma, Southeast Asia, and Indonesia.

olive-brown ground •

• *conical shape*

Egg size 58–75 x 43–55 mm	Clutch size 3–6	Incubation ♂♀ 28–30 days

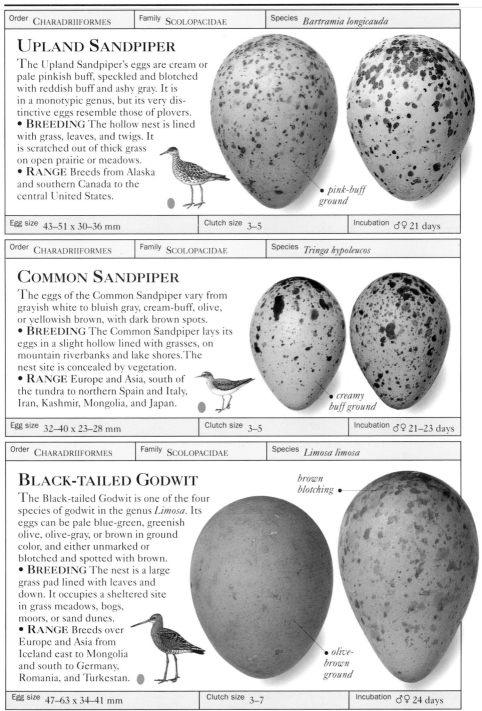

| Order CHARADRIIFORMES | Family SCOLOPACIDAE | Species *Bartramia longicauda* |

UPLAND SANDPIPER

The Upland Sandpiper's eggs are cream or pale pinkish buff, speckled and blotched with reddish buff and ashy gray. It is in a monotypic genus, but its very distinctive eggs resemble those of plovers.
• **BREEDING** The hollow nest is lined with grass, leaves, and twigs. It is scratched out of thick grass on open prairie or meadows.
• **RANGE** Breeds from Alaska and southern Canada to the central United States.

• *pink-buff ground*

| Egg size 43–51 x 30–36 mm | Clutch size 3–5 | Incubation ♂♀ 21 days |

| Order CHARADRIIFORMES | Family SCOLOPACIDAE | Species *Tringa hypoleucos* |

COMMON SANDPIPER

The eggs of the Common Sandpiper vary from grayish white to bluish gray, cream-buff, olive, or yellowish brown, with dark brown spots.
• **BREEDING** The Common Sandpiper lays its eggs in a slight hollow lined with grasses, on mountain riverbanks and lake shores. The nest site is concealed by vegetation.
• **RANGE** Europe and Asia, south of the tundra to northern Spain and Italy, Iran, Kashmir, Mongolia, and Japan.

• *creamy buff ground*

| Egg size 32–40 x 23–28 mm | Clutch size 3–5 | Incubation ♂♀ 21–23 days |

| Order CHARADRIIFORMES | Family SCOLOPACIDAE | Species *Limosa limosa* |

BLACK-TAILED GODWIT

brown blotching •

The Black-tailed Godwit is one of the four species of godwit in the genus *Limosa*. Its eggs can be pale blue-green, greenish olive, olive-gray, or brown in ground color, and either unmarked or blotched and spotted with brown.
• **BREEDING** The nest is a large grass pad lined with leaves and down. It occupies a sheltered site in grass meadows, bogs, moors, or sand dunes.
• **RANGE** Breeds over Europe and Asia from Iceland east to Mongolia and south to Germany, Romania, and Turkestan.

• *olive-brown ground*

| Egg size 47–63 x 34–41 mm | Clutch size 3–7 | Incubation ♂♀ 24 days |

Order CHARADRIIFORMES	Family SCOLOPACIDAE	Species *Tringa totanus*

REDSHANK

The Redshank's eggs vary from bluish or grayish white through stone-buff and yellowish or reddish ochre to yellowish brown or pale green, blotched and spotted in brown. The markings can form a cap at the larger end.
• **BREEDING** The eggs are laid in a hollow lined with dry grass, in rough pastures or meadows, marshes, and moorland edges, or occasionally on the coast. The nest has a canopy and side entrance to help conceal it.
• **RANGE** Breeds from Iceland and Scandinavia, south to the Mediterranean, across Siberia to China and the Himalayas.

marks form cap at larger end

conical shape

Egg size 41–49 x 28–33 mm	Clutch size 3–5	Incubation ♂♀ 23–24 days

Order CHARADRIIFORMES	Family SCOLOPACIDAE	Species *Scolopax rusticola*

COMMON WOODCOCK

The Common Woodcock's eggs are grayish white, buff, or warm pinkish brown, spotted in shades of chestnut with ashy gray underlying marks.
• **BREEDING** The eggs are laid in a hollow on mossy ground, lined with dead leaves. The hollow is situated in woodland, often at the base of a tree, but it can also be found in open areas or in deep heather.
• **RANGE** Breeds in the British Isles and Scandinavia, south to the Pyrenees, east to the Balkans, and across Asia to the Himalayas, and Japan.

underlying gray marks

chestnut spots

Egg size 40–49 x 31–36 mm	Clutch size 3–6	Incubation ♀ 20–22 days

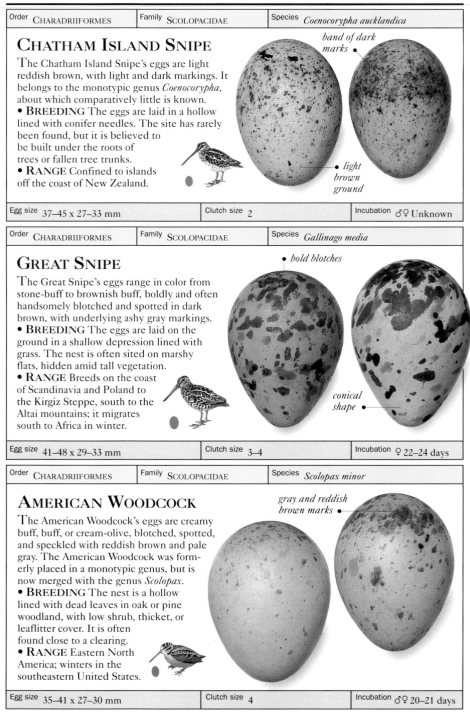

| Order CHARADRIIFORMES | Family SCOLOPACIDAE | Species *Coenocorypha aucklandica* |

CHATHAM ISLAND SNIPE

The Chatham Island Snipe's eggs are light reddish brown, with light and dark markings. It belongs to the monotypic genus *Coenocorypha*, about which comparatively little is known.
• **BREEDING** The eggs are laid in a hollow lined with conifer needles. The site has rarely been found, but it is believed to be built under the roots of trees or fallen tree trunks.
• **RANGE** Confined to islands off the coast of New Zealand.

band of dark marks •

• light brown ground

| Egg size 37–45 x 27–33 mm | Clutch size 2 | Incubation ♂♀ Unknown |

| Order CHARADRIIFORMES | Family SCOLOPACIDAE | Species *Gallinago media* |

GREAT SNIPE

The Great Snipe's eggs range in color from stone-buff to brownish buff, boldly and often handsomely blotched and spotted in dark brown, with underlying ashy gray markings.
• **BREEDING** The eggs are laid on the ground in a shallow depression lined with grass. The nest is often sited on marshy flats, hidden amid tall vegetation.
• **RANGE** Breeds on the coast of Scandinavia and Poland to the Kirgiz Steppe, south to the Altai mountains; it migrates south to Africa in winter.

• bold blotches

conical shape •

| Egg size 41–48 x 29–33 mm | Clutch size 3–4 | Incubation ♀ 22–24 days |

| Order CHARADRIIFORMES | Family SCOLOPACIDAE | Species *Scolopax minor* |

AMERICAN WOODCOCK

The American Woodcock's eggs are creamy buff, buff, or cream-olive, blotched, spotted, and speckled with reddish brown and pale gray. The American Woodcock was formerly placed in a monotypic genus, but is now merged with the genus *Scolopax*.
• **BREEDING** The nest is a hollow lined with dead leaves in oak or pine woodland, with low shrub, thicket, or leaflitter cover. It is often found close to a clearing.
• **RANGE** Eastern North America; winters in the southeastern United States.

gray and reddish brown marks •

| Egg size 35–41 x 27–30 mm | Clutch size 4 | Incubation ♂♀ 20–21 days |

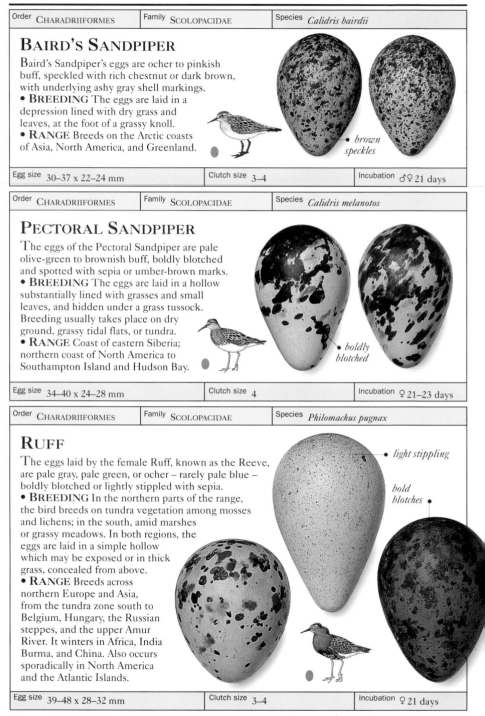

Order CHARADRIIFORMES	Family SCOLOPACIDAE	Species *Calidris bairdii*

BAIRD'S SANDPIPER

Baird's Sandpiper's eggs are ocher to pinkish
buff, speckled with rich chestnut or dark brown,
with underlying ashy gray shell markings.
• **BREEDING** The eggs are laid in a
depression lined with dry grass and
leaves, at the foot of a grassy knoll.
• **RANGE** Breeds on the Arctic coasts
of Asia, North America, and Greenland.

• *brown speckles*

Egg size 30–37 x 22–24 mm	Clutch size 3–4	Incubation ♂♀ 21 days

Order CHARADRIIFORMES	Family SCOLOPACIDAE	Species *Calidris melanotos*

PECTORAL SANDPIPER

The eggs of the Pectoral Sandpiper are pale
olive-green to brownish buff, boldly blotched
and spotted with sepia or umber-brown marks.
• **BREEDING** The eggs are laid in a hollow
substantially lined with grasses and small
leaves, and hidden under a grass tussock.
Breeding usually takes place on dry
ground, grassy tidal flats, or tundra.
• **RANGE** Coast of eastern Siberia;
northern coast of North America to
Southampton Island and Hudson Bay.

• *boldly blotched*

Egg size 34–40 x 24–28 mm	Clutch size 4	Incubation ♀ 21–23 days

Order CHARADRIIFORMES	Family SCOLOPACIDAE	Species *Philomachus pugnax*

RUFF

light stippling

The eggs laid by the female Ruff, known as the Reeve,
are pale gray, pale green, or ocher – rarely pale blue –
boldly blotched or lightly stippled with sepia.
• **BREEDING** In the northern parts of the range,
the bird breeds on tundra vegetation among mosses
and lichens; in the south, amid marshes
or grassy meadows. In both regions, the
eggs are laid in a simple hollow
which may be exposed or in thick
grass, concealed from above.
• **RANGE** Breeds across
northern Europe and Asia,
from the tundra zone south to
Belgium, Hungary, the Russian
steppes, and the upper Amur
River. It winters in Africa, India
Burma, and China. Also occurs
sporadically in North America
and the Atlantic Islands.

bold blotches •

Egg size 39–48 x 28–32 mm	Clutch size 3–4	Incubation ♀ 21 days

Order CHARADRIIFORMES	Family RECURVIROSTRIDAE	Species *Himantopus himantopus*

BLACK-WINGED STILT

The eggs of the Black-winged Stilt have a whitish stone to pale brown ground, with black blotches and spots and a few ashy shell marks. The eggs of the seven other species in the genus, which include the avocets and the Ibisbill (see below and p.102), are all similar. Even the eggs of the Banded Stilt *(Cladorhynchus leucocephalus)* are similar in appearance to that of a typical stilt beneath their superficial chalky white coating.

• **BREEDING** The nest is usually situated in or near shallow water, especially amid brackish marshland. The type of nest built varies. On the shore it is a simple hollow lined with a few dead reeds; in water it may be a substantial structure made out of stalks and mud.

• **RANGE** The Mediterranean, Africa, Madagascar, Russia, the Arabian peninsula, China, India, and southern Asia to Malaysia.

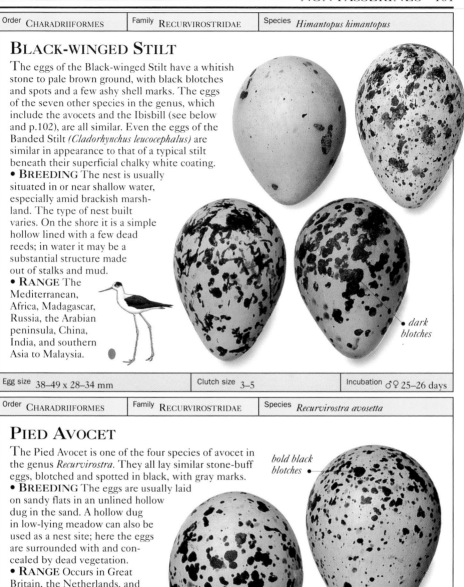

• *dark blotches*

Egg size 38–49 x 28–34 mm	Clutch size 3–5	Incubation ♂♀ 25–26 days

Order CHARADRIIFORMES	Family RECURVIROSTRIDAE	Species *Recurvirostra avosetta*

PIED AVOCET

The Pied Avocet is one of the four species of avocet in the genus *Recurvirostra*. They all lay similar stone-buff eggs, blotched and spotted in black, with gray marks.

bold black blotches •

• **BREEDING** The eggs are usually laid on sandy flats in an unlined hollow dug in the sand. A hollow dug in low-lying meadow can also be used as a nest site; here the eggs are surrounded with and concealed by dead vegetation.

• **RANGE** Occurs in Great Britain, the Netherlands, and the Mediterranean; east to the Black and Caspian Seas; over Asia, Turkestan, and northern China. It winters in Africa, southern China, and India.

•*clay-buff ground*

Egg size 43–55 x 31–38 mm	Clutch size 3–5	Incubation ♂♀ 22–24 days

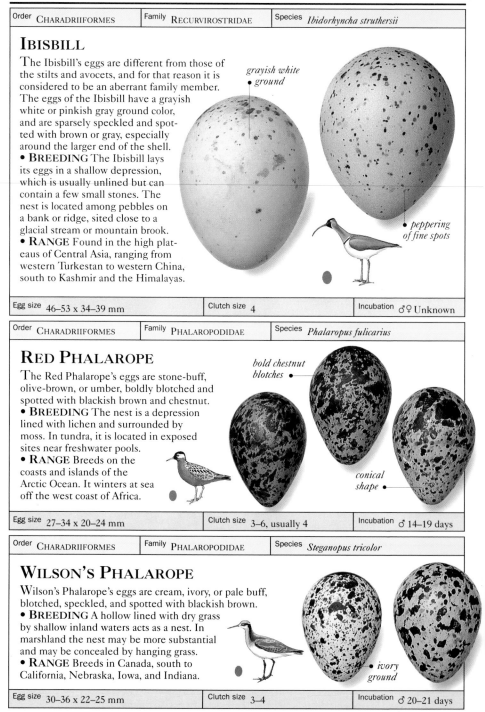

| Order CHARADRIIFORMES | Family RECURVIROSTRIDAE | Species *Ibidorhyncha struthersii* |

IBISBILL

The Ibisbill's eggs are different from those of the stilts and avocets, and for that reason it is considered to be an aberrant family member. The eggs of the Ibisbill have a grayish white or pinkish gray ground color, and are sparsely speckled and spotted with brown or gray, especially around the larger end of the shell.
• **BREEDING** The Ibisbill lays its eggs in a shallow depression, which is usually unlined but can contain a few small stones. The nest is located among pebbles on a bank or ridge, sited close to a glacial stream or mountain brook.
• **RANGE** Found in the high plateaus of Central Asia, ranging from western Turkestan to western China, south to Kashmir and the Himalayas.

grayish white ground

peppering of fine spots

| Egg size 46–53 x 34–39 mm | Clutch size 4 | Incubation ♂♀ Unknown |

| Order CHARADRIIFORMES | Family PHALAROPODIDAE | Species *Phalaropus fulicarius* |

RED PHALAROPE

The Red Phalarope's eggs are stone-buff, olive-brown, or umber, boldly blotched and spotted with blackish brown and chestnut.
• **BREEDING** The nest is a depression lined with lichen and surrounded by moss. In tundra, it is located in exposed sites near freshwater pools.
• **RANGE** Breeds on the coasts and islands of the Arctic Ocean. It winters at sea off the west coast of Africa.

bold chestnut blotches

conical shape

| Egg size 27–34 x 20–24 mm | Clutch size 3–6, usually 4 | Incubation ♂ 14–19 days |

| Order CHARADRIIFORMES | Family PHALAROPODIDAE | Species *Steganopus tricolor* |

WILSON'S PHALAROPE

Wilson's Phalarope's eggs are cream, ivory, or pale buff, blotched, speckled, and spotted with blackish brown.
• **BREEDING** A hollow lined with dry grass by shallow inland waters acts as a nest. In marshland the nest may be more substantial and may be concealed by hanging grass.
• **RANGE** Breeds in Canada, south to California, Nebraska, Iowa, and Indiana.

ivory ground

| Egg size 30–36 x 22–25 mm | Clutch size 3–4 | Incubation ♂ 20–21 days |

Order CHARADRIIFORMES	Family DROMADIDAE	Species *Dromas ardeola*

CRAB PLOVER

The single egg of the Crab Plover is plain white and very large in relation to the size of the bird. The egg is also quite unlike those of any other member of the order Charadriiformes.
• **BREEDING** Breeds colonially, laying its egg in a hole made by crabs in sandbanks on coral reefs.
• **RANGE** The northern and western shores and islands of the Indian Ocean, the Red Sea and Persian Gulf, south to Natal, and east to India.

plain, smooth shell

Egg size 58–69 x 41–47 mm	Clutch size 1	Incubation Unknown

Order CHARADRIIFORMES	Family BURHINIDAE	Species *Burhinus oedicnemus*

STONE CURLEW

sepia-brown spots and blotches

The eggs of the Stone Curlew are light yellowish stone to pale brown in ground color, blotched, spotted, and streaked in sepia. The streaks and scrawls are characteristic of the eggs in this family.
• **BREEDING** The Stone Curlew lays its eggs on bare ground in exposed sites, downs, sandy flats, heaths, and farmland. In all these locations, both parents and eggs are well camouflaged.
• **RANGE** Breeds from the Canary Islands over much of Europe and North Africa, east to the Kirgiz Steppe, India, and Southeast Asia.

pale brown ground

speckled surface

bold blotches

Egg size 43–61 x 32–43 mm	Clutch size 2–3	Incubation ♂♀ 25–27 days

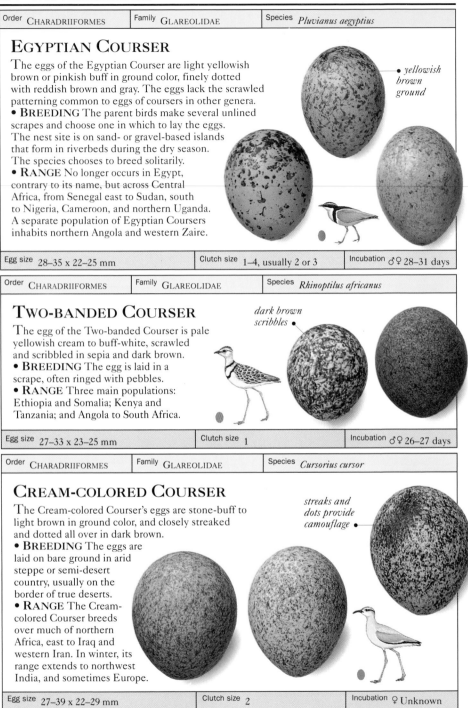

Order CHARADRIIFORMES	Family GLAREOLIDAE	Species *Pluvianus aegyptius*

EGYPTIAN COURSER

The eggs of the Egyptian Courser are light yellowish brown or pinkish buff in ground color, finely dotted with reddish brown and gray. The eggs lack the scrawled patterning common to eggs of coursers in other genera.
• **BREEDING** The parent birds make several unlined scrapes and choose one in which to lay the eggs. The nest site is on sand- or gravel-based islands that form in riverbeds during the dry season. The species chooses to breed solitarily.
• **RANGE** No longer occurs in Egypt, contrary to its name, but across Central Africa, from Senegal east to Sudan, south to Nigeria, Cameroon, and northern Uganda. A separate population of Egyptian Coursers inhabits northern Angola and western Zaire.

yellowish brown ground

Egg size 28–35 x 22–25 mm	Clutch size 1–4, usually 2 or 3	Incubation ♂♀ 28–31 days

Order CHARADRIIFORMES	Family GLAREOLIDAE	Species *Rhinoptilus africanus*

TWO-BANDED COURSER

The egg of the Two-banded Courser is pale yellowish cream to buff-white, scrawled and scribbled in sepia and dark brown.
• **BREEDING** The egg is laid in a scrape, often ringed with pebbles.
• **RANGE** Three main populations: Ethiopia and Somalia; Kenya and Tanzania; and Angola to South Africa.

dark brown scribbles

Egg size 27–33 x 23–25 mm	Clutch size 1	Incubation ♂♀ 26–27 days

Order CHARADRIIFORMES	Family GLAREOLIDAE	Species *Cursorius cursor*

CREAM-COLORED COURSER

The Cream-colored Courser's eggs are stone-buff to light brown in ground color, and closely streaked and dotted all over in dark brown.
• **BREEDING** The eggs are laid on bare ground in arid steppe or semi-desert country, usually on the border of true deserts.
• **RANGE** The Cream-colored Courser breeds over much of northern Africa, east to Iraq and western Iran. In winter, its range extends to northwest India, and sometimes Europe.

streaks and dots provide camouflage

Egg size 27–39 x 22–29 mm	Clutch size 2	Incubation ♀ Unknown

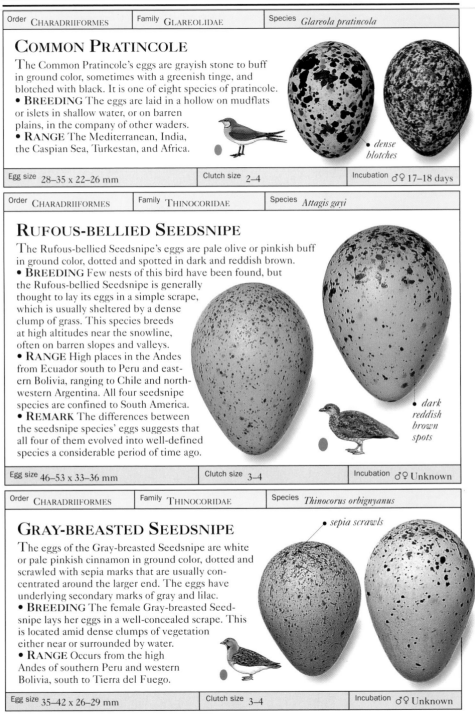

| Order CHARADRIIFORMES | Family GLAREOLIDAE | Species *Glareola pratincola* |

COMMON PRATINCOLE

The Common Pratincole's eggs are grayish stone to buff in ground color, sometimes with a greenish tinge, and blotched with black. It is one of eight species of pratincole.
• **BREEDING** The eggs are laid in a hollow on mudflats or islets in shallow water, or on barren plains, in the company of other waders.
• **RANGE** The Mediterranean, India, the Caspian Sea, Turkestan, and Africa.

• *dense blotches*

| Egg size 28–35 x 22–26 mm | Clutch size 2–4 | Incubation ♂♀ 17–18 days |

| Order CHARADRIIFORMES | Family THINOCORIDAE | Species *Attagis gayi* |

RUFOUS-BELLIED SEEDSNIPE

The Rufous-bellied Seedsnipe's eggs are pale olive or pinkish buff in ground color, dotted and spotted in dark and reddish brown.
• **BREEDING** Few nests of this bird have been found, but the Rufous-bellied Seedsnipe is generally thought to lay its eggs in a simple scrape, which is usually sheltered by a dense clump of grass. This species breeds at high altitudes near the snowline, often on barren slopes and valleys.
• **RANGE** High places in the Andes from Ecuador south to Peru and eastern Bolivia, ranging to Chile and northwestern Argentina. All four seedsnipe species are confined to South America.
• **REMARK** The differences between the seedsnipe species' eggs suggests that all four of them evolved into well-defined species a considerable period of time ago.

• *dark reddish brown spots*

| Egg size 46–53 x 33–36 mm | Clutch size 3–4 | Incubation ♂♀ Unknown |

| Order CHARADRIIFORMES | Family THINOCORIDAE | Species *Thinocorus orbignyanus* |

GRAY-BREASTED SEEDSNIPE

• *sepia scrawls*

The eggs of the Gray-breasted Seedsnipe are white or pale pinkish cinnamon in ground color, dotted and scrawled with sepia marks that are usually concentrated around the larger end. The eggs have underlying secondary marks of gray and lilac.
• **BREEDING** The female Gray-breasted Seedsnipe lays her eggs in a well-concealed scrape. This is located amid dense clumps of vegetation either near or surrounded by water.
• **RANGE** Occurs from the high Andes of southern Peru and western Bolivia, south to Tierra del Fuego.

| Egg size 35–42 x 26–29 mm | Clutch size 3–4 | Incubation ♂♀ Unknown |

Order CHARADRIIFORMES	Family CHIONIDIDAE	Species *Chionis alba*

SNOWY SHEATHBILL

The eggs of the Snowy Sheathbill are creamy white, and heavily blotched, spotted, and speckled with black or brown. They are similar to those of the only other *Chionis* species, the Lesser Sheathbill (*C. minor*).
• **BREEDING** The eggs are laid in a hole lined with an untidy collection of debris, including broken eggshells, stones, and lichen, among rocks on coasts and islands.
• **RANGE** Coasts of southern Argentina, and islands between them and Antarctica.

• *brown blotches*

Egg size 55–58 x 36–38 mm	Clutch size 2–3	Incubation ♂♀ Unknown

Order CHARADRIIFORMES	Family STERCORARIIDAE	Species *Catharacta skua*

GREAT SKUA

The eggs of the Great Skua vary from olive-gray to reddish brown (or sometimes very pale gray, white, or pale blue), sparsely blotched or spotted with dark brown; occasionally an egg is unmarked. Similar color variations and marks occur in the eggs of gulls, to which skuas and jaegers are related.
• **BREEDING** The eggs are laid in a depression, either scantily lined with vegetation or unlined. The nest is found on the ground, amid heather, moss, or rough pasture.
• **RANGE** Breeds in Iceland, the Faeroe, the Orkney, and the Shetland Islands, and perhaps also in Greenland and on Baffin Island. It winters at sea in the temperate Atlantic. Closely related species occur in the Antarctic.

• *sparse blotches on olive-gray ground*

Egg size 62–78 x 44–53 mm	Clutch size 1–3, usually 2	Incubation ♂♀ 28 days

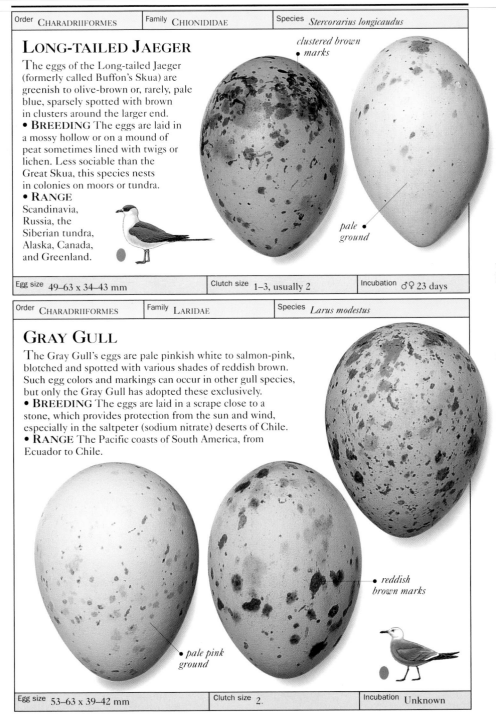

| Order CHARADRIIFORMES | Family CHIONIDIDAE | Species *Stercorarius longicaudus* |

LONG-TAILED JAEGER

The eggs of the Long-tailed Jaeger
(formerly called Buffon's Skua) are
greenish to olive-brown or, rarely, pale
blue, sparsely spotted with brown
in clusters around the larger end.
• **BREEDING** The eggs are laid in
a mossy hollow or on a mound of
peat sometimes lined with twigs or
lichen. Less sociable than the
Great Skua, this species nests
in colonies on moors or tundra.
• **RANGE**
Scandinavia,
Russia, the
Siberian tundra,
Alaska, Canada,
and Greenland.

clustered brown
• *marks*

pale •
ground

| Egg size 49–63 x 34–43 mm | Clutch size 1–3, usually 2 | Incubation ♂♀ 23 days |

| Order CHARADRIIFORMES | Family LARIDAE | Species *Larus modestus* |

GRAY GULL

The Gray Gull's eggs are pale pinkish white to salmon-pink,
blotched and spotted with various shades of reddish brown.
Such egg colors and markings can occur in other gull species,
but only the Gray Gull has adopted these exclusively.
• **BREEDING** The eggs are laid in a scrape close to a
stone, which provides protection from the sun and wind,
especially in the saltpeter (sodium nitrate) deserts of Chile.
• **RANGE** The Pacific coasts of South America, from
Ecuador to Chile.

• *reddish*
brown marks

• *pale pink*
ground

| Egg size 53–63 x 39–42 mm | Clutch size 2. | Incubation Unknown |

Order CHARADRIIFORMES	Family LARIDAE	Species *Larus argentatus*

HERRING GULL

The eggs of the Herring Gull range from blue-gray to olive and umber-brown, blotched and spotted in varying shades of brown. Rarely, a clutch may be pink, and spotted in reddish brown. Larger gulls, such as the Herring Gull, tend to have more variable eggs than smaller gulls. They also have a higher proportion of light-colored eggs because there is less need for camouflage in the large, aggressive species.
• **BREEDING** Breeding usually takes place in colonies of considerable size on sea cliff ledges, sand dunes, gravel beaches, and small, grassy marine islands. They can also be found inland, within range of an expanse of water, such as a freshwater lake. The nest is a heap of material, including grass, heathers, and seaweed.
• **RANGE** Widespread over the seas of the northern hemisphere: north to most Arctic coasts; south to the Caribbean Sea, the Canary Islands, the Mediterranean, the Red, Black, and Caspian Seas; and on inland lakes eastwards across Central Asia to Lake Baikal. A number of distinct geographical races or quasi-species of Herring Gull occur.

• *blue-gray ground*

• *reddish brown blotches on pale pink ground*

• *blurred gray underlying marks*

Egg size 58–86 x 43–54 mm	Clutch size 2–6, usually 3	Incubation ♂♀ 25–27 days

Order CHARADRIIFORMES	Family LARIDAE	Species *Larus minutus*

LITTLE GULL

The Little Gull's eggs are yellowish buff to olive-brown, blotched and spotted in dark brown; very rarely, a clutch may have a blue ground color.
• **BREEDING** The nest is a haphazard heap of dead sedge, rushes, or reeds next to freshwater lakes and marshes. Breeding usually takes place in large colonies.
• **RANGE** Breeds from Central Sweden east across Asia to the Sea of Okhotsk; south to Denmark, Central Russia, and Lake Baikal; also in northeastern North America.

olive-brown ground color

deep brown marks

Egg size 37–45 x 27–32 mm	Clutch size 2–7	Incubation ♂♀ Unknown

Order CHARADRIIFORMES	Family LARIDAE	Species *Larus marinus*

GREAT BLACK-BACKED GULL

The eggs of the Great Black-backed Gull are stone-buff to olive-brown, blotched and spotted in dark brown and gray-green; less frequently, the ground is blue. Rarely, pink eggs are produced.
• **BREEDING** Where the species is numerous it will nest in colonies on the tops of rock stacks and islands, but many pairs nest solitarily. Heather, sticks, seaweed, and grass are heaped together to make a large nest.
• **RANGE** Breeds on North Atlantic coasts south to North Carolina and the adjacent shores of the Arctic Ocean.

intricate shell markings

pale gray ground

Egg size 69–85 x 49–57 mm	Clutch size 2–5	Incubation ♂♀ 26–28 days

Order CHARADRIIFORMES	Family LARIDAE	Species *Rhodosthethia rosea*

ROSS'S GULL

The eggs of Ross's Gull are olive-brown, sparsely blotched with blurred umber-brown markings.
• **BREEDING** The nest is a construction of dry grasses and sedge, sometimes with a few birch or willow leaves or moss as lining. It is built up above the bog surface, in swampy tundra on low-lying islands in deltas of Arctic rivers, where terns often also breed.
• **RANGE** Breeds in the mouths and valleys of rivers in eastern Siberia, and occasionally further east in Greenland. It winters south to the northern United States.

• *olive-brown ground*

Egg size 41–46 x 30–33 mm	Clutch size 2–3	Incubation ♂♀ c.21 days

Order CHARADRIIFORMES	Family LARIDAE	Species *Rissa tridactyla*

KITTIWAKE

The eggs of the Kittiwake (or Black-legged Kittiwake) are pale bluish gray to yellowish stone or brown, either blotched with brown and gray marks all over or plain.
• **BREEDING** The eggs are laid in a cup-shaped nest of moss, grass, and seaweed. The nest sits on a ledge of a cliff, mostly on the coast but sometimes inland; rarely, on the roof or windowledge of a tall building.
• **RANGE** Breeds from the northern coasts of the Northern Hemisphere south to the Gulf of St. Lawrence, Iceland, and France.

gray underlying marks •

• *plain gray ground*

• *brown and gray blotches*

Egg size 51–63 x 37–44 mm	Clutch size 1–3	Incubation ♂♀ 21–24 days

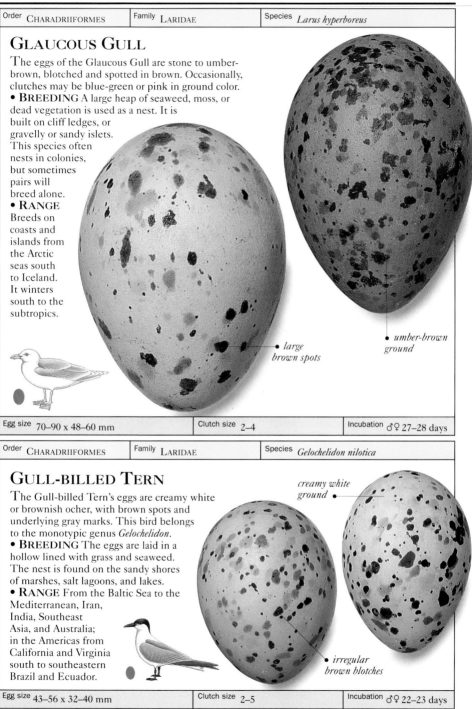

Order CHARADRIIFORMES	Family LARIDAE	Species *Larus hyperboreus*

GLAUCOUS GULL

The eggs of the Glaucous Gull are stone to umber-brown, blotched and spotted in brown. Occasionally, clutches may be blue-green or pink in ground color.
• **BREEDING** A large heap of seaweed, moss, or dead vegetation is used as a nest. It is built on cliff ledges, or gravelly or sandy islets. This species often nests in colonies, but sometimes pairs will breed alone.
• **RANGE** Breeds on coasts and islands from the Arctic seas south to Iceland. It winters south to the subtropics.

• *umber-brown ground*

• *large brown spots*

Egg size 70–90 x 48–60 mm	Clutch size 2–4	Incubation ♂♀ 27–28 days

Order CHARADRIIFORMES	Family LARIDAE	Species *Gelochelidon nilotica*

GULL-BILLED TERN

The Gull-billed Tern's eggs are creamy white or brownish ocher, with brown spots and underlying gray marks. This bird belongs to the monotypic genus *Gelochelidon*.
• **BREEDING** The eggs are laid in a hollow lined with grass and seaweed. The nest is found on the sandy shores of marshes, salt lagoons, and lakes.
• **RANGE** From the Baltic Sea to the Mediterranean, Iran, India, Southeast Asia, and Australia; in the Americas from California and Virginia south to southeastern Brazil and Ecuador.

creamy white ground •

• *irregular brown blotches*

Egg size 43–56 x 32–40 mm	Clutch size 2–5	Incubation ♂♀ 22–23 days

Order CHARADRIIFORMES	Family LARIDAE	Species *Larus ridibundus*

BLACK-HEADED GULL

The eggs of the Black-headed Gull are variable in ground color, ranging from light buffish stone to umber, blotched, spotted, and streaked with dark brown pigmentation. Occasionally, a pale blue egg is laid, which can be unmarked.
• **BREEDING** The nest is a loose heap of vegetation. Its size varies as it is added to even after the young have hatched. It is sited on the ground, among sand hills by the sea or on top of gravel banks, often around inland lakes and pools, or marine islets; rarely, on shed roofs or even in bushes.
• **RANGE** The Black-headed Gull breeds from northern Europe south to Sardinia and east across Central Asia to Kamchatka, Central Russia, and northeastern China. In winter it can also be found in North America.

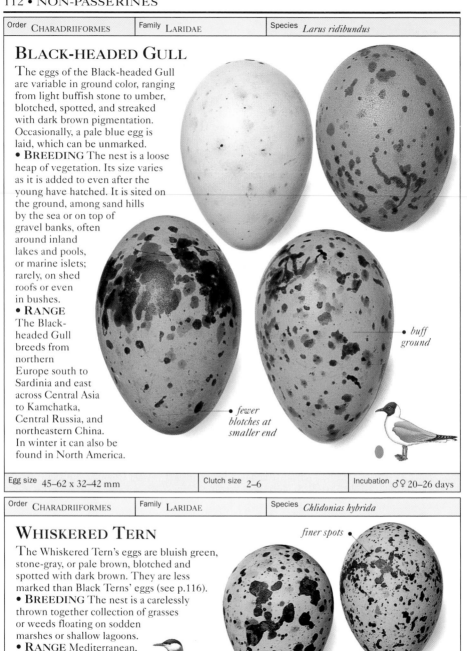

• *buff ground*

• *fewer blotches at smaller end*

Egg size 45–62 x 32–42 mm	Clutch size 2–6	Incubation ♂♀ 20–26 days

Order CHARADRIIFORMES	Family LARIDAE	Species *Chlidonias hybrida*

WHISKERED TERN

finer spots •

The Whiskered Tern's eggs are bluish green, stone-gray, or pale brown, blotched and spotted with dark brown. They are less marked than Black Terns' eggs (see p.116).
• **BREEDING** The nest is a carelessly thrown together collection of grasses or weeds floating on sodden marshes or shallow lagoons.
• **RANGE** Mediterranean, India, China, Madagascar, south to South Africa, Indonesia, and Australia.

• *brown and gray blotches*

Egg size 34–44 x 26–30 mm	Clutch size 2–4	Incubation ♂♀ Unknown

Order CHARADRIIFORMES	Family LARIDAE	Species *Anous stolidus*

BROWN NODDY

The Brown Noddy's single egg is white, grayish, or pinkish, sparsely blotched and spotted with reddish brown and with delicate underlying lavender markings.
• **BREEDING** The nest is a substantial structure of sticks and seaweed. It is usually built in a tree or shrub, but where these are not available, rocky islets, coral atolls, or cliff ledges are used. The Brown Noddy breeds in colonies, often in the company of several other species of tern.
• **RANGE** Breeds on small islands off the west coast of Mexico, Central America, and the Caribbean. Also breeds in the Red Sea, the Indian Ocean, and the Pacific Ocean south to Australia.

pink-buff ground color •

• *veiled lavender marks*

Egg size 47–58 x 32–39 mm	Clutch size 1	Incubation ♂♀ 32–36 days

Order CHARADRIIFORMES	Family LARIDAE	Species *Sterna hirundo*

COMMON TERN

large, dark • *brown blotches*

The eggs of the Common Tern are stone to gray or brown, blotched with dark brown and gray marks.
• **BREEDING** The eggs are laid in an unlined hollow scratched in the sand or gravel, on sand dunes, gravel banks, salt marshes, rocky islets, or lake shores. Breeding often takes place in huge colonies.
• **RANGE** Northern Canada and the United States, locally on the Atlantic and Gulf coasts, and the West Indies. Also the British Isles to Siberia, and the Middle East.

Egg size 35–48 x 26–32 mm	Clutch size 2–4	Incubation ♂♀ 21–26 days

Order CHARADRIIFORMES	Family LARIDAE	Species *Sterna bergii*

GREATER CRESTED TERN

The eggs of the Greater Crested Tern (or Swift Tern) vary greatly in basic coloration. They range from olive-yellow to buff or cream in ground color, and are usually blotched, spotted, and scrawled with black, brown, and gray, with secondary underlying marks of gray and lilac.

elliptical to conical shape •

• **BREEDING** The Greater Crested Tern lays its eggs in a nest that is a mere scrape in the sand, and rarely has any lining. The nest is usually located on offshore or coastal islands, and may sometimes be partly concealed among weeds. This tern breeds in dense colonies, most often in association with other species of tern or with other seabirds.

• **RANGE** Southern Africa and Madagascar, ranging north to the Red Sea, and east from islands in the Indian Ocean to Southeast Asia, New Guinea, Australia, and the western Pacific Ocean.

• cream ground color

intricate brown markings •

smooth, matte shell •

Egg size 53–68 x 38–46 mm	Clutch size 1–3	Incubation Unknown

Order CHARADRIIFORMES	Family LARIDAE	Species *Sterna bengalensis*

LESSER CRESTED TERN

The elliptical eggs of the Lesser Crested Tern are variable in coloration. They may be anything from a basic white to yellow, pink, and buff, blotched, splashed, and spotted in brown and black pigment, with underlying secondary marks of gray and lilac.

• **BREEDING** The eggs are laid in the sand in a simple, unlined, shallow scrape. Although the birds usually occur inshore on sandy and rocky coasts and estuaries, the chosen nest site is always situated on offshore islands, where the birds breed in huge colonies. These terns are so closely crowded together within the nest site that incubating birds almost touch one another – although each pair guards its tiny space jealously.

• **RANGE** Widespread during the breeding season, extending from the Mediterranean and the Red Sea over the coasts and islands of the Indian Ocean, south to Indonesia, and Australia.

• *matte shell*

• *elliptical in shape*

variable brown and black blotching •

• *pinkish white ground*

Egg size 46–62 x 33–39 mm	Clutch size 1, rarely 2	Incubation ♂♀ 21–26 days

Order CHARADRIIFORMES	Family LARIDAE	Species *Gygis alba*

FAIRY TERN

The Fairy Tern, also known as the White Tern, forms a monotypic genus. Its single, oval egg is grayish white to grayish pink or buff in ground color, and is lavishly blotched, spotted, and scrawled with a variety of black and reddish brown shell markings.
• **BREEDING** The Fairy Tern is remarkable for not building a nest of any description. Instead the lone egg is simply laid on to the bare branch of a tree or on to bare rock. In the Maldive Islands, the Fairy Tern is reputed to lay its egg on a banana leaf.
• **RANGE** This species breeds in scattered locations on many islands throughout the tropical oceans: the Atlantic, the Indian, and the western Pacific.

• *buff ground color*

• *intricate shell markings*

Egg size 35–47 x 28–35 mm	Clutch size 1	Incubation ♂♀ 30–32 days

Order CHARADRIIFORMES	Family LARIDAE	Species *Chlidonias niger*

BLACK TERN

dark brown • *marks*

The Black Tern's eggs are white, ocher, brown, or greenish, blotched with blackish brown marks that can form a zone at the larger end. They are smaller and darker than those of the Whiskered Tern (see p.112).
• **BREEDING** The nest is a floating pile of waterweeds and reeds, sited in shallow water in marshes and lagoons. Sometimes the Black Tern breeds on dry ground, in a scrape lined with dead grass or reeds.
• **RANGE** North America from central Canada, to the northern United States. Winters from Panama to Central South America, and tropical Africa.

pale • *ground color*

Egg size 30–40 x 22–27 mm	Clutch size 2–4	Incubation ♂♀ 14–16 days

Order CHARADRIIFORMES	Family LARIDAE	Species *Larosterna inca*

INCA TERN

The Inca Tern's eggs are browner than those of other terns, and are blotched and spotted in dark brown, which in some cases merge into black marks.
• **BREEDING** The Inca Tern nests in a variety of locations on offshore islands, including rock crevices, natural holes amid guano deposits, and burrows formerly occupied by petrels or penguins. Inca Terns have even been reported nesting in disused barges.
• **RANGE** The coasts of Peru and Chile in South America.

darker ground than other terns

gray underlying marks

Egg size 48–54 x 35–43 mm	Clutch size 1–2	Incubation Unknown

Order CHARADRIIFORMES	Family RHYNCHOPIDAE	Species *Rhynchops niger*

BLACK SKIMMER

The eggs of the Black Skimmer range in ground color from pale pinkish buff, creamy brown, or pale salmon to grayish or greenish white. They are blotched and spotted with large dark brown or reddish brown marks.
• **BREEDING** The eggs are laid in an unlined scrape in the sand, mostly on the banks of large rivers, some-times a considerable distance upstream. They breed in colonies, often in association with terns.
• **RANGE** Atlantic and Gulf coasts of the United States from New Jersey to Florida and Texas. South through the Caribbean and Central America to southern Chile and Central Argentina.

pinkish buff ground

dark brown blotches

Egg size 39–51 x 30–36 mm	Clutch size 3–7	Incubation ♀ Unknown

Order CHARADRIIFORMES	Family ALCIDAE	Species *Alle alle*

DOVEKIE

The eggs of the Dovekie, or Little Auk have a pale blue tinge, but this is difficult to capture on film. They can be unmarked or they may have a few yellow-brown spots or streaks.
• **BREEDING** The Dovekie makes no nest. The eggs are laid in chinks and holes among the rocks and scree at great heights on cliffs, usually on the coast but sometimes inland. They breed together in large colonies.
• **RANGE** Throughout the Arctic Ocean: Greenland, Iceland, Jan Mayen Land, Spitsbergen, Franz Joseph Land, Bear Island, and Novaya Zemlya. It winters at sea in the North Atlantic.
• **REMARK** This family is peculiar to the colder waters of the Northern Hemisphere.

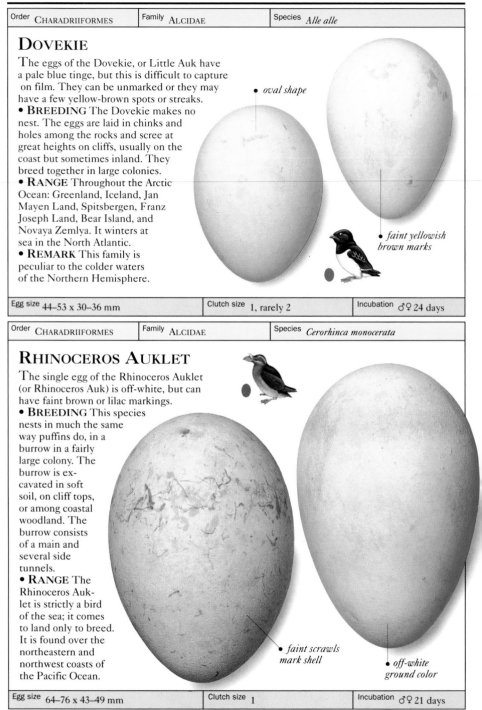

• *oval shape*

• *faint yellowish brown marks*

Egg size 44–53 x 30–36 mm	Clutch size 1, rarely 2	Incubation ♂♀ 24 days

Order CHARADRIIFORMES	Family ALCIDAE	Species *Cerorhinca monocerata*

RHINOCEROS AUKLET

The single egg of the Rhinoceros Auklet (or Rhinoceros Auk) is off-white, but can have faint brown or lilac markings.
• **BREEDING** This species nests in much the same way puffins do, in a burrow in a fairly large colony. The burrow is ex- cavated in soft soil, on cliff tops, or among coastal woodland. The burrow consists of a main and several side tunnels.
• **RANGE** The Rhinoceros Auk- let is strictly a bird of the sea; it comes to land only to breed. It is found over the northeastern and northwest coasts of the Pacific Ocean.

• *faint scrawls mark shell*

• *off-white ground color*

Egg size 64–76 x 43–49 mm	Clutch size 1	Incubation ♂♀ 21 days

Order CHARADRIIFORMES	Family ALCIDAE	Species *Alca torda*

RAZORBILL

The Razorbill lays either a single egg or a clutch of two. These range in ground color from light brown to white – sometimes greenish or pale mauve – blotched, scrawled, and streaked in brown or black. They are not unlike the Common Murre's eggs (see p.121) but are less variable within the species despite their wide range of color.
• **BREEDING** No nest is built. The eggs are laid in a crevice or hole, usually in the shelter of a large rock on sea cliffs, although they can be laid among shoreline rocks and boulders. The Razorbill often breeds in large colonies, usually in association with guillemots.
• **RANGE** The coasts of the North Atlantic: on the American side from southern Greenland to the Bay of Fundy; and on the east from Iceland and the White Sea to the British Isles and Brittany (northern France).

black and brown scrawls and streaks

cream ground color

blurred gray-brown streaks

Egg size 63–83 x 42–52 mm	Clutch size 1, rarely 2	Incubation ♂♀ 25 days

Order CHARADRIIFORMES	Family ALCIDAE	Species *Pinguinus impennis*

GREAT AUK

The huge single egg of the now-extinct Great Auk – a bird that in recent years has become almost as famous for being extinct as the Dodo – varied widely in basic coloration, ranging from brown, green, or blue, to yellowish stone or white. These were irregularly spotted, blotched, and streaked with brown or black. The eggs resembled those of the Common Murre (opposite) but were about twice the size. About 75 Great Auk eggs have survived in collections. The egg featured here, however, is, a painted model.

• **BREEDING** The Great Auk made no actual nest. The egg was simply laid on bare rock on low-lying rocky islets and island coasts of the North Atlantic where there were few if any natural predators; as the birds were unable to fly, they were virtually defenseless.

• **RANGE** Extinct. The Great Auk's ultimate demise occurred in the mid-19th century (the exact date is a matter of some debate by historians and ornithologists alike) after it had been slaughtered for food, in huge numbers, by passing mariners. In historic times, the Great Auk was known to breed on Funk Island off Newfoundland, to Iceland, St. Kilda, the Faroe Islands, and the Orkney Islands. It ranged widely over the waters of the North Atlantic. Recent bone excavations indicate that in prehistoric times the Great Auk's breeding range was even more extensive.

intricate scribbles
• *unique to each egg*

pyriform shape •

REPLICA
OF GREAT
AUK EGG

Egg size 111–140 x 69–83 mm	Clutch size 1	Incubation Unknown

Order CHARADRIIFORMES	Family ALCIDAE	Species *Uria aalge*

COMMON MURRE

The sizeable egg of the Common Murre or Guillemot is extremely variable in coloration, ranging from blue or green or bright reddish brown, to warm ocher, pale blue, cream, or white, sparsely or heavily marked with blotches, spots, zones, or interlaced lines in light yellowish brown, bright reddish brown, dark brown, or black. It has been suggested that this variation enables the birds to recognize their own eggs.

• **BREEDING** The single egg is laid directly onto bare rock on cliffs or the tops of rocky stacks. The birds breed in colonies.

• **RANGE** Widespread over the coasts and islands of the North Atlantic, ranging from Bear Island south to Portugal and Nova Scotia; also in the Baltic Sea and the Bering Sea to California and Japan.

• **REMARK** The pointed shape of the egg causes it to roll in a circle, meaning that it is less likely to fall off a steep cliff ledge.

• *thick blotching*

• *gray-blue ground*

pyriform shape •

• *intricately detailed markings*

Egg size 70–92 x 43–56 mm	Clutch size 1	Incubation ♂♀ 28–30 days

Order CHARADRIIFORMES	Family ALCIDAE	Species *Cepphus grylle*

BLACK GUILLEMOT

The Black Guillemot's oval to elliptical eggs are off-white, tinged with bluish green, cream, or buff, blotched and spotted with blackish or chestnut markings and with underlying gray marks.
• **BREEDING** The Black Guillemot builds no nest: the eggs are laid in rough crevices on cliffs, among boulders, or even in holes in masonry (such as old sea walls).
• **RANGE** Coasts of the North Atlantic and Arctic Oceans, south to Maine and the British Isles.

buff ground color

bold, dark blotching

Egg size 53–66 x 35–43 mm	Clutch size 2	Incubation ♂♀ 21 days

Order CHARADRIIFORMES	Family ALCIDAE	Species *Synthliboramphus antiquus*

ANCIENT AUKLET

The largish, elliptical eggs of the Ancient Auklet vary from bluish milky white to cream or yellowish buff in ground color, spotted and streaked in brown, fawn, or lilac-gray. They resemble the eggs of the sandgrouse (see p.124) more than those of other members of the family Alcidae.
• **BREEDING** A grass-lined nest is built in a burrow. It is excavated in soft soil under a tussock of grass, either on the tops of cliffs or islands or in crevices.
• **RANGE** Breeds on the coasts and islands of the North Pacific Ocean, the Sea of Okhotsk, and the Bering Sea.

pale buff ground

fine speckles

Egg size 57–64 x 36–42 mm	Clutch size 1–2	Incubation ♂♀ Unknown

Order CHARADRIIFORMES	Family ALCIDAE	Species *Aethia pusilla*

LEAST AUKLET

The single egg of the Least Auklet is pure white
but often becomes stained in the nesting crevice.
In form, though not in size, it resembles the eggs
of the Crested Auklet and the Whiskered Auklet.
• **BREEDING** The egg is laid on rock, in crevices
in or under rocks on beaches and in cliffs.
• **RANGE** Occurs in the northern North
Pacific Ocean, the Bering Sea, Cape
Lisburne, and the Aleutian Islands.
• **REMARK** The Least Auklet may
well be the smallest of all seabirds.

plain •
white ground

Egg size 38–42 x 27–30 mm	Clutch size 1	Incubation Unknown

Order CHARADRIIFORMES	Family ALCIDAE	Species *Fratercula arctica*

ATLANTIC PUFFIN

The large eggs (similar to those of the Horned
Puffin and Tufted Puffin) are white in ground
color but often have ghostly brown or lilac
markings. Occasionally the eggs may be
pigmented with chestnut-brown blotches.
• **BREEDING** The parent birds excavate
or re-use old burrows on grassy coastal or
island slopes. The nest is simply a slight
depression in the floor within the burrow.
• **RANGE** Breeds from northern Greenland,
Spitsbergen, and Franz Josef Land south to
the British Isles, to Brittany (France) in
the east, and to Nova Scotia in the west.

• blurred
chestnut-
brown
blotches

• ghostly
lilac
markings

Egg size 56–69 x 38–46 mm	Clutch size 1, rarely 2	Incubation ♀ 40–43 days

Order COLUMBIFORMES	Family PTEROCLIDAE	Species *Syrrhaptes paradoxus*

PALLAS'S SANDGROUSE

The oval to elliptical eggs of Pallas's Sandgrouse are stone-buff to yellow-brown with darker brown speckles and spots and a few ashy shell markings.
• **BREEDING** Breeds in large colonies. The nest is a mere scrape, generally unlined, found amid steppe or semidesert in Central Asia, or, during one of its incursions westward to Europe, in coastal dunes and farmland.
• **RANGE** Central Asia from southeastern Russia to Mongolia and China. Occasionally Europe.

intricate scribbles

Egg size 39–46 x 27–32 mm	Clutch size 2–4, usually 3	Incubation ♂♀ 23–28 days

Order COLUMBIFORMES	Family PTEROCLIDAE	Species *Pterocles alchata*

PIN-TAILED SANDGROUSE

The oval eggs of the Pin-tailed Sandgrouse are pale creamy buff or warm reddish buff in ground color, blotched in reddish or dark brown, and with gray secondary markings.
• **BREEDING** The eggs are laid on bare ground in dry, open, flat terrain, especially dried-out marshes or edges of sand dunes.
• **RANGE** The Iberian peninsula, to North Africa, Asia Minor, Afghanistan, and northwestern India.

cream-buff ground

brown blotches

Egg size 39–51 x 28–34 mm	Clutch size 2–3	Incubation ♂♀ 21–23 days

Order COLUMBIFORMES	Family PTEROCLIDAE	Species *Pterocles indicus*

PAINTED SANDGROUSE

The oval to elliptical eggs of the Painted Sandgrouse are pinkish cream to salmon-buff in ground color, sparsely blotched and speckled in brownish red, with secondary markings of grayish lavender.
• **BREEDING** The nest is a simple scrape on stony ground amid rocky terrain, scrub jungle, or forest. It is often sheltered by grass or a small bush and may be quite far from water.
• **RANGE** Over much of the Indian Subcontinent.

• deep salmon-buff ground

Egg size 32–41 x 23–27 mm	Clutch size 2–3	Incubation ♂♀ Unknown

Order COLUMBIFORMES	Family COLUMBIDAE	Species *Columba palumbus*

WOOD PIGEON

Like those of almost all pigeons, the eggs of the Wood Pigeon are plain white. The most likely explanation for the puzzling lack of pigmentation is that since the eggs are rarely left uncovered in the nest, there is no need for cryptic coloration.
• **BREEDING** A lattice of small twigs forms the nest. It is so frail that the eggs can often be seen from beneath. The nest is situated in most tree types in forests, or in hedgerows.
• **RANGE** Europe, Scandinavia, Russia, North Africa, western Asia, Iran, the Himalayas, and India.

• *pure white ground*

• *oval shape*

Egg size 37–47 x 25–32 mm	Clutch size 2	Incubation ♂♀ 17 days

Order COLUMBIFORMES	Family COLUMBIDAE	Species *Oena capensis*

NAMAQUA DOVE

The eggs laid by the Namaqua Dove are pale yellow or creamy buff. The color is exceptional for this family, which predominantly lays white eggs.
• **BREEDING** The nest, made from a circular platform of twigs and roots, is situated in bushes or grassy tufts in tropical savannah scrubland.
• **RANGE** Tropical Africa south of the Sahara, except the rain forest; also the Arabian peninsula and Madagascar.

• *creamy buff ground*

Egg size 19–23 x 14–18 mm	Clutch size 2	Incubation ♂♀ Unknown

Order COLUMBIFORMES	Family PSITTACIDAE	Species *Psittacula krameri*

ROSE-RINGED PARAKEET

Like other members of the family Psittacidae, the Rose-ringed Parakeet lays pure white eggs.
• **BREEDING** The parakeet nests in holes, most often one formerly excavated by a woodpecker or a barbet, in trees amid forests and woodland. In India, nests are unlined; in Africa, some nests appear to be lined with kapok.
• **RANGE** In tropical Africa, from Senegal east to the Sudan, south to Ethiopia and Cameroon; in Asia, from India to Southeast Asia and southeastern China. It is now also feral in countries to which it is not native.

matte • surface

plain • ground

Egg size 28–34 x 22–26 mm	Clutch size 2–6	Incubation ♂♀ 22–24 days

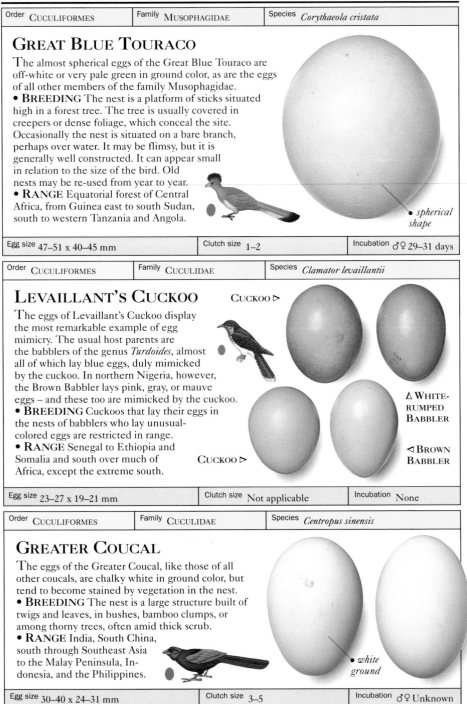

Order CUCULIFORMES	Family MUSOPHAGIDAE	Species *Corythaeola cristata*

GREAT BLUE TOURACO

The almost spherical eggs of the Great Blue Touraco are off-white or very pale green in ground color, as are the eggs of all other members of the family Musophagidae.
• **BREEDING** The nest is a platform of sticks situated high in a forest tree. The tree is usually covered in creepers or dense foliage, which conceal the site. Occasionally the nest is situated on a bare branch, perhaps over water. It may be flimsy, but it is generally well constructed. It can appear small in relation to the size of the bird. Old nests may be re-used from year to year.
• **RANGE** Equatorial forest of Central Africa, from Guinea east to south Sudan, south to western Tanzania and Angola.

• *spherical shape*

Egg size 47–51 x 40–45 mm	Clutch size 1–2	Incubation ♂♀ 29–31 days

Order CUCULIFORMES	Family CUCULIDAE	Species *Clamator levaillantii*

LEVAILLANT'S CUCKOO

CUCKOO ▷

The eggs of Levaillant's Cuckoo display the most remarkable example of egg mimicry. The usual host parents are the babblers of the genus *Turdoides*, almost all of which lay blue eggs, duly mimicked by the cuckoo. In northern Nigeria, however, the Brown Babbler lays pink, gray, or mauve eggs – and these too are mimicked by the cuckoo.
• **BREEDING** Cuckoos that lay their eggs in the nests of babblers who lay unusual-colored eggs are restricted in range.
• **RANGE** Senegal to Ethiopia and Somalia and south over much of Africa, except the extreme south.

△ WHITE-RUMPED BABBLER

◁ BROWN BABBLER

CUCKOO ▷

Egg size 23–27 x 19–21 mm	Clutch size Not applicable	Incubation None

Order CUCULIFORMES	Family CUCULIDAE	Species *Centropus sinensis*

GREATER COUCAL

The eggs of the Greater Coucal, like those of all other coucals, are chalky white in ground color, but tend to become stained by vegetation in the nest.
• **BREEDING** The nest is a large structure built of twigs and leaves, in bushes, bamboo clumps, or among thorny trees, often amid thick scrub.
• **RANGE** India, South China, south through Southeast Asia to the Malay Peninsula, Indonesia, and the Philippines.

• *white ground*

Egg size 30–40 x 24–31 mm	Clutch size 3–5	Incubation ♂♀ Unknown

Order CUCULIFORMES	Family CUCULIDAE	Species *Clamator glandarius*

GREAT SPOTTED CUCKOO

The eggs are very pale bluish green, thickly dotted in light liver-brown or reddish brown. They are not unlike those of the Common Magpie (see p.245).
• **BREEDING** This species tends especially to parasitize the nests of the crow family, although the actual host depends on the geographical area of breeding.
• **RANGE** Breeds in southern Europe, the Mediterranean, southern and eastern Africa, and the Middle East.

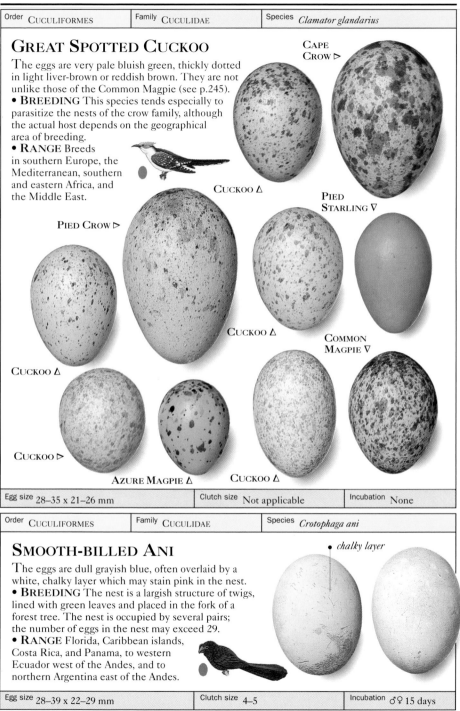

CAPE CROW ▷

CUCKOO △

PIED STARLING ▽

PIED CROW ▷

CUCKOO △

CUCKOO △

COMMON MAGPIE ▽

CUCKOO △

CUCKOO ▷

AZURE MAGPIE △

CUCKOO △

Egg size 28–35 x 21–26 mm	Clutch size Not applicable	Incubation None

Order CUCULIFORMES	Family CUCULIDAE	Species *Crotophaga ani*

SMOOTH-BILLED ANI

The eggs are dull grayish blue, often overlaid by a white, chalky layer which may stain pink in the nest.
• **BREEDING** The nest is a largish structure of twigs, lined with green leaves and placed in the fork of a forest tree. The nest is occupied by several pairs; the number of eggs in the nest may exceed 29.
• **RANGE** Florida, Caribbean islands, Costa Rica, and Panama, to western Ecuador west of the Andes, and to northern Argentina east of the Andes.

• *chalky layer*

Egg size 28–39 x 22–29 mm	Clutch size 4–5	Incubation ♂♀ 15 days

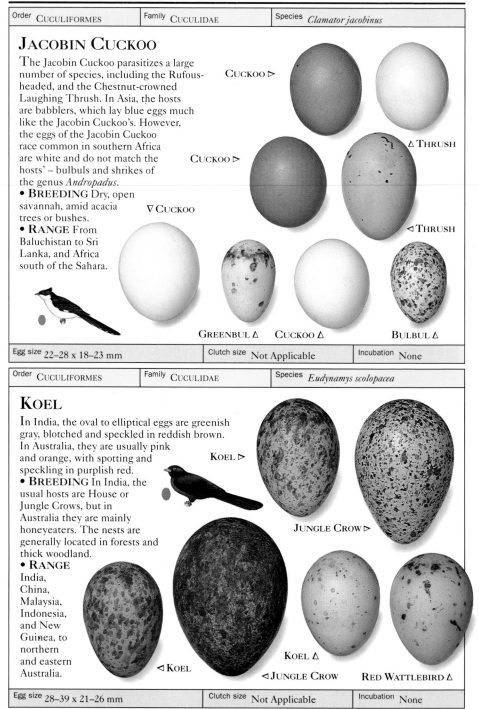

| Order CUCULIFORMES | Family CUCULIDAE | Species *Clamator jacobinus* |

JACOBIN CUCKOO

The Jacobin Cuckoo parasitizes a large number of species, including the Rufous-headed, and the Chestnut-crowned Laughing Thrush. In Asia, the hosts are babblers, which lay blue eggs much like the Jacobin Cuckoo's. However, the eggs of the Jacobin Cuckoo race common in southern Africa are white and do not match the hosts' – bulbuls and shrikes of the genus *Andropadus*.
• **BREEDING** Dry, open savannah, amid acacia trees or bushes.
• **RANGE** From Baluchistan to Sri Lanka, and Africa south of the Sahara.

CUCKOO ▷

CUCKOO ▷

▽ CUCKOO

△ THRUSH

◁ THRUSH

GREENBUL △   CUCKOO △   BULBUL △

| Egg size 22–28 x 18–23 mm | Clutch size Not Applicable | Incubation None |

| Order CUCULIFORMES | Family CUCULIDAE | Species *Eudynamys scolopacea* |

KOEL

In India, the oval to elliptical eggs are greenish gray, blotched and speckled in reddish brown. In Australia, they are usually pink and orange, with spotting and speckling in purplish red.
• **BREEDING** In India, the usual hosts are House or Jungle Crows, but in Australia they are mainly honeyeaters. The nests are generally located in forests and thick woodland.
• **RANGE** India, China, Malaysia, Indonesia, and New Guinea, to northern and eastern Australia.

KOEL ▷

JUNGLE CROW ▷

◁ KOEL

KOEL △

◁ JUNGLE CROW   RED WATTLEBIRD △

| Egg size 28–39 x 21–26 mm | Clutch size Not Applicable | Incubation None |

Order CUCULIFORMES	Family CUCULIDAE	Species *Cuculus canorus*

COMMON CUCKOO

The eggs of this species vary greatly in color and markings, and mimic the eggs of the host to a greater or lesser extent. An individual cuckoo cannot alter the color of its eggs to match those of the host, as is sometimes believed.

• **BREEDING** Each hen Cuckoo confines her activities to a certain area, and usually lays in the nest of one particular host. However, in cases where she is unable to find the nests of the host she seeks, her eggs will be laid in the nests of other species, regardless of the fact that they do not match.

• **RANGE** The British Isles, Finland, northern Russia, and Siberia, east to China and Japan, south to the Mediterranean, North Africa, India, and Southeast Asia.

CUCKOO △

△ DUNNOCK

△ CUCKOO △ ROBIN

△ CUCKOO △ CHAFFINCH △ CUCKOO △ SKYLARK △ CUCKOO △ GREAT REED WARBLER

CUCKOO ▷

RED-BACKED SHRIKE △ △ CUCKOO △ WINTER WREN

△ CUCKOO △ COMMON REDSTART △ CUCKOO △ TREE PIPIT △ CUCKOO △ RED-BACKED SHRIKE

CUCKOO ▷

△ RED BLACKSTART △ CUCKOO △ BRAMBLING

Egg size 19–27 x 14–19 mm	Clutch size Not Applicable	Incubation None

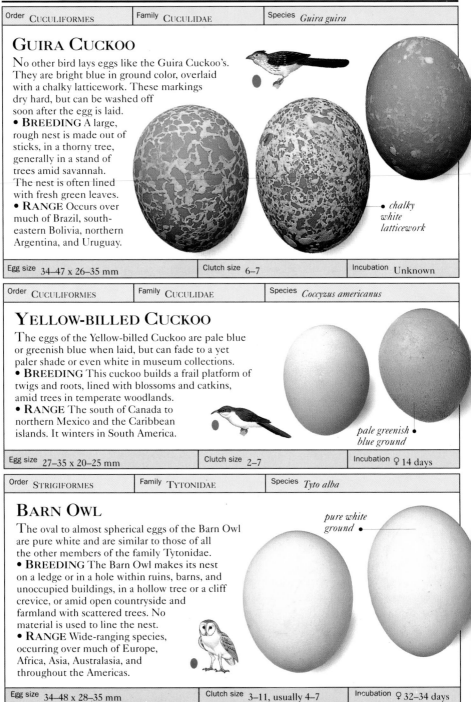

Order CUCULIFORMES	Family CUCULIDAE	Species *Guira guira*

GUIRA CUCKOO

No other bird lays eggs like the Guira Cuckoo's. They are bright blue in ground color, overlaid with a chalky latticework. These markings dry hard, but can be washed off soon after the egg is laid.
• **BREEDING** A large, rough nest is made out of sticks, in a thorny tree, generally in a stand of trees amid savannah. The nest is often lined with fresh green leaves.
• **RANGE** Occurs over much of Brazil, south-eastern Bolivia, northern Argentina, and Uruguay.

• chalky white latticework

Egg size 34–47 x 26–35 mm	Clutch size 6–7	Incubation Unknown

Order CUCULIFORMES	Family CUCULIDAE	Species *Coccyzus americanus*

YELLOW-BILLED CUCKOO

The eggs of the Yellow-billed Cuckoo are pale blue or greenish blue when laid, but can fade to a yet paler shade or even white in museum collections.
• **BREEDING** This cuckoo builds a frail platform of twigs and roots, lined with blossoms and catkins, amid trees in temperate woodlands.
• **RANGE** The south of Canada to northern Mexico and the Caribbean islands. It winters in South America.

pale greenish • blue ground

Egg size 27–35 x 20–25 mm	Clutch size 2–7	Incubation ♀ 14 days

Order STRIGIFORMES	Family TYTONIDAE	Species *Tyto alba*

BARN OWL

The oval to almost spherical eggs of the Barn Owl are pure white and are similar to those of all the other members of the family Tytonidae.
• **BREEDING** The Barn Owl makes its nest on a ledge or in a hole within ruins, barns, and unoccupied buildings, in a hollow tree or a cliff crevice, or amid open countryside and farmland with scattered trees. No material is used to line the nest.
• **RANGE** Wide-ranging species, occurring over much of Europe, Africa, Asia, Australasia, and throughout the Americas.

pure white ground •

Egg size 34–48 x 28–35 mm	Clutch size 3–11, usually 4–7	Incubation ♀ 32–34 days

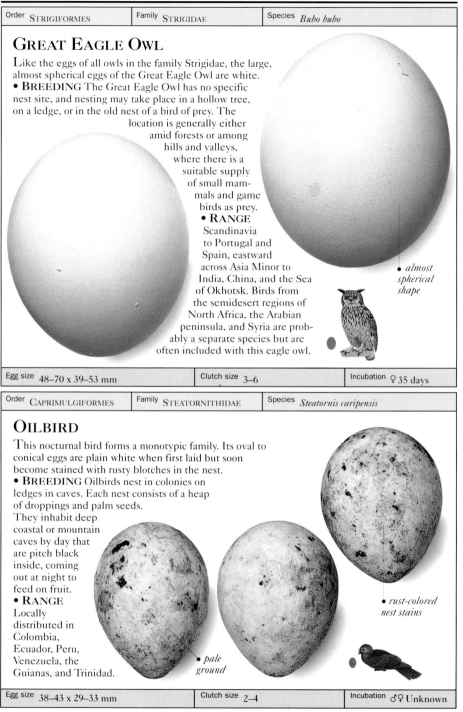

Order STRIGIFORMES	Family STRIGIDAE	Species *Bubo bubo*

GREAT EAGLE OWL

Like the eggs of all owls in the family Strigidae, the large, almost spherical eggs of the Great Eagle Owl are white.
• **BREEDING** The Great Eagle Owl has no specific nest site, and nesting may take place in a hollow tree, on a ledge, or in the old nest of a bird of prey. The location is generally either amid forests or among hills and valleys, where there is a suitable supply of small mammals and game birds as prey.
• **RANGE** Scandinavia to Portugal and Spain, eastward across Asia Minor to India, China, and the Sea of Okhotsk. Birds from the semidesert regions of North Africa, the Arabian peninsula, and Syria are probably a separate species but are often included with this eagle owl.

• *almost spherical shape*

Egg size 48–70 x 39–53 mm	Clutch size 3–6	Incubation ♀ 35 days

Order CAPRIMULGIFORMES	Family STEATORNITHIDAE	Species *Steatornis caripensis*

OILBIRD

This nocturnal bird forms a monotypic family. Its oval to conical eggs are plain white when first laid but soon become stained with rusty blotches in the nest.
• **BREEDING** Oilbirds nest in colonies on ledges in caves. Each nest consists of a heap of droppings and palm seeds. They inhabit deep coastal or mountain caves by day that are pitch black inside, coming out at night to feed on fruit.
• **RANGE** Locally distributed in Colombia, Ecuador, Peru, Venezuela, the Guianas, and Trinidad.

• *rust-colored nest stains*

• *pale ground*

Egg size 38–43 x 29–33 mm	Clutch size 2–4	Incubation ♂♀ Unknown

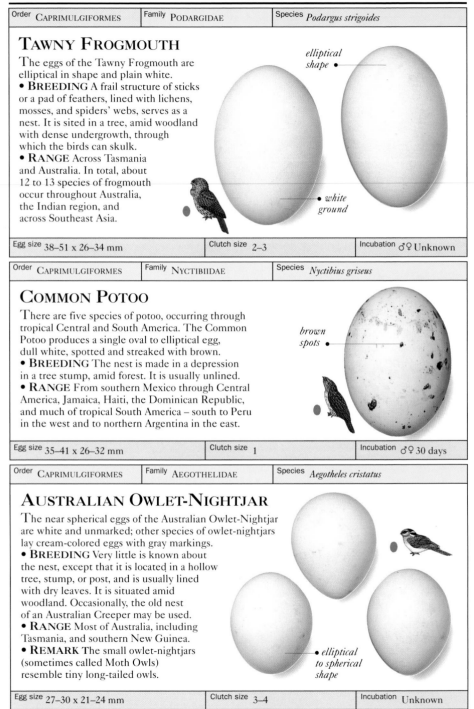

Order CAPRIMULGIFORMES	Family PODARGIDAE	Species *Podargus strigoides*

TAWNY FROGMOUTH

The eggs of the Tawny Frogmouth are elliptical in shape and plain white.
• **BREEDING** A frail structure of sticks or a pad of feathers, lined with lichens, mosses, and spiders' webs, serves as a nest. It is sited in a tree, amid woodland with dense undergrowth, through which the birds can skulk.
• **RANGE** Across Tasmania and Australia. In total, about 12 to 13 species of frogmouth occur throughout Australia, the Indian region, and across Southeast Asia.

elliptical shape •

• *white ground*

Egg size 38–51 x 26–34 mm	Clutch size 2–3	Incubation ♂♀ Unknown

Order CAPRIMULGIFORMES	Family NYCTIBIIDAE	Species *Nyctibius griseus*

COMMON POTOO

There are five species of potoo, occurring through tropical Central and South America. The Common Potoo produces a single oval to elliptical egg, dull white, spotted and streaked with brown.
• **BREEDING** The nest is made in a depression in a tree stump, amid forest. It is usually unlined.
• **RANGE** From southern Mexico through Central America, Jamaica, Haiti, the Dominican Republic, and much of tropical South America – south to Peru in the west and to northern Argentina in the east.

brown spots •

Egg size 35–41 x 26–32 mm	Clutch size 1	Incubation ♂♀ 30 days

Order CAPRIMULGIFORMES	Family AEGOTHELIDAE	Species *Aegotheles cristatus*

AUSTRALIAN OWLET-NIGHTJAR

The near spherical eggs of the Australian Owlet-Nightjar are white and unmarked; other species of owlet-nightjars lay cream-colored eggs with gray markings.
• **BREEDING** Very little is known about the nest, except that it is located in a hollow tree, stump, or post, and is usually lined with dry leaves. It is situated amid woodland. Occasionally, the old nest of an Australian Creeper may be used.
• **RANGE** Most of Australia, including Tasmania, and southern New Guinea.
• **REMARK** The small owlet-nightjars (sometimes called Moth Owls) resemble tiny long-tailed owls.

• *elliptical to spherical shape*

Egg size 27–30 x 21–24 mm	Clutch size 3–4	Incubation Unknown

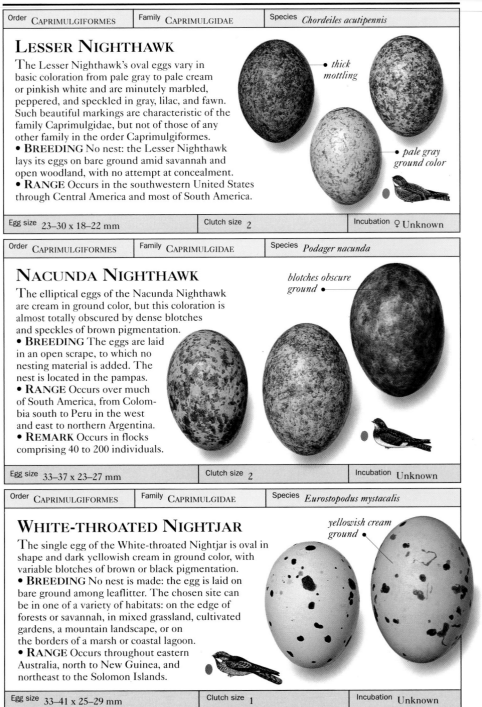

| Order CAPRIMULGIFORMES | Family CAPRIMULGIDAE | Species *Chordeiles acutipennis* |

LESSER NIGHTHAWK

The Lesser Nighthawk's oval eggs vary in basic coloration from pale gray to pale cream or pinkish white and are minutely marbled, peppered, and speckled in gray, lilac, and fawn. Such beautiful markings are characteristic of the family Caprimulgidae, but not of those of any other family in the order Caprimulgiformes.
• **BREEDING** No nest: the Lesser Nighthawk lays its eggs on bare ground amid savannah and open woodland, with no attempt at concealment.
• **RANGE** Occurs in the southwestern United States through Central America and most of South America.

thick mottling

pale gray ground color

| Egg size 23–30 x 18–22 mm | Clutch size 2 | Incubation ♀ Unknown |

| Order CAPRIMULGIFORMES | Family CAPRIMULGIDAE | Species *Podager nacunda* |

NACUNDA NIGHTHAWK

The elliptical eggs of the Nacunda Nighthawk are cream in ground color, but this coloration is almost totally obscured by dense blotches and speckles of brown pigmentation.
• **BREEDING** The eggs are laid in an open scrape, to which no nesting material is added. The nest is located in the pampas.
• **RANGE** Occurs over much of South America, from Colombia south to Peru in the west and east to northern Argentina.
• **REMARK** Occurs in flocks comprising 40 to 200 individuals.

blotches obscure ground

| Egg size 33–37 x 23–27 mm | Clutch size 2 | Incubation Unknown |

| Order CAPRIMULGIFORMES | Family CAPRIMULGIDAE | Species *Eurostopodus mystacalis* |

WHITE-THROATED NIGHTJAR

The single egg of the White-throated Nightjar is oval in shape and dark yellowish cream in ground color, with variable blotches of brown or black pigmentation.
• **BREEDING** No nest is made: the egg is laid on bare ground among leaflitter. The chosen site can be in one of a variety of habitats: on the edge of forests or savannah, in mixed grassland, cultivated gardens, a mountain landscape, or on the borders of a marsh or coastal lagoon.
• **RANGE** Occurs throughout eastern Australia, north to New Guinea, and northeast to the Solomon Islands.

yellowish cream ground

| Egg size 33–41 x 25–29 mm | Clutch size 1 | Incubation Unknown |

Order CAPRIMULGIFORMES	Family CAPRIMULGIDAE	Species *Eurostopodus macrotis*

GREAT-EARED NIGHTJAR

The oval to cylindrical egg of the Great-eared Nightjar is either pale yellowish cream or rosy pink in ground color with very pale mottling.
• **BREEDING** No nest: the egg is laid on bare ground, amid thin forest or bamboo jungle. The bird may occupy the same site year after year.
• **RANGE** Discontinuous range in southern India, through Southeast Asia to the Philippines; and on to Sulawesi and Simalur.

pale mottling

Egg size 37–44 x 27–31 mm	Clutch size 1	Incubation Unknown

Order CAPRIMULGIFORMES	Family CAPRIMULGIDAE	Species *Caprimulgus indicus*

INDIAN NIGHTJAR

The Indian Nightjar's oval to elliptical eggs vary in color according to geographical race. Some are white in ground color, marbled in dark gray or grayish brown; others are creamy to buff, spattered irregularly with reddish brown marks.
• **BREEDING** Indian Nightjars do not build nests: the eggs are laid on bare ground amid forests and woodland.
• **RANGE** Indian Subcontinent east to China and southeastern Siberia, and south through Southeast Asia to Sumatra, Java, and Borneo. There is an isolated population on the Palau islands, north-east of the Philippines.

warm buff ground

reddish brown mottling

Egg size 26–34 x 20–24 mm	Clutch size 2	Incubation ♂♀ 17 days

Order CAPRIMULGIFORMES	Family CAPRIMULGIDAE	Species *Caprimulgus europaeus*

EUROPEAN NIGHTJAR

The eggs are often oval in shape, and vary in coloration between grayish white and cream, less commonly bluish or pink-ish white, blotched and marbled in pale yellow-brown or lead-gray.
• **BREEDING** The nest is simply a scrape on bare ground in heaths, on commons, in woodland glades, and occasionally on sand hills.
• **RANGE** Breeds over Europe and temperate Asia, south to the Mediterranean and Baluchistan.

lead-gray marbling

Egg size 27–36 x 20–24 mm	Clutch size 2	Incubation ♂♀ 18 days

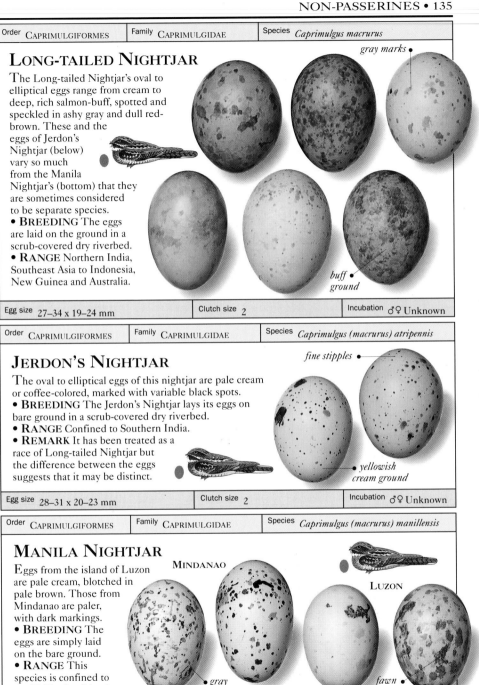

| Order CAPRIMULGIFORMES | Family CAPRIMULGIDAE | Species *Caprimulgus macrurus* |

LONG-TAILED NIGHTJAR

gray marks

The Long-tailed Nightjar's oval to elliptical eggs range from cream to deep, rich salmon-buff, spotted and speckled in ashy gray and dull red-brown. These and the eggs of Jerdon's Nightjar (below) vary so much from the Manila Nightjar's (bottom) that they are sometimes considered to be separate species.
• **BREEDING** The eggs are laid on the ground in a scrub-covered dry riverbed.
• **RANGE** Northern India, Southeast Asia to Indonesia, New Guinea and Australia.

buff ground

| Egg size 27–34 x 19–24 mm | Clutch size 2 | Incubation ♂♀ Unknown |

| Order CAPRIMULGIFORMES | Family CAPRIMULGIDAE | Species *Caprimulgus (macrurus) atripennis* |

JERDON'S NIGHTJAR

fine stipples

The oval to elliptical eggs of this nightjar are pale cream or coffee-colored, marked with variable black spots.
• **BREEDING** The Jerdon's Nightjar lays its eggs on bare ground in a scrub-covered dry riverbed.
• **RANGE** Confined to Southern India.
• **REMARK** It has been treated as a race of Long-tailed Nightjar but the difference between the eggs suggests that it may be distinct.

yellowish cream ground

| Egg size 28–31 x 20–23 mm | Clutch size 2 | Incubation ♂♀ Unknown |

| Order CAPRIMULGIFORMES | Family CAPRIMULGIDAE | Species *Caprimulgus (macrurus) manillensis* |

MANILA NIGHTJAR

MINDANAO

LUZON

Eggs from the island of Luzon are pale cream, blotched in pale brown. Those from Mindanao are paler, with dark markings.
• **BREEDING** The eggs are simply laid on the bare ground.
• **RANGE** This species is confined to the Philippine Islands.

gray spots

fawn blotches

| Egg size 28–29 x 20–21 mm | Clutch size 2 | Incubation Unknown |

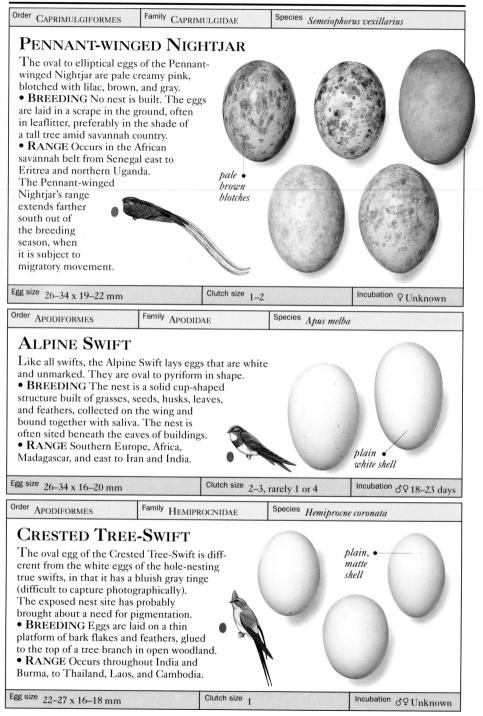

Order CAPRIMULGIFORMES	Family CAPRIMULGIDAE	Species *Semeiophorus vexillarius*

PENNANT-WINGED NIGHTJAR

The oval to elliptical eggs of the Pennant-winged Nightjar are pale creamy pink, blotched with lilac, brown, and gray.
• **BREEDING** No nest is built. The eggs are laid in a scrape in the ground, often in leaflitter, preferably in the shade of a tall tree amid savannah country.
• **RANGE** Occurs in the African savannah belt from Senegal east to Eritrea and northern Uganda. The Pennant-winged Nightjar's range extends farther south out of the breeding season, when it is subject to migratory movement.

pale • brown blotches

Egg size 26–34 x 19–22 mm	Clutch size 1–2	Incubation ♀ Unknown

Order APODIFORMES	Family APODIDAE	Species *Apus melba*

ALPINE SWIFT

Like all swifts, the Alpine Swift lays eggs that are white and unmarked. They are oval to pyriform in shape.
• **BREEDING** The nest is a solid cup-shaped structure built of grasses, seeds, husks, leaves, and feathers, collected on the wing and bound together with saliva. The nest is often sited beneath the eaves of buildings.
• **RANGE** Southern Europe, Africa, Madagascar, and east to Iran and India.

plain • white shell

Egg size 26–34 x 16–20 mm	Clutch size 2–3, rarely 1 or 4	Incubation ♂♀ 18–23 days

Order APODIFORMES	Family HEMIPROCNIDAE	Species *Hemiprocne coronata*

CRESTED TREE-SWIFT

The oval egg of the Crested Tree-Swift is different from the white eggs of the hole-nesting true swifts, in that it has a bluish gray tinge (difficult to capture photographically). The exposed nest site has probably brought about a need for pigmentation.
• **BREEDING** Eggs are laid on a thin platform of bark flakes and feathers, glued to the top of a tree branch in open woodland.
• **RANGE** Occurs throughout India and Burma, to Thailand, Laos, and Cambodia.

plain, • matte shell

Egg size 22–27 x 16–18 mm	Clutch size 1	Incubation ♂♀ Unknown

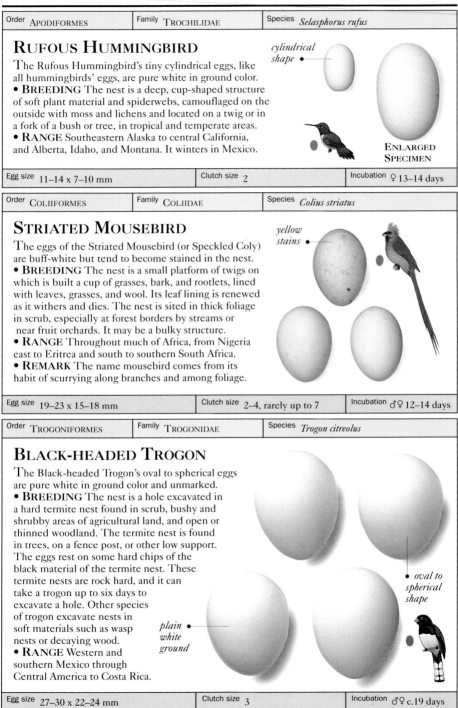

Order APODIFORMES	Family TROCHILIDAE	Species *Selasphorus rufus*

RUFOUS HUMMINGBIRD

cylindrical shape

The Rufous Hummingbird's tiny cylindrical eggs, like all hummingbirds' eggs, are pure white in ground color.
• **BREEDING** The nest is a deep, cup-shaped structure of soft plant material and spiderwebs, camouflaged on the outside with moss and lichens and located on a twig or in a fork of a bush or tree, in tropical and temperate areas.
• **RANGE** Southeastern Alaska to central California, and Alberta, Idaho, and Montana. It winters in Mexico.

ENLARGED SPECIMEN

Egg size 11–14 x 7–10 mm	Clutch size 2	Incubation ♀ 13–14 days

Order COLIIFORMES	Family COLIIDAE	Species *Colius striatus*

STRIATED MOUSEBIRD

yellow stains

The eggs of the Striated Mousebird (or Speckled Coly) are buff-white but tend to become stained in the nest.
• **BREEDING** The nest is a small platform of twigs on which is built a cup of grasses, bark, and rootlets, lined with leaves, grasses, and wool. Its leaf lining is renewed as it withers and dies. The nest is sited in thick foliage in scrub, especially at forest borders by streams or near fruit orchards. It may be a bulky structure.
• **RANGE** Throughout much of Africa, from Nigeria east to Eritrea and south to southern South Africa.
• **REMARK** The name mousebird comes from its habit of scurrying along branches and among foliage.

Egg size 19–23 x 15–18 mm	Clutch size 2–4, rarely up to 7	Incubation ♂♀ 12–14 days

Order TROGONIFORMES	Family TROGONIDAE	Species *Trogon citreolus*

BLACK-HEADED TROGON

The Black-headed Trogon's oval to spherical eggs are pure white in ground color and unmarked.
• **BREEDING** The nest is a hole excavated in a hard termite nest found in scrub, bushy and shrubby areas of agricultural land, and open or thinned woodland. The termite nest is found in trees, on a fence post, or other low support. The eggs rest on some hard chips of the black material of the termite nest. These termite nests are rock hard, and it can take a trogon up to six days to excavate a hole. Other species of trogon excavate nests in soft materials such as wasp nests or decaying wood.
• **RANGE** Western and southern Mexico through Central America to Costa Rica.

oval to spherical shape

plain white ground

Egg size 27–30 x 22–24 mm	Clutch size 3	Incubation ♂♀ c.19 days

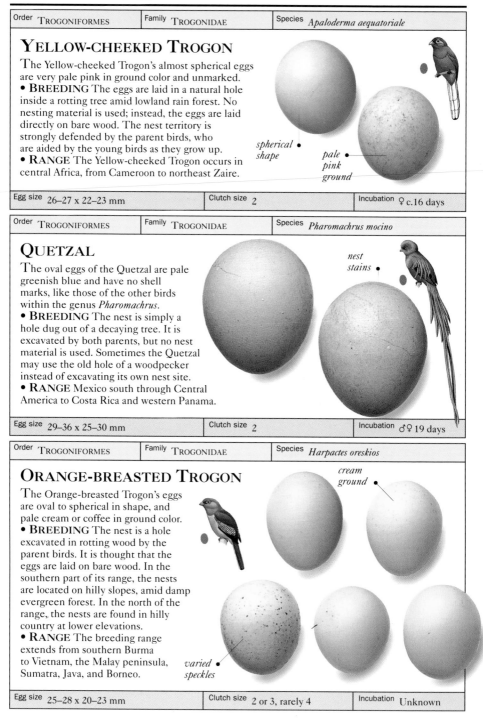

Order TROGONIFORMES	Family TROGONIDAE	Species *Apaloderma aequatoriale*

YELLOW-CHEEKED TROGON

The Yellow-cheeked Trogon's almost spherical eggs are very pale pink in ground color and unmarked.
• BREEDING The eggs are laid in a natural hole inside a rotting tree amid lowland rain forest. No nesting material is used; instead, the eggs are laid directly on bare wood. The nest territory is strongly defended by the parent birds, who are aided by the young birds as they grow up.
• RANGE The Yellow-cheeked Trogon occurs in central Africa, from Cameroon to northeast Zaire.

spherical • shape

pale • pink ground

Egg size 26–27 x 22–23 mm	Clutch size 2	Incubation ♀ c.16 days

Order TROGONIFORMES	Family TROGONIDAE	Species *Pharomachrus mocino*

QUETZAL

The oval eggs of the Quetzal are pale greenish blue and have no shell marks, like those of the other birds within the genus *Pharomachrus*.
• BREEDING The nest is simply a hole dug out of a decaying tree. It is excavated by both parents, but no nest material is used. Sometimes the Quetzal may use the old hole of a woodpecker instead of excavating its own nest site.
• RANGE Mexico south through Central America to Costa Rica and western Panama.

nest stains •

Egg size 29–36 x 25–30 mm	Clutch size 2	Incubation ♂♀ 19 days

Order TROGONIFORMES	Family TROGONIDAE	Species *Harpactes oreskios*

ORANGE-BREASTED TROGON

The Orange-breasted Trogon's eggs are oval to spherical in shape, and pale cream or coffee in ground color.
• BREEDING The nest is a hole excavated in rotting wood by the parent birds. It is thought that the eggs are laid on bare wood. In the southern part of its range, the nests are located on hilly slopes, amid damp evergreen forest. In the north of the range, the nests are found in hilly country at lower elevations.
• RANGE The breeding range extends from southern Burma to Vietnam, the Malay peninsula, Sumatra, Java, and Borneo.

cream ground •

varied • speckles

Egg size 25–28 x 20–23 mm	Clutch size 2 or 3, rarely 4	Incubation Unknown

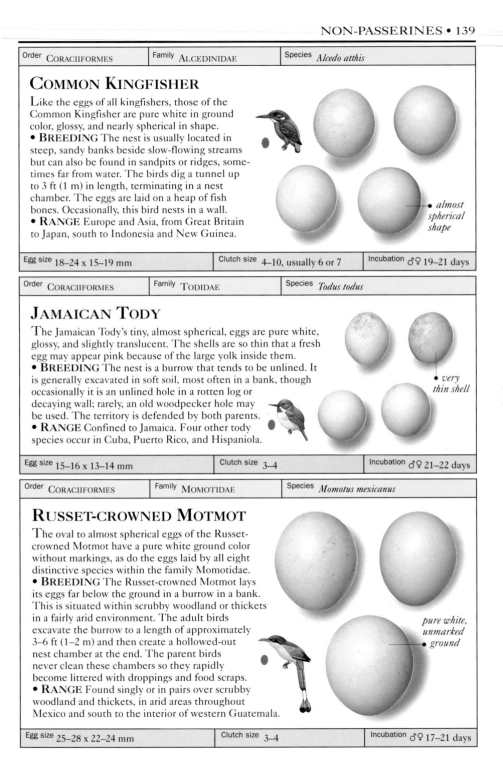

| Order CORACIIFORMES | Family ALCEDINIDAE | Species *Alcedo atthis* |

COMMON KINGFISHER

Like the eggs of all kingfishers, those of the
Common Kingfisher are pure white in ground
color, glossy, and nearly spherical in shape.
• **BREEDING** The nest is usually located in
steep, sandy banks beside slow-flowing streams
but can also be found in sandpits or ridges, sometimes far from water. The birds dig a tunnel up
to 3 ft (1 m) in length, terminating in a nest
chamber. The eggs are laid on a heap of fish
bones. Occasionally, this bird nests in a wall.
• **RANGE** Europe and Asia, from Great Britain
to Japan, south to Indonesia and New Guinea.

*almost
spherical
shape*

| Egg size 18–24 x 15–19 mm | Clutch size 4–10, usually 6 or 7 | Incubation ♂♀ 19–21 days |

| Order CORACIIFORMES | Family TODIDAE | Species *Todus todus* |

JAMAICAN TODY

The Jamaican Tody's tiny, almost spherical, eggs are pure white,
glossy, and slightly translucent. The shells are so thin that a fresh
egg may appear pink because of the large yolk inside them.
• **BREEDING** The nest is a burrow that tends to be unlined. It
is generally excavated in soft soil, most often in a bank, though
occasionally it is an unlined hole in a rotten log or
decaying wall; rarely, an old woodpecker hole may
be used. The territory is defended by both parents.
• **RANGE** Confined to Jamaica. Four other tody
species occur in Cuba, Puerto Rico, and Hispaniola.

*very
thin shell*

| Egg size 15–16 x 13–14 mm | Clutch size 3–4 | Incubation ♂♀ 21–22 days |

| Order CORACIIFORMES | Family MOMOTIDAE | Species *Momotus mexicanus* |

RUSSET-CROWNED MOTMOT

The oval to almost spherical eggs of the Russet-
crowned Motmot have a pure white ground color
without markings, as do the eggs laid by all eight
distinctive species within the family Momotidae.
• **BREEDING** The Russet-crowned Motmot lays
its eggs far below the ground in a burrow in a bank.
This is situated within scrubby woodland or thickets
in a fairly arid environment. The adult birds
excavate the burrow to a length of approximately
3–6 ft (1–2 m) and then create a hollowed-out
nest chamber at the end. The parent birds
never clean these chambers so they rapidly
become littered with droppings and food scraps.
• **RANGE** Found singly or in pairs over scrubby
woodland and thickets, in arid areas throughout
Mexico and south to the interior of western Guatemala.

*pure white,
unmarked
ground*

| Egg size 25–28 x 22–24 mm | Clutch size 3–4 | Incubation ♂♀ 17–21 days |

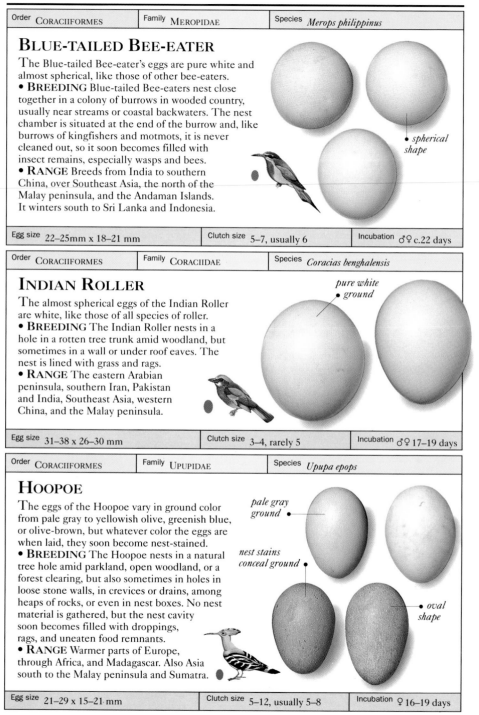

| Order CORACIIFORMES | Family MEROPIDAE | Species *Merops philippinus* |

BLUE-TAILED BEE-EATER

The Blue-tailed Bee-eater's eggs are pure white and almost spherical, like those of other bee-eaters.
• **BREEDING** Blue-tailed Bee-eaters nest close together in a colony of burrows in wooded country, usually near streams or coastal backwaters. The nest chamber is situated at the end of the burrow and, like burrows of kingfishers and motmots, it is never cleaned out, so it soon becomes filled with insect remains, especially wasps and bees.
• **RANGE** Breeds from India to southern China, over Southeast Asia, the north of the Malay peninsula, and the Andaman Islands. It winters south to Sri Lanka and Indonesia.

• spherical shape

| Egg size 22–25mm x 18–21 mm | Clutch size 5–7, usually 6 | Incubation ♂♀ c.22 days |

| Order CORACIIFORMES | Family CORACIIDAE | Species *Coracias benghalensis* |

INDIAN ROLLER

pure white • ground

The almost spherical eggs of the Indian Roller are white, like those of all species of roller.
• **BREEDING** The Indian Roller nests in a hole in a rotten tree trunk amid woodland, but sometimes in a wall or under roof eaves. The nest is lined with grass and rags.
• **RANGE** The eastern Arabian peninsula, southern Iran, Pakistan and India, Southeast Asia, western China, and the Malay peninsula.

| Egg size 31–38 x 26–30 mm | Clutch size 3–4, rarely 5 | Incubation ♂♀ 17–19 days |

| Order CORACIIFORMES | Family UPUPIDAE | Species *Upupa epops* |

HOOPOE

pale gray ground •

The eggs of the Hoopoe vary in ground color from pale gray to yellowish olive, greenish blue, or olive-brown, but whatever color the eggs are when laid, they soon become nest-stained.
• **BREEDING** The Hoopoe nests in a natural tree hole amid parkland, open woodland, or a forest clearing, but also sometimes in holes in loose stone walls, in crevices or drains, among heaps of rocks, or even in nest boxes. No nest material is gathered, but the nest cavity soon becomes filled with droppings, rags, and uneaten food remnants.
• **RANGE** Warmer parts of Europe, through Africa, and Madagascar. Also Asia south to the Malay peninsula and Sumatra.

nest stains conceal ground •

• oval shape

| Egg size 21–29 x 15–21 mm | Clutch size 5–12, usually 5–8 | Incubation ♀ 16–19 days |

Order CORACIIFORMES	Family PHOENICULIDAE	Species *Phoeniculus purpureus*

GREEN WOOD-HOOPOE

The oval eggs of the large and noisy Green Wood-Hoopoe range from greenish blue through to turquoise in ground color.
• **BREEDING** The nest is simply a hole in a tree, fence post, or building, amid savannah or open woodland, especially near streams. The eggs are laid on rotten wood chips within the cavity. Usually a new location for the nest is found for each successive season, although a pair may use the same hole again.
• **RANGE** Occurs throughout most of Africa south of the Sahara, except forest and desert regions.

blue ground

Egg size 22–27mm x 16–19 mm	Clutch size 2–5, usually 3–4	Incubation ♀ 17–18 days

Order CORACIIFORMES	Family BUCEROTIDAE	Species *Aceros nipalensis*

RUFOUS-NECKED HORNBILL

The Rufous-necked Hornbill's largish egg is white, but becomes heavily stained by nest material during incubation.
• **BREEDING** Like most species of hornbill, the bird nests in a natural tree hole, amid tropical forests and woodland. The female walls up the entrance to the hole from inside, using her own excrement mixed with fruit pulp; mud may be added to the outside of the hole until a narrow slit is left, through which the male feeds the female during incubation.
• **RANGE** The foothills of the Himalayas, south to northern Thailand, Laos, and Vietnam.

white eggs are stained in nest

Egg size 54–68 x 39–46 mm	Clutch size 1–2	Incubation ♀ Unknown

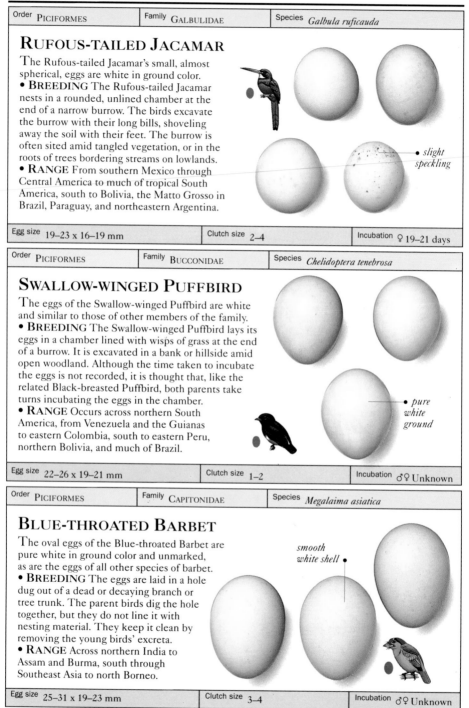

Order PICIFORMES	Family GALBULIDAE	Species *Galbula ruficauda*

RUFOUS-TAILED JACAMAR

The Rufous-tailed Jacamar's small, almost spherical, eggs are white in ground color.
• **BREEDING** The Rufous-tailed Jacamar nests in a rounded, unlined chamber at the end of a narrow burrow. The birds excavate the burrow with their long bills, shoveling away the soil with their feet. The burrow is often sited amid tangled vegetation, or in the roots of trees bordering streams on lowlands.
• **RANGE** From southern Mexico through Central America to much of tropical South America, south to Bolivia, the Matto Grosso in Brazil, Paraguay, and northeastern Argentina.

• *slight speckling*

Egg size 19–23 x 16–19 mm	Clutch size 2–4	Incubation ♀ 19–21 days

Order PICIFORMES	Family BUCCONIDAE	Species *Chelidoptera tenebrosa*

SWALLOW-WINGED PUFFBIRD

The eggs of the Swallow-winged Puffbird are white and similar to those of other members of the family.
• **BREEDING** The Swallow-winged Puffbird lays its eggs in a chamber lined with wisps of grass at the end of a burrow. It is excavated in a bank or hillside amid open woodland. Although the time taken to incubate the eggs is not recorded, it is thought that, like the related Black-breasted Puffbird, both parents take turns incubating the eggs in the chamber.
• **RANGE** Occurs across northern South America, from Venezuela and the Guianas to eastern Colombia, south to eastern Peru, northern Bolivia, and much of Brazil.

• *pure white ground*

Egg size 22–26 x 19–21 mm	Clutch size 1–2	Incubation ♂♀ Unknown

Order PICIFORMES	Family CAPITONIDAE	Species *Megalaima asiatica*

BLUE-THROATED BARBET

The oval eggs of the Blue-throated Barbet are pure white in ground color and unmarked, as are the eggs of all other species of barbet.
• **BREEDING** The eggs are laid in a hole dug out of a dead or decaying branch or tree trunk. The parent birds dig the hole together, but they do not line it with nesting material. They keep it clean by removing the young birds' excreta.
• **RANGE** Across northern India to Assam and Burma, south through Southeast Asia to north Borneo.

smooth white shell •

Egg size 25–31 x 19–23 mm	Clutch size 3–4	Incubation ♂♀ Unknown

Order PICIFORMES	Family INDICATORIDAE	Species *Indicator indicator*

GREATER HONEYGUIDE

The Greater Honeyguide lays white eggs. Although it is a nest parasite, the white eggs do not always match those of the host.
• **BREEDING** The Greater Honeyguide parasitizes a number of species, most of which live in forests. It may destroy the host bird's eggs when laying its own, or the host's chicks may be killed by the young honeyguide, which bites the host's chicks with a very sharp hook on its bill.
• **RANGE** Occurs in Africa south of the Sahara, although it is absent from the lowland forests of West Africa and the mountain forests of East Africa.

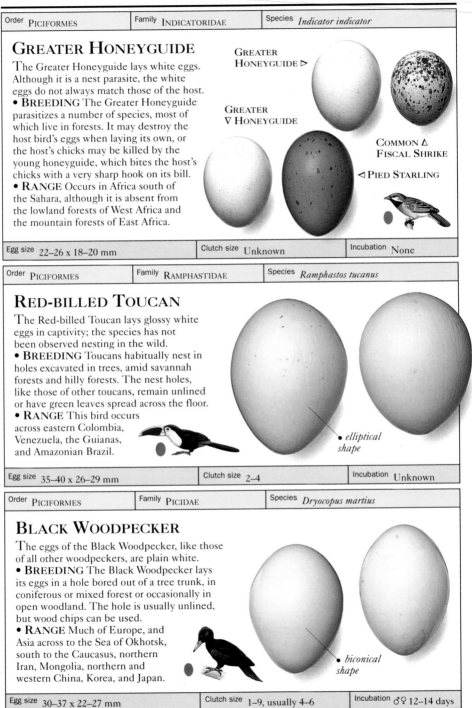

GREATER HONEYGUIDE ▷

GREATER ▽ HONEYGUIDE

COMMON △ FISCAL SHRIKE

◁ PIED STARLING

Egg size 22–26 x 18–20 mm	Clutch size Unknown	Incubation None

Order PICIFORMES	Family RAMPHASTIDAE	Species *Ramphastos tucanus*

RED-BILLED TOUCAN

The Red-billed Toucan lays glossy white eggs in captivity; the species has not been observed nesting in the wild.
• **BREEDING** Toucans habitually nest in holes excavated in trees, amid savannah forests and hilly forests. The nest holes, like those of other toucans, remain unlined or have green leaves spread across the floor.
• **RANGE** This bird occurs across eastern Colombia, Venezuela, the Guianas, and Amazonian Brazil.

• *elliptical shape*

Egg size 35–40 x 26–29 mm	Clutch size 2–4	Incubation Unknown

Order PICIFORMES	Family PICIDAE	Species *Dryocopus martius*

BLACK WOODPECKER

The eggs of the Black Woodpecker, like those of all other woodpeckers, are plain white.
• **BREEDING** The Black Woodpecker lays its eggs in a hole bored out of a tree trunk, in coniferous or mixed forest or occasionally in open woodland. The hole is usually unlined, but wood chips can be used.
• **RANGE** Much of Europe, and Asia across to the Sea of Okhotsk, south to the Caucasus, northern Iran, Mongolia, northern and western China, Korea, and Japan.

• *biconical shape*

Egg size 30–37 x 22–27 mm	Clutch size 1–9, usually 4–6	Incubation ♂♀ 12–14 days

PASSERINES

Order PASSERIFORMES	Family EURYLAIMIDAE	Species *Smithornis capensis*

AFRICAN BROADBILL

The African Broadbill's eggs are pure white in ground color, and glossy, like those of the other two species in its genus.
• BREEDING The bulky nest is an untidy dome of leaves, grass, and moss. It is lined and has a side entrance. The nest is placed just above the ground on a low branch.
• RANGE Forested parts of Africa south of the Sahara.

white ground

Egg size 20–25 x 15–16 mm	Clutch size 3	Incubation Unknown

Order PASSERIFORMES	Family EURYLAIMIDAE	Species *Corydon sumatranus*

DUSKY BROADBILL

The eggs of the Dusky Broadbill are pinkish white in ground color, thickly blotched and dotted with variable yellowish brown pigmentation and underlying pale lavender markings.
• BREEDING The nest is an enclosed structure (with a side entrance hole) of loosely-woven pear-shaped, dead creepers, lined with flat strips of palm leaves. The nest hangs from a tree branch in thick jungle.
• RANGE Watercourses and damp ravines in Southeast Asia, to Burma, Thailand, the Malay peninsula, Sumatra, Borneo, and the North Natoena Islands.

dense mottling

Egg size 26–31 x 20–24 mm	Clutch size 3	Incubation Unknown

Order PASSERIFORMES	Family EURYLAIMIDAE	Species *Eurylaimus javanicus*

BANDED BROADBILL

The eggs of the Banded Broadbill are white or creamy white in ground color, variably spotted with reddish or purplish brown.
• BREEDING The nest is a ragged, globular structure with a side entrance. It hangs from a tree branch, close to the trunk, about 70 ft (20 m) from the ground. The nest tree is located in dense jungle, near water.
• RANGE Occurs from Southeast Asia through southern Burma and the Malay peninsula, and south to Sumatra, Java, and Borneo.

creamy white ground

Egg size 26–30 x 17–20 mm	Clutch size 2–3	Incubation Unknown

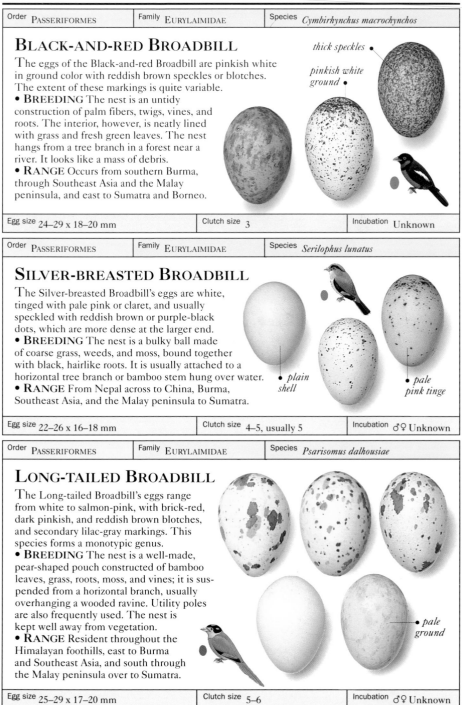

| Order PASSERIFORMES | Family EURYLAIMIDAE | Species *Cymbirhynchus macrorhynchos* |

BLACK-AND-RED BROADBILL

The eggs of the Black-and-red Broadbill are pinkish white in ground color with reddish brown speckles or blotches. The extent of these markings is quite variable.
• BREEDING The nest is an untidy construction of palm fibers, twigs, vines, and roots. The interior, however, is neatly lined with grass and fresh green leaves. The nest hangs from a tree branch in a forest near a river. It looks like a mass of debris.
• RANGE Occurs from southern Burma, through Southeast Asia and the Malay peninsula, and east to Sumatra and Borneo.

thick speckles

pinkish white ground

| Egg size 24–29 x 18–20 mm | Clutch size 3 | Incubation Unknown |

| Order PASSERIFORMES | Family EURYLAIMIDAE | Species *Serilophus lunatus* |

SILVER-BREASTED BROADBILL

The Silver-breasted Broadbill's eggs are white, tinged with pale pink or claret, and usually speckled with reddish brown or purple-black dots, which are more dense at the larger end.
• BREEDING The nest is a bulky ball made of coarse grass, weeds, and moss, bound together with black, hairlike roots. It is usually attached to a horizontal tree branch or bamboo stem hung over water.
• RANGE From Nepal across to China, Burma, Southeast Asia, and the Malay peninsula to Sumatra.

plain shell

pale pink tinge

| Egg size 22–26 x 16–18 mm | Clutch size 4–5, usually 5 | Incubation ♂♀ Unknown |

| Order PASSERIFORMES | Family EURYLAIMIDAE | Species *Psarisomus dalhousiae* |

LONG-TAILED BROADBILL

The Long-tailed Broadbill's eggs range from white to salmon-pink, with brick-red, dark pinkish, and reddish brown blotches, and secondary lilac-gray markings. This species forms a monotypic genus.
• BREEDING The nest is a well-made, pear-shaped pouch constructed of bamboo leaves, grass, roots, moss, and vines; it is suspended from a horizontal branch, usually overhanging a wooded ravine. Utility poles are also frequently used. The nest is kept well away from vegetation.
• RANGE Resident throughout the Himalayan foothills, east to Burma and Southeast Asia, and south through the Malay peninsula over to Sumatra.

pale ground

| Egg size 25–29 x 17–20 mm | Clutch size 5–6 | Incubation ♂♀ Unknown |

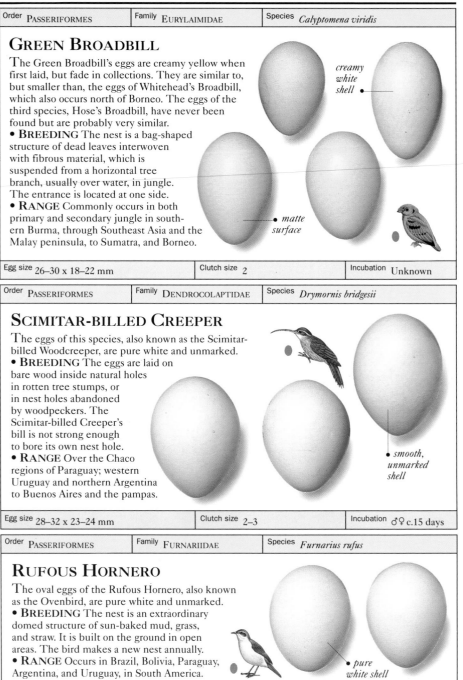

| Order PASSERIFORMES | Family EURYLAIMIDAE | Species *Calyptomena viridis* |

GREEN BROADBILL

The Green Broadbill's eggs are creamy yellow when first laid, but fade in collections. They are similar to, but smaller than, the eggs of Whitehead's Broadbill, which also occurs north of Borneo. The eggs of the third species, Hose's Broadbill, have never been found but are probably very similar.

• **BREEDING** The nest is a bag-shaped structure of dead leaves interwoven with fibrous material, which is suspended from a horizontal tree branch, usually over water, in jungle. The entrance is located at one side.

• **RANGE** Commonly occurs in both primary and secondary jungle in southern Burma, through Southeast Asia and the Malay peninsula, to Sumatra, and Borneo.

creamy white shell •

matte surface

| Egg size 26–30 x 18–22 mm | Clutch size 2 | Incubation Unknown |

| Order PASSERIFORMES | Family DENDROCOLAPTIDAE | Species *Drymornis bridgesii* |

SCIMITAR-BILLED CREEPER

The eggs of this species, also known as the Scimitar-billed Woodcreeper, are pure white and unmarked.

• **BREEDING** The eggs are laid on bare wood inside natural holes in rotten tree stumps, or in nest holes abandoned by woodpeckers. The Scimitar-billed Creeper's bill is not strong enough to bore its own nest hole.

• **RANGE** Over the Chaco regions of Paraguay; western Uruguay and northern Argentina to Buenos Aires and the pampas.

smooth, unmarked shell

| Egg size 28–32 x 23–24 mm | Clutch size 2–3 | Incubation ♂♀ c.15 days |

| Order PASSERIFORMES | Family FURNARIIDAE | Species *Furnarius rufus* |

RUFOUS HORNERO

The oval eggs of the Rufous Hornero, also known as the Ovenbird, are pure white and unmarked.

• **BREEDING** The nest is an extraordinary domed structure of sun-baked mud, grass, and straw. It is built on the ground in open areas. The bird makes a new nest annually.

• **RANGE** Occurs in Brazil, Bolivia, Paraguay, Argentina, and Uruguay, in South America.

pure white shell

| Egg size 25–32 x 18–23 mm | Clutch size 3–5 | Incubation Unknown |

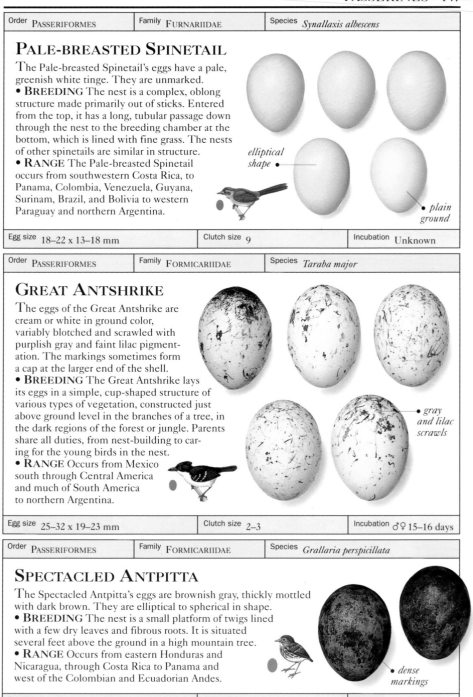

| Order PASSERIFORMES | Family FURNARIIDAE | Species *Synallaxis albescens* |

PALE-BREASTED SPINETAIL

The Pale-breasted Spinetail's eggs have a pale, greenish white tinge. They are unmarked.
• **BREEDING** The nest is a complex, oblong structure made primarily out of sticks. Entered from the top, it has a long, tubular passage down through the nest to the breeding chamber at the bottom, which is lined with fine grass. The nests of other spinetails are similar in structure.
• **RANGE** The Pale-breasted Spinetail occurs from southwestern Costa Rica, to Panama, Colombia, Venezuela, Guyana, Surinam, Brazil, and Bolivia to western Paraguay and northern Argentina.

elliptical shape •

• *plain ground*

| Egg size 18–22 x 13–18 mm | Clutch size 9 | Incubation Unknown |

| Order PASSERIFORMES | Family FORMICARIIDAE | Species *Taraba major* |

GREAT ANTSHRIKE

The eggs of the Great Antshrike are cream or white in ground color, variably blotched and scrawled with purplish gray and faint lilac pigmentation. The markings sometimes form a cap at the larger end of the shell.
• **BREEDING** The Great Antshrike lays its eggs in a simple, cup-shaped structure of various types of vegetation, constructed just above ground level in the branches of a tree, in the dark regions of the forest or jungle. Parents share all duties, from nest-building to caring for the young birds in the nest.
• **RANGE** Occurs from Mexico south through Central America and much of South America to northern Argentina.

• *gray and lilac scrawls*

| Egg size 25–32 x 19–23 mm | Clutch size 2–3 | Incubation ♂♀ 15–16 days |

| Order PASSERIFORMES | Family FORMICARIIDAE | Species *Grallaria perspicillata* |

SPECTACLED ANTPITTA

The Spectacled Antpitta's eggs are brownish gray, thickly mottled with dark brown. They are elliptical to spherical in shape.
• **BREEDING** The nest is a small platform of twigs lined with a few dry leaves and fibrous roots. It is situated several feet above the ground in a high mountain tree.
• **RANGE** Occurs from eastern Honduras and Nicaragua, through Costa Rica to Panama and west of the Colombian and Ecuadorian Andes.

• *dense markings*

| Egg size 25–27 x 20–21 mm | Clutch size 2 | Incubation ♂♀ Unknown |

Order PASSERIFORMES	Family CONOPOPHAGIDAE	Species *Conopophaga lineata*

RUFOUS GNATEATER

• *buff ground*

The Rufous Gnateater's oval to conical eggs are buff in ground color, with occasional darker markings.
• **BREEDING** The simple, cup-shaped nest is made of sticks and moss, and sited in forest trees.
• **RANGE** Occurs throughout southeastern Brazil, eastern Paraguay, and northern Argentina.

Egg size 21–23 x 17–18 mm	Clutch size 2	Incubation Unknown

Order PASSERIFORMES	Family RHINOCRYPTIDAE	Species *Scytalopus magellanicus*

ANDEAN TAPACULO

plain white • *ground*

The Andean Tapaculo's eggs are plain white, but can be spotted or speckled due to staining.
• **BREEDING** The bird builds a rounded nest of root fibers, moss, and lichens which it lodges in a tree between the outer bark and the trunk, or among tangled roots of a fallen tree, amid forested mountains. Other tapaculos nest in rock crevices, thorn bushes, or tunnels.
• **RANGE** Extends along the Andes, from Colombia and Venezuela south to Tierra del Fuego; also found in the Falkland Islands, southeast of South America.

Egg size 20–22 x 15–17 mm	Clutch size 2–3	Incubation ♂♀ Unknown

Order PASSERIFORMES	Family COTINGIDAE	Species *Rupicola rupicola*

ORANGE COCK-OF-THE-ROCK

The Orange Cock-of-the-Rock's eggs are basically pale buffish brown to very pale buff or off-white, blotched and spotted in dark brown, with underlying pale lilac-gray markings. Occasionally, the markings on the shell may be scrawled.
• **BREEDING** The nest is a cup or bracket of mud and vegetable matter, attached to a rockface. It is built in a cave or on the leeward side of a huge boulder to shelter the nest from the weather.
• **RANGE** Mountain forests of eastern Colombia, southern Venezuela, Guyana, Surinam, French Guiana, and northern Brazil.

• *buff ground*

• *dark brown blotches*

Egg size 40–45 x 30–33 mm	Clutch size 2	Incubation ♀ 27–28 days

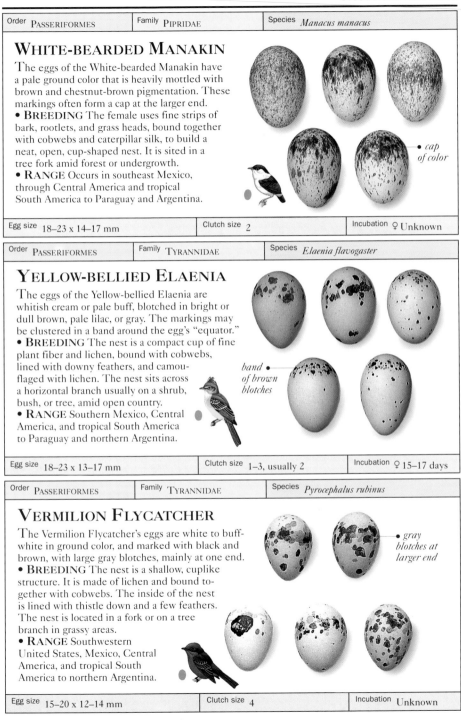

Order PASSERIFORMES	Family PIPRIDAE	Species *Manacus manacus*

WHITE-BEARDED MANAKIN

The eggs of the White-bearded Manakin have a pale ground color that is heavily mottled with brown and chestnut-brown pigmentation. These markings often form a cap at the larger end.
• **BREEDING** The female uses fine strips of bark, rootlets, and grass heads, bound together with cobwebs and caterpillar silk, to build a neat, open, cup-shaped nest. It is sited in a tree fork amid forest or undergrowth.
• **RANGE** Occurs in southeast Mexico, through Central America and tropical South America to Paraguay and Argentina.

cap of color

Egg size 18–23 x 14–17 mm	Clutch size 2	Incubation ♀ Unknown

Order PASSERIFORMES	Family TYRANNIDAE	Species *Elaenia flavogaster*

YELLOW-BELLIED ELAENIA

The eggs of the Yellow-bellied Elaenia are whitish cream or pale buff, blotched in bright or dull brown, pale lilac, or gray. The markings may be clustered in a band around the egg's "equator."
• **BREEDING** The nest is a compact cup of fine plant fiber and lichen, bound with cobwebs, lined with downy feathers, and camouflaged with lichen. The nest sits across a horizontal branch usually on a shrub, bush, or tree, amid open country.
• **RANGE** Southern Mexico, Central America, and tropical South America to Paraguay and northern Argentina.

band of brown blotches

Egg size 18–23 x 13–17 mm	Clutch size 1–3, usually 2	Incubation ♀ 15–17 days

Order PASSERIFORMES	Family TYRANNIDAE	Species *Pyrocephalus rubinus*

VERMILION FLYCATCHER

The Vermilion Flycatcher's eggs are white to buff-white in ground color, and marked with black and brown, with large gray blotches, mainly at one end.
• **BREEDING** The nest is a shallow, cuplike structure. It is made of lichen and bound together with cobwebs. The inside of the nest is lined with thistle down and a few feathers. The nest is located in a fork or on a tree branch in grassy areas.
• **RANGE** Southwestern United States, Mexico, Central America, and tropical South America to northern Argentina.

gray blotches at larger end

Egg size 15–20 x 12–14 mm	Clutch size 4	Incubation Unknown

Order PASSERIFORMES	Family TYRANNIDAE	Species *Xolmis coronata*

BLACK-CROWNED MONJITA

The eggs of the Black-crowned Monjita are pure white in ground color with large, dark red spots. They can also occasionally have dark red lines and zigzags marking the shell.
• **BREEDING** The Black-crowned Monjita lays its eggs in a rather shallow nest of vegetation. The nest is situated in scrub, brush, thickets, and grassland shrubbery on lowland terrain in open country.
• **RANGE** Occurs throughout eastern Bolivia, and ranges south to Paraguay, Uruguay, southern Brazil, and northern Argentina, particularly the pampas.

dark red spots

Egg size 24–28 x 18–19 mm	Clutch size 4–5, usually 4	Incubation Unknown

Order PASSERIFORMES	Family TYRANNIDAE	Species *Xolmis irupero*

WHITE MONJITA

The White Monjita's eggs are creamy white with a few small reddish spots occasionally scattered over the surface.
• **BREEDING** Unlike others of the genus, the White Monjita nests in a hole lined with feathers, usually in a tree branch or trunk. In some areas, the eggs are often laid in the old "oven" nest of a hornero, or a similar structure made by another species of that family (see p.146).
• **RANGE** Occurs throughout eastern Bolivia, Paraguay, Uruguay, eastern and southern Brazil, and northern Argentina.

creamy white ground

Egg size 21–25 x 15–18 mm	Clutch size 3–4	Incubation Unknown

Order PASSERIFORMES	Family TYRANNIDAE	Species *Myiarchus crinitus*

CRESTED FLYCATCHER

The Crested Flycatcher's eggs are creamy white to pinkish buff, blotched, streaked, and scratched with claret, liver-brown, purple, or lavender marks.
• **BREEDING** The nest is often situated in natural tree holes, but sometimes in old woodpecker nests in forests and woodland, or even in isolated trees near human habitation. It is filled with leaves, hair, bark fiber, and other assorted materials.
• **RANGE** The United States, southern Canada, eastern Mexico, and Cuba.

dark streaks

Egg size 20–26 x 15–18 mm	Clutch size 4–8, usually 5	Incubation ♀ 13–15 days

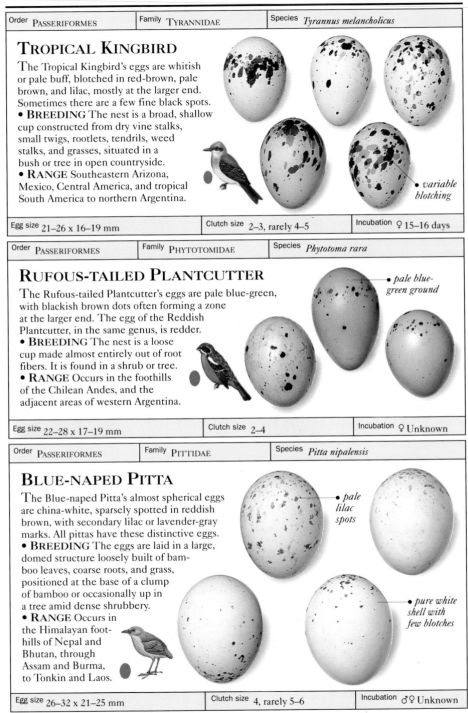

Order PASSERIFORMES	Family TYRANNIDAE	Species *Tyrannus melancholicus*

TROPICAL KINGBIRD

The Tropical Kingbird's eggs are whitish or pale buff, blotched in red-brown, pale brown, and lilac, mostly at the larger end. Sometimes there are a few fine black spots.
• **BREEDING** The nest is a broad, shallow cup constructed from dry vine stalks, small twigs, rootlets, tendrils, weed stalks, and grasses, situated in a bush or tree in open countryside.
• **RANGE** Southeastern Arizona, Mexico, Central America, and tropical South America to northern Argentina.

• *variable blotching*

Egg size 21–26 x 16–19 mm	Clutch size 2–3, rarely 4–5	Incubation ♀ 15–16 days

Order PASSERIFORMES	Family PHYTOTOMIDAE	Species *Phytotoma rara*

RUFOUS-TAILED PLANTCUTTER

• *pale blue-green ground*

The Rufous-tailed Plantcutter's eggs are pale blue-green, with blackish brown dots often forming a zone at the larger end. The egg of the Reddish Plantcutter, in the same genus, is redder.
• **BREEDING** The nest is a loose cup made almost entirely out of root fibers. It is found in a shrub or tree.
• **RANGE** Occurs in the foothills of the Chilean Andes, and the adjacent areas of western Argentina.

Egg size 22–28 x 17–19 mm	Clutch size 2–4	Incubation ♀ Unknown

Order PASSERIFORMES	Family PITTIDAE	Species *Pitta nipalensis*

BLUE-NAPED PITTA

The Blue-naped Pitta's almost spherical eggs are china-white, sparsely spotted in reddish brown, with secondary lilac or lavender-gray marks. All pittas have these distinctive eggs.
• **BREEDING** The eggs are laid in a large, domed structure loosely built of bamboo leaves, coarse roots, and grass, positioned at the base of a clump of bamboo or occasionally up in a tree amid dense shrubbery.
• **RANGE** Occurs in the Himalayan foothills of Nepal and Bhutan, through Assam and Burma, to Tonkin and Laos.

• *pale lilac spots*

• *pure white shell with few blotches*

Egg size 26–32 x 21–25 mm	Clutch size 4, rarely 5–6	Incubation ♂♀ Unknown

Order PASSERIFORMES	Family ACANTHISITTIDAE	Species *Acanthisitta chloris*

RIFLEMAN

The eggs laid by the Rifleman – a tiny, wrenlike bird – are plain white and very smooth and matte in texture and appearance.
• **BREEDING** Roots, leaves, and feathers are used to construct a domed, pear-shaped nest in a tree hole or among ground roots.
• **RANGE** Mountain ranges throughout North Island, South Island, Stewart Island, and Codfish Island, in New Zealand.

• *plain white shell*

Egg size 16 x 12–13 mm	Clutch size 4–5	Incubation Unknown

Order PASSERIFORMES	Family PHILEPITTIDAE	Species *Philepitta castanea*

VELVETY ASITY

The eggs of the Velvety Asity are plain white in ground color with variable brown and orange-brown markings.
• **BREEDING** The nest is a pear-shaped structure woven out of mosses and palm fibers. It is lined with dead leaves. The nest is suspended from a horizontal tree branch in humid rain forest. The entrance to the nest is situated at one side, and is sheltered by a porch.
• **RANGE** Confined to the humid forests of eastern Madagascar. The other three species of the family Philepittidae also inhabit the island of Madagascar.

white ground color •

• *orange-brown stains*

Egg size 24–29 x 18–19 mm	Clutch size 3	Incubation Unknown

Order PASSERIFORMES	Family MENURIDAE	Species *Menura novaehollandiae*

SUPERB LYREBIRD

The Superb Lyrebird's single egg varies in ground color from light gray or brown-gray, to dark gray, spotted and streaked with darker gray. This coloration is unique in birds.
• **BREEDING** The nest is an elaborate structure built on a foundation of sticks the sides of which curve upwards, meeting on top. It has a roof of green moss that extends to conceal the entrance. The female lays her egg in a ball of dry bark, ferns, and moss lined with rootlets. She also collects feathers that help to incubate the egg. The nest site is near running water, within humid forests.
• **RANGE** Eastern Australia, from Queensland to Victoria.

large, dark gray spots •

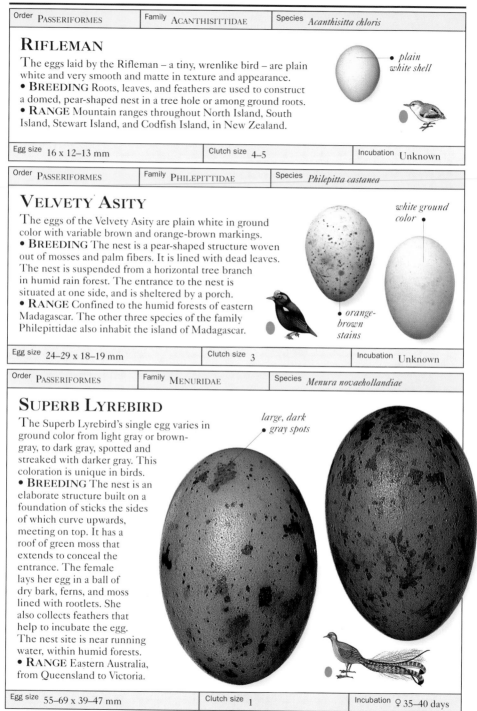

Egg size 55–69 x 39–47 mm	Clutch size 1	Incubation ♀ 35–40 days

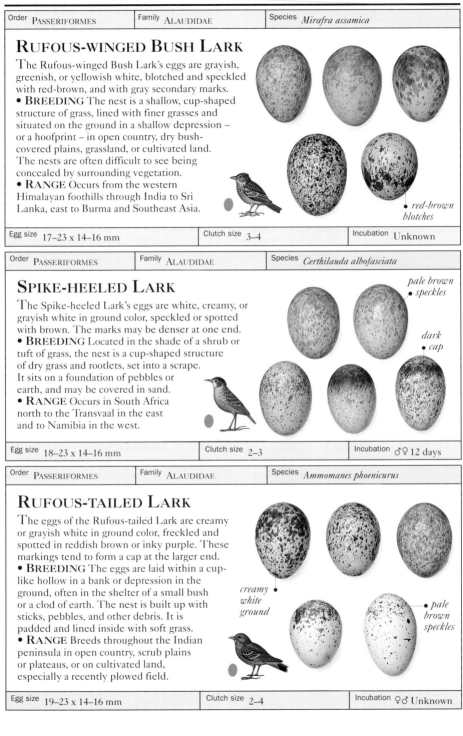

Order PASSERIFORMES	Family ALAUDIDAE	Species *Mirafra assamica*

RUFOUS-WINGED BUSH LARK

The Rufous-winged Bush Lark's eggs are grayish, greenish, or yellowish white, blotched and speckled with red-brown, and with gray secondary marks.
• **BREEDING** The nest is a shallow, cup-shaped structure of grass, lined with finer grasses and situated on the ground in a shallow depression – or a hoofprint – in open country, dry bush-covered plains, grassland, or cultivated land. The nests are often difficult to see being concealed by surrounding vegetation.
• **RANGE** Occurs from the western Himalayan foothills through India to Sri Lanka, east to Burma and Southeast Asia.

red-brown blotches

Egg size 17–23 x 14–16 mm	Clutch size 3–4	Incubation Unknown

Order PASSERIFORMES	Family ALAUDIDAE	Species *Certhilauda albofasciata*

SPIKE-HEELED LARK

pale brown speckles

The Spike-heeled Lark's eggs are white, creamy, or grayish white in ground color, speckled or spotted with brown. The marks may be denser at one end.
• **BREEDING** Located in the shade of a shrub or tuft of grass, the nest is a cup-shaped structure of dry grass and rootlets, set into a scrape. It sits on a foundation of pebbles or earth, and may be covered in sand.
• **RANGE** Occurs in South Africa north to the Transvaal in the east and to Namibia in the west.

dark cap

Egg size 18–23 x 14–16 mm	Clutch size 2–3	Incubation ♂♀ 12 days

Order PASSERIFORMES	Family ALAUDIDAE	Species *Ammomanes phoenicurus*

RUFOUS-TAILED LARK

The eggs of the Rufous-tailed Lark are creamy or grayish white in ground color, freckled and spotted in reddish brown or inky purple. These markings tend to form a cap at the larger end.
• **BREEDING** The eggs are laid within a cup-like hollow in a bank or depression in the ground, often in the shelter of a small bush or a clod of earth. The nest is built up with sticks, pebbles, and other debris. It is padded and lined inside with soft grass.
• **RANGE** Breeds throughout the Indian peninsula in open country, scrub plains or plateaus, or on cultivated land, especially a recently plowed field.

creamy white ground

pale brown speckles

Egg size 19–23 x 14–16 mm	Clutch size 2–4	Incubation ♀♂ Unknown

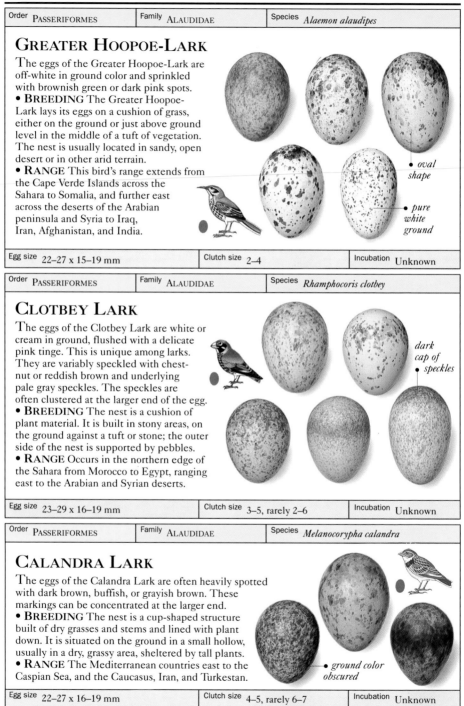

Order PASSERIFORMES	Family ALAUDIDAE	Species *Alaemon alaudipes*

GREATER HOOPOE-LARK

The eggs of the Greater Hoopoe-Lark are off-white in ground color and sprinkled with brownish green or dark pink spots.
• **BREEDING** The Greater Hoopoe-Lark lays its eggs on a cushion of grass, either on the ground or just above ground level in the middle of a tuft of vegetation. The nest is usually located in sandy, open desert or in other arid terrain.
• **RANGE** This bird's range extends from the Cape Verde Islands across the Sahara to Somalia, and further east across the deserts of the Arabian peninsula and Syria to Iraq, Iran, Afghanistan, and India.

• *oval shape*
• *pure white ground*

Egg size 22–27 x 15–19 mm	Clutch size 2–4	Incubation Unknown

Order PASSERIFORMES	Family ALAUDIDAE	Species *Rhamphocoris clotbey*

CLOTBEY LARK

The eggs of the Clotbey Lark are white or cream in ground, flushed with a delicate pink tinge. This is unique among larks. They are variably speckled with chestnut or reddish brown and underlying pale gray speckles. The speckles are often clustered at the larger end of the egg.
• **BREEDING** The nest is a cushion of plant material. It is built in stony areas, on the ground against a tuft or stone; the outer side of the nest is supported by pebbles.
• **RANGE** Occurs in the northern edge of the Sahara from Morocco to Egypt, ranging east to the Arabian and Syrian deserts.

dark cap of • *speckles*

Egg size 23–29 x 16–19 mm	Clutch size 3–5, rarely 2–6	Incubation Unknown

Order PASSERIFORMES	Family ALAUDIDAE	Species *Melanocorypha calandra*

CALANDRA LARK

The eggs of the Calandra Lark are often heavily spotted with dark brown, buffish, or grayish brown. These markings can be concentrated at the larger end.
• **BREEDING** The nest is a cup-shaped structure built of dry grasses and stems and lined with plant down. It is situated on the ground in a small hollow, usually in a dry, grassy area, sheltered by tall plants.
• **RANGE** The Mediterranean countries east to the Caspian Sea, and the Caucasus, Iran, and Turkestan.

• *ground color obscured*

Egg size 22–27 x 16–19 mm	Clutch size 4–5, rarely 6–7	Incubation Unknown

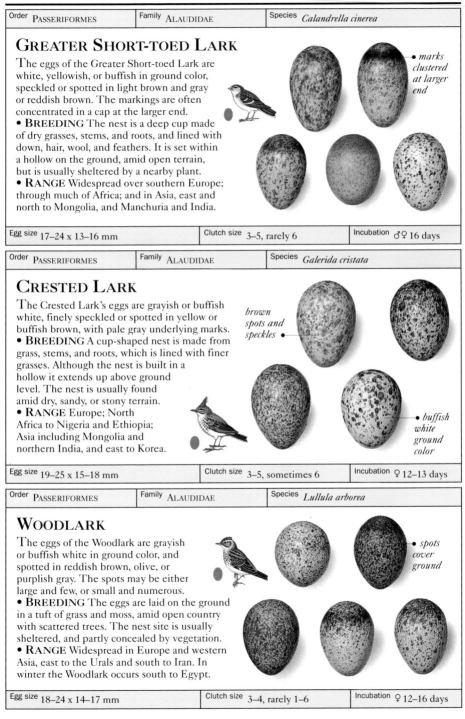

| Order PASSERIFORMES | Family ALAUDIDAE | Species *Calandrella cinerea* |

GREATER SHORT-TOED LARK

The eggs of the Greater Short-toed Lark are white, yellowish, or buffish in ground color, speckled or spotted in light brown and gray or reddish brown. The markings are often concentrated in a cap at the larger end.
• **BREEDING** The nest is a deep cup made of dry grasses, stems, and roots, and lined with down, hair, wool, and feathers. It is set within a hollow on the ground, amid open terrain, but is usually sheltered by a nearby plant.
• **RANGE** Widespread over southern Europe; through much of Africa; and in Asia, east and north to Mongolia, and Manchuria and India.

• *marks clustered at larger end*

| Egg size 17–24 x 13–16 mm | Clutch size 3–5, rarely 6 | Incubation ♂♀ 16 days |

| Order PASSERIFORMES | Family ALAUDIDAE | Species *Galerida cristata* |

CRESTED LARK

The Crested Lark's eggs are grayish or buffish white, finely speckled or spotted in yellow or buffish brown, with pale gray underlying marks.
• **BREEDING** A cup-shaped nest is made from grass, stems, and roots, which is lined with finer grasses. Although the nest is built in a hollow it extends up above ground level. The nest is usually found amid dry, sandy, or stony terrain.
• **RANGE** Europe; North Africa to Nigeria and Ethiopia; Asia including Mongolia and northern India, and east to Korea.

brown spots and speckles •

• *buffish white ground color*

| Egg size 19–25 x 15–18 mm | Clutch size 3–5, sometimes 6 | Incubation ♀ 12–13 days |

| Order PASSERIFORMES | Family ALAUDIDAE | Species *Lullula arborea* |

WOODLARK

The eggs of the Woodlark are grayish or buffish white in ground color, and spotted in reddish brown, olive, or purplish gray. The spots may be either large and few, or small and numerous.
• **BREEDING** The eggs are laid on the ground in a tuft of grass and moss, amid open country with scattered trees. The nest site is usually sheltered, and partly concealed by vegetation.
• **RANGE** Widespread in Europe and western Asia, east to the Urals and south to Iran. In winter the Woodlark occurs south to Egypt.

• *spots cover ground*

| Egg size 18–24 x 14–17 mm | Clutch size 3–4, rarely 1–6 | Incubation ♀ 12–16 days |

Order PASSERIFORMES	Family ALAUDIDAE	Species *Alauda arvensis*

SKYLARK

The Skylark's eggs appear in a variety of colors and patterns. They may be dull grayish white, buff, or greenish in ground color, and heavily spotted with greatly variable brown or olive markings.
• **BREEDING** The nest is a shallow cup-shaped structure. It is composed solely of grass, and lined with finer grasses or, occasionally, hair, and set in a slight depression excavated in the ground. It is some- times sheltered by a grass tuft, and is generally located amid open country, especially grassland, farmland, heaths, moors, and sometimes dunes.
• **RANGE** Occurs over much of Europe, south to the mountains of North Africa, and east to Japan, northern India, and China.

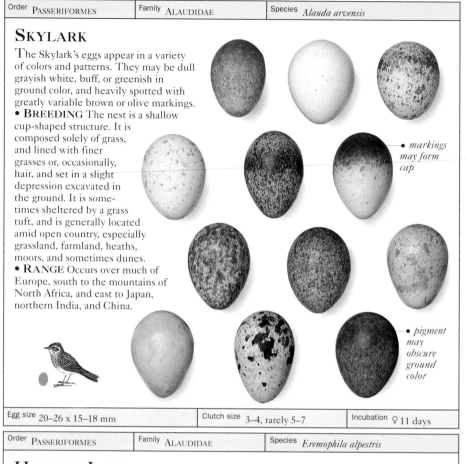

• *markings may form cap*

• *pigment may obscure ground color*

Egg size 20–26 x 15–18 mm	Clutch size 3–4, rarely 5–7	Incubation ♀ 11 days

Order PASSERIFORMES	Family ALAUDIDAE	Species *Eremophila alpestris*

HORNED LARK

Also known as the Shore Lark, this species' eggs have a pale greenish white ground color, and are heavily speckled with buffish brown, often with a black hairline, and sometimes with bolder spots or dark pigmentation zones.
• **BREEDING** The nest is located in a hollow, often in the shelter of a plant or rock, amid open areas of tundra or barren high ground. It is a loose cup of dry grass and plant stems, lined with hair and plant down. Small pebbles or pellets of peat may be placed around the nest to strengthen the outer edges.
• **RANGE** Occurs widely over much of the Northern Hemisphere, ranging east to northern India and south to Colombia in South America.

• *buffish brown speckles*

Egg size 19–26 x 14–18 mm	Clutch size 2–7, usually 4	Incubation ♀ 10–14 days

Order PASSERIFORMES	Family HIRUNDINIDAE	Species *Hirundo rustica*

BARN SWALLOW

The eggs of the Barn Swallow are white in ground color, and are sparsely spotted or blotched with reddish brown, pale lilac, or gray markings.
• **BREEDING** The nest is constructed of mud pellets mixed with fragments of vegetation, and is lined with feathers. The natural site for the nest is a cave, but rafters and girders in barns or bridges can be used.
• **RANGE** Breeds throughout Europe, northern Africa, Asia, and northern North America, migrating south to the tropical Southern Hemisphere during winter.

large, reddish brown blotches

Egg size 16–23 x 12–15 mm	Clutch size 4–5, rarely 3–8	Incubation ♀ 14–16 days

Order PASSERIFORMES	Family MOTACILLIDAE	Species *Dendronanthus indicus*

FOREST WAGTAIL

The Forest Wagtail's eggs are pale yellowish gray, blotched and dotted in brown or black, with underlying gray markings. It is the only species in its genus and is not closely related to other species of wagtail.
• **BREEDING** The nest is sited on a horizontal tree branch (usually an oak) in forest or woodland. It is constructed of an outer mask of grass stalks, horsehair, cobwebs, and lichens, with a lining of wool, fur, and more horsehair.
• **RANGE** Breeds in eastern Asia, from Siberia south to north China and Korea.

yellow-gray ground

pale gray marks

Egg size 17–20 x 14–15 mm	Clutch size 5	Incubation Unknown

Order PASSERIFORMES	Family MOTACILLIDAE	Species *Motacilla flava*

YELLOW WAGTAIL

The eggs of the Yellow Wagtail are pale buff or grayish in ground color, but they are often so heavily speckled in buff or brown that the ground may be almost obscured.
• **BREEDING** The cup-shaped nest is made of grasses, stems, roots, and other vegetable matter, lined with hair, fur, or wool. It is set in a hollow in the ground or in vegetation amid marshland, damp grassland, salt marshes, or cultivated land, often, though not necessarily, near water.
• **RANGE** Widespread throughout Europe and Asia, but winters south to Central and southern Africa, India, Sri Lanka, and Indonesia.

dark mottling

heavily clouded ground

pale buff ground

Egg size 16–22 x 12–16 mm	Clutch size 5–6, rarely 7	Incubation ♀ 12–14 days

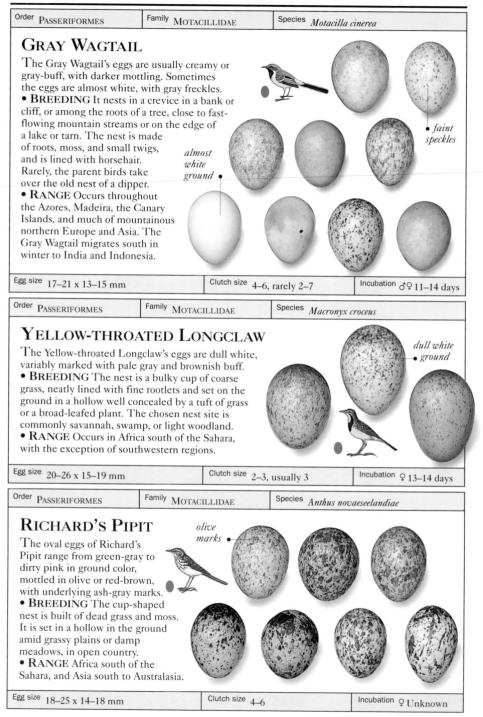

Order PASSERIFORMES	Family MOTACILLIDAE	Species *Motacilla cinerea*

GRAY WAGTAIL

The Gray Wagtail's eggs are usually creamy or
gray-buff, with darker mottling. Sometimes
the eggs are almost white, with gray freckles.
• **BREEDING** It nests in a crevice in a bank or
cliff, or among the roots of a tree, close to fast-
flowing mountain streams or on the edge of
a lake or tarn. The nest is made
of roots, moss, and small twigs,
and is lined with horsehair.
Rarely, the parent birds take
over the old nest of a dipper.
• **RANGE** Occurs throughout
the Azores, Madeira, the Canary
Islands, and much of mountainous
northern Europe and Asia. The
Gray Wagtail migrates south in
winter to India and Indonesia.

*almost
white
ground* •

• *faint
speckles*

Egg size 17–21 x 13–15 mm	Clutch size 4–6, rarely 2–7	Incubation ♂♀ 11–14 days

Order PASSERIFORMES	Family MOTACILLIDAE	Species *Macronyx croceus*

YELLOW-THROATED LONGCLAW

The Yellow-throated Longclaw's eggs are dull white,
variably marked with pale gray and brownish buff.
• **BREEDING** The nest is a bulky cup of coarse
grass, neatly lined with fine rootlets and set on the
ground in a hollow well concealed by a tuft of grass
or a broad-leafed plant. The chosen nest site is
commonly savannah, swamp, or light woodland.
• **RANGE** Occurs in Africa south of the Sahara,
with the exception of southwestern regions.

*dull white
• ground*

Egg size 20–26 x 15–19 mm	Clutch size 2–3, usually 3	Incubation ♀ 13–14 days

Order PASSERIFORMES	Family MOTACILLIDAE	Species *Anthus novaeseelandiae*

RICHARD'S PIPIT

*olive
marks* •

The oval eggs of Richard's
Pipit range from green-gray to
dirty pink in ground color,
mottled in olive or red-brown,
with underlying ash-gray marks.
• **BREEDING** The cup-shaped
nest is built of dead grass and moss.
It is set in a hollow in the ground
amid grassy plains or damp
meadows, in open country.
• **RANGE** Africa south of the
Sahara, and Asia south to Australasia.

Egg size 18–25 x 14–18 mm	Clutch size 4–6	Incubation ♀ Unknown

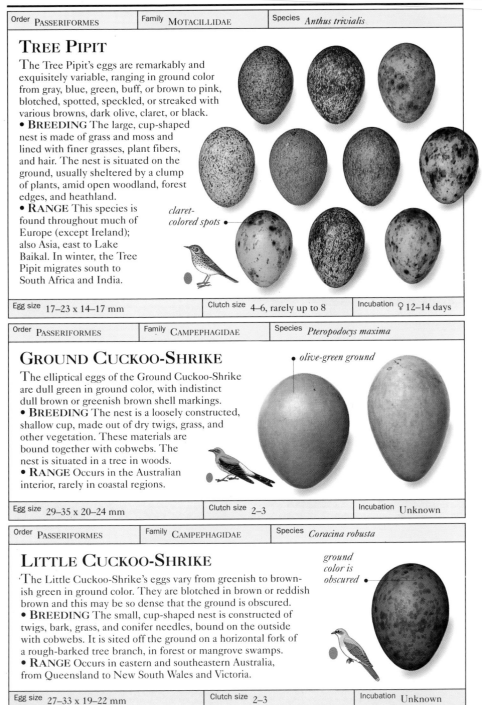

Order PASSERIFORMES	Family MOTACILLIDAE	Species *Anthus trivialis*

TREE PIPIT

The Tree Pipit's eggs are remarkably and exquisitely variable, ranging in ground color from gray, blue, green, buff, or brown to pink, blotched, spotted, speckled, or streaked with various browns, dark olive, claret, or black.
• **BREEDING** The large, cup-shaped nest is made of grass and moss and lined with finer grasses, plant fibers, and hair. The nest is situated on the ground, usually sheltered by a clump of plants, amid open woodland, forest edges, and heathland.
• **RANGE** This species is found throughout much of Europe (except Ireland); also Asia, east to Lake Baikal. In winter, the Tree Pipit migrates south to South Africa and India.

claret-colored spots •

Egg size 17–23 x 14–17 mm	Clutch size 4–6, rarely up to 8	Incubation ♀ 12–14 days

Order PASSERIFORMES	Family CAMPEPHAGIDAE	Species *Pteropodocys maxima*

GROUND CUCKOO-SHRIKE

• olive-green ground

The elliptical eggs of the Ground Cuckoo-Shrike are dull green in ground color, with indistinct dull brown or greenish brown shell markings.
• **BREEDING** The nest is a loosely constructed, shallow cup, made out of dry twigs, grass, and other vegetation. These materials are bound together with cobwebs. The nest is situated in a tree in woods.
• **RANGE** Occurs in the Australian interior, rarely in coastal regions.

Egg size 29–35 x 20–24 mm	Clutch size 2–3	Incubation Unknown

Order PASSERIFORMES	Family CAMPEPHAGIDAE	Species *Coracina robusta*

LITTLE CUCKOO-SHRIKE

ground color is obscured •

The Little Cuckoo-Shrike's eggs vary from greenish to brownish green in ground color. They are blotched in brown or reddish brown and this may be so dense that the ground is obscured.
• **BREEDING** The small, cup-shaped nest is constructed of twigs, bark, grass, and conifer needles, bound on the outside with cobwebs. It is sited off the ground on a horizontal fork of a rough-barked tree branch, in forest or mangrove swamps.
• **RANGE** Occurs in eastern and southeastern Australia, from Queensland to New South Wales and Victoria.

Egg size 27–33 x 19–22 mm	Clutch size 2–3	Incubation Unknown

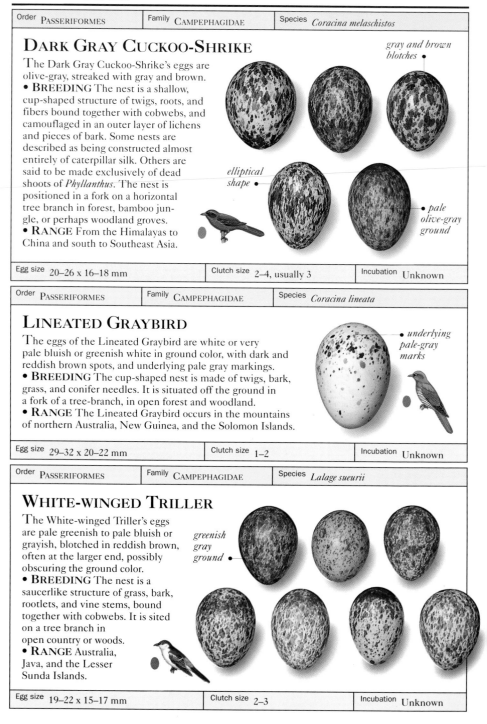

Order PASSERIFORMES	Family CAMPEPHAGIDAE	Species *Coracina melaschistos*

DARK GRAY CUCKOO-SHRIKE

The Dark Gray Cuckoo-Shrike's eggs are olive-gray, streaked with gray and brown.
• **BREEDING** The nest is a shallow, cup-shaped structure of twigs, roots, and fibers bound together with cobwebs, and camouflaged in an outer layer of lichens and pieces of bark. Some nests are described as being constructed almost entirely of caterpillar silk. Others are said to be made exclusively of dead shoots of *Phyllanthus*. The nest is positioned in a fork on a horizontal tree branch in forest, bamboo jungle, or perhaps woodland groves.
• **RANGE** From the Himalayas to China and south to Southeast Asia.

gray and brown blotches

elliptical shape

pale olive-gray ground

Egg size 20–26 x 16–18 mm	Clutch size 2–4, usually 3	Incubation Unknown

Order PASSERIFORMES	Family CAMPEPHAGIDAE	Species *Coracina lineata*

LINEATED GRAYBIRD

The eggs of the Lineated Graybird are white or very pale bluish or greenish white in ground color, with dark and reddish brown spots, and underlying pale gray markings.
• **BREEDING** The cup-shaped nest is made of twigs, bark, grass, and conifer needles. It is situated off the ground in a fork of a tree-branch, in open forest and woodland.
• **RANGE** The Lineated Graybird occurs in the mountains of northern Australia, New Guinea, and the Solomon Islands.

underlying pale-gray marks

Egg size 29–32 x 20–22 mm	Clutch size 1–2	Incubation Unknown

Order PASSERIFORMES	Family CAMPEPHAGIDAE	Species *Lalage sueurii*

WHITE-WINGED TRILLER

The White-winged Triller's eggs are pale greenish to pale bluish or grayish, blotched in reddish brown, often at the larger end, possibly obscuring the ground color.
• **BREEDING** The nest is a saucerlike structure of grass, bark, rootlets, and vine stems, bound together with cobwebs. It is sited on a tree branch in open country or woods.
• **RANGE** Australia, Java, and the Lesser Sunda Islands.

greenish gray ground

Egg size 19–22 x 15–17 mm	Clutch size 2–3	Incubation Unknown

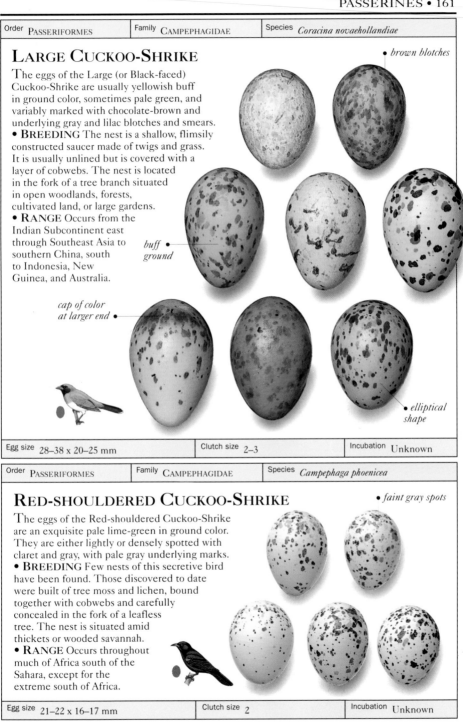

| Order PASSERIFORMES | Family CAMPEPHAGIDAE | Species *Coracina novaehollandiae* |

LARGE CUCKOO-SHRIKE

• *brown blotches*

The eggs of the Large (or Black-faced) Cuckoo-Shrike are usually yellowish buff in ground color, sometimes pale green, and variably marked with chocolate-brown and underlying gray and lilac blotches and smears.
• **BREEDING** The nest is a shallow, flimsily constructed saucer made of twigs and grass. It is usually unlined but is covered with a layer of cobwebs. The nest is located in the fork of a tree branch situated in open woodlands, forests, cultivated land, or large gardens.
• **RANGE** Occurs from the Indian Subcontinent east through Southeast Asia to southern China, south to Indonesia, New Guinea, and Australia.

buff • *ground*

cap of color at larger end •

• *elliptical shape*

| Egg size 28–38 x 20–25 mm | Clutch size 2–3 | Incubation Unknown |

| Order PASSERIFORMES | Family CAMPEPHAGIDAE | Species *Campephaga phoenicea* |

RED-SHOULDERED CUCKOO-SHRIKE

• *faint gray spots*

The eggs of the Red-shouldered Cuckoo-Shrike are an exquisite pale lime-green in ground color. They are either lightly or densely spotted with claret and gray, with pale gray underlying marks.
• **BREEDING** Few nests of this secretive bird have been found. Those discovered to date were built of tree moss and lichen, bound together with cobwebs and carefully concealed in the fork of a leafless tree. The nest is situated amid thickets or wooded savannah.
• **RANGE** Occurs throughout much of Africa south of the Sahara, except for the extreme south of Africa.

| Egg size 21–22 x 16–17 mm | Clutch size 2 | Incubation Unknown |

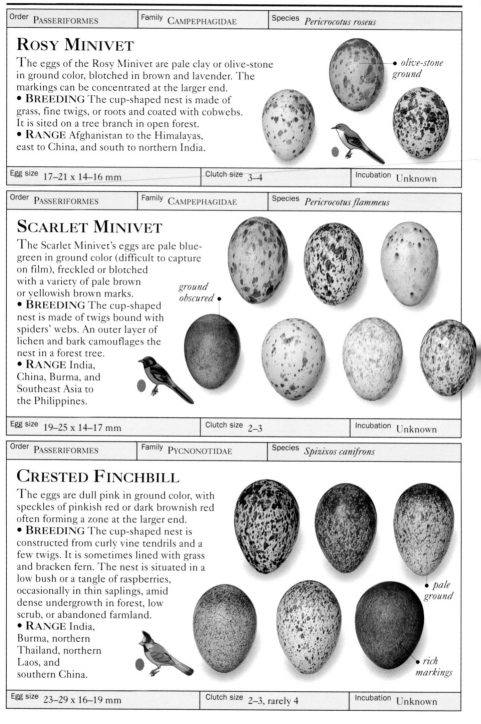

Order PASSERIFORMES	Family CAMPEPHAGIDAE	Species *Pericrocotus roseus*

ROSY MINIVET

The eggs of the Rosy Minivet are pale clay or olive-stone in ground color, blotched in brown and lavender. The markings can be concentrated at the larger end.
• **BREEDING** The cup-shaped nest is made of grass, fine twigs, or roots and coated with cobwebs. It is sited on a tree branch in open forest.
• **RANGE** Afghanistan to the Himalayas, east to China, and south to northern India.

olive-stone ground

Egg size 17–21 x 14–16 mm	Clutch size 3–4	Incubation Unknown

Order PASSERIFORMES	Family CAMPEPHAGIDAE	Species *Pericrocotus flammeus*

SCARLET MINIVET

The Scarlet Minivet's eggs are pale blue-green in ground color (difficult to capture on film), freckled or blotched with a variety of pale brown or yellowish brown marks.
• **BREEDING** The cup-shaped nest is made of twigs bound with spiders' webs. An outer layer of lichen and bark camouflages the nest in a forest tree.
• **RANGE** India, China, Burma, and Southeast Asia to the Philippines.

ground obscured

Egg size 19–25 x 14–17 mm	Clutch size 2–3	Incubation Unknown

Order PASSERIFORMES	Family PYCNONOTIDAE	Species *Spizixos canifrons*

CRESTED FINCHBILL

The eggs are dull pink in ground color, with speckles of pinkish red or dark brownish red often forming a zone at the larger end.
• **BREEDING** The cup-shaped nest is constructed from curly vine tendrils and a few twigs. It is sometimes lined with grass and bracken fern. The nest is situated in a low bush or a tangle of raspberries, occasionally in thin saplings, amid dense undergrowth in forest, low scrub, or abandoned farmland.
• **RANGE** India, Burma, northern Thailand, northern Laos, and southern China.

pale ground

rich markings

Egg size 23–29 x 16–19 mm	Clutch size 2–3, rarely 4	Incubation Unknown

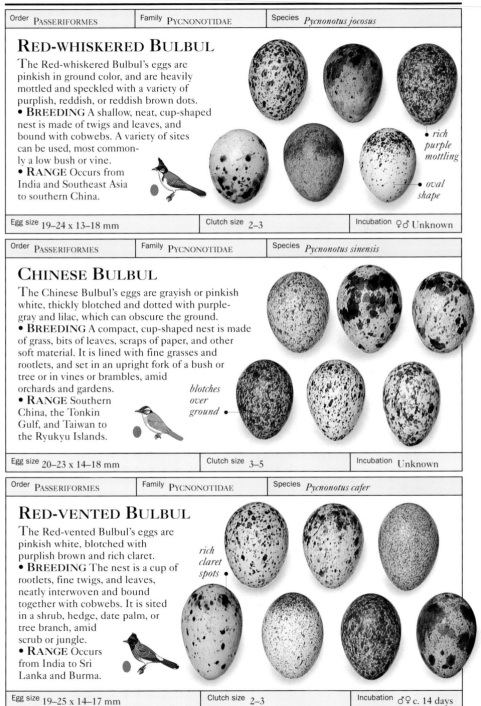

Order PASSERIFORMES	Family PYCNONOTIDAE	Species *Pycnonotus jocosus*

RED-WHISKERED BULBUL

The Red-whiskered Bulbul's eggs are
pinkish in ground color, and are heavily
mottled and speckled with a variety of
purplish, reddish, or reddish brown dots.
• BREEDING A shallow, neat, cup-shaped
nest is made of twigs and leaves, and
bound with cobwebs. A variety of sites
can be used, most common-
ly a low bush or vine.
• RANGE Occurs from
India and Southeast Asia
to southern China.

rich purple mottling

oval shape

Egg size 19–24 x 13–18 mm	Clutch size 2–3	Incubation ♀♂ Unknown

Order PASSERIFORMES	Family PYCNONOTIDAE	Species *Pycnonotus sinensis*

CHINESE BULBUL

The Chinese Bulbul's eggs are grayish or pinkish
white, thickly blotched and dotted with purple-
gray and lilac, which can obscure the ground.
• BREEDING A compact, cup-shaped nest is made
of grass, bits of leaves, scraps of paper, and other
soft material. It is lined with fine grasses and
rootlets, and set in an upright fork of a bush or
tree or in vines or brambles, amid
orchards and gardens.
• RANGE Southern
China, the Tonkin
Gulf, and Taiwan to
the Ryukyu Islands.

blotches over ground

Egg size 20–23 x 14–18 mm	Clutch size 3–5	Incubation Unknown

Order PASSERIFORMES	Family PYCNONOTIDAE	Species *Pycnonotus cafer*

RED-VENTED BULBUL

The Red-vented Bulbul's eggs are
pinkish white, blotched with
purplish brown and rich claret.
• BREEDING The nest is a cup of
rootlets, fine twigs, and leaves,
neatly interwoven and bound
together with cobwebs. It is sited
in a shrub, hedge, date palm, or
tree branch, amid
scrub or jungle.
• RANGE Occurs
from India to Sri
Lanka and Burma.

rich claret spots

Egg size 19–25 x 14–17 mm	Clutch size 2–3	Incubation ♂♀ c. 14 days

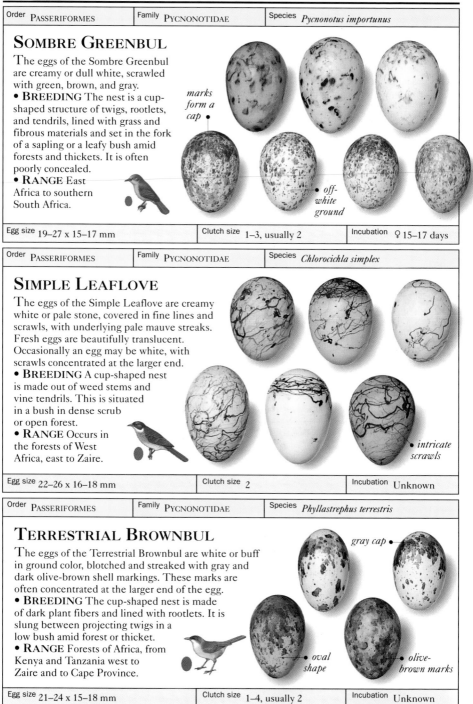

Order PASSERIFORMES	Family PYCNONOTIDAE	Species *Pycnonotus importunus*

SOMBRE GREENBUL

The eggs of the Sombre Greenbul
are creamy or dull white, scrawled
with green, brown, and gray.
• **BREEDING** The nest is a cup-
shaped structure of twigs, rootlets,
and tendrils, lined with grass and
fibrous materials and set in the fork
of a sapling or a leafy bush amid
forests and thickets. It is often
poorly concealed.
• **RANGE** East
Africa to southern
South Africa.

marks form a cap •

• off-white ground

Egg size 19–27 x 15–17 mm	Clutch size 1–3, usually 2	Incubation ♀ 15–17 days

Order PASSERIFORMES	Family PYCNONOTIDAE	Species *Chlorocichla simplex*

SIMPLE LEAFLOVE

The eggs of the Simple Leaflove are creamy
white or pale stone, covered in fine lines and
scrawls, with underlying pale mauve streaks.
Fresh eggs are beautifully translucent.
Occasionally an egg may be white, with
scrawls concentrated at the larger end.
• **BREEDING** A cup-shaped nest
is made out of weed stems and
vine tendrils. This is situated
in a bush in dense scrub
or open forest.
• **RANGE** Occurs in
the forests of West
Africa, east to Zaire.

• intricate scrawls

Egg size 22–26 x 16–18 mm	Clutch size 2	Incubation Unknown

Order PASSERIFORMES	Family PYCNONOTIDAE	Species *Phyllastrephus terrestris*

TERRESTRIAL BROWNBUL

The eggs of the Terrestrial Brownbul are white or buff
in ground color, blotched and streaked with gray and
dark olive-brown shell markings. These marks are
often concentrated at the larger end of the egg.
• **BREEDING** The cup-shaped nest is made
of dark plant fibers and lined with rootlets. It is
slung between projecting twigs in a
low bush amid forest or thicket.
• **RANGE** Forests of Africa, from
Kenya and Tanzania west to
Zaire and to Cape Province.

gray cap •

• oval shape

• olive-brown marks

Egg size 21–24 x 15–18 mm	Clutch size 1–4, usually 2	Incubation Unknown

Order PASSERIFORMES	Family PYCNONOTIDAE	Species *Phyllastrephus flavostriatus*

YELLOW-STREAKED GREENBUL

The Yellow-streaked Greenbul's oval
or elliptical eggs are pinkish, buff,
gray, or mauve in ground color,
spotted and streaked in reddish
brown, brown, purple, and slate-gray.
• BREEDING A cup-shaped nest is
constructed of twigs and rootlets, bound
together with cobwebs and camouflaged
with lichen. It is situated in a tree fork
or among vines or large leaves.
• RANGE The forests of eastern and
southern Africa, from southern Kenya west
to Zaire and on to eastern Cape Province.

• *pale pink ground*

• *glossy surface*

Egg size 22–24 x 16–17 mm	Clutch size 2–3	Incubation Unknown

Order PASSERIFORMES	Family PYCNONOTIDAE	Species *Hypsipetes indicus*

YELLOW-BROWED BULBUL

The Yellow-browed Bulbul's eggs are creamy
pink to warm salmon in ground color and
often blotched, speckled, and freckled
over the surface in various shades of red.
• BREEDING The nest is a flimsy
hammock of grass and skeletal leaves slung
across the fork of a tree branch in forests. It
is lined with grass or black roots and
camouflaged with moss and cobwebs.
• RANGE Southern India and Sri Lanka.

creamy ground •

red freckles over surface •

Egg size 21–25 x 15–17 mm	Clutch size 2–3	Incubation Unknown

Order PASSERIFORMES	Family PYCNONOTIDAE	Species *Hypsipetes madagascariensis*

BLACK BULBUL

The Black Bulbul's eggs are very pale cream
to pink, blotched all over in red-brown,
chocolate-brown, or purple-brown, with
underlying lavender and dark gray marks.
• BREEDING The nest is a flimsy cup of
grass, leaves, moss, bark fibers, and
lichen, bound with cobwebs and lined
with rootlets, fine grass, bark shavings,
or pine needles. It is sited in the fork
of a tree branch amid forest.
• RANGE Occurs in
Madagascar, Sri Lanka,
India, Burma, South-
east Asia, southern
China, and Taiwan.

dark freckles •

chocolate-brown blotches •

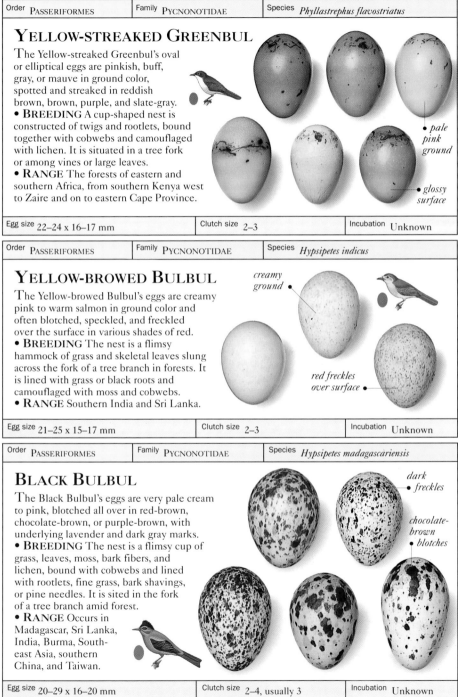

Egg size 20–29 x 16–20 mm	Clutch size 2–4, usually 3	Incubation Unknown

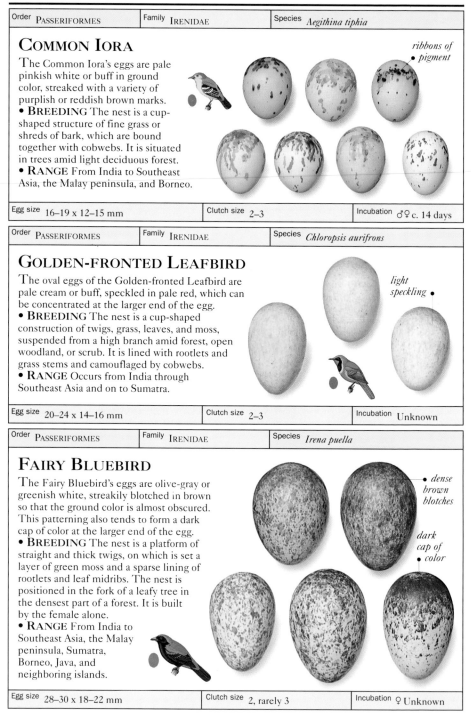

Order PASSERIFORMES	Family IRENIDAE	Species *Aegithina tiphia*

COMMON IORA

ribbons of pigment

The Common Iora's eggs are pale pinkish white or buff in ground color, streaked with a variety of purplish or reddish brown marks.
• **BREEDING** The nest is a cup-shaped structure of fine grass or shreds of bark, which are bound together with cobwebs. It is situated in trees amid light deciduous forest.
• **RANGE** From India to Southeast Asia, the Malay peninsula, and Borneo.

Egg size 16–19 x 12–15 mm	Clutch size 2–3	Incubation ♂♀ c. 14 days

Order PASSERIFORMES	Family IRENIDAE	Species *Chloropsis aurifrons*

GOLDEN-FRONTED LEAFBIRD

light speckling

The oval eggs of the Golden-fronted Leafbird are pale cream or buff, speckled in pale red, which can be concentrated at the larger end of the egg.
• **BREEDING** The nest is a cup-shaped construction of twigs, grass, leaves, and moss, suspended from a high branch amid forest, open woodland, or scrub. It is lined with rootlets and grass stems and camouflaged by cobwebs.
• **RANGE** Occurs from India through Southeast Asia and on to Sumatra.

Egg size 20–24 x 14–16 mm	Clutch size 2–3	Incubation Unknown

Order PASSERIFORMES	Family IRENIDAE	Species *Irena puella*

FAIRY BLUEBIRD

dense brown blotches

The Fairy Bluebird's eggs are olive-gray or greenish white, streakily blotched in brown so that the ground color is almost obscured. This patterning also tends to form a dark cap of color at the larger end of the egg.
• **BREEDING** The nest is a platform of straight and thick twigs, on which is set a layer of green moss and a sparse lining of rootlets and leaf midribs. The nest is positioned in the fork of a leafy tree in the densest part of a forest. It is built by the female alone.
• **RANGE** From India to Southeast Asia, the Malay peninsula, Sumatra, Borneo, Java, and neighboring islands.

dark cap of color

Egg size 28–30 x 18–22 mm	Clutch size 2, rarely 3	Incubation ♀ Unknown

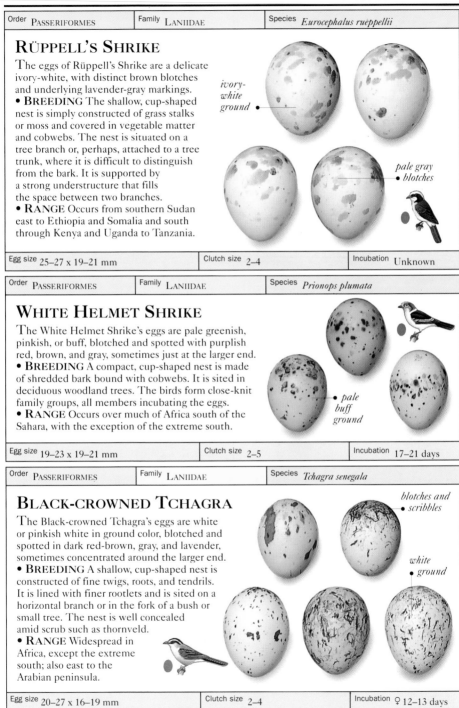

| Order PASSERIFORMES | Family LANIIDAE | Species *Eurocephalus rueppellii* |

RÜPPELL'S SHRIKE

The eggs of Rüppell's Shrike are a delicate ivory-white, with distinct brown blotches and underlying lavender-gray markings.
• **BREEDING** The shallow, cup-shaped nest is simply constructed of grass stalks or moss and covered in vegetable matter and cobwebs. The nest is situated on a tree branch or, perhaps, attached to a tree trunk, where it is difficult to distinguish from the bark. It is supported by a strong understructure that fills the space between two branches.
• **RANGE** Occurs from southern Sudan east to Ethiopia and Somalia and south through Kenya and Uganda to Tanzania.

ivory-white ground •

pale gray • *blotches*

| Egg size 25–27 x 19–21 mm | Clutch size 2–4 | Incubation Unknown |

| Order PASSERIFORMES | Family LANIIDAE | Species *Prionops plumata* |

WHITE HELMET SHRIKE

The White Helmet Shrike's eggs are pale greenish, pinkish, or buff, blotched and spotted with purplish red, brown, and gray, sometimes just at the larger end.
• **BREEDING** A compact, cup-shaped nest is made of shredded bark bound with cobwebs. It is sited in deciduous woodland trees. The birds form close-knit family groups, all members incubating the eggs.
• **RANGE** Occurs over much of Africa south of the Sahara, with the exception of the extreme south.

• *pale buff ground*

| Egg size 19–23 x 19–21 mm | Clutch size 2–5 | Incubation 17–21 days |

| Order PASSERIFORMES | Family LANIIDAE | Species *Tchagra senegala* |

BLACK-CROWNED TCHAGRA

blotches and • *scribbles*

The Black-crowned Tchagra's eggs are white or pinkish white in ground color, blotched and spotted in dark red-brown, gray, and lavender, sometimes concentrated around the larger end.
• **BREEDING** A shallow, cup-shaped nest is constructed of fine twigs, roots, and tendrils. It is lined with finer rootlets and is sited on a horizontal branch or in the fork of a bush or small tree. The nest is well concealed amid scrub such as thornveld.
• **RANGE** Widespread in Africa, except the extreme south; also east to the Arabian peninsula.

white • *ground*

| Egg size 20–27 x 16–19 mm | Clutch size 2–4 | Incubation ♀ 12–13 days |

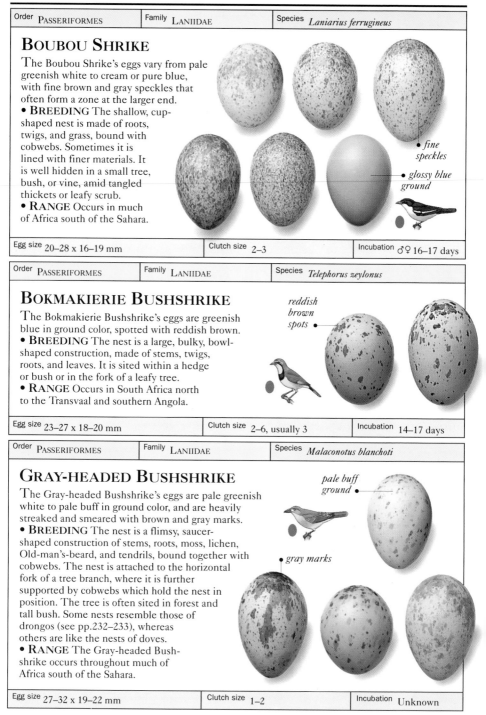

Order PASSERIFORMES	Family LANIIDAE	Species *Laniarius ferrugineus*

BOUBOU SHRIKE

The Boubou Shrike's eggs vary from pale greenish white to cream or pure blue, with fine brown and gray speckles that often form a zone at the larger end.
• **BREEDING** The shallow, cup-shaped nest is made of roots, twigs, and grass, bound with cobwebs. Sometimes it is lined with finer materials. It is well hidden in a small tree, bush, or vine, amid tangled thickets or leafy scrub.
• **RANGE** Occurs in much of Africa south of the Sahara.

• *fine speckles*

• *glossy blue ground*

Egg size 20–28 x 16–19 mm	Clutch size 2–3	Incubation ♂♀ 16–17 days

Order PASSERIFORMES	Family LANIIDAE	Species *Telephorus zeylonus*

BOKMAKIERIE BUSHSHRIKE

The Bokmakierie Bushshrike's eggs are greenish blue in ground color, spotted with reddish brown.
• **BREEDING** The nest is a large, bulky, bowl-shaped construction, made of stems, twigs, roots, and leaves. It is sited within a hedge or bush or in the fork of a leafy tree.
• **RANGE** Occurs in South Africa north to the Transvaal and southern Angola.

reddish brown spots •

Egg size 23–27 x 18–20 mm	Clutch size 2–6, usually 3	Incubation 14–17 days

Order PASSERIFORMES	Family LANIIDAE	Species *Malaconotus blanchoti*

GRAY-HEADED BUSHSHRIKE

The Gray-headed Bushshrike's eggs are pale greenish white to pale buff in ground color, and are heavily streaked and smeared with brown and gray marks.
• **BREEDING** The nest is a flimsy, saucer-shaped construction of stems, roots, moss, lichen, Old-man's-beard, and tendrils, bound together with cobwebs. The nest is attached to the horizontal fork of a tree branch, where it is further supported by cobwebs which hold the nest in position. The tree is often sited in forest and tall bush. Some nests resemble those of drongos (see pp.232–233), whereas others are like the nests of doves.
• **RANGE** The Gray-headed Bush-shrike occurs throughout much of Africa south of the Sahara.

pale buff ground •

• *gray marks*

Egg size 27–32 x 19–22 mm	Clutch size 1–2	Incubation Unknown

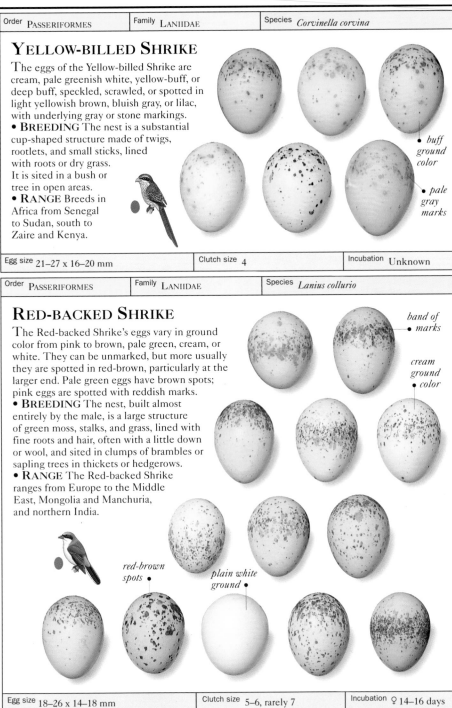

Order PASSERIFORMES	Family LANIIDAE	Species *Corvinella corvina*

YELLOW-BILLED SHRIKE

The eggs of the Yellow-billed Shrike are cream, pale greenish white, yellow-buff, or deep buff, speckled, scrawled, or spotted in light yellowish brown, bluish gray, or lilac, with underlying gray or stone markings.
• BREEDING The nest is a substantial cup-shaped structure made of twigs, rootlets, and small sticks, lined with roots or dry grass. It is sited in a bush or tree in open areas.
• RANGE Breeds in Africa from Senegal to Sudan, south to Zaire and Kenya.

buff ground color

pale gray marks

Egg size 21–27 x 16–20 mm	Clutch size 4	Incubation Unknown

Order PASSERIFORMES	Family LANIIDAE	Species *Lanius collurio*

RED-BACKED SHRIKE

The Red-backed Shrike's eggs vary in ground color from pink to brown, pale green, cream, or white. They can be unmarked, but more usually they are spotted in red-brown, particularly at the larger end. Pale green eggs have brown spots; pink eggs are spotted with reddish marks.
• BREEDING The nest, built almost entirely by the male, is a large structure of green moss, stalks, and grass, lined with fine roots and hair, often with a little down or wool, and sited in clumps of brambles or sapling trees in thickets or hedgerows.
• RANGE The Red-backed Shrike ranges from Europe to the Middle East, Mongolia and Manchuria, and northern India.

band of marks

cream ground color

red-brown spots

plain white ground

Egg size 18–26 x 14–18 mm	Clutch size 5–6, rarely 7	Incubation ♀ 14–16 days

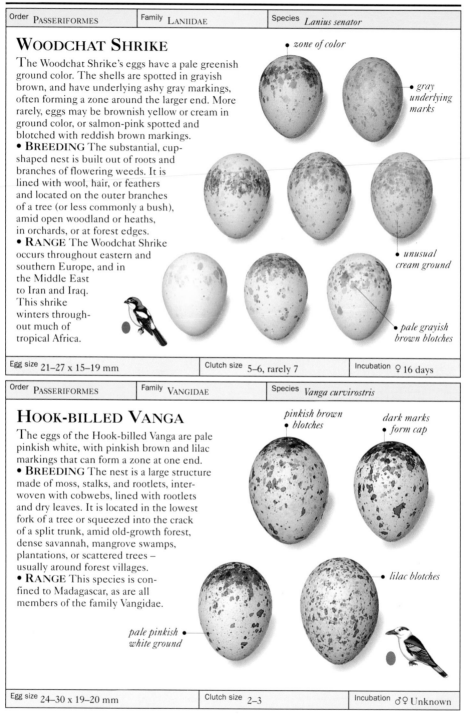

| Order PASSERIFORMES | Family LANIIDAE | Species *Lanius senator* |

WOODCHAT SHRIKE

The Woodchat Shrike's eggs have a pale greenish ground color. The shells are spotted in grayish brown, and have underlying ashy gray markings, often forming a zone around the larger end. More rarely, eggs may be brownish yellow or cream in ground color, or salmon-pink spotted and blotched with reddish brown markings.
• **BREEDING** The substantial, cup-shaped nest is built out of roots and branches of flowering weeds. It is lined with wool, hair, or feathers and located on the outer branches of a tree (or less commonly a bush), amid open woodland or heaths, in orchards, or at forest edges.
• **RANGE** The Woodchat Shrike occurs throughout eastern and southern Europe, and in the Middle East to Iran and Iraq. This shrike winters through-out much of tropical Africa.

• *zone of color*

• *gray underlying marks*

• *unusual cream ground*

• *pale grayish brown blotches*

| Egg size 21–27 x 15–19 mm | Clutch size 5–6, rarely 7 | Incubation ♀ 16 days |

| Order PASSERIFORMES | Family VANGIDAE | Species *Vanga curvirostris* |

HOOK-BILLED VANGA

The eggs of the Hook-billed Vanga are pale pinkish white, with pinkish brown and lilac markings that can form a zone at one end.
• **BREEDING** The nest is a large structure made of moss, stalks, and rootlets, inter-woven with cobwebs, lined with rootlets and dry leaves. It is located in the lowest fork of a tree or squeezed into the crack of a split trunk, amid old-growth forest, dense savannah, mangrove swamps, plantations, or scattered trees – usually around forest villages.
• **RANGE** This species is con-fined to Madagascar, as are all members of the family Vangidae.

pinkish brown • blotches

dark marks • form cap

• *lilac blotches*

pale pinkish • white ground

| Egg size 24–30 x 19–20 mm | Clutch size 2–3 | Incubation ♂♀ Unknown |

Order PASSERIFORMES	Family BOMBYCILLIDAE	Species *Bombycilla garrulus*

BOHEMIAN WAXWING

The eggs of the Bohemian Waxwing are ashy gray or ashy blue (occasionally buffish) in ground color, sparsely spotted in black or blackish brown. These markings may have blurred brownish edges. The shells also have gray underlying secondary markings.

• **BREEDING** The Bohemian Waxwing constructs a slight, cup-shaped nest that is built of pine or spruce twigs, reindeer moss, and grass and lined with a little hair, down, or feathers. The nest is situated in a tree, the favored site being usually amid open coniferous or birch forest.

• **RANGE** This bird inhabits forests throughout northern Europe, Asia, and North America from Alaska and northern Canada. In winter it ranges south over the United States, Central Europe, and across Asia to China and Japan.

ashy gray ground

blurred spots and blotches

elliptical shape

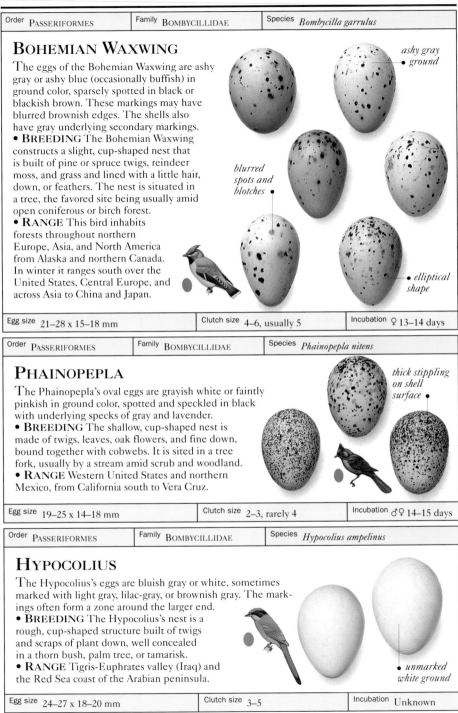

Egg size 21–28 x 15–18 mm	Clutch size 4–6, usually 5	Incubation ♀ 13–14 days

Order PASSERIFORMES	Family BOMBYCILLIDAE	Species *Phainopepla nitens*

PHAINOPEPLA

The Phainopepla's oval eggs are grayish white or faintly pinkish in ground color, spotted and speckled in black with underlying specks of gray and lavender.

• **BREEDING** The shallow, cup-shaped nest is made of twigs, leaves, oak flowers, and fine down, bound together with cobwebs. It is sited in a tree fork, usually by a stream amid scrub and woodland.

• **RANGE** Western United States and northern Mexico, from California south to Vera Cruz.

thick stippling on shell surface

Egg size 19–25 x 14–18 mm	Clutch size 2–3, rarely 4	Incubation ♂♀ 14–15 days

Order PASSERIFORMES	Family BOMBYCILLIDAE	Species *Hypocolius ampelinus*

HYPOCOLIUS

The Hypocolius's eggs are bluish gray or white, sometimes marked with light gray, lilac-gray, or brownish gray. The markings often form a zone around the larger end.

• **BREEDING** The Hypocolius's nest is a rough, cup-shaped structure built of twigs and scraps of plant down, well concealed in a thorn bush, palm tree, or tamarisk.

• **RANGE** Tigris-Euphrates valley (Iraq) and the Red Sea coast of the Arabian peninsula.

unmarked white ground

Egg size 24–27 x 18–20 mm	Clutch size 3–5	Incubation Unknown

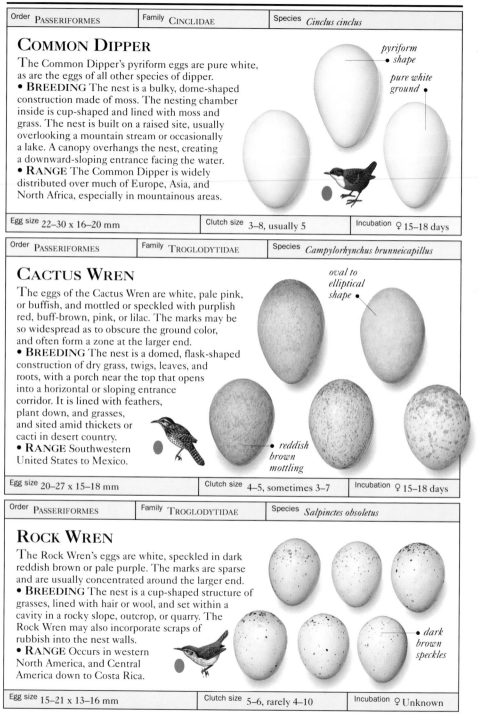

Order PASSERIFORMES	Family CINCLIDAE	Species *Cinclus cinclus*

COMMON DIPPER

The Common Dipper's pyriform eggs are pure white, as are the eggs of all other species of dipper.
• **BREEDING** The nest is a bulky, dome-shaped construction made of moss. The nesting chamber inside is cup-shaped and lined with moss and grass. The nest is built on a raised site, usually overlooking a mountain stream or occasionally a lake. A canopy overhangs the nest, creating a downward-sloping entrance facing the water.
• **RANGE** The Common Dipper is widely distributed over much of Europe, Asia, and North Africa, especially in mountainous areas.

pyriform shape

pure white ground

Egg size 22–30 x 16–20 mm	Clutch size 3–8, usually 5	Incubation ♀ 15–18 days

Order PASSERIFORMES	Family TROGLODYTIDAE	Species *Campylorhynchus brunneicapillus*

CACTUS WREN

The eggs of the Cactus Wren are white, pale pink, or buffish, and mottled or speckled with purplish red, buff-brown, pink, or lilac. The marks may be so widespread as to obscure the ground color, and often form a zone at the larger end.
• **BREEDING** The nest is a domed, flask-shaped construction of dry grass, twigs, leaves, and roots, with a porch near the top that opens into a horizontal or sloping entrance corridor. It is lined with feathers, plant down, and grasses, and sited amid thickets or cacti in desert country.
• **RANGE** Southwestern United States to Mexico.

oval to elliptical shape

reddish brown mottling

Egg size 20–27 x 15–18 mm	Clutch size 4–5, sometimes 3–7	Incubation ♀ 15–18 days

Order PASSERIFORMES	Family TROGLODYTIDAE	Species *Salpinctes obsoletus*

ROCK WREN

The Rock Wren's eggs are white, speckled in dark reddish brown or pale purple. The marks are sparse and are usually concentrated around the larger end.
• **BREEDING** The nest is a cup-shaped structure of grasses, lined with hair or wool, and set within a cavity in a rocky slope, outcrop, or quarry. The Rock Wren may also incorporate scraps of rubbish into the nest walls.
• **RANGE** Occurs in western North America, and Central America down to Costa Rica.

dark brown speckles

Egg size 15–21 x 13–16 mm	Clutch size 5–6, rarely 4–10	Incubation ♀ Unknown

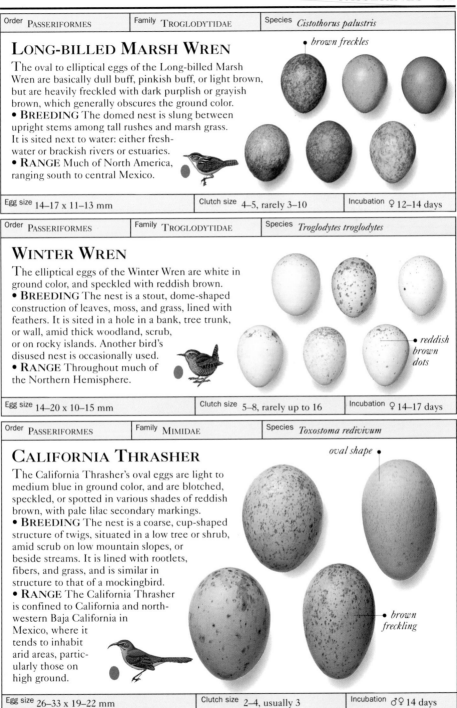

Order PASSERIFORMES	Family TROGLODYTIDAE	Species *Cistothorus palustris*

LONG-BILLED MARSH WREN

• *brown freckles*

The oval to elliptical eggs of the Long-billed Marsh Wren are basically dull buff, pinkish buff, or light brown, but are heavily freckled with dark purplish or grayish brown, which generally obscures the ground color.
• **BREEDING** The domed nest is slung between upright stems among tall rushes and marsh grass. It is sited next to water: either fresh-water or brackish rivers or estuaries.
• **RANGE** Much of North America, ranging south to central Mexico.

Egg size 14–17 x 11–13 mm	Clutch size 4–5, rarely 3–10	Incubation ♀ 12–14 days

Order PASSERIFORMES	Family TROGLODYTIDAE	Species *Troglodytes troglodytes*

WINTER WREN

The elliptical eggs of the Winter Wren are white in ground color, and speckled with reddish brown.
• **BREEDING** The nest is a stout, dome-shaped construction of leaves, moss, and grass, lined with feathers. It is sited in a hole in a bank, tree trunk, or wall, amid thick woodland, scrub, or on rocky islands. Another bird's disused nest is occasionally used.
• **RANGE** Throughout much of the Northern Hemisphere.

• *reddish brown dots*

Egg size 14–20 x 10–15 mm	Clutch size 5–8, rarely up to 16	Incubation ♀ 14–17 days

Order PASSERIFORMES	Family MIMIDAE	Species *Toxostoma redivivum*

CALIFORNIA THRASHER

oval shape •

The California Thrasher's oval eggs are light to medium blue in ground color, and are blotched, speckled, or spotted in various shades of reddish brown, with pale lilac secondary markings.
• **BREEDING** The nest is a coarse, cup-shaped structure of twigs, situated in a low tree or shrub, amid scrub on low mountain slopes, or beside streams. It is lined with rootlets, fibers, and grass, and is similar in structure to that of a mockingbird.
• **RANGE** The California Thrasher is confined to California and north-western Baja California in Mexico, where it tends to inhabit arid areas, partic-ularly those on high ground.

• *brown freckling*

Egg size 26–33 x 19–22 mm	Clutch size 2–4, usually 3	Incubation ♂♀ 14 days

Order PASSERIFORMES	Family MIMIDAE	Species *Donacobius atricapillus*

BLACK-CAPPED MOCKINGTHRUSH

The eggs of the Black-capped Mockingthrush are purplish white, but almost entirely covered in reddish and purplish blotches and spots, which are often more concentrated at the larger end.
• **BREEDING** The nest is a deep, bulky, tightly woven cup of strips of dead grass, fibers, and other plant materials, lined with fine grass blades, grass-flowers, and rootlets (or other available materials, such as lizard skin), and held in place between rigid stems, in overgrown marshland.
• **RANGE** Eastern Panama and much of tropical South America east of the Andes, south to Argentina.

bright reddish mottling

glossy surface

Egg size 21–24 x 16–18 mm	Clutch size 2	Incubation ♀ 17 days

Order PASSERIFORMES	Family MIMIDAE	Species *Dumatella carolinensis*

GRAY CATBIRD

The eggs of the Gray Catbird are deep blue or grayish blue in ground color, and unmarked.
• **BREEDING** The nest is a cup-shaped structure of sticks, weeds, leaves, and grass, and sometimes string, cotton, or rags. It is lined with rootlets, bark, pine needles, decayed leaves, and hair, and is often situated in a tree in woodland.
• **RANGE** This species breeds throughout southern Canada and the northern United States. It winters from the southern United States to central Panama and the West Indies.

grayish blue ground

glossy surface

Egg size 21–26 x 15–18 mm	Clutch size 3–5, usually 4	Incubation ♀ 12–13 days

Order PASSERIFORMES	Family MIMIDAE	Species *Mimus polyglottos*

NORTHERN MOCKINGBIRD

The Northern Mockingbird's eggs are pale to greenish blue, sometimes with a pink tinge (though these shades are difficult to photograph). The eggs are speckled with chestnut-brown.
• **BREEDING** The cup-shaped nest is built of natural and manmade materials. It is sited in a forest tree.
• **RANGE** United States, Mexico, and the West Indies.

variable shades of blotching

Egg size 21–27 x 17–19 mm	Clutch size 3–5, rarely 6	Incubation ♀ 11–14 days

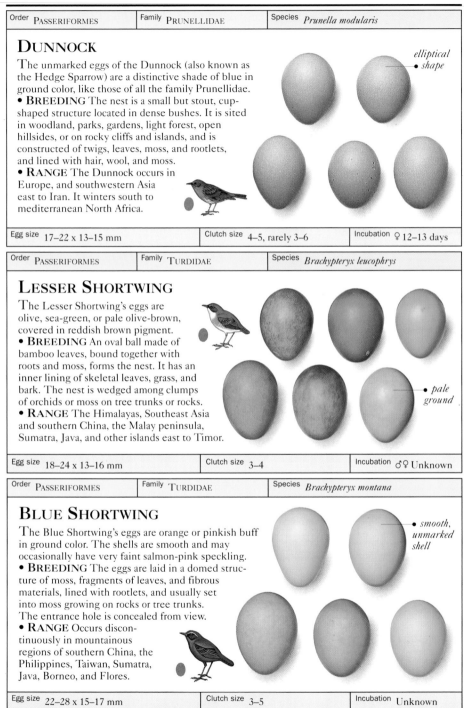

| Order PASSERIFORMES | Family PRUNELLIDAE | Species *Prunella modularis* |

DUNNOCK

The unmarked eggs of the Dunnock (also known as the Hedge Sparrow) are a distinctive shade of blue in ground color, like those of all the family Prunellidae.
• **BREEDING** The nest is a small but stout, cup-shaped structure located in dense bushes. It is sited in woodland, parks, gardens, light forest, open hillsides, or on rocky cliffs and islands, and is constructed of twigs, leaves, moss, and rootlets, and lined with hair, wool, and moss.
• **RANGE** The Dunnock occurs in Europe, and southwestern Asia east to Iran. It winters south to mediterranean North Africa.

elliptical shape

| Egg size 17–22 x 13–15 mm | Clutch size 4–5, rarely 3–6 | Incubation ♀ 12–13 days |

| Order PASSERIFORMES | Family TURDIDAE | Species *Brachypteryx leucophrys* |

LESSER SHORTWING

The Lesser Shortwing's eggs are olive, sea-green, or pale olive-brown, covered in reddish brown pigment.
• **BREEDING** An oval ball made of bamboo leaves, bound together with roots and moss, forms the nest. It has an inner lining of skeletal leaves, grass, and bark. The nest is wedged among clumps of orchids or moss on tree trunks or rocks.
• **RANGE** The Himalayas, Southeast Asia and southern China, the Malay peninsula, Sumatra, Java, and other islands east to Timor.

pale ground

| Egg size 18–24 x 13–16 mm | Clutch size 3–4 | Incubation ♂♀ Unknown |

| Order PASSERIFORMES | Family TURDIDAE | Species *Brachypteryx montana* |

BLUE SHORTWING

The Blue Shortwing's eggs are orange or pinkish buff in ground color. The shells are smooth and may occasionally have very faint salmon-pink speckling.
• **BREEDING** The eggs are laid in a domed struc-ture of moss, fragments of leaves, and fibrous materials, lined with rootlets, and usually set into moss growing on rocks or tree trunks. The entrance hole is concealed from view.
• **RANGE** Occurs discon-tinuously in mountainous regions of southern China, the Philippines, Taiwan, Sumatra, Java, Borneo, and Flores.

smooth, unmarked shell

| Egg size 22–28 x 15–17 mm | Clutch size 3–5 | Incubation Unknown |

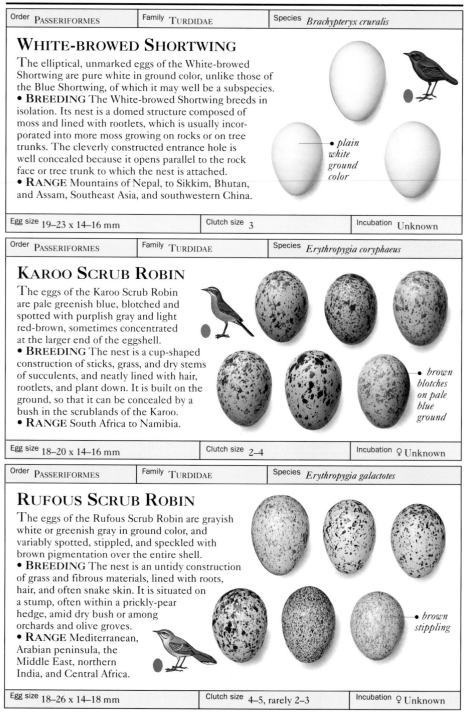

Order PASSERIFORMES	Family TURDIDAE	Species *Brachypteryx cruralis*

WHITE-BROWED SHORTWING

The elliptical, unmarked eggs of the White-browed Shortwing are pure white in ground color, unlike those of the Blue Shortwing, of which it may well be a subspecies.
• **BREEDING** The White-browed Shortwing breeds in isolation. Its nest is a domed structure composed of moss and lined with rootlets, which is usually incorporated into more moss growing on rocks or on tree trunks. The cleverly constructed entrance hole is well concealed because it opens parallel to the rock face or tree trunk to which the nest is attached.
• **RANGE** Mountains of Nepal, to Sikkim, Bhutan, and Assam, Southeast Asia, and southwestern China.

• *plain white ground color*

Egg size 19–23 x 14–16 mm	Clutch size 3	Incubation Unknown

Order PASSERIFORMES	Family TURDIDAE	Species *Erythropygia coryphaeus*

KAROO SCRUB ROBIN

The eggs of the Karoo Scrub Robin are pale greenish blue, blotched and spotted with purplish gray and light red-brown, sometimes concentrated at the larger end of the eggshell.
• **BREEDING** The nest is a cup-shaped construction of sticks, grass, and dry stems of succulents, and neatly lined with hair, rootlets, and plant down. It is built on the ground, so that it can be concealed by a bush in the scrublands of the Karoo.
• **RANGE** South Africa to Namibia.

• *brown blotches on pale blue ground*

Egg size 18–20 x 14–16 mm	Clutch size 2–4	Incubation ♀ Unknown

Order PASSERIFORMES	Family TURDIDAE	Species *Erythropygia galactotes*

RUFOUS SCRUB ROBIN

The eggs of the Rufous Scrub Robin are grayish white or greenish gray in ground color, and variably spotted, stippled, and speckled with brown pigmentation over the entire shell.
• **BREEDING** The nest is an untidy construction of grass and fibrous materials, lined with roots, hair, and often snake skin. It is situated on a stump, often within a prickly-pear hedge, amid dry bush or among orchards and olive groves.
• **RANGE** Mediterranean, Arabian peninsula, the Middle East, northern India, and Central Africa.

• *brown stippling*

Egg size 18–26 x 14–18 mm	Clutch size 4–5, rarely 2–3	Incubation ♀ Unknown

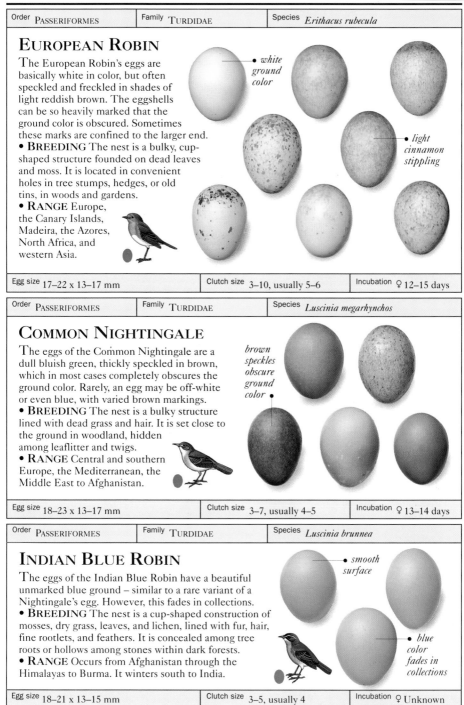

Order PASSERIFORMES	Family TURDIDAE	Species *Erithacus rubecula*

EUROPEAN ROBIN

The European Robin's eggs are basically white in color, but often speckled and freckled in shades of light reddish brown. The eggshells can be so heavily marked that the ground color is obscured. Sometimes these marks are confined to the larger end.
• **BREEDING** The nest is a bulky, cup-shaped structure founded on dead leaves and moss. It is located in convenient holes in tree stumps, hedges, or old tins, in woods and gardens.
• **RANGE** Europe, the Canary Islands, Madeira, the Azores, North Africa, and western Asia.

• *white ground color*

• *light cinnamon stippling*

Egg size 17–22 x 13–17 mm	Clutch size 3–10, usually 5–6	Incubation ♀ 12–15 days

Order PASSERIFORMES	Family TURDIDAE	Species *Luscinia megarhynchos*

COMMON NIGHTINGALE

The eggs of the Common Nightingale are a dull bluish green, thickly speckled in brown, which in most cases completely obscures the ground color. Rarely, an egg may be off-white or even blue, with varied brown markings.
• **BREEDING** The nest is a bulky structure lined with dead grass and hair. It is set close to the ground in woodland, hidden among leaflitter and twigs.
• **RANGE** Central and southern Europe, the Mediterranean, the Middle East to Afghanistan.

brown speckles obscure ground color •

Egg size 18–23 x 13–17 mm	Clutch size 3–7, usually 4–5	Incubation ♀ 13–14 days

Order PASSERIFORMES	Family TURDIDAE	Species *Luscinia brunnea*

INDIAN BLUE ROBIN

The eggs of the Indian Blue Robin have a beautiful unmarked blue ground – similar to a rare variant of a Nightingale's egg. However, this fades in collections.
• **BREEDING** The nest is a cup-shaped construction of mosses, dry grass, leaves, and lichen, lined with fur, hair, fine rootlets, and feathers. It is concealed among tree roots or hollows among stones within dark forests.
• **RANGE** Occurs from Afghanistan through the Himalayas to Burma. It winters south to India.

• *smooth surface*

• *blue color fades in collections*

Egg size 18–21 x 13–15 mm	Clutch size 3–5, usually 4	Incubation ♀ Unknown

Order PASSERIFORMES	Family TURDIDAE	Species *Tarsiger cyanurus*

RED-FLANKED BLUETAIL

The Red-flanked Bluetail, also known as the Orange-flanked Bush-Robin, lays white eggs, sometimes unmarked, but usually speckled or finely mottled with pale red-brown or purplish marks often around the larger end.
• **BREEDING** The cup-shaped nest is made of grass, roots, and moss, lined with wool, musk deer hair, or pine needles. It is set in a bank, or in a fallen log, amid coniferous or birchwood forest.
• **RANGE** Occurs in northern Europe and Asia, from Lapland to Kamchatka, south to Afghanistan, the Himalayas, and western China.

white ground

faint marks

Egg size 16–19 x 13–15 mm	Clutch size 3–5, rarely 7	Incubation ♀ Unknown

Order PASSERIFORMES	Family TURDIDAE	Species *Cossypha natalensis*

NATAL ROBIN-CHAT

The Natal Robin-Chat's eggs vary in color, from a uniform chocolate-brown to olive-green or turquoise, sometimes mottled in brown or olive.
• **BREEDING** The nest is a cup-shaped structure of dead leaves, twigs, and moss, lined with rootlets and plant fibers. A hollow tree stump, rock crevice, hanging vine, or the ground can be used as suitable nest sites, amid dense forest, parkland, or large gardens.
• **RANGE** Occurs in eastern and southern Africa from the Sudan west to Zaire and Angola, and further south to southern South Africa.

olive-green shell

slight sheen on smooth surface

Egg size 20–25 x 14–18 mm	Clutch size 1–4, usually 3	Incubation ♀ 13–15 days

Order PASSERIFORMES.	Family TURDIDAE	Species *Copsychus saularis*

MAGPIE-ROBIN

The eggs of the Magpie-Robin are pale blue-green in ground color, blotched in reddish brown, with underlying pale lavender and purple-gray markings.
• **BREEDING** The nest is a cup of vegetation and debris, lined with the same, set in a hole in a tree, bank, or wall, under eaves, or in a rainwater pipe, in forest, jungle, gardens, or orchards.
• **RANGE** India, Southeast Asia, China, the Malay peninsula, Indonesia, and the Philippines.

boldly blotched surface

pale blue ground

Egg size 18–27 x 15–18 mm	Clutch size 3–6, usually 4 or 5	Incubation ♂♀ 12–13 days

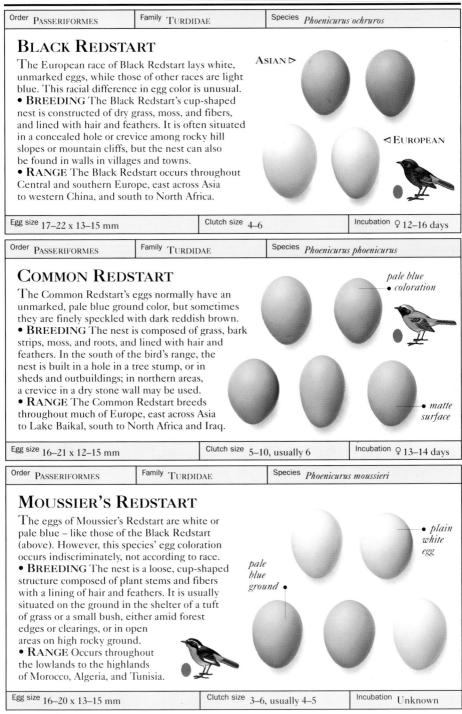

Order PASSERIFORMES	Family TURDIDAE	Species *Phoenicurus ochruros*

BLACK REDSTART

ASIAN ▷

The European race of Black Redstart lays white, unmarked eggs, while those of other races are light blue. This racial difference in egg color is unusual.
• **BREEDING** The Black Redstart's cup-shaped nest is constructed of dry grass, moss, and fibers, and lined with hair and feathers. It is often situated in a concealed hole or crevice among rocky hill slopes or mountain cliffs, but the nest can also be found in walls in villages and towns.
• **RANGE** The Black Redstart occurs throughout Central and southern Europe, east across Asia to western China, and south to North Africa.

◁ EUROPEAN

Egg size 17–22 x 13–15 mm	Clutch size 4–6	Incubation ♀ 12–16 days

Order PASSERIFORMES	Family TURDIDAE	Species *Phoenicurus phoenicurus*

COMMON REDSTART

pale blue
• *coloration*

The Common Redstart's eggs normally have an unmarked, pale blue ground color, but sometimes they are finely speckled with dark reddish brown.
• **BREEDING** The nest is composed of grass, bark strips, moss, and roots, and lined with hair and feathers. In the south of the bird's range, the nest is built in a hole in a tree stump, or in sheds and outbuildings; in northern areas, a crevice in a dry stone wall may be used.
• **RANGE** The Common Redstart breeds throughout much of Europe, east across Asia to Lake Baikal, south to North Africa and Iraq.

• *matte surface*

Egg size 16–21 x 12–15 mm	Clutch size 5–10, usually 6	Incubation ♀ 13–14 days

Order PASSERIFORMES	Family TURDIDAE	Species *Phoenicurus moussieri*

MOUSSIER'S REDSTART

The eggs of Moussier's Redstart are white or pale blue – like those of the Black Redstart (above). However, this species' egg coloration occurs indiscriminately, not according to race.
• **BREEDING** The nest is a loose, cup-shaped structure composed of plant stems and fibers with a lining of hair and feathers. It is usually situated on the ground in the shelter of a tuft of grass or a small bush, either amid forest edges or clearings, or in open areas on high rocky ground.
• **RANGE** Occurs throughout the lowlands to the highlands of Morocco, Algeria, and Tunisia.

• *plain white egg*

pale blue ground •

Egg size 16–20 x 13–15 mm	Clutch size 3–6, usually 4–5	Incubation Unknown

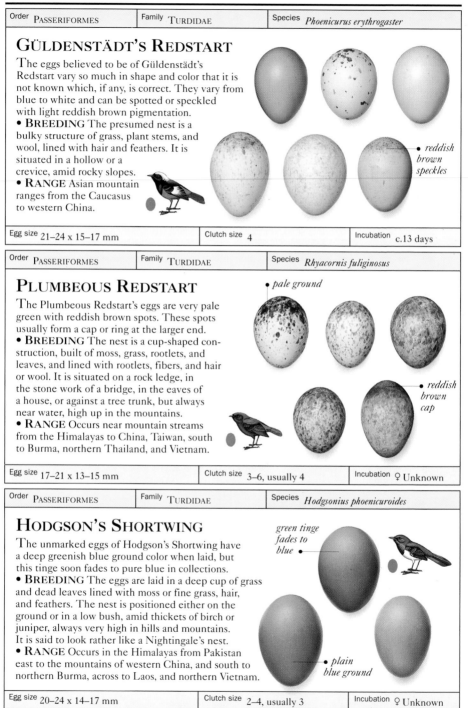

| Order PASSERIFORMES | Family TURDIDAE | Species *Phoenicurus erythrogaster* |

GÜLDENSTÄDT'S REDSTART

The eggs believed to be of Güldenstädt's
Redstart vary so much in shape and color that it is
not known which, if any, is correct. They vary from
blue to white and can be spotted or speckled
with light reddish brown pigmentation.
• **BREEDING** The presumed nest is a
bulky structure of grass, plant stems, and
wool, lined with hair and feathers. It is
situated in a hollow or a
crevice, amid rocky slopes.
• **RANGE** Asian mountain
ranges from the Caucasus
to western China.

• *reddish brown speckles*

| Egg size 21–24 x 15–17 mm | Clutch size 4 | Incubation c.13 days |

| Order PASSERIFORMES | Family TURDIDAE | Species *Rhyacornis fuliginosus* |

PLUMBEOUS REDSTART

• *pale ground*

The Plumbeous Redstart's eggs are very pale
green with reddish brown spots. These spots
usually form a cap or ring at the larger end.
• **BREEDING** The nest is a cup-shaped construction, built of moss, grass, rootlets, and
leaves, and lined with rootlets, fibers, and hair
or wool. It is situated on a rock ledge, in
the stone work of a bridge, in the eaves of
a house, or against a tree trunk, but always
near water, high up in the mountains.
• **RANGE** Occurs near mountain streams
from the Himalayas to China, Taiwan, south
to Burma, northern Thailand, and Vietnam.

• *reddish brown cap*

| Egg size 17–21 x 13–15 mm | Clutch size 3–6, usually 4 | Incubation ♀ Unknown |

| Order PASSERIFORMES | Family TURDIDAE | Species *Hodgsonius phoenicuroides* |

HODGSON'S SHORTWING

green tinge fades to blue •

The unmarked eggs of Hodgson's Shortwing have
a deep greenish blue ground color when laid, but
this tinge soon fades to pure blue in collections.
• **BREEDING** The eggs are laid in a deep cup of grass
and dead leaves lined with moss or fine grass, hair,
and feathers. The nest is positioned either on the
ground or in a low bush, amid thickets of birch or
juniper, always very high in hills and mountains.
It is said to look rather like a Nightingale's nest.
• **RANGE** Occurs in the Himalayas from Pakistan
east to the mountains of western China, and south to
northern Burma, across to Laos, and northern Vietnam.

• *plain blue ground*

| Egg size 20–24 x 14–17 mm | Clutch size 2–4, usually 3 | Incubation ♀ Unknown |

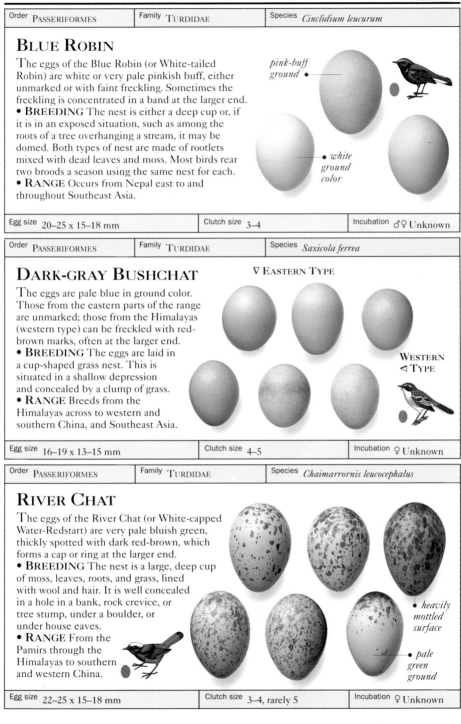

Order PASSERIFORMES	Family TURDIDAE	Species *Cinclidium leucurum*

BLUE ROBIN

The eggs of the Blue Robin (or White-tailed Robin) are white or very pale pinkish buff, either unmarked or with faint freckling. Sometimes the freckling is concentrated in a band at the larger end.
• **BREEDING** The nest is either a deep cup or, if it is in an exposed situation, such as among the roots of a tree overhanging a stream, it may be domed. Both types of nest are made of rootlets mixed with dead leaves and moss. Most birds rear two broods a season using the same nest for each.
• **RANGE** Occurs from Nepal east to and throughout Southeast Asia.

pink-buff ground •

• *white ground color*

Egg size 20–25 x 15–18 mm	Clutch size 3–4	Incubation ♂♀ Unknown

Order PASSERIFORMES	Family TURDIDAE	Species *Saxicola ferrea*

DARK-GRAY BUSHCHAT

∇ **EASTERN TYPE**

The eggs are pale blue in ground color. Those from the eastern parts of the range are unmarked; those from the Himalayas (western type) can be freckled with red-brown marks, often at the larger end.
• **BREEDING** The eggs are laid in a cup-shaped grass nest. This is situated in a shallow depression and concealed by a clump of grass.
• **RANGE** Breeds from the Himalayas across to western and southern China, and Southeast Asia.

WESTERN ◁ **TYPE**

Egg size 16–19 x 13–15 mm	Clutch size 4–5	Incubation ♀ Unknown

Order PASSERIFORMES	Family TURDIDAE	Species *Chaimarrornis leucocephalus*

RIVER CHAT

The eggs of the River Chat (or White-capped Water-Redstart) are very pale bluish green, thickly spotted with dark red-brown, which forms a cap or ring at the larger end.
• **BREEDING** The nest is a large, deep cup of moss, leaves, roots, and grass, lined with wool and hair. It is well concealed in a hole in a bank, rock crevice, or tree stump, under a boulder, or under house eaves.
• **RANGE** From the Pamirs through the Himalayas to southern and western China.

• *heavily mottled surface*

• *pale green ground*

Egg size 22–25 x 15–18 mm	Clutch size 3–4, rarely 5	Incubation ♀ Unknown

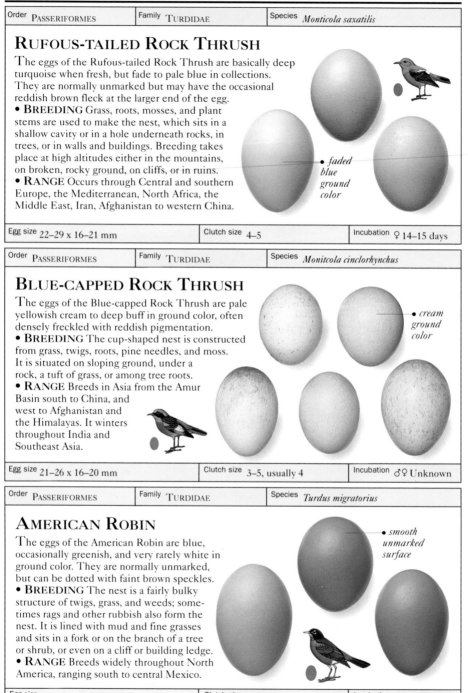

Order PASSERIFORMES	Family TURDIDAE	Species *Monticola saxatilis*

RUFOUS-TAILED ROCK THRUSH

The eggs of the Rufous-tailed Rock Thrush are basically deep turquoise when fresh, but fade to pale blue in collections. They are normally unmarked but may have the occasional reddish brown fleck at the larger end of the egg.
• **BREEDING** Grass, roots, mosses, and plant stems are used to make the nest, which sits in a shallow cavity or in a hole underneath rocks, in trees, or in walls and buildings. Breeding takes place at high altitudes either in the mountains, on broken, rocky ground, on cliffs, or in ruins.
• **RANGE** Occurs through Central and southern Europe, the Mediterranean, North Africa, the Middle East, Iran, Afghanistan to western China.

• *faded blue ground color*

Egg size 22–29 x 16–21 mm	Clutch size 4–5	Incubation ♀ 14–15 days

Order PASSERIFORMES	Family TURDIDAE	Species *Monitcola cinclorhynchus*

BLUE-CAPPED ROCK THRUSH

The eggs of the Blue-capped Rock Thrush are pale yellowish cream to deep buff in ground color, often densely freckled with reddish pigmentation.
• **BREEDING** The cup-shaped nest is constructed from grass, twigs, roots, pine needles, and moss. It is situated on sloping ground, under a rock, a tuft of grass, or among tree roots.
• **RANGE** Breeds in Asia from the Amur Basin south to China, and west to Afghanistan and the Himalayas. It winters throughout India and Southeast Asia.

• *cream ground color*

Egg size 21–26 x 16–20 mm	Clutch size 3–5, usually 4	Incubation ♂♀ Unknown

Order PASSERIFORMES	Family TURDIDAE	Species *Turdus migratorius*

AMERICAN ROBIN

The eggs of the American Robin are blue, occasionally greenish, and very rarely white in ground color. They are normally unmarked, but can be dotted with faint brown speckles.
• **BREEDING** The nest is a fairly bulky structure of twigs, grass, and weeds; some-times rags and other rubbish also form the nest. It is lined with mud and fine grasses and sits in a fork or on the branch of a tree or shrub, or even on a cliff or building ledge.
• **RANGE** Breeds widely throughout North America, ranging south to central Mexico.

• *smooth unmarked surface*

Egg size 24–33 x 17–23 mm	Clutch size 3–7, usually 4	Incubation ♀ 11–14 days

Order PASSERIFORMES	Family TURDIDAE	Species *Turdus merula*

EURASIAN BLACKBIRD

The eggs of the western subspecies of Blackbird (*Turdus merula merula*) are light blue or white in ground color, sometimes unmarked but usually thickly spotted and mottled in reddish brown; occasionally the shell has a slightly greenish or pinkish tint. Eggs from China (*T. merula mandarinus*) are pinkish in color, and very similar to those of a Mistle Thrush (see p.184). Eggs laid by the birds of southern India (*T. merula nigropileus*) are browner. These groups were once treated as separate species; the variation in eggs suggests this opinion may have been justified.

• **BREEDING** The nest is a large, stoutly built cup of plant stems, grass, leaves, twigs, and roots, lined with a solid layer of mud, and then dry grass.

• **RANGE** Europe, Asia, northern Africa, the Azores, Madeira, the Canary Islands, and east to the Pamirs and the Himalayas. Isolated populations occur in southern India and southwest China.

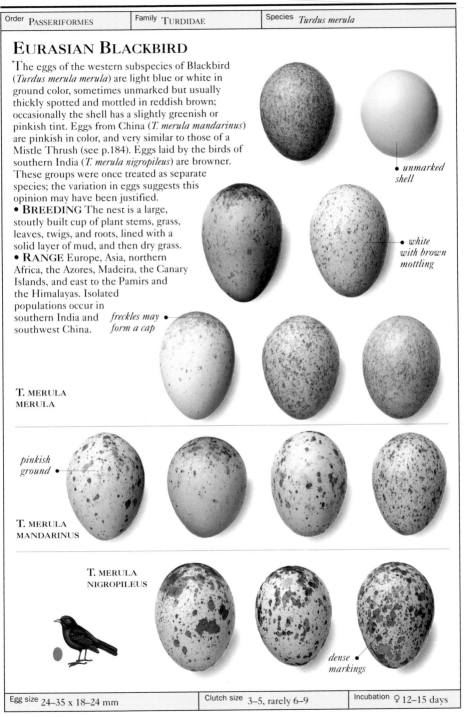

• *unmarked shell*

• *white with brown mottling*

freckles may form a cap •

T. MERULA MERULA

pinkish ground •

T. MERULA MANDARINUS

T. MERULA NIGROPILEUS

dense markings •

Egg size 24–35 x 18–24 mm	Clutch size 3–5, rarely 6–9	Incubation ♀ 12–15 days

Order PASSERIFORMES	Family TURDIDAE	Species *Turdus viscivorus*

MISTLE THRUSH

The eggs of the Mistle Thrush are pinkish cream or, more rarely, pale greenish blue in ground color. They are blotched and spotted with various shades of brown and have underlying pale lilac markings.
• **BREEDING** The nest is constructed of roots and moss. These materials are cemented together with mud and lined with grass, lichens, scraps of wool, linen, rags, and feathers. It is built in a fork or on a branch of a tree, usually at quite a considerable height from the ground, but also in bushes or in a rock-cleft near the coast. During the breeding season, the Mistle Thrush also frequents woods, plantations, orchards, and timberland.
• **RANGE** Breeds through much of Europe and southern Asia, south to the Mediterranean and east to Afghanistan, Pakistan, and the Himalayas. Northern populations migrate south in winter.

• *pale greenish blue ground*

brown spots and • *blotches*

Egg size 26–34 x 20–24 mm	Clutch size 3–6, usually 4	Incubation ♀ 13–14 days

Order PASSERIFORMES	Family TURDIDAE	Species *Turdus philomelos*

SONG THRUSH

The Song Thrush's eggs are clear blue, scantily spotted and dotted with black, most often around the larger end. Rarely, eggs are white in ground color with reddish brown spots.
• **BREEDING** The nest is a well-built construction made of grass, twigs, moss, leaves, and rootlets, solidified with mud and lined with a hard and very distinctive coating of mud, rotten wood, and dung mixed with saliva and pulverized. The nest sits in hedgerows, bushes, trees, or ivy banks, or on the ground.
• **RANGE** Europe, the Mediterranean, northern Iran, Asia, and western China.

• *oval shape*

rare white • *variety*

Egg size 23–31 x 18–23 mm	Clutch size 3–9, usually 4 or 5	Incubation ♂♀ 13–14 days

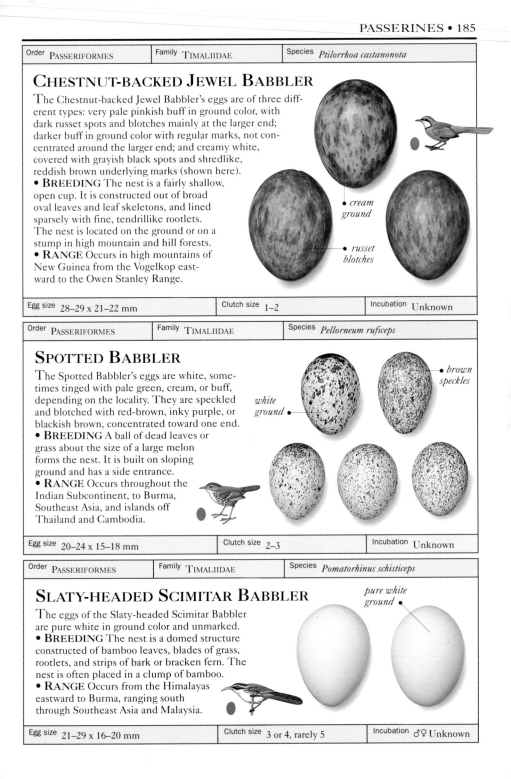

Order PASSERIFORMES	Family TIMALIIDAE	Species *Ptilorrhoa castanonota*

CHESTNUT-BACKED JEWEL BABBLER

The Chestnut-backed Jewel Babbler's eggs are of three different types: very pale pinkish buff in ground color, with dark russet spots and blotches mainly at the larger end; darker buff in ground color with regular marks, not concentrated around the larger end; and creamy white, covered with grayish black spots and shredlike, reddish brown underlying marks (shown here).
• **BREEDING** The nest is a fairly shallow, open cup. It is constructed out of broad oval leaves and leaf skeletons, and lined sparsely with fine, tendrillike rootlets. The nest is located on the ground or on a stump in high mountain and hill forests.
• **RANGE** Occurs in high mountains of New Guinea from the Vogelkop eastward to the Owen Stanley Range.

• *cream ground*

• *russet blotches*

Egg size 28–29 x 21–22 mm	Clutch size 1–2	Incubation Unknown

Order PASSERIFORMES	Family TIMALIIDAE	Species *Pellorneum ruficeps*

SPOTTED BABBLER

The Spotted Babbler's eggs are white, sometimes tinged with pale green, cream, or buff, depending on the locality. They are speckled and blotched with red-brown, inky purple, or blackish brown, concentrated toward one end.
• **BREEDING** A ball of dead leaves or grass about the size of a large melon forms the nest. It is built on sloping ground and has a side entrance.
• **RANGE** Occurs throughout the Indian Subcontinent, to Burma, Southeast Asia, and islands off Thailand and Cambodia.

white ground •

• *brown speckles*

Egg size 20–24 x 15–18 mm	Clutch size 2–3	Incubation Unknown

Order PASSERIFORMES	Family TIMALIIDAE	Species *Pomatorhinus schisticeps*

SLATY-HEADED SCIMITAR BABBLER

The eggs of the Slaty-headed Scimitar Babbler are pure white in ground color and unmarked.
• **BREEDING** The nest is a domed structure constructed of bamboo leaves, blades of grass, rootlets, and strips of bark or bracken fern. The nest is often placed in a clump of bamboo.
• **RANGE** Occurs from the Himalayas eastward to Burma, ranging south through Southeast Asia and Malaysia.

pure white ground •

Egg size 21–29 x 16–20 mm	Clutch size 3 or 4, rarely 5	Incubation ♂♀ Unknown

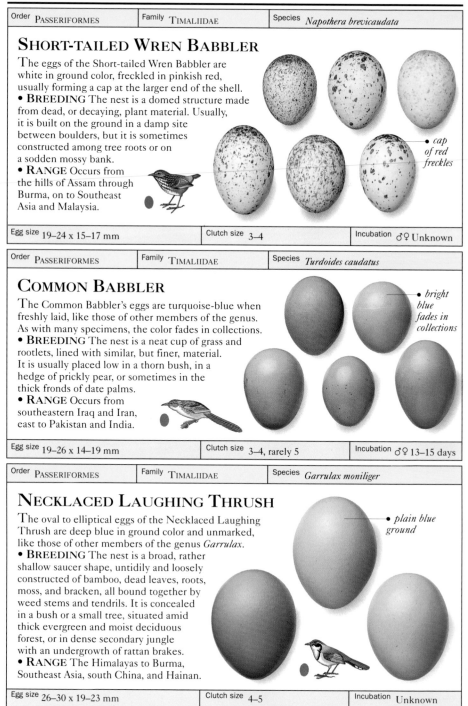

Order PASSERIFORMES	Family TIMALIIDAE	Species *Napothera brevicaudata*

SHORT-TAILED WREN BABBLER

The eggs of the Short-tailed Wren Babbler are white in ground color, freckled in pinkish red, usually forming a cap at the larger end of the shell.
• **BREEDING** The nest is a domed structure made from dead, or decaying, plant material. Usually, it is built on the ground in a damp site between boulders, but it is sometimes constructed among tree roots or on a sodden mossy bank.
• **RANGE** Occurs from the hills of Assam through Burma, on to Southeast Asia and Malaysia.

cap of red freckles

Egg size 19–24 x 15–17 mm	Clutch size 3–4	Incubation ♂♀ Unknown

Order PASSERIFORMES	Family TIMALIIDAE	Species *Turdoides caudatus*

COMMON BABBLER

The Common Babbler's eggs are turquoise-blue when freshly laid, like those of other members of the genus. As with many specimens, the color fades in collections.
• **BREEDING** The nest is a neat cup of grass and rootlets, lined with similar, but finer, material. It is usually placed low in a thorn bush, in a hedge of prickly pear, or sometimes in the thick fronds of date palms.
• **RANGE** Occurs from southeastern Iraq and Iran, east to Pakistan and India.

bright blue fades in collections

Egg size 19–26 x 14–19 mm	Clutch size 3–4, rarely 5	Incubation ♂♀ 13–15 days

Order PASSERIFORMES	Family TIMALIIDAE	Species *Garrulax moniliger*

NECKLACED LAUGHING THRUSH

The oval to elliptical eggs of the Necklaced Laughing Thrush are deep blue in ground color and unmarked, like those of other members of the genus *Garrulax*.
• **BREEDING** The nest is a broad, rather shallow saucer shape, untidily and loosely constructed of bamboo, dead leaves, roots, moss, and bracken, all bound together by weed stems and tendrils. It is concealed in a bush or a small tree, situated amid thick evergreen and moist deciduous forest, or in dense secondary jungle with an undergrowth of rattan brakes.
• **RANGE** The Himalayas to Burma, Southeast Asia, south China, and Hainan.

plain blue ground

Egg size 26–30 x 19–23 mm	Clutch size 4–5	Incubation Unknown

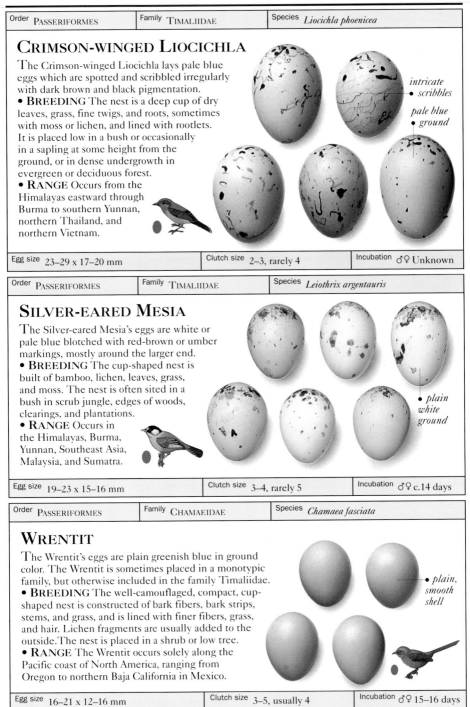

Order PASSERIFORMES	Family TIMALIIDAE	Species *Liocichla phoenicea*

CRIMSON-WINGED LIOCICHLA

The Crimson-winged Liocichla lays pale blue eggs which are spotted and scribbled irregularly with dark brown and black pigmentation.
• **BREEDING** The nest is a deep cup of dry leaves, grass, fine twigs, and roots, sometimes with moss or lichen, and lined with rootlets. It is placed low in a bush or occasionally in a sapling at some height from the ground, or in dense undergrowth in evergreen or deciduous forest.
• **RANGE** Occurs from the Himalayas eastward through Burma to southern Yunnan, northern Thailand, and northern Vietnam.

intricate
• *scribbles*

pale blue
• *ground*

Egg size 23–29 x 17–20 mm	Clutch size 2–3, rarely 4	Incubation ♂♀ Unknown

Order PASSERIFORMES	Family TIMALIIDAE	Species *Leiothrix argentauris*

SILVER-EARED MESIA

The Silver-eared Mesia's eggs are white or pale blue blotched with red-brown or umber markings, mostly around the larger end.
• **BREEDING** The cup-shaped nest is built of bamboo, lichen, leaves, grass, and moss. The nest is often sited in a bush in scrub jungle, edges of woods, clearings, and plantations.
• **RANGE** Occurs in the Himalayas, Burma, Yunnan, Southeast Asia, Malaysia, and Sumatra.

• *plain white ground*

Egg size 19–23 x 15–16 mm	Clutch size 3–4, rarely 5	Incubation ♂♀ c.14 days

Order PASSERIFORMES	Family CHAMAEIDAE	Species *Chamaea fasciata*

WRENTIT

The Wrentit's eggs are plain greenish blue in ground color. The Wrentit is sometimes placed in a monotypic family, but otherwise included in the family Timaliidae.
• **BREEDING** The well-camouflaged, compact, cup-shaped nest is constructed of bark fibers, bark strips, stems, and grass, and is lined with finer fibers, grass, and hair. Lichen fragments are usually added to the outside.The nest is placed in a shrub or low tree.
• **RANGE** The Wrentit occurs solely along the Pacific coast of North America, ranging from Oregon to northern Baja California in Mexico.

• *plain, smooth shell*

Egg size 16–21 x 12–16 mm	Clutch size 3–5, usually 4	Incubation ♂♀ 15–16 days

Order PASSERIFORMES	Family PARADOXORNITHIDAE	Species *Panurus biarmicus*

BEARDED PARROTBILL

The Bearded Parrotbill's eggs are creamy white, sparsely sprinkled with tiny, short streaks, scrawls, and specks of dark brown, usually very thinly and finely laid on.
• **BREEDING** Breeding takes place in stands of reeds and sedges in swampy ground. The nest is a deep cup built out of the dead leaves of reeds and sedges and lined with reed flower heads and sometimes feathers. The nest is located fairly low down near the edge of the stand and is often situated over water.
• **RANGE** Central and southern Europe, eastward through Turkey, southern Russia, Iran, and Turkestan to Inner Mongolia and Manchuria.

short brown streaks

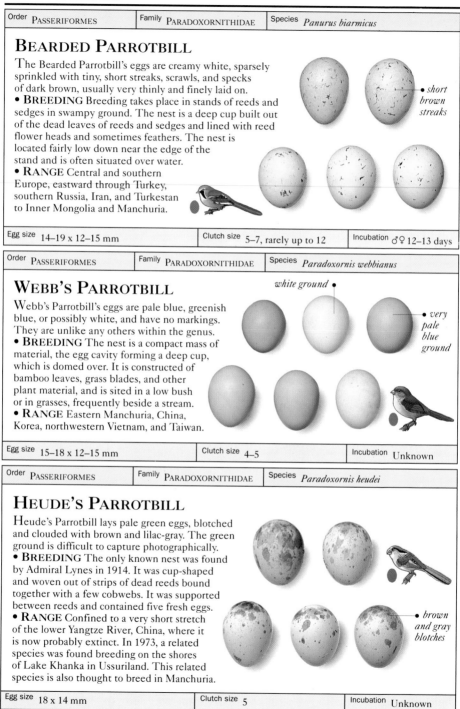

Egg size 14–19 x 12–15 mm	Clutch size 5–7, rarely up to 12	Incubation ♂♀ 12–13 days

Order PASSERIFORMES	Family PARADOXORNITHIDAE	Species *Paradoxornis webbianus*

WEBB'S PARROTBILL

white ground

Webb's Parrotbill's eggs are pale blue, greenish blue, or possibly white, and have no markings. They are unlike any others within the genus.
• **BREEDING** The nest is a compact mass of material, the egg cavity forming a deep cup, which is domed over. It is constructed of bamboo leaves, grass blades, and other plant material, and is sited in a low bush or in grasses, frequently near a stream.
• **RANGE** Eastern Manchuria, China, Korea, northwestern Vietnam, and Taiwan.

very pale blue ground

Egg size 15–18 x 12–15 mm	Clutch size 4–5	Incubation Unknown

Order PASSERIFORMES	Family PARADOXORNITHIDAE	Species *Paradoxornis heudei*

HEUDE'S PARROTBILL

Heude's Parrotbill lays pale green eggs, blotched and clouded with brown and lilac-gray. The green ground is difficult to capture photographically.
• **BREEDING** The only known nest was found by Admiral Lynes in 1914. It was cup-shaped and woven out of strips of dead reeds bound together with a few cobwebs. It was supported between reeds and contained five fresh eggs.
• **RANGE** Confined to a very short stretch of the lower Yangtze River, China, where it is now probably extinct. In 1973, a related species was found breeding on the shores of Lake Khanka in Ussuriland. This related species is also thought to breed in Manchuria.

brown and gray blotches

Egg size 18 x 14 mm	Clutch size 5	Incubation Unknown

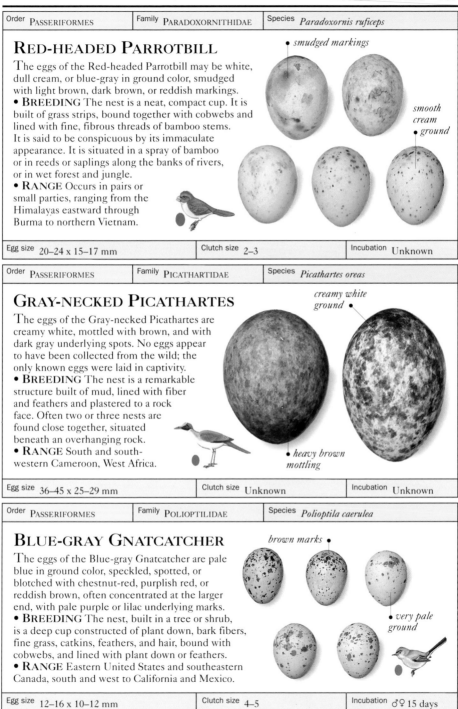

| Order PASSERIFORMES | Family PARADOXORNITHIDAE | Species *Paradoxornis ruficeps* |

RED-HEADED PARROTBILL

• smudged markings

The eggs of the Red-headed Parrotbill may be white, dull cream, or blue-gray in ground color, smudged with light brown, dark brown, or reddish markings.
• **BREEDING** The nest is a neat, compact cup. It is built of grass strips, bound together with cobwebs and lined with fine, fibrous threads of bamboo stems. It is said to be conspicuous by its immaculate appearance. It is situated in a spray of bamboo or in reeds or saplings along the banks of rivers, or in wet forest and jungle.
• **RANGE** Occurs in pairs or small parties, ranging from the Himalayas eastward through Burma to northern Vietnam.

smooth cream
• ground

| Egg size 20–24 x 15–17 mm | Clutch size 2–3 | Incubation Unknown |

| Order PASSERIFORMES | Family PICATHARTIDAE | Species *Picathartes oreas* |

GRAY-NECKED PICATHARTES

creamy white ground •

The eggs of the Gray-necked Picathartes are creamy white, mottled with brown, and with dark gray underlying spots. No eggs appear to have been collected from the wild; the only known eggs were laid in captivity.
• **BREEDING** The nest is a remarkable structure built of mud, lined with fiber and feathers and plastered to a rock face. Often two or three nests are found close together, situated beneath an overhanging rock.
• **RANGE** South and south-western Cameroon, West Africa.

• heavy brown mottling

| Egg size 36–45 x 25–29 mm | Clutch size Unknown | Incubation Unknown |

| Order PASSERIFORMES | Family POLIOPTILIDAE | Species *Polioptila caerulea* |

BLUE-GRAY GNATCATCHER

brown marks •

The eggs of the Blue-gray Gnatcatcher are pale blue in ground color, speckled, spotted, or blotched with chestnut-red, purplish red, or reddish brown, often concentrated at the larger end, with pale purple or lilac underlying marks.
• **BREEDING** The nest, built in a tree or shrub, is a deep cup constructed of plant down, bark fibers, fine grass, catkins, feathers, and hair, bound with cobwebs, and lined with plant down or feathers.
• **RANGE** Eastern United States and southeastern Canada, south and west to California and Mexico.

• very pale ground

| Egg size 12–16 x 10–12 mm | Clutch size 4–5 | Incubation ♂♀ 15 days |

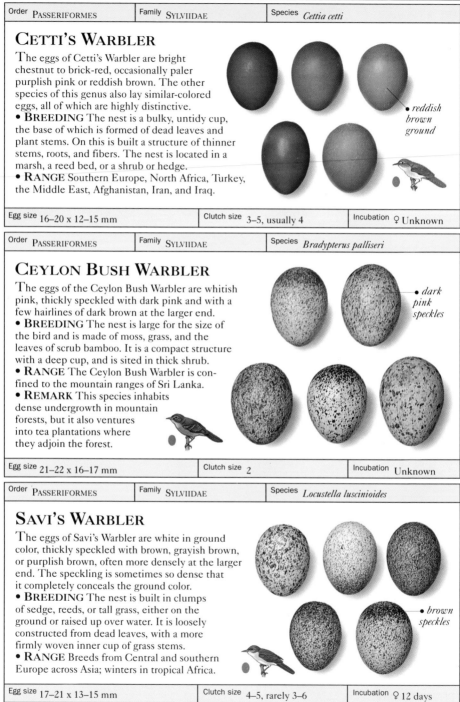

Order PASSERIFORMES	Family SYLVIIDAE	Species *Cettia cetti*

CETTI'S WARBLER

The eggs of Cetti's Warbler are bright chestnut to brick-red, occasionally paler purplish pink or reddish brown. The other species of this genus also lay similar-colored eggs, all of which are highly distinctive.
• **BREEDING** The nest is a bulky, untidy cup, the base of which is formed of dead leaves and plant stems. On this is built a structure of thinner stems, roots, and fibers. The nest is located in a marsh, a reed bed, or a shrub or hedge.
• **RANGE** Southern Europe, North Africa, Turkey, the Middle East, Afghanistan, Iran, and Iraq.

• *reddish brown ground*

Egg size 16–20 x 12–15 mm	Clutch size 3–5, usually 4	Incubation ♀ Unknown

Order PASSERIFORMES	Family SYLVIIDAE	Species *Bradypterus palliseri*

CEYLON BUSH WARBLER

The eggs of the Ceylon Bush Warbler are whitish pink, thickly speckled with dark pink and with a few hairlines of dark brown at the larger end.
• **BREEDING** The nest is large for the size of the bird and is made of moss, grass, and the leaves of scrub bamboo. It is a compact structure with a deep cup, and is sited in thick shrub.
• **RANGE** The Ceylon Bush Warbler is confined to the mountain ranges of Sri Lanka.
• **REMARK** This species inhabits dense undergrowth in mountain forests, but it also ventures into tea plantations where they adjoin the forest.

• *dark pink speckles*

Egg size 21–22 x 16–17 mm	Clutch size 2	Incubation Unknown

Order PASSERIFORMES	Family SYLVIIDAE	Species *Locustella luscinioides*

SAVI'S WARBLER

The eggs of Savi's Warbler are white in ground color, thickly speckled with brown, grayish brown, or purplish brown, often more densely at the larger end. The speckling is sometimes so dense that it completely conceals the ground color.
• **BREEDING** The nest is built in clumps of sedge, reeds, or tall grass, either on the ground or raised up over water. It is loosely constructed from dead leaves, with a more firmly woven inner cup of grass stems.
• **RANGE** Breeds from Central and southern Europe across Asia; winters in tropical Africa.

• *brown speckles*

Egg size 17–21 x 13–15 mm	Clutch size 4–5, rarely 3–6	Incubation ♀ 12 days

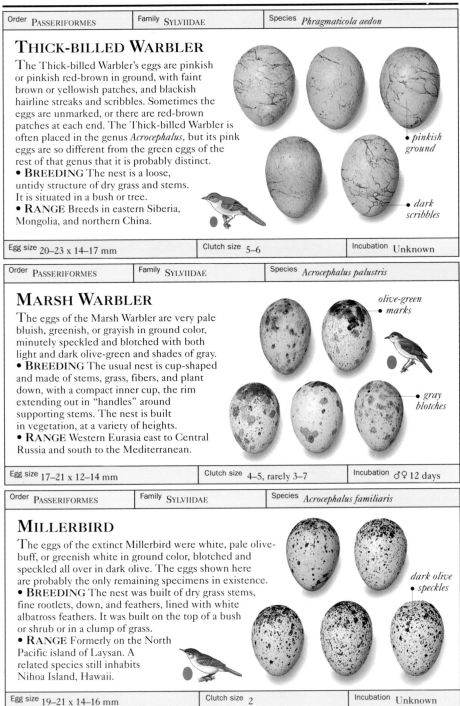

| Order PASSERIFORMES | Family SYLVIIDAE | Species *Phragmaticola aedon* |

THICK-BILLED WARBLER

The Thick-billed Warbler's eggs are pinkish or pinkish red-brown in ground, with faint brown or yellowish patches, and blackish hairline streaks and scribbles. Sometimes the eggs are unmarked, or there are red-brown patches at each end. The Thick-billed Warbler is often placed in the genus *Acrocephalus*, but its pink eggs are so different from the green eggs of the rest of that genus that it is probably distinct.
• **BREEDING** The nest is a loose, untidy structure of dry grass and stems. It is situated in a bush or tree.
• **RANGE** Breeds in eastern Siberia, Mongolia, and northern China.

• *pinkish ground*

• *dark scribbles*

| Egg size 20–23 x 14–17 mm | Clutch size 5–6 | Incubation Unknown |

| Order PASSERIFORMES | Family SYLVIIDAE | Species *Acrocephalus palustris* |

MARSH WARBLER

The eggs of the Marsh Warbler are very pale bluish, greenish, or grayish in ground color, minutely speckled and blotched with both light and dark olive-green and shades of gray.
• **BREEDING** The usual nest is cup-shaped and made of stems, grass, fibers, and plant down, with a compact inner cup, the rim extending out in "handles" around supporting stems. The nest is built in vegetation, at a variety of heights.
• **RANGE** Western Eurasia east to Central Russia and south to the Mediterranean.

olive-green • *marks*

• *gray blotches*

| Egg size 17–21 x 12–14 mm | Clutch size 4–5, rarely 3–7 | Incubation ♂♀ 12 days |

| Order PASSERIFORMES | Family SYLVIIDAE | Species *Acrocephalus familiaris* |

MILLERBIRD

The eggs of the extinct Millerbird were white, pale olive-buff, or greenish white in ground color, blotched and speckled all over in dark olive. The eggs shown here are probably the only remaining specimens in existence.
• **BREEDING** The nest was built of dry grass stems, fine rootlets, down, and feathers, lined with white albatross feathers. It was built on the top of a bush or shrub or in a clump of grass.
• **RANGE** Formerly on the North Pacific island of Laysan. A related species still inhabits Nihoa Island, Hawaii.

dark olive • *speckles*

| Egg size 19–21 x 14–16 mm | Clutch size 2 | Incubation Unknown |

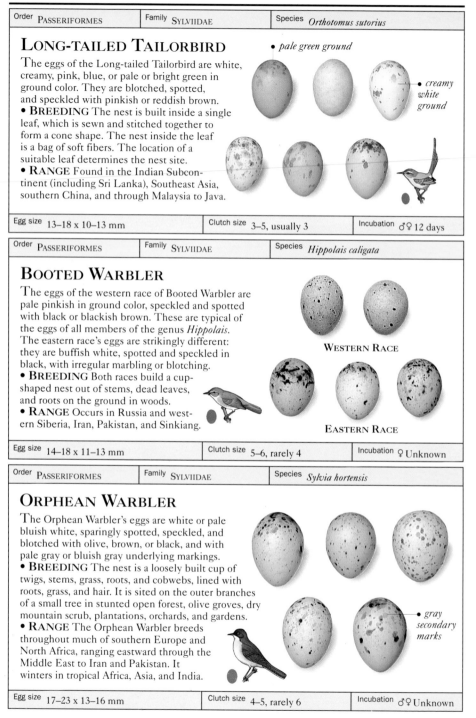

Order PASSERIFORMES	Family SYLVIIDAE	Species *Orthotomus sutorius*

LONG-TAILED TAILORBIRD

• *pale green ground*

The eggs of the Long-tailed Tailorbird are white, creamy, pink, blue, or pale or bright green in ground color. They are blotched, spotted, and speckled with pinkish or reddish brown.

• *creamy white ground*

• **BREEDING** The nest is built inside a single leaf, which is sewn and stitched together to form a cone shape. The nest inside the leaf is a bag of soft fibers. The location of a suitable leaf determines the nest site.

• **RANGE** Found in the Indian Subcontinent (including Sri Lanka), Southeast Asia, southern China, and through Malaysia to Java.

Egg size 13–18 x 10–13 mm	Clutch size 3–5, usually 3	Incubation ♂♀ 12 days

Order PASSERIFORMES	Family SYLVIIDAE	Species *Hippolais caligata*

BOOTED WARBLER

The eggs of the western race of Booted Warbler are pale pinkish in ground color, speckled and spotted with black or blackish brown. These are typical of the eggs of all members of the genus *Hippolais*. The eastern race's eggs are strikingly different: they are buffish white, spotted and speckled in black, with irregular marbling or blotching.

WESTERN RACE

• **BREEDING** Both races build a cup-shaped nest out of stems, dead leaves, and roots on the ground in woods.

• **RANGE** Occurs in Russia and western Siberia, Iran, Pakistan, and Sinkiang.

EASTERN RACE

Egg size 14–18 x 11–13 mm	Clutch size 5–6, rarely 4	Incubation ♀ Unknown

Order PASSERIFORMES	Family SYLVIIDAE	Species *Sylvia hortensis*

ORPHEAN WARBLER

The Orphean Warbler's eggs are white or pale bluish white, sparingly spotted, speckled, and blotched with olive, brown, or black, and with pale gray or bluish gray underlying markings.

• **BREEDING** The nest is a loosely built cup of twigs, stems, grass, roots, and cobwebs, lined with roots, grass, and hair. It is sited on the outer branches of a small tree in stunted open forest, olive groves, dry mountain scrub, plantations, orchards, and gardens.

• *gray secondary marks*

• **RANGE** The Orphean Warbler breeds throughout much of southern Europe and North Africa, ranging eastward through the Middle East to Iran and Pakistan. It winters in tropical Africa, Asia, and India.

Egg size 17–23 x 13–16 mm	Clutch size 4–5, rarely 6	Incubation ♂♀ Unknown

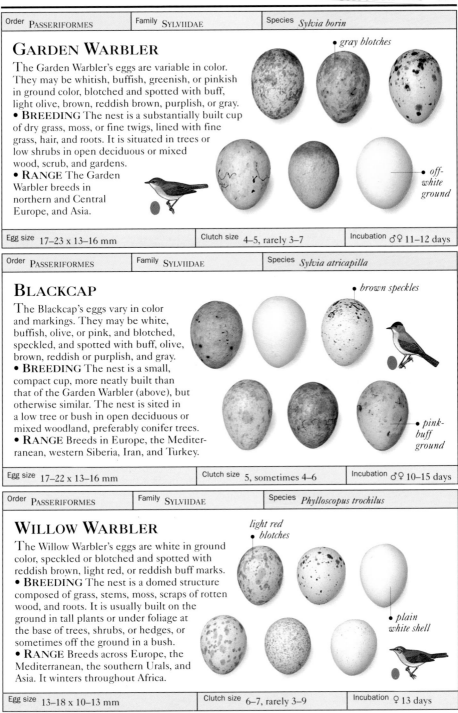

| Order PASSERIFORMES | Family SYLVIIDAE | Species *Sylvia borin* |

GARDEN WARBLER

• *gray blotches*

The Garden Warbler's eggs are variable in color. They may be whitish, buffish, greenish, or pinkish in ground color, blotched and spotted with buff, light olive, brown, reddish brown, purplish, or gray.
• **BREEDING** The nest is a substantially built cup of dry grass, moss, or fine twigs, lined with fine grass, hair, and roots. It is situated in trees or low shrubs in open deciduous or mixed wood, scrub, and gardens.
• **RANGE** The Garden Warbler breeds in northern and Central Europe, and Asia.

• *off-white ground*

| Egg size 17–23 x 13–16 mm | Clutch size 4–5, rarely 3–7 | Incubation ♂♀ 11–12 days |

| Order PASSERIFORMES | Family SYLVIIDAE | Species *Sylvia atricapilla* |

BLACKCAP

• *brown speckles*

The Blackcap's eggs vary in color and markings. They may be white, buffish, olive, or pink, and blotched, speckled, and spotted with buff, olive, brown, reddish or purplish, and gray.
• **BREEDING** The nest is a small, compact cup, more neatly built than that of the Garden Warbler (above), but otherwise similar. The nest is sited in a low tree or bush in open deciduous or mixed woodland, preferably conifer trees.
• **RANGE** Breeds in Europe, the Mediterranean, western Siberia, Iran, and Turkey.

• *pink-buff ground*

| Egg size 17–22 x 13–16 mm | Clutch size 5, sometimes 4–6 | Incubation ♂♀ 10–15 days |

| Order PASSERIFORMES | Family SYLVIIDAE | Species *Phylloscopus trochilus* |

WILLOW WARBLER

light red • *blotches*

The Willow Warbler's eggs are white in ground color, speckled or blotched and spotted with reddish brown, light red, or reddish buff marks.
• **BREEDING** The nest is a domed structure composed of grass, stems, moss, scraps of rotten wood, and roots. It is usually built on the ground in tall plants or under foliage at the base of trees, shrubs, or hedges, or sometimes off the ground in a bush.
• **RANGE** Breeds across Europe, the Mediterranean, the southern Urals, and Asia. It winters throughout Africa.

• *plain white shell*

| Egg size 13–18 x 10–13 mm | Clutch size 6–7, rarely 3–9 | Incubation ♀ 13 days |

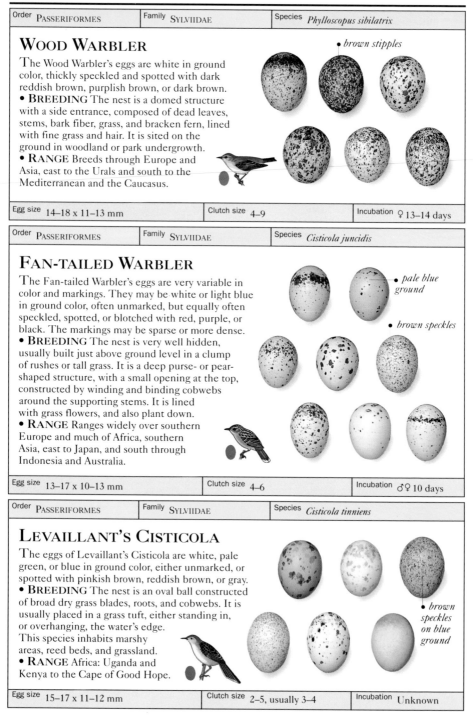

| Order PASSERIFORMES | Family SYLVIIDAE | Species *Phylloscopus sibilatrix* |

WOOD WARBLER

• *brown stipples*

The Wood Warbler's eggs are white in ground color, thickly speckled and spotted with dark reddish brown, purplish brown, or dark brown.
• **BREEDING** The nest is a domed structure with a side entrance, composed of dead leaves, stems, bark fiber, grass, and bracken fern, lined with fine grass and hair. It is sited on the ground in woodland or park undergrowth.
• **RANGE** Breeds through Europe and Asia, east to the Urals and south to the Mediterranean and the Caucasus.

| Egg size 14–18 x 11–13 mm | Clutch size 4–9 | Incubation ♀ 13–14 days |

| Order PASSERIFORMES | Family SYLVIIDAE | Species *Cisticola juncidis* |

FAN-TAILED WARBLER

The Fan-tailed Warbler's eggs are very variable in color and markings. They may be white or light blue in ground color, often unmarked, but equally often speckled, spotted, or blotched with red, purple, or black. The markings may be sparse or more dense.
• **BREEDING** The nest is very well hidden, usually built just above ground level in a clump of rushes or tall grass. It is a deep purse- or pear-shaped structure, with a small opening at the top, constructed by winding and binding cobwebs around the supporting stems. It is lined with grass flowers, and also plant down.
• **RANGE** Ranges widely over southern Europe and much of Africa, southern Asia, east to Japan, and south through Indonesia and Australia.

• *pale blue ground*

• *brown speckles*

| Egg size 13–17 x 10–13 mm | Clutch size 4–6 | Incubation ♂♀ 10 days |

| Order PASSERIFORMES | Family SYLVIIDAE | Species *Cisticola tinniens* |

LEVAILLANT'S CISTICOLA

The eggs of Levaillant's Cisticola are white, pale green, or blue in ground color, either unmarked, or spotted with pinkish brown, reddish brown, or gray.
• **BREEDING** The nest is an oval ball constructed of broad dry grass blades, roots, and cobwebs. It is usually placed in a grass tuft, either standing in, or overhanging, the water's edge. This species inhabits marshy areas, reed beds, and grassland.
• **RANGE** Africa: Uganda and Kenya to the Cape of Good Hope.

• *brown speckles on blue ground*

| Egg size 15–17 x 11–12 mm | Clutch size 2–5, usually 3–4 | Incubation Unknown |

Order PASSERIFORMES	Family SYLVIIDAE	Species *Cisticola erythrops*

RED-FACED CISTICOLA

The eggs of the Red-faced Cisticola are blue, greenish blue, or white in ground color, and are blotched or speckled with red-brown and gray. These markings are often concentrated at the larger end, and form a cap of color.
• **BREEDING** The nest of the Red-faced Cisticola is an oval-shaped ball of leaves, containing a cup made out of dry grass, plant down, and cobwebs. The parent birds gain access to the nest through an entrance in the side of the oval ball of leaves near the top. The nest is situated in the broad leaves of a herb or shrub, usually in or among tall, rank vegetation in marshes, along the borders of rivers, or in cultivated fields some distance away from water.
• **RANGE** The Red-faced Cisticola occurs throughout much of Africa south of the Sahara.

• brown speckles

brown • blotches

cap of color •

pale blue ground •

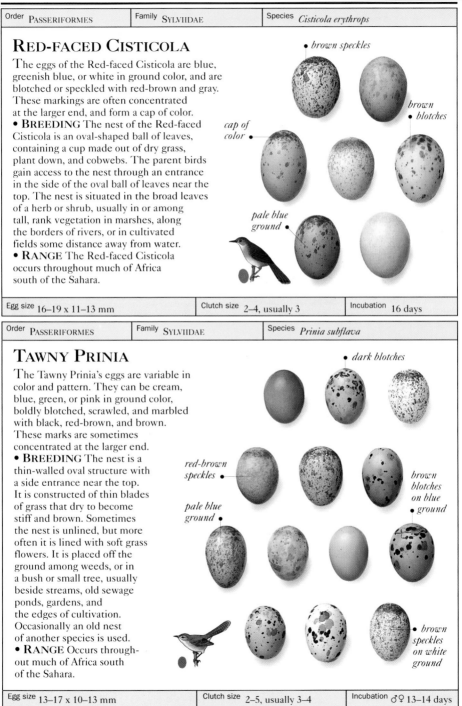

Egg size 16–19 x 11–13 mm	Clutch size 2–4, usually 3	Incubation 16 days

Order PASSERIFORMES	Family SYLVIIDAE	Species *Prinia subflava*

TAWNY PRINIA

The Tawny Prinia's eggs are variable in color and pattern. They can be cream, blue, green, or pink in ground color, boldly blotched, scrawled, and marbled with black, red-brown, and brown. These marks are sometimes concentrated at the larger end.
• **BREEDING** The nest is a thin-walled oval structure with a side entrance near the top. It is constructed of thin blades of grass that dry to become stiff and brown. Sometimes the nest is unlined, but more often it is lined with soft grass flowers. It is placed off the ground among weeds, or in a bush or small tree, usually beside streams, old sewage ponds, gardens, and the edges of cultivation. Occasionally an old nest of another species is used.
• **RANGE** Occurs through-out much of Africa south of the Sahara.

• dark blotches

red-brown speckles •

pale blue ground •

brown blotches on blue • ground

• brown speckles on white ground

Egg size 13–17 x 10–13 mm	Clutch size 2–5, usually 3–4	Incubation ♂♀ 13–14 days

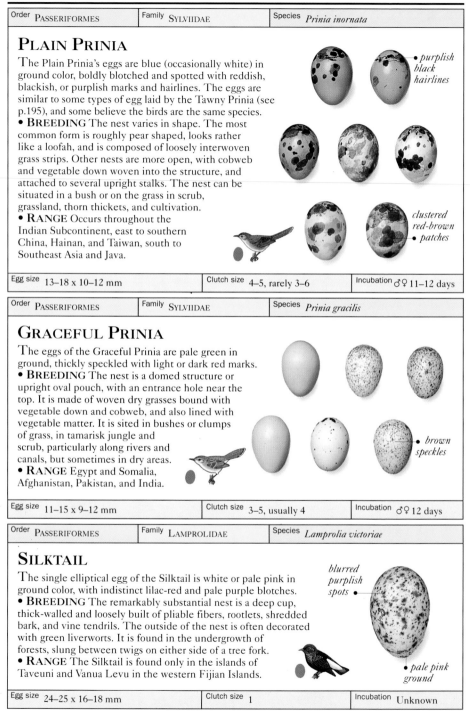

Order PASSERIFORMES	Family SYLVIIDAE	Species *Prinia inornata*

PLAIN PRINIA

The Plain Prinia's eggs are blue (occasionally white) in ground color, boldly blotched and spotted with reddish, blackish, or purplish marks and hairlines. The eggs are similar to some types of egg laid by the Tawny Prinia (see p.195), and some believe the birds are the same species.
• **BREEDING** The nest varies in shape. The most common form is roughly pear shaped, looks rather like a loofah, and is composed of loosely interwoven grass strips. Other nests are more open, with cobweb and vegetable down woven into the structure, and attached to several upright stalks. The nest can be situated in a bush or on the grass in scrub, grassland, thorn thickets, and cultivation.
• **RANGE** Occurs throughout the Indian Subcontinent, east to southern China, Hainan, and Taiwan, south to Southeast Asia and Java.

• *purplish black hairlines*

clustered red-brown
• *patches*

Egg size 13–18 x 10–12 mm	Clutch size 4–5, rarely 3–6	Incubation ♂♀ 11–12 days

Order PASSERIFORMES	Family SYLVIIDAE	Species *Prinia gracilis*

GRACEFUL PRINIA

The eggs of the Graceful Prinia are pale green in ground, thickly speckled with light or dark red marks.
• **BREEDING** The nest is a domed structure or upright oval pouch, with an entrance hole near the top. It is made of woven dry grasses bound with vegetable down and cobweb, and also lined with vegetable matter. It is sited in bushes or clumps of grass, in tamarisk jungle and scrub, particularly along rivers and canals, but sometimes in dry areas.
• **RANGE** Egypt and Somalia, Afghanistan, Pakistan, and India.

• *brown speckles*

Egg size 11–15 x 9–12 mm	Clutch size 3–5, usually 4	Incubation ♂♀ 12 days

Order PASSERIFORMES	Family LAMPROLIDAE	Species *Lamprolia victoriae*

SILKTAIL

The single elliptical egg of the Silktail is white or pale pink in ground color, with indistinct lilac-red and pale purple blotches.
• **BREEDING** The remarkably substantial nest is a deep cup, thick-walled and loosely built of pliable fibers, rootlets, shredded bark, and vine tendrils. The outside of the nest is often decorated with green liverworts. It is found in the undergrowth of forests, slung between twigs on either side of a tree fork.
• **RANGE** The Silktail is found only in the islands of Taveuni and Vanua Levu in the western Fijian Islands.

blurred purplish spots •

• *pale pink ground*

Egg size 24–25 x 16–18 mm	Clutch size 1	Incubation Unknown

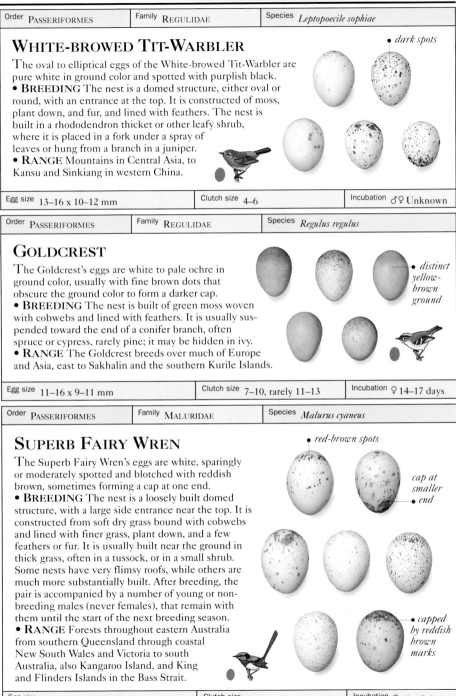

| Order PASSERIFORMES | Family REGULIDAE | Species *Leptopoecile sophiae* |

WHITE-BROWED TIT-WARBLER

• *dark spots*

The oval to elliptical eggs of the White-browed Tit-Warbler are pure white in ground color and spotted with purplish black.
• **BREEDING** The nest is a domed structure, either oval or round, with an entrance at the top. It is constructed of moss, plant down, and fur, and lined with feathers. The nest is built in a rhododendron thicket or other leafy shrub, where it is placed in a fork under a spray of leaves or hung from a branch in a juniper.
• **RANGE** Mountains in Central Asia, to Kansu and Sinkiang in western China.

| Egg size 13–16 x 10–12 mm | Clutch size 4–6 | Incubation ♂♀ Unknown |

| Order PASSERIFORMES | Family REGULIDAE | Species *Regulus regulus* |

GOLDCREST

The Goldcrest's eggs are white to pale ochre in ground color, usually with fine brown dots that obscure the ground color to form a darker cap.
• **BREEDING** The nest is built of green moss woven with cobwebs and lined with feathers. It is usually suspended toward the end of a conifer branch, often spruce or cypress, rarely pine; it may be hidden in ivy.
• **RANGE** The Goldcrest breeds over much of Europe and Asia, east to Sakhalin and the southern Kurile Islands.

• *distinct yellow-brown ground*

| Egg size 11–16 x 9–11 mm | Clutch size 7–10, rarely 11–13 | Incubation ♀ 14–17 days |

| Order PASSERIFORMES | Family MALURIDAE | Species *Malurus cyaneus* |

SUPERB FAIRY WREN

The Superb Fairy Wren's eggs are white, sparingly or moderately spotted and blotched with reddish brown, sometimes forming a cap at one end.
• **BREEDING** The nest is a loosely built domed structure, with a large side entrance near the top. It is constructed from soft dry grass bound with cobwebs and lined with finer grass, plant down, and a few feathers or fur. It is usually built near the ground in thick grass, often in a tussock, or in a small shrub. Some nests have very flimsy roofs, while others are much more substantially built. After breeding, the pair is accompanied by a number of young or non-breeding males (never females), that remain with them until the start of the next breeding season.
• **RANGE** Forests throughout eastern Australia from southern Queensland through coastal New South Wales and Victoria to south Australia, also Kangaroo Island, and King and Flinders Islands in the Bass Strait.

• *red-brown spots*

cap at smaller
• *end*

• *capped by reddish brown marks*

| Egg size 15–19 x 11–14 mm | Clutch size 3–4 | Incubation ♀ 13–15 days |

Order PASSERIFORMES	Family EPHTHIANURIDAE	Species *Ephthianura albifrons*

WHITE-FRONTED CHAT

The White-fronted Chat lays eggs that are white or pale pinkish white, sparingly spotted and blotched with dark reddish brown and reddish black.
• **BREEDING** The nest is a neat cup of fine twigs, coarse grass, and rootlets. It is lined with fine grass and hair picked off barbed wire fences. The nest is hidden low down in a shrub.
• **RANGE** Occurs in Tasmania, southern Australia, and Queensland.

loose cluster of spots at larger end

Egg size 15–18 x 11–14 mm	Clutch size 2–4, usually 3	Incubation Unknown

Order PASSERIFORMES	Family ACANTHIZIDAE	Species *Dasyornis broadbenti*

RUFOUS BRISTLEBIRD

The eggs of the Rufous Bristlebird are pale brown or brownish white in ground color, and spotted and blotched in purplish brown with a reddish hue that can obscure this paler ground.
• **BREEDING** The nest is a large, loosely built oval structure, which stands on one end and has a pointed top with a large side entrance hole close by. It is constructed of fine stiff pieces of grass stalk and other coarse grasses and is lined with finer grass. The nest is found close to the ground in a tuft of grass, in a small, dense shrub.
• **RANGE** This species occurs in coastal regions of Victoria and southwestern Australia.

dark marks cover pale brown ground

oval to elliptical shape

Egg size 27–32 x 20–21 mm	Clutch size 2	Incubation Unknown

Order PASSERIFORMES	Family ACANTHIZIDAE	Species *Origma solitaria*

ROCK WARBLER

The Rock Warbler's eggs are pure white in ground color, occasionally with a few blackish spots at the larger end.
• **BREEDING** The nest is a domed structure with an entrance at the side, made of dry grass, bark, rootlets, and moss, bound with cobwebs, and lined with feathers, plant down, or fur. It is suspended from the top and placed in dark recesses beneath an overhanging rock ledge, in a cave, under a bridge, or occasionally in a deserted building.
• **RANGE** Found solely in the sandstone hills of eastern New South Wales, in Australia.

plain white shell

Egg size 19–22 x 15–16 mm	Clutch size 3	Incubation Unknown

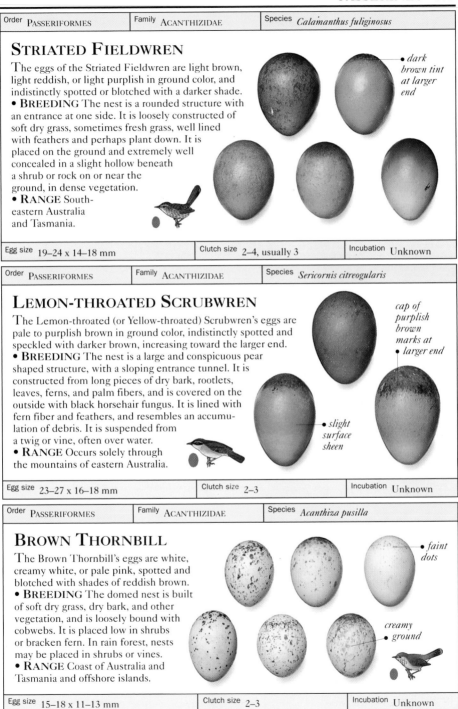

| Order | PASSERIFORMES | Family | ACANTHIZIDAE | Species | *Calamanthus fuliginosus* |

STRIATED FIELDWREN

The eggs of the Striated Fieldwren are light brown,
light reddish, or light purplish in ground color, and
indistinctly spotted or blotched with a darker shade.

• **BREEDING** The nest is a rounded structure with
an entrance at one side. It is loosely constructed of
soft dry grass, sometimes fresh grass, well lined
with feathers and perhaps plant down. It is
placed on the ground and extremely well
concealed in a slight hollow beneath
a shrub or rock on or near the
ground, in dense vegetation.

• **RANGE** South-
eastern Australia
and Tasmania.

*• dark
brown tint
at larger
end*

| Egg size | 19–24 x 14–18 mm | Clutch size | 2–4, usually 3 | Incubation | Unknown |

| Order | PASSERIFORMES | Family | ACANTHIZIDAE | Species | *Sericornis citreogularis* |

LEMON-THROATED SCRUBWREN

The Lemon-throated (or Yellow-throated) Scrubwren's eggs are
pale to purplish brown in ground color, indistinctly spotted and
speckled with darker brown, increasing toward the larger end.

• **BREEDING** The nest is a large and conspicuous pear
shaped structure, with a sloping entrance tunnel. It is
constructed from long pieces of dry bark, rootlets,
leaves, ferns, and palm fibers, and is covered on the
outside with black horsehair fungus. It is lined with
fern fiber and feathers, and resembles an accumu-
lation of debris. It is suspended from
a twig or vine, often over water.

• **RANGE** Occurs solely through
the mountains of eastern Australia.

*cap of
purplish
brown
marks at
• larger end*

*• slight
surface
sheen*

| Egg size | 23–27 x 16–18 mm | Clutch size | 2–3 | Incubation | Unknown |

| Order | PASSERIFORMES | Family | ACANTHIZIDAE | Species | *Acanthiza pusilla* |

BROWN THORNBILL

The Brown Thornbill's eggs are white,
creamy white, or pale pink, spotted and
blotched with shades of reddish brown.

• **BREEDING** The domed nest is built
of soft dry grass, dry bark, and other
vegetation, and is loosely bound with
cobwebs. It is placed low in shrubs
or bracken fern. In rain forest, nests
may be placed in shrubs or vines.

• **RANGE** Coast of Australia and
Tasmania and offshore islands.

*• faint
dots*

*creamy
• ground*

| Egg size | 15–18 x 11–13 mm | Clutch size | 2–3 | Incubation | Unknown |

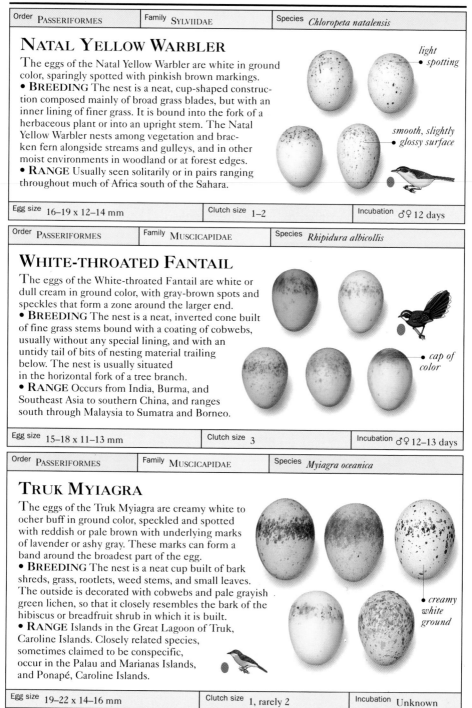

Order PASSERIFORMES	Family SYLVIIDAE	Species *Chloropeta natalensis*

NATAL YELLOW WARBLER

The eggs of the Natal Yellow Warbler are white in ground color, sparingly spotted with pinkish brown markings.
• **BREEDING** The nest is a neat, cup-shaped construction composed mainly of broad grass blades, but with an inner lining of finer grass. It is bound into the fork of a herbaceous plant or into an upright stem. The Natal Yellow Warbler nests among vegetation and bracken fern alongside streams and gulleys, and in other moist environments in woodland or at forest edges.
• **RANGE** Usually seen solitarily or in pairs ranging throughout much of Africa south of the Sahara.

light • *spotting*

smooth, slightly • *glossy surface*

Egg size 16–19 x 12–14 mm	Clutch size 1–2	Incubation ♂♀ 12 days

Order PASSERIFORMES	Family MUSCICAPIDAE	Species *Rhipidura albicollis*

WHITE-THROATED FANTAIL

The eggs of the White-throated Fantail are white or dull cream in ground color, with gray-brown spots and speckles that form a zone around the larger end.
• **BREEDING** The nest is a neat, inverted cone built of fine grass stems bound with a coating of cobwebs, usually without any special lining, and with an untidy tail of bits of nesting material trailing below. The nest is usually situated in the horizontal fork of a tree branch.
• **RANGE** Occurs from India, Burma, and Southeast Asia to southern China, and ranges south through Malaysia to Sumatra and Borneo.

cap of • *color*

Egg size 15–18 x 11–13 mm	Clutch size 3	Incubation ♂♀ 12–13 days

Order PASSERIFORMES	Family MUSCICAPIDAE	Species *Myiagra oceanica*

TRUK MYIAGRA

The eggs of the Truk Myiagra are creamy white to ocher buff in ground color, speckled and spotted with reddish or pale brown with underlying marks of lavender or ashy gray. These marks can form a band around the broadest part of the egg.
• **BREEDING** The nest is a neat cup built of bark shreds, grass, rootlets, weed stems, and small leaves. The outside is decorated with cobwebs and pale grayish green lichen, so that it closely resembles the bark of the hibiscus or breadfruit shrub in which it is built.
• **RANGE** Islands in the Great Lagoon of Truk, Caroline Islands. Closely related species, sometimes claimed to be conspecific, occur in the Palau and Marianas Islands, and Ponapé, Caroline Islands.

creamy • *white* *ground*

Egg size 19–22 x 14–16 mm	Clutch size 1, rarely 2	Incubation Unknown

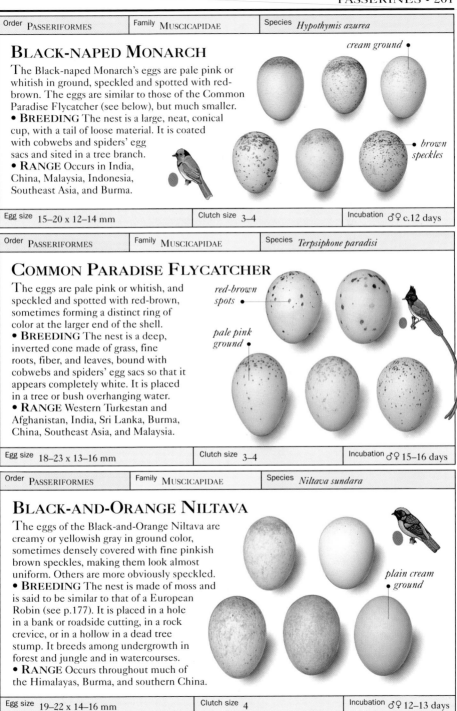

Order PASSERIFORMES	Family MUSCICAPIDAE	Species *Hypothymis azurea*

BLACK-NAPED MONARCH

The Black-naped Monarch's eggs are pale pink or whitish in ground, speckled and spotted with red-brown. The eggs are similar to those of the Common Paradise Flycatcher (see below), but much smaller.
• **BREEDING** The nest is a large, neat, conical cup, with a tail of loose material. It is coated with cobwebs and spiders' egg sacs and sited in a tree branch.
• **RANGE** Occurs in India, China, Malaysia, Indonesia, Southeast Asia, and Burma.

cream ground •

• *brown speckles*

Egg size 15–20 x 12–14 mm	Clutch size 3–4	Incubation ♂♀ c.12 days

Order PASSERIFORMES	Family MUSCICAPIDAE	Species *Terpsiphone paradisi*

COMMON PARADISE FLYCATCHER

The eggs are pale pink or whitish, and speckled and spotted with red-brown, sometimes forming a distinct ring of color at the larger end of the shell.
• **BREEDING** The nest is a deep, inverted cone made of grass, fine roots, fiber, and leaves, bound with cobwebs and spiders' egg sacs so that it appears completely white. It is placed in a tree or bush overhanging water.
• **RANGE** Western Turkestan and Afghanistan, India, Sri Lanka, Burma, China, Southeast Asia, and Malaysia.

red-brown spots •

pale pink ground •

Egg size 18–23 x 13–16 mm	Clutch size 3–4	Incubation ♂♀ 15–16 days

Order PASSERIFORMES	Family MUSCICAPIDAE	Species *Niltava sundara*

BLACK-AND-ORANGE NILTAVA

The eggs of the Black-and-Orange Niltava are creamy or yellowish gray in ground color, sometimes densely covered with fine pinkish brown speckles, making them look almost uniform. Others are more obviously speckled.
• **BREEDING** The nest is made of moss and is said to be similar to that of a European Robin (see p.177). It is placed in a hole in a bank or roadside cutting, in a rock crevice, or in a hollow in a dead tree stump. It breeds among undergrowth in forest and jungle and in watercourses.
• **RANGE** Occurs throughout much of the Himalayas, Burma, and southern China.

plain cream • *ground*

Egg size 19–22 x 14–16 mm	Clutch size 4	Incubation ♂♀ 12–13 days

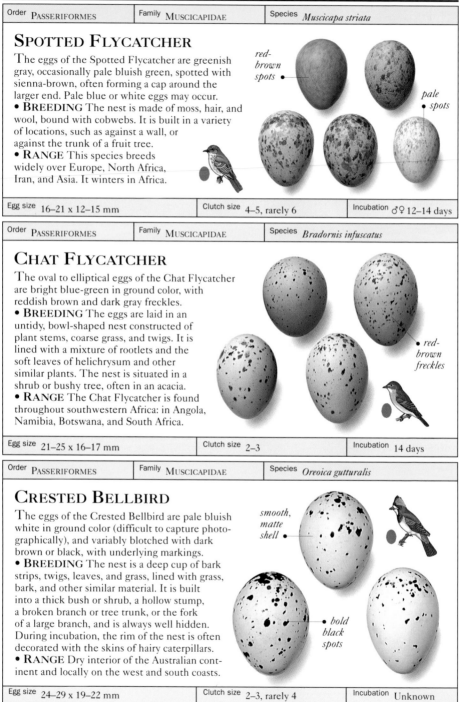

Order PASSERIFORMES	Family MUSCICAPIDAE	Species *Muscicapa striata*

SPOTTED FLYCATCHER

The eggs of the Spotted Flycatcher are greenish gray, occasionally pale bluish green, spotted with sienna-brown, often forming a cap around the larger end. Pale blue or white eggs may occur.
• **BREEDING** The nest is made of moss, hair, and wool, bound with cobwebs. It is built in a variety of locations, such as against a wall, or against the trunk of a fruit tree.
• **RANGE** This species breeds widely over Europe, North Africa, Iran, and Asia. It winters in Africa.

red-brown spots

pale spots

Egg size 16–21 x 12–15 mm	Clutch size 4–5, rarely 6	Incubation ♂♀ 12–14 days

Order PASSERIFORMES	Family MUSCICAPIDAE	Species *Bradornis infuscatus*

CHAT FLYCATCHER

The oval to elliptical eggs of the Chat Flycatcher are bright blue-green in ground color, with reddish brown and dark gray freckles.
• **BREEDING** The eggs are laid in an untidy, bowl-shaped nest constructed of plant stems, coarse grass, and twigs. It is lined with a mixture of rootlets and the soft leaves of helichrysum and other similar plants. The nest is situated in a shrub or bushy tree, often in an acacia.
• **RANGE** The Chat Flycatcher is found throughout southwestern Africa: in Angola, Namibia, Botswana, and South Africa.

red-brown freckles

Egg size 21–25 x 16–17 mm	Clutch size 2–3	Incubation 14 days

Order PASSERIFORMES	Family MUSCICAPIDAE	Species *Oreoica gutturalis*

CRESTED BELLBIRD

The eggs of the Crested Bellbird are pale bluish white in ground color (difficult to capture photographically), and variably blotched with dark brown or black, with underlying markings.
• **BREEDING** The nest is a deep cup of bark strips, twigs, leaves, and grass, lined with grass, bark, and other similar material. It is built into a thick bush or shrub, a hollow stump, a broken branch or tree trunk, or the fork of a large branch, and is always well hidden. During incubation, the rim of the nest is often decorated with the skins of hairy caterpillars.
• **RANGE** Dry interior of the Australian continent and locally on the west and south coasts.

smooth, matte shell

bold black spots

Egg size 24–29 x 19–22 mm	Clutch size 2–3, rarely 4	Incubation Unknown

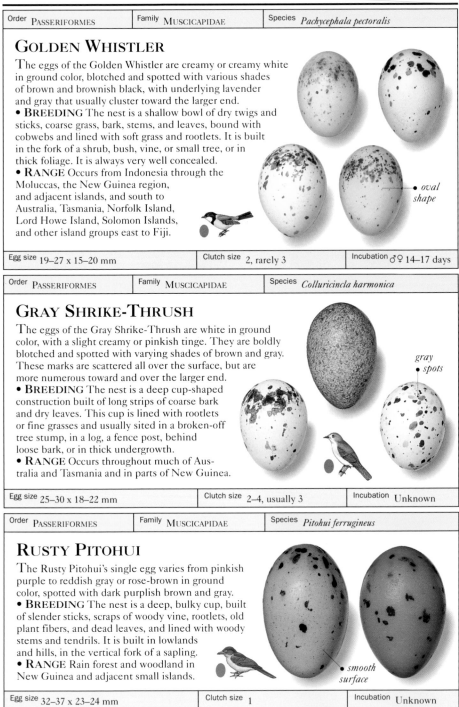

Order PASSERIFORMES	Family MUSCICAPIDAE	Species *Pachycephala pectoralis*

GOLDEN WHISTLER

The eggs of the Golden Whistler are creamy or creamy white in ground color, blotched and spotted with various shades of brown and brownish black, with underlying lavender and gray that usually cluster toward the larger end.
• **BREEDING** The nest is a shallow bowl of dry twigs and sticks, coarse grass, bark, stems, and leaves, bound with cobwebs and lined with soft grass and rootlets. It is built in the fork of a shrub, bush, vine, or small tree, or in thick foliage. It is always very well concealed.
• **RANGE** Occurs from Indonesia through the Moluccas, the New Guinea region, and adjacent islands, and south to Australia, Tasmania, Norfolk Island, Lord Howe Island, Solomon Islands, and other island groups east to Fiji.

• *oval shape*

Egg size 19–27 x 15–20 mm	Clutch size 2, rarely 3	Incubation ♂♀ 14–17 days

Order PASSERIFORMES	Family MUSCICAPIDAE	Species *Colluricincla harmonica*

GRAY SHRIKE-THRUSH

The eggs of the Gray Shrike-Thrush are white in ground color, with a slight creamy or pinkish tinge. They are boldly blotched and spotted with varying shades of brown and gray. These marks are scattered all over the surface, but are more numerous toward and over the larger end.
• **BREEDING** The nest is a deep cup-shaped construction built of long strips of coarse bark and dry leaves. This cup is lined with rootlets or fine grasses and usually sited in a broken-off tree stump, in a log, a fence post, behind loose bark, or in thick undergrowth.
• **RANGE** Occurs throughout much of Australia and Tasmania and in parts of New Guinea.

gray spots

Egg size 25–30 x 18–22 mm	Clutch size 2–4, usually 3	Incubation Unknown

Order PASSERIFORMES	Family MUSCICAPIDAE	Species *Pitohui ferrugineus*

RUSTY PITOHUI

The Rusty Pitohui's single egg varies from pinkish purple to reddish gray or rose-brown in ground color, spotted with dark purplish brown and gray.
• **BREEDING** The nest is a deep, bulky cup, built of slender sticks, scraps of woody vine, rootlets, old plant fibers, and dead leaves, and lined with woody stems and tendrils. It is built in lowlands and hills, in the vertical fork of a sapling.
• **RANGE** Rain forest and woodland in New Guinea and adjacent small islands.

smooth surface

Egg size 32–37 x 23–24 mm	Clutch size 1	Incubation Unknown

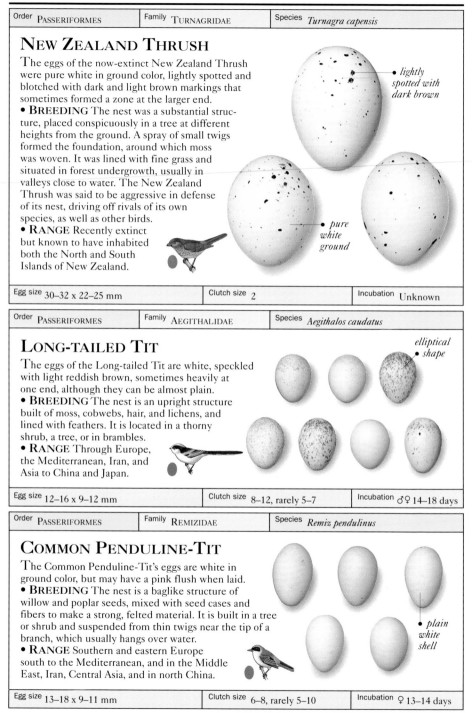

Order PASSERIFORMES	Family TURNAGRIDAE	Species *Turnagra capensis*

NEW ZEALAND THRUSH

The eggs of the now-extinct New Zealand Thrush were pure white in ground color, lightly spotted and blotched with dark and light brown markings that sometimes formed a zone at the larger end.
• **BREEDING** The nest was a substantial structure, placed conspicuously in a tree at different heights from the ground. A spray of small twigs formed the foundation, around which moss was woven. It was lined with fine grass and situated in forest undergrowth, usually in valleys close to water. The New Zealand Thrush was said to be aggressive in defense of its nest, driving off rivals of its own species, as well as other birds.
• **RANGE** Recently extinct but known to have inhabited both the North and South Islands of New Zealand.

lightly spotted with dark brown

pure white ground

Egg size 30–32 x 22–25 mm	Clutch size 2	Incubation Unknown

Order PASSERIFORMES	Family AEGITHALIDAE	Species *Aegithalos caudatus*

LONG-TAILED TIT

The eggs of the Long-tailed Tit are white, speckled with light reddish brown, sometimes heavily at one end, although they can be almost plain.
• **BREEDING** The nest is an upright structure built of moss, cobwebs, hair, and lichens, and lined with feathers. It is located in a thorny shrub, a tree, or in brambles.
• **RANGE** Through Europe, the Mediterranean, Iran, and Asia to China and Japan.

elliptical shape

Egg size 12–16 x 9–12 mm	Clutch size 8–12, rarely 5–7	Incubation ♂♀ 14–18 days

Order PASSERIFORMES	Family REMIZIDAE	Species *Remiz pendulinus*

COMMON PENDULINE-TIT

The Common Penduline-Tit's eggs are white in ground color, but may have a pink flush when laid.
• **BREEDING** The nest is a baglike structure of willow and poplar seeds, mixed with seed cases and fibers to make a strong, felted material. It is built in a tree or shrub and suspended from thin twigs near the tip of a branch, which usually hangs over water.
• **RANGE** Southern and eastern Europe south to the Mediterranean, and in the Middle East, Iran, Central Asia, and in north China.

plain white shell

Egg size 13–18 x 9–11 mm	Clutch size 6–8, rarely 5–10	Incubation ♀ 13–14 days

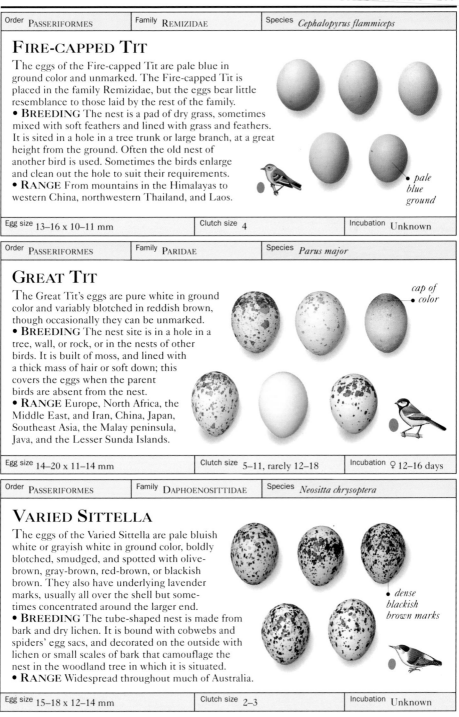

Order PASSERIFORMES	Family REMIZIDAE	Species *Cephalopyrus flammiceps*

FIRE-CAPPED TIT

The eggs of the Fire-capped Tit are pale blue in ground color and unmarked. The Fire-capped Tit is placed in the family Remizidae, but the eggs bear little resemblance to those laid by the rest of the family.
• BREEDING The nest is a pad of dry grass, sometimes mixed with soft feathers and lined with grass and feathers. It is sited in a hole in a tree trunk or large branch, at a great height from the ground. Often the old nest of another bird is used. Sometimes the birds enlarge and clean out the hole to suit their requirements.
• RANGE From mountains in the Himalayas to western China, northwestern Thailand, and Laos.

pale blue ground

Egg size 13–16 x 10–11 mm	Clutch size 4	Incubation Unknown

Order PASSERIFORMES	Family PARIDAE	Species *Parus major*

GREAT TIT

The Great Tit's eggs are pure white in ground color and variably blotched in reddish brown, though occasionally they can be unmarked.
• BREEDING The nest site is in a hole in a tree, wall, or rock, or in the nests of other birds. It is built of moss, and lined with a thick mass of hair or soft down; this covers the eggs when the parent birds are absent from the nest.
• RANGE Europe, North Africa, the Middle East, and Iran, China, Japan, Southeast Asia, the Malay peninsula, Java, and the Lesser Sunda Islands.

cap of color

Egg size 14–20 x 11–14 mm	Clutch size 5–11, rarely 12–18	Incubation ♀ 12–16 days

Order PASSERIFORMES	Family DAPHOENOSITTIDAE	Species *Neositta chrysoptera*

VARIED SITTELLA

The eggs of the Varied Sittella are pale bluish white or grayish white in ground color, boldly blotched, smudged, and spotted with olive-brown, gray-brown, red-brown, or blackish brown. They also have underlying lavender marks, usually all over the shell but sometimes concentrated around the larger end.
• BREEDING The tube-shaped nest is made from bark and dry lichen. It is bound with cobwebs and spiders' egg sacs, and decorated on the outside with lichen or small scales of bark that camouflage the nest in the woodland tree in which it is situated.
• RANGE Widespread throughout much of Australia.

dense blackish brown marks

Egg size 15–18 x 12–14 mm	Clutch size 2–3	Incubation Unknown

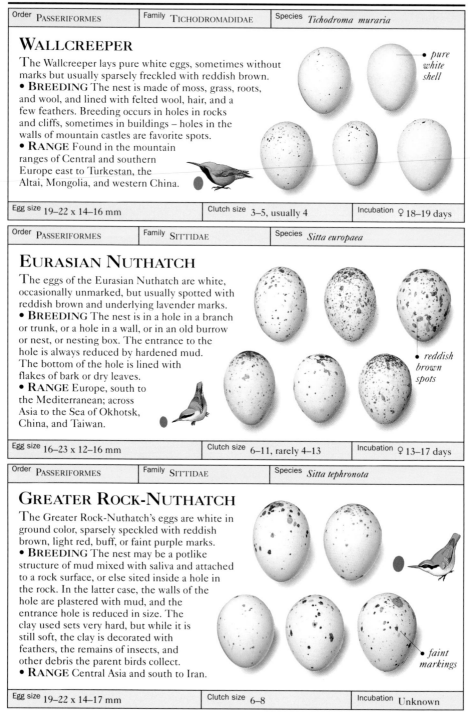

Order PASSERIFORMES	Family TICHODROMADIDAE	Species *Tichodroma muraria*

WALLCREEPER

The Wallcreeper lays pure white eggs, sometimes without marks but usually sparsely freckled with reddish brown.
• **BREEDING** The nest is made of moss, grass, roots, and wool, and lined with felted wool, hair, and a few feathers. Breeding occurs in holes in rocks and cliffs, sometimes in buildings – holes in the walls of mountain castles are favorite spots.
• **RANGE** Found in the mountain ranges of Central and southern Europe east to Turkestan, the Altai, Mongolia, and western China.

• *pure white shell*

Egg size 19–22 x 14–16 mm	Clutch size 3–5, usually 4	Incubation ♀ 18–19 days

Order PASSERIFORMES	Family SITTIDAE	Species *Sitta europaea*

EURASIAN NUTHATCH

The eggs of the Eurasian Nuthatch are white, occasionally unmarked, but usually spotted with reddish brown and underlying lavender marks.
• **BREEDING** The nest is in a hole in a branch or trunk, or a hole in a wall, in an old burrow or nest, or nesting box. The entrance to the hole is always reduced by hardened mud. The bottom of the hole is lined with flakes of bark or dry leaves.
• **RANGE** Europe, south to the Mediterranean; across Asia to the Sea of Okhotsk, China, and Taiwan.

• *reddish brown spots*

Egg size 16–23 x 12–16 mm	Clutch size 6–11, rarely 4–13	Incubation ♀ 13–17 days

Order PASSERIFORMES	Family SITTIDAE	Species *Sitta tephronota*

GREATER ROCK-NUTHATCH

The Greater Rock-Nuthatch's eggs are white in ground color, sparsely speckled with reddish brown, light red, buff, or faint purple marks.
• **BREEDING** The nest may be a potlike structure of mud mixed with saliva and attached to a rock surface, or else sited inside a hole in the rock. In the latter case, the walls of the hole are plastered with mud, and the entrance hole is reduced in size. The clay used sets very hard, but while it is still soft, the clay is decorated with feathers, the remains of insects, and other debris the parent birds collect.
• **RANGE** Central Asia and south to Iran.

• *faint markings*

Egg size 19–22 x 14–17 mm	Clutch size 6–8	Incubation Unknown

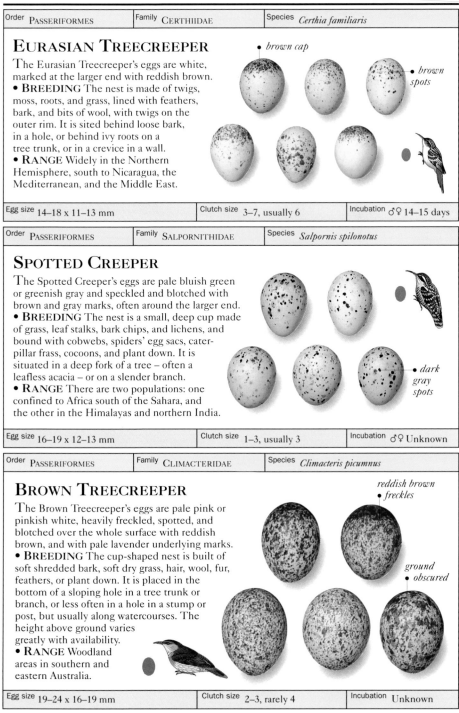

| Order | PASSERIFORMES | Family | CERTHIIDAE | Species | *Certhia familiaris* |

EURASIAN TREECREEPER

• *brown cap*

The Eurasian Treecreeper's eggs are white, marked at the larger end with reddish brown.
• **BREEDING** The nest is made of twigs, moss, roots, and grass, lined with feathers, bark, and bits of wool, with twigs on the outer rim. It is sited behind loose bark, in a hole, or behind ivy roots on a tree trunk, or in a crevice in a wall.
• **RANGE** Widely in the Northern Hemisphere, south to Nicaragua, the Mediterranean, and the Middle East.

• *brown spots*

| Egg size 14–18 x 11–13 mm | Clutch size 3–7, usually 6 | Incubation ♂♀ 14–15 days |

| Order | PASSERIFORMES | Family | SALPORNITHIDAE | Species | *Salpornis spilonotus* |

SPOTTED CREEPER

The Spotted Creeper's eggs are pale bluish green or greenish gray and speckled and blotched with brown and gray marks, often around the larger end.
• **BREEDING** The nest is a small, deep cup made of grass, leaf stalks, bark chips, and lichens, and bound with cobwebs, spiders' egg sacs, caterpillar frass, cocoons, and plant down. It is situated in a deep fork of a tree – often a leafless acacia – or on a slender branch.
• **RANGE** There are two populations: one confined to Africa south of the Sahara, and the other in the Himalayas and northern India.

• *dark gray spots*

| Egg size 16–19 x 12–13 mm | Clutch size 1–3, usually 3 | Incubation ♂♀ Unknown |

| Order | PASSERIFORMES | Family | CLIMACTERIDAE | Species | *Climacteris picumnus* |

BROWN TREECREEPER

reddish brown
• *freckles*

The Brown Treecreeper's eggs are pale pink or pinkish white, heavily freckled, spotted, and blotched over the whole surface with reddish brown, and with pale lavender underlying marks.
• **BREEDING** The cup-shaped nest is built of soft shredded bark, soft dry grass, hair, wool, fur, feathers, or plant down. It is placed in the bottom of a sloping hole in a tree trunk or branch, or less often in a hole in a stump or post, but usually along watercourses. The height above ground varies greatly with availability.
• **RANGE** Woodland areas in southern and eastern Australia.

ground
• *obscured*

| Egg size 19–24 x 16–19 mm | Clutch size 2–3, rarely 4 | Incubation Unknown |

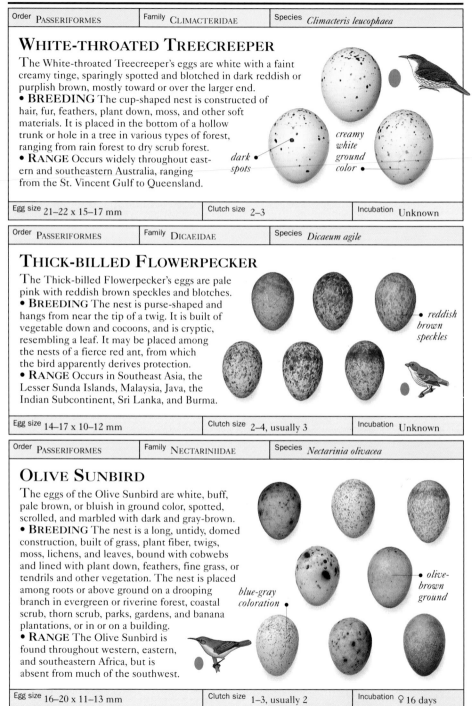

Order PASSERIFORMES	Family CLIMACTERIDAE	Species *Climacteris leucophaea*

WHITE-THROATED TREECREEPER

The White-throated Treecreeper's eggs are white with a faint creamy tinge, sparingly spotted and blotched in dark reddish or purplish brown, mostly toward or over the larger end.
• **BREEDING** The cup-shaped nest is constructed of hair, fur, feathers, plant down, moss, and other soft materials. It is placed in the bottom of a hollow trunk or hole in a tree in various types of forest, ranging from rain forest to dry scrub forest.
• **RANGE** Occurs widely throughout eastern and southeastern Australia, ranging from the St. Vincent Gulf to Queensland.

dark spots

creamy white ground color

Egg size 21–22 x 15–17 mm	Clutch size 2–3	Incubation Unknown

Order PASSERIFORMES	Family DICAEIDAE	Species *Dicaeum agile*

THICK-BILLED FLOWERPECKER

The Thick-billed Flowerpecker's eggs are pale pink with reddish brown speckles and blotches.
• **BREEDING** The nest is purse-shaped and hangs from near the tip of a twig. It is built of vegetable down and cocoons, and is cryptic, resembling a leaf. It may be placed among the nests of a fierce red ant, from which the bird apparently derives protection.
• **RANGE** Occurs in Southeast Asia, the Lesser Sunda Islands, Malaysia, Java, the Indian Subcontinent, Sri Lanka, and Burma.

reddish brown speckles

Egg size 14–17 x 10–12 mm	Clutch size 2–4, usually 3	Incubation Unknown

Order PASSERIFORMES	Family NECTARINIIDAE	Species *Nectarinia olivacea*

OLIVE SUNBIRD

The eggs of the Olive Sunbird are white, buff, pale brown, or bluish in ground color, spotted, scrolled, and marbled with dark and gray-brown.
• **BREEDING** The nest is a long, untidy, domed construction, built of grass, plant fiber, twigs, moss, lichens, and leaves, bound with cobwebs and lined with plant down, feathers, fine grass, or tendrils and other vegetation. The nest is placed among roots or above ground on a drooping branch in evergreen or riverine forest, coastal scrub, thorn scrub, parks, gardens, and banana plantations, or in or on a building.
• **RANGE** The Olive Sunbird is found throughout western, eastern, and southeastern Africa, but is absent from much of the southwest.

blue-gray coloration

olive-brown ground

Egg size 16–20 x 11–13 mm	Clutch size 1–3, usually 2	Incubation ♀ 16 days

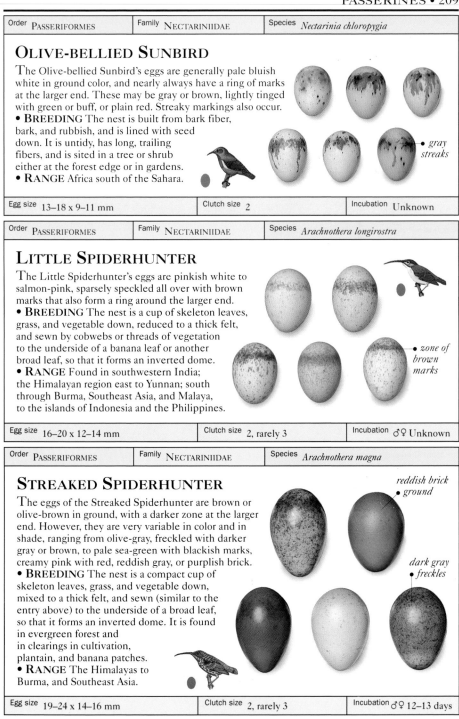

Order PASSERIFORMES	Family NECTARINIIDAE	Species *Nectarinia chloropygia*

OLIVE-BELLIED SUNBIRD

The Olive-bellied Sunbird's eggs are generally pale bluish white in ground color, and nearly always have a ring of marks at the larger end. These may be gray or brown, lightly tinged with green or buff, or plain red. Streaky markings also occur.
• **BREEDING** The nest is built from bark fiber, bark, and rubbish, and is lined with seed down. It is untidy, has long, trailing fibers, and is sited in a tree or shrub either at the forest edge or in gardens.
• **RANGE** Africa south of the Sahara.

gray streaks

Egg size 13–18 x 9–11 mm	Clutch size 2	Incubation Unknown

Order PASSERIFORMES	Family NECTARINIIDAE	Species *Arachnothera longirostra*

LITTLE SPIDERHUNTER

The Little Spiderhunter's eggs are pinkish white to salmon-pink, sparsely speckled all over with brown marks that also form a ring around the larger end.
• **BREEDING** The nest is a cup of skeleton leaves, grass, and vegetable down, reduced to a thick felt, and sewn by cobwebs or threads of vegetation to the underside of a banana leaf or another broad leaf, so that it forms an inverted dome.
• **RANGE** Found in southwestern India; the Himalayan region east to Yunnan; south through Burma, Southeast Asia, and Malaya, to the islands of Indonesia and the Philippines.

zone of brown marks

Egg size 16–20 x 12–14 mm	Clutch size 2, rarely 3	Incubation ♂♀ Unknown

Order PASSERIFORMES	Family NECTARINIIDAE	Species *Arachnothera magna*

STREAKED SPIDERHUNTER

reddish brick ground

The eggs of the Streaked Spiderhunter are brown or olive-brown in ground, with a darker zone at the larger end. However, they are very variable in color and in shade, ranging from olive-gray, freckled with darker gray or brown, to pale sea-green with blackish marks, creamy pink with red, reddish gray, or purplish brick.
• **BREEDING** The nest is a compact cup of skeleton leaves, grass, and vegetable down, mixed to a thick felt, and sewn (similar to the entry above) to the underside of a broad leaf, so that it forms an inverted dome. It is found in evergreen forest and in clearings in cultivation, plantain, and banana patches.
• **RANGE** The Himalayas to Burma, and Southeast Asia.

dark gray freckles

Egg size 19–24 x 14–16 mm	Clutch size 2, rarely 3	Incubation ♂♀ 12–13 days

Order PASSERIFORMES	Family NECTARINIIDAE	Species *Arachnothera chrysogenys*

YELLOW-EARED SPIDERHUNTER

• *ring of marks*

The eggs of the Yellow-eared Spiderhunter are grayish white in ground color, streaked and scribbled with sepia and grayish brown.
• **BREEDING** The nest is a dome-shaped construction, sometimes with an entrance tunnel. It is often hung from the undersurface of a palm frond or banana leaf in the upper stories of forest, forest edge, and sometimes woody gardens.
• **RANGE** Occurs through extreme southern Burma, south across the Malay peninsula to Sumatra, Java, and Borneo.

Egg size 21 x 15 mm	Clutch size 2	Incubation Unknown

Order PASSERIFORMES	Family ZOSTEROPIDAE	Species *Zosterops palpebrosa*

ORIENTAL WHITE-EYE

The eggs of all species of white-eye are similar in appearance, differing only in the tone of blue of the ground color. This tone is very pale, and is difficult to capture photographically.
• **BREEDING** The small, fragile cup-shaped nest is constructed of grass, rootlets, moss, lichen, cobwebs, and vegetable down, and lined with hair. It is either slung in a fork or in a cluster of leaves at the end of a tree branch.
• **RANGE** India, Sri Lanka, Burma, Yunnan, Szechwan, Southeast Asia, the Malay peninsula, and Indonesia.

• *plain shell*

Egg size 12–18 x 10–13 mm	Clutch size 2–4, usually 3	Incubation ♂♀ 10–11 days

Order PASSERIFORMES	Family MELIPHAGIDAE	Species *Philemon novaeguineae*

LEATHERHEAD

bold blotches •

The Leatherhead's eggs are pinkish or creamy white, spotted with brown, reddish brown, and light purple.
• **BREEDING** The nest is a large, bulky, loosely built cup of thin stems, tendrils, weathered bark fibers, and leaves, lined with fine, semiwoody stems. Sometimes paper, rags, scraps of plastic, and Spanish moss are used. The nest is slung by its edges across a slender tree fork among foliage.
• **RANGE** Aru Islands, western Papuan Islands, and parts of New Guinea and Australia.

• *ground may be obscured*

Egg size 28–34 x 21–24 mm	Clutch size 2–3	Incubation 17 days

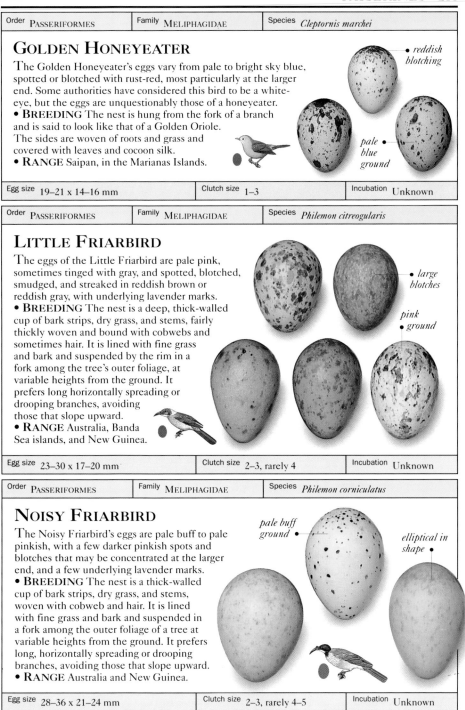

| Order PASSERIFORMES | Family MELIPHAGIDAE | Species *Cleptornis marchei* |

GOLDEN HONEYEATER

The Golden Honeyeater's eggs vary from pale to bright sky blue, spotted or blotched with rust-red, most particularly at the larger end. Some authorities have considered this bird to be a white-eye, but the eggs are unquestionably those of a honeyeater.
• **BREEDING** The nest is hung from the fork of a branch and is said to look like that of a Golden Oriole. The sides are woven of roots and grass and covered with leaves and cocoon silk.
• **RANGE** Saipan, in the Marianas Islands.

• reddish blotching

pale • blue ground

| Egg size 19–21 x 14–16 mm | Clutch size 1–3 | Incubation Unknown |

| Order PASSERIFORMES | Family MELIPHAGIDAE | Species *Philemon citreogularis* |

LITTLE FRIARBIRD

The eggs of the Little Friarbird are pale pink, sometimes tinged with gray, and spotted, blotched, smudged, and streaked in reddish brown or reddish gray, with underlying lavender marks.
• **BREEDING** The nest is a deep, thick-walled cup of bark strips, dry grass, and stems, fairly thickly woven and bound with cobwebs and sometimes hair. It is lined with fine grass and bark and suspended by the rim in a fork among the tree's outer foliage, at variable heights from the ground. It prefers long horizontally spreading or drooping branches, avoiding those that slope upward.
• **RANGE** Australia, Banda Sea islands, and New Guinea.

• large blotches

pink • ground

| Egg size 23–30 x 17–20 mm | Clutch size 2–3, rarely 4 | Incubation Unknown |

| Order PASSERIFORMES | Family MELIPHAGIDAE | Species *Philemon corniculatus* |

NOISY FRIARBIRD

The Noisy Friarbird's eggs are pale buff to pale pinkish, with a few darker pinkish spots and blotches that may be concentrated at the larger end, and a few underlying lavender marks.
• **BREEDING** The nest is a thick-walled cup of bark strips, dry grass, and stems, woven with cobweb and hair. It is lined with fine grass and bark and suspended in a fork among the outer foliage of a tree at variable heights from the ground. It prefers long, horizontally spreading or drooping branches, avoiding those that slope upward.
• **RANGE** Australia and New Guinea.

pale buff ground •

elliptical in shape •

| Egg size 28–36 x 21–24 mm | Clutch size 2–3, rarely 4–5 | Incubation Unknown |

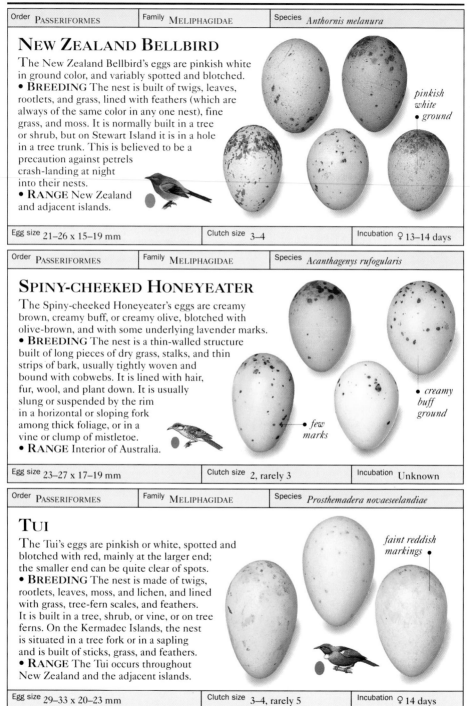

Order PASSERIFORMES	Family MELIPHAGIDAE	Species *Anthornis melanura*

NEW ZEALAND BELLBIRD

The New Zealand Bellbird's eggs are pinkish white in ground color, and variably spotted and blotched.
• **BREEDING** The nest is built of twigs, leaves, rootlets, and grass, lined with feathers (which are always of the same color in any one nest), fine grass, and moss. It is normally built in a tree or shrub, but on Stewart Island it is in a hole in a tree trunk. This is believed to be a precaution against petrels crash-landing at night into their nests.
• **RANGE** New Zealand and adjacent islands.

pinkish white • ground

Egg size 21–26 x 15–19 mm	Clutch size 3–4	Incubation ♀ 13–14 days

Order PASSERIFORMES	Family MELIPHAGIDAE	Species *Acanthagenys rufogularis*

SPINY-CHEEKED HONEYEATER

The Spiny-cheeked Honeyeater's eggs are creamy brown, creamy buff, or creamy olive, blotched with olive-brown, and with some underlying lavender marks.
• **BREEDING** The nest is a thin-walled structure built of long pieces of dry grass, stalks, and thin strips of bark, usually tightly woven and bound with cobwebs. It is lined with hair, fur, wool, and plant down. It is usually slung or suspended by the rim in a horizontal or sloping fork among thick foliage, or in a vine or clump of mistletoe.
• **RANGE** Interior of Australia.

few marks

creamy buff ground

Egg size 23–27 x 17–19 mm	Clutch size 2, rarely 3	Incubation Unknown

Order PASSERIFORMES	Family MELIPHAGIDAE	Species *Prosthemadera novaeseelandiae*

TUI

The Tui's eggs are pinkish or white, spotted and blotched with red, mainly at the larger end; the smaller end can be quite clear of spots.
• **BREEDING** The nest is made of twigs, rootlets, leaves, moss, and lichen, and lined with grass, tree-fern scales, and feathers. It is built in a tree, shrub, or vine, or on tree ferns. On the Kermadec Islands, the nest is situated in a tree fork or in a sapling and is built of sticks, grass, and feathers.
• **RANGE** The Tui occurs throughout New Zealand and the adjacent islands.

faint reddish markings •

Egg size 29–33 x 20–23 mm	Clutch size 3–4, rarely 5	Incubation ♀ 14 days

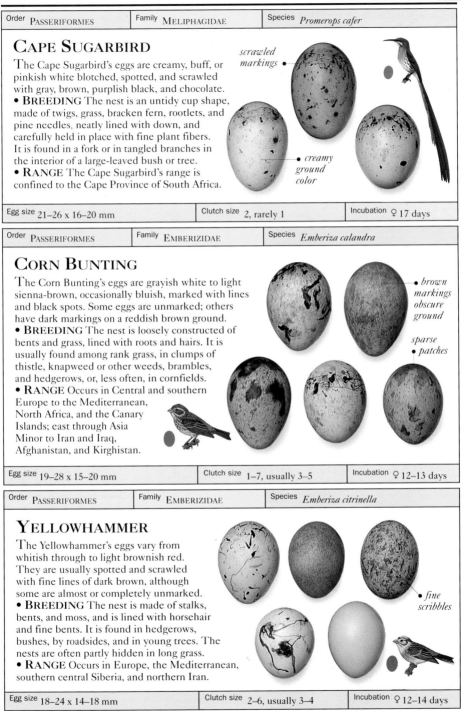

| Order PASSERIFORMES | Family MELIPHAGIDAE | Species *Promerops cafer* |

CAPE SUGARBIRD

The Cape Sugarbird's eggs are creamy, buff, or pinkish white blotched, spotted, and scrawled with gray, brown, purplish black, and chocolate.
• **BREEDING** The nest is an untidy cup shape, made of twigs, grass, bracken fern, rootlets, and pine needles, neatly lined with down, and carefully held in place with fine plant fibers. It is found in a fork or in tangled branches in the interior of a large-leaved bush or tree.
• **RANGE** The Cape Sugarbird's range is confined to the Cape Province of South Africa.

scrawled markings

creamy ground color

| Egg size 21–26 x 16–20 mm | Clutch size 2, rarely 1 | Incubation ♀ 17 days |

| Order PASSERIFORMES | Family EMBERIZIDAE | Species *Emberiza calandra* |

CORN BUNTING

The Corn Bunting's eggs are grayish white to light sienna-brown, occasionally bluish, marked with lines and black spots. Some eggs are unmarked; others have dark markings on a reddish brown ground.
• **BREEDING** The nest is loosely constructed of bents and grass, lined with roots and hairs. It is usually found among rank grass, in clumps of thistle, knapweed or other weeds, brambles, and hedgerows, or, less often, in cornfields.
• **RANGE** Occurs in Central and southern Europe to the Mediterranean, North Africa, and the Canary Islands; east through Asia Minor to Iran and Iraq, Afghanistan, and Kirghistan.

brown markings obscure ground

sparse patches

| Egg size 19–28 x 15–20 mm | Clutch size 1–7, usually 3–5 | Incubation ♀ 12–13 days |

| Order PASSERIFORMES | Family EMBERIZIDAE | Species *Emberiza citrinella* |

YELLOWHAMMER

The Yellowhammer's eggs vary from whitish through to light brownish red. They are usually spotted and scrawled with fine lines of dark brown, although some are almost or completely unmarked.
• **BREEDING** The nest is made of stalks, bents, and moss, and is lined with horsehair and fine bents. It is found in hedgerows, bushes, by roadsides, and in young trees. The nests are often partly hidden in long grass.
• **RANGE** Occurs in Europe, the Mediterranean, southern central Siberia, and northern Iran.

fine scribbles

| Egg size 18–24 x 14–18 mm | Clutch size 2–6, usually 3–4 | Incubation ♀ 12–14 days |

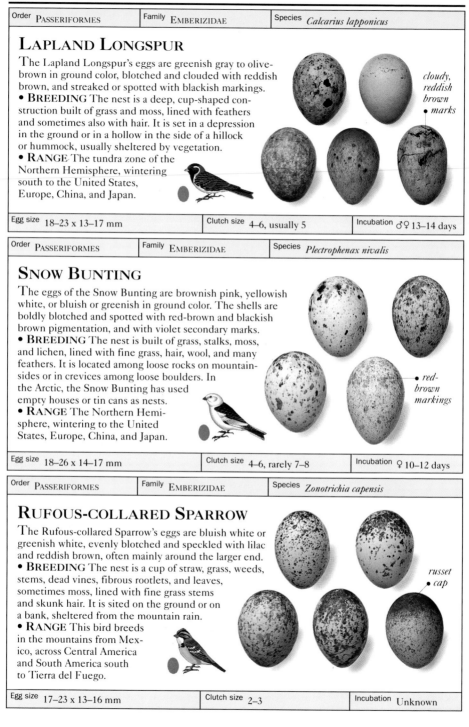

Order PASSERIFORMES	Family EMBERIZIDAE	Species *Calcarius lapponicus*

LAPLAND LONGSPUR

The Lapland Longspur's eggs are greenish gray to olive-brown in ground color, blotched and clouded with reddish brown, and streaked or spotted with blackish markings.
• **BREEDING** The nest is a deep, cup-shaped construction built of grass and moss, lined with feathers and sometimes also with hair. It is set in a depression in the ground or in a hollow in the side of a hillock or hummock, usually sheltered by vegetation.
• **RANGE** The tundra zone of the Northern Hemisphere, wintering south to the United States, Europe, China, and Japan.

cloudy, reddish brown marks

Egg size 18–23 x 13–17 mm	Clutch size 4–6, usually 5	Incubation ♂♀ 13–14 days

Order PASSERIFORMES	Family EMBERIZIDAE	Species *Plectrophenax nivalis*

SNOW BUNTING

The eggs of the Snow Bunting are brownish pink, yellowish white, or bluish or greenish in ground color. The shells are boldly blotched and spotted with red-brown and blackish brown pigmentation, and with violet secondary marks.
• **BREEDING** The nest is built of grass, stalks, moss, and lichen, lined with fine grass, hair, wool, and many feathers. It is located among loose rocks on mountainsides or in crevices among loose boulders. In the Arctic, the Snow Bunting has used empty houses or tin cans as nests.
• **RANGE** The Northern Hemisphere, wintering to the United States, Europe, China, and Japan.

red-brown markings

Egg size 18–26 x 14–17 mm	Clutch size 4–6, rarely 7–8	Incubation ♀ 10–12 days

Order PASSERIFORMES	Family EMBERIZIDAE	Species *Zonotrichia capensis*

RUFOUS-COLLARED SPARROW

The Rufous-collared Sparrow's eggs are bluish white or greenish white, evenly blotched and speckled with lilac and reddish brown, often mainly around the larger end.
• **BREEDING** The nest is a cup of straw, grass, weeds, stems, dead vines, fibrous rootlets, and leaves, sometimes moss, lined with fine grass stems and skunk hair. It is sited on the ground or on a bank, sheltered from the mountain rain.
• **RANGE** This bird breeds in the mountains from Mexico, across Central America and South America south to Tierra del Fuego.

russet cap

Egg size 17–23 x 13–16 mm	Clutch size 2–3	Incubation Unknown

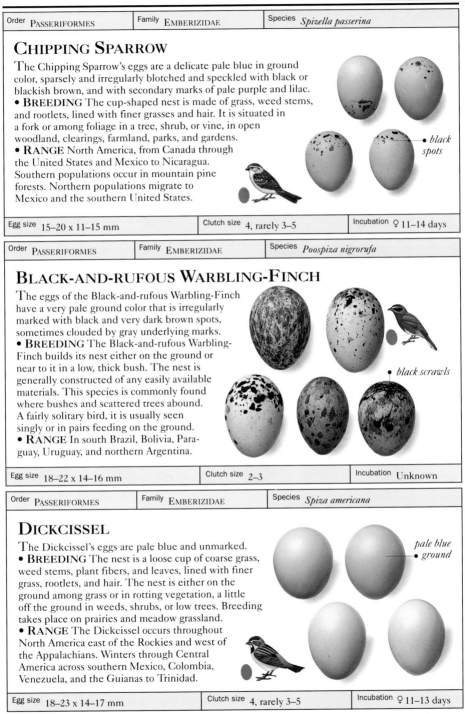

| Order PASSERIFORMES | Family EMBERIZIDAE | Species *Spizella passerina* |

CHIPPING SPARROW

The Chipping Sparrow's eggs are a delicate pale blue in ground color, sparsely and irregularly blotched and speckled with black or blackish brown, and with secondary marks of pale purple and lilac.
• **BREEDING** The cup-shaped nest is made of grass, weed stems, and rootlets, lined with finer grasses and hair. It is situated in a fork or among foliage in a tree, shrub, or vine, in open woodland, clearings, farmland, parks, and gardens.
• **RANGE** North America, from Canada through the United States and Mexico to Nicaragua. Southern populations occur in mountain pine forests. Northern populations migrate to Mexico and the southern United States.

• black spots

| Egg size 15–20 x 11–15 mm | Clutch size 4, rarely 3–5 | Incubation ♀ 11–14 days |

| Order PASSERIFORMES | Family EMBERIZIDAE | Species *Poospiza nigrorufa* |

BLACK-AND-RUFOUS WARBLING-FINCH

The eggs of the Black-and-rufous Warbling-Finch have a very pale ground color that is irregularly marked with black and very dark brown spots, sometimes clouded by gray underlying marks.
• **BREEDING** The Black-and-rufous Warbling-Finch builds its nest either on the ground or near to it in a low, thick bush. The nest is generally constructed of any easily available materials. This species is commonly found where bushes and scattered trees abound. A fairly solitary bird, it is usually seen singly or in pairs feeding on the ground.
• **RANGE** In south Brazil, Bolivia, Paraguay, Uruguay, and northern Argentina.

• black scrawls

| Egg size 18–22 x 14–16 mm | Clutch size 2–3 | Incubation Unknown |

| Order PASSERIFORMES | Family EMBERIZIDAE | Species *Spiza americana* |

DICKCISSEL

The Dickcissel's eggs are pale blue and unmarked.
• **BREEDING** The nest is a loose cup of coarse grass, weed stems, plant fibers, and leaves, lined with finer grass, rootlets, and hair. The nest is either on the ground among grass or in rotting vegetation, a little off the ground in weeds, shrubs, or low trees. Breeding takes place on prairies and meadow grassland.
• **RANGE** The Dickcissel occurs throughout North America east of the Rockies and west of the Appalachians. Winters through Central America across southern Mexico, Colombia, Venezuela, and the Guianas to Trinidad.

pale blue • ground

| Egg size 18–23 x 14–17 mm | Clutch size 4, rarely 3–5 | Incubation ♀ 11–13 days |

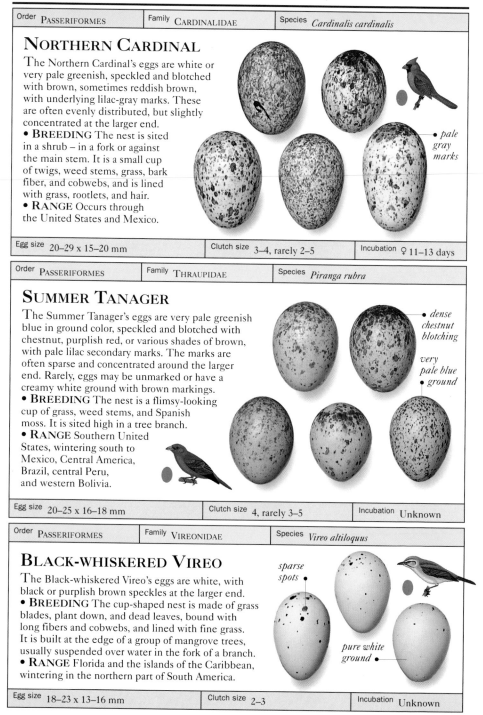

Order PASSERIFORMES	Family CARDINALIDAE	Species *Cardinalis cardinalis*

NORTHERN CARDINAL

The Northern Cardinal's eggs are white or
very pale greenish, speckled and blotched
with brown, sometimes reddish brown,
with underlying lilac-gray marks. These
are often evenly distributed, but slightly
concentrated at the larger end.
• **BREEDING** The nest is sited
in a shrub – in a fork or against
the main stem. It is a small cup
of twigs, weed stems, grass, bark
fiber, and cobwebs, and is lined
with grass, rootlets, and hair.
• **RANGE** Occurs through
the United States and Mexico.

pale gray marks

Egg size 20–29 x 15–20 mm	Clutch size 3–4, rarely 2–5	Incubation ♀ 11–13 days

Order PASSERIFORMES	Family THRAUPIDAE	Species *Piranga rubra*

SUMMER TANAGER

The Summer Tanager's eggs are very pale greenish
blue in ground color, speckled and blotched with
chestnut, purplish red, or various shades of brown,
with pale lilac secondary marks. The marks are
often sparse and concentrated around the larger
end. Rarely, eggs may be unmarked or have a
creamy white ground with brown markings.
• **BREEDING** The nest is a flimsy-looking
cup of grass, weed stems, and Spanish
moss. It is sited high in a tree branch.
• **RANGE** Southern United
States, wintering south to
Mexico, Central America,
Brazil, central Peru,
and western Bolivia.

dense chestnut blotching

very pale blue ground

Egg size 20–25 x 16–18 mm	Clutch size 4, rarely 3–5	Incubation Unknown

Order PASSERIFORMES	Family VIREONIDAE	Species *Vireo altiloquus*

BLACK-WHISKERED VIREO

The Black-whiskered Vireo's eggs are white, with
black or purplish brown speckles at the larger end.
• **BREEDING** The cup-shaped nest is made of grass
blades, plant down, and dead leaves, bound with
long fibers and cobwebs, and lined with fine grass.
It is built at the edge of a group of mangrove trees,
usually suspended over water in the fork of a branch.
• **RANGE** Florida and the islands of the Caribbean,
wintering in the northern part of South America.

sparse spots

pure white ground

Egg size 18–23 x 13–16 mm	Clutch size 2–3	Incubation Unknown

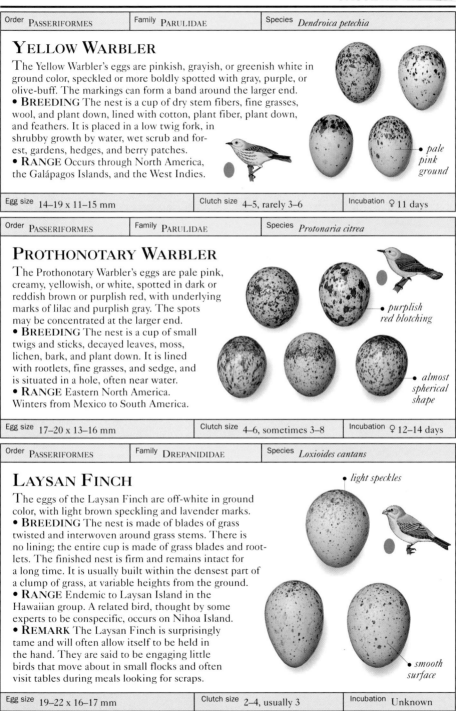

| Order PASSERIFORMES | Family PARULIDAE | Species *Dendroica petechia* |

YELLOW WARBLER

The Yellow Warbler's eggs are pinkish, grayish, or greenish white in ground color, speckled or more boldly spotted with gray, purple, or olive-buff. The markings can form a band around the larger end.
• **BREEDING** The nest is a cup of dry stem fibers, fine grasses, wool, and plant down, lined with cotton, plant fiber, plant down, and feathers. It is placed in a low twig fork, in shrubby growth by water, wet scrub and forest, gardens, hedges, and berry patches.
• **RANGE** Occurs through North America, the Galápagos Islands, and the West Indies.

• *pale pink ground*

| Egg size 14–19 x 11–15 mm | Clutch size 4–5, rarely 3–6 | Incubation ♀ 11 days |

| Order PASSERIFORMES | Family PARULIDAE | Species *Protonaria citrea* |

PROTHONOTARY WARBLER

The Prothonotary Warbler's eggs are pale pink, creamy, yellowish, or white, spotted in dark or reddish brown or purplish red, with underlying marks of lilac and purplish gray. The spots may be concentrated at the larger end.
• **BREEDING** The nest is a cup of small twigs and sticks, decayed leaves, moss, lichen, bark, and plant down. It is lined with rootlets, fine grasses, and sedge, and is situated in a hole, often near water.
• **RANGE** Eastern North America. Winters from Mexico to South America.

• *purplish red blotching*

• *almost spherical shape*

| Egg size 17–20 x 13–16 mm | Clutch size 4–6, sometimes 3–8 | Incubation ♀ 12–14 days |

| Order PASSERIFORMES | Family DREPANIDIDAE | Species *Loxioides cantans* |

LAYSAN FINCH

• *light speckles*

The eggs of the Laysan Finch are off-white in ground color, with light brown speckling and lavender marks.
• **BREEDING** The nest is made of blades of grass twisted and interwoven around grass stems. There is no lining; the entire cup is made of grass blades and rootlets. The finished nest is firm and remains intact for a long time. It is usually built within the densest part of a clump of grass, at variable heights from the ground.
• **RANGE** Endemic to Laysan Island in the Hawaiian group. A related bird, thought by some experts to be conspecific, occurs on Nihoa Island.
• **REMARK** The Laysan Finch is surprisingly tame and will often allow itself to be held in the hand. They are said to be engaging little birds that move about in small flocks and often visit tables during meals looking for scraps.

• *smooth surface*

| Egg size 19–22 x 16–17 mm | Clutch size 2–4, usually 3 | Incubation Unknown |

Order PASSERIFORMES	Family ICTERIDAE	Species *Icterus bullockii*

NORTHERN ORIOLE

The eggs of Northern Oriole are very pale in ground color and scribbled and scrawled with black or dark purplish marks that are underlaid with lilac or gray. These fine, dark marks often form a wreath of scribbling around the larger end of the eggshell.
• **BREEDING** The nest is a deep pouch built of long pieces of plant fiber, vine bark, hair, and bits of string. It is suspended in a tree fork, usually at the end of a branch, sometimes in mistletoe.
• **RANGE** Bullock's Oriole breeds in North America west of the Rocky Mountains, ranging south to Mexico.

intricate scribbles

Egg size 20–25 x 15–16 mm	Clutch size 4–5, rarely 3 or 6	Incubation ♀ c.14 days

Order PASSERIFORMES	Family ICTERIDAE	Species *Agelaius phoeniceus*

RED-WINGED BLACKBIRD

The eggs of the Red-winged Blackbird are very pale blue in ground color (difficult to capture photographically), sometimes tinged with pink or purplish and sparsely marked with black, dark brown, or purple. They can also have under-lying pale brown, lilac, or gray shell marks, or indistinct purple or brown clouding.
• **BREEDING** The nest is a deep cup of leaves and stems woven around twigs or grass stems. It is sited in rushes, sedges, and grass, in swamp or marshes.
• **RANGE** North America.

smudged blotches

pale gray marks

Egg size 20–27 x 15–20 mm	Clutch size 4, rarely 3 or 5	Incubation ♀ 10–12 days

Order PASSERIFORMES	Family ICTERIDAE	Species *Leistes militaris*

RED-BREASTED BLACKBIRD

The oval eggs of the Red-breasted Blackbird are pale bluish or grayish blue in ground color, but this color is covered by pale or darker reddish brown spots and blotches.
• **BREEDING** The nest is a deep, cup-shaped construction made of grass stems, and lined with finer grass and plant down. It is situated on the ground in a clump of grass. The birds push their way through the grass to form an entrance tunnel to the nest.
• **RANGE** Inhabits open fields, pastures, rice paddies, and wet savannah in eastern Panama and tropical South America, south to Uruguay and northern Argentina.

thick mottling

pale ground is obscured

Egg size 21–25 x 15–18 mm	Clutch size 3, rarely 2 or 4	Incubation Unknown

| Order PASSERIFORMES | Family ICTERIDAE | Species *Molothrus bonariensis* |

SHINY COWBIRD

The eggs of the Shiny Cowbird are almost spherical and are very variable in ground color. They may be white, cream, light bluish white, greenish white, or light brown, and spotted, blotched, or speckled with various shades of brown or purplish gray, though unmarked eggs are always white in ground color. Although cowbirds are parasitic, their eggs do not normally match those of the host species.
• **BREEDING** The Shiny Cowbird is promiscuous and a nest parasite. It lays principally in the nests of ovenbirds and woodhewers, although nearly 150 species of South American birds have been recorded as hosts. Usually only one egg is laid by a female in any one nest, but more than one female may lay in the same nest. Each female is capable of laying up to 30 eggs per season.
• **RANGE** From central Argentina and Chile to the West Indies; recently arrived in the southwestern United States, eastern Panama, and South America.

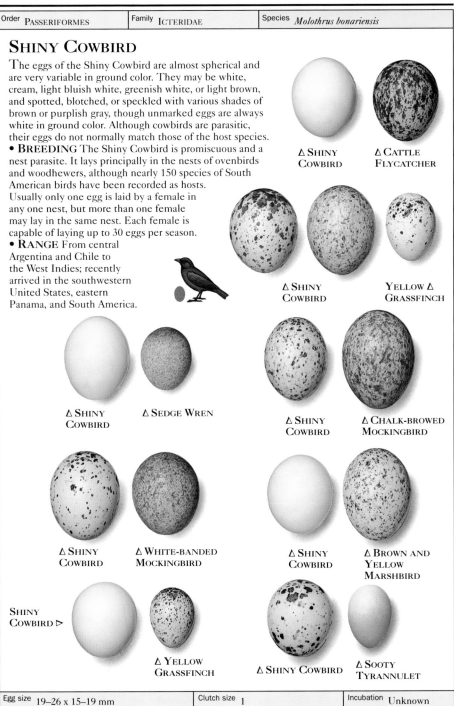

△ SHINY COWBIRD △ CATTLE FLYCATCHER

△ SHINY COWBIRD YELLOW △ GRASSFINCH

△ SHINY COWBIRD △ SEDGE WREN

△ SHINY COWBIRD △ CHALK-BROWED MOCKINGBIRD

△ SHINY COWBIRD △ WHITE-BANDED MOCKINGBIRD

△ SHINY COWBIRD △ BROWN AND YELLOW MARSHBIRD

SHINY COWBIRD ▷

△ YELLOW GRASSFINCH △ SHINY COWBIRD △ SOOTY TYRANNULET

| Egg size 19–26 x 15–19 mm | Clutch size 1 | Incubation Unknown |

Order PASSERIFORMES	Family ICTERIDAE	Species *Molothrus ater*

BROWN-HEADED COWBIRD

The eggs of the Brown-headed Cowbird are white or faintly bluish or greenish in ground color, finely speckled or mottled with brown, red, or purplish brown, with underlying lilac marks. Sometimes the color can be concentrated at the larger end. Unlike the Common Cuckoo (see p.129), the eggs of cowbirds do not normally match those of the host.
• **BREEDING** The Brown-headed Cowbird is promiscuous and a nest parasite, laying principally in the nests of finches, vireos, warblers, and fly-catchers. A total of a further 220 species of North American birds have been recorded as hosts. Normally only one egg is laid by a female in any single nest, but more than one female may lay in the same host's nest.
• **RANGE** Breeds from southern Canada south to central Mexico.

• *bluish tinge*

◁ DICKCISSEL

△ BROWN-HEADED COWBIRD

brown
• *mottling*

sparse
• *marks*

△ BROWN-HEADED COWBIRD

△ LARK SPARROW

△ BROWN-HEADED COWBIRD

△ BELL'S VIREO

Egg size 18–25 x 13–17 mm	Clutch size 1	Incubation 11–12 days

Order PASSERIFORMES	Family FRINGILLIDAE	Species *Fringilla coelebs*

CHAFFINCH

The Chaffinch's eggs' ground coloration ranges from pale greenish blue or brownish stone to, less often, clear pale blue or light olive, some-times tinged with pink. They can be sparsely spotted, streaked, scrawled, and blotched with dark chestnut, often with smudged pinkish edges. Occasionally, the eggs are unmarked.
• **BREEDING** The neat, cup-shaped nest is constructed of moss, lichen, grass, roots, and feathers, bound with cobwebs and decorated on the outside with lichen and flakes of bark. It is lined with feathers, rootlets, wool, fur, and plant down. The Chaffinch's nest is normally located in the fork of a tree or in a tall shrub in deciduous and coniferous woodland, gardens, hedgerows, thickets, and bushy parks.
• **RANGE** Occurs over much of Europe, the islands of the Mediterranean, the Azores, Madeira, the Canary Islands, and North Africa, to Iran.

smudged pinkish marks •

greenish blue
• *ground*

brownish
• *ground*

Egg size 16–24 x 13–16 mm	Clutch size 4–5, rarely 2–8	Incubation ♀ 11–13 days

Order PASSERIFORMES	Family FRINGILLIDAE	Species *Fringilla teydea*

BLUE CHAFFINCH

The eggs of the Blue Chaffinch are nearly always pale blue in ground color, marked with chestnut or purple spots and with fainter blotching of the same color. The eggs are larger than those of the Chaffinch (opposite) and are less variable in color.
• **BREEDING** The nest is cup-shaped and is constructed using pine needles, twigs, and lichen, lined with hair, feathers, and plant down. It is situated on a tree branch in pine forests.
• **RANGE** The pine forests of Tenerife and Gran Canaria, in the Canary Islands.
• **REMARK** The Blue Chaffinch is related to the Common Chaffinch. It was one of the first chaffinches to immigrate to the Canary Islands.

pale blue ground •

chestnut spots at larger end •

Egg size 22–26 x 15–17mm	Clutch size 1–2	Incubation ♀ 14 days

Order PASSERIFORMES	Family FRINGILLIDAE	Species *Serinus serinus*

EUROPEAN SERIN

The European Serin's eggs are very pale blue and may have a slight greenish tinge. They are speckled and scrawled in purplish and brownish red, with paler lilac marks, mainly confined to the larger end.
• **BREEDING** The neat, cup-shaped nest is made of plant stems, roots, moss, and lichen, sited near the end of a branch of a tree or bush.
• **RANGE** Occurs throughout western and Central Europe (including the Ukraine), south to the Mediterranean and its islands, ranging to North Africa.

• *pale green tinge*

Egg size 14–17 x 11–13 mm	Clutch size 4, rarely 3–5	Incubation ♀ 13 days

Order PASSERIFORMES	Family FRINGILLIDAE	Species *Carduelis carduelis*

EUROPEAN GOLDFINCH

The European Goldfinch's eggs are such a pale shade of blue that they appear white when photographed. Most eggs are spotted, speckled, blotched, and streaked with purplish black, red, or pink marks that can be confined to the larger end.
• **BREEDING** The cup-shaped nest is made out of moss, roots, grass, lichen, and wool. It is sited in a tree or shrub.
• **RANGE** Europe south to the Mediterranean, and east to Iran and Lake Baikal.

• *dark spots*

Egg size 14–19 x 11–14 mm	Clutch size 4–6, rarely 3–7	Incubation ♀ 12–14 days

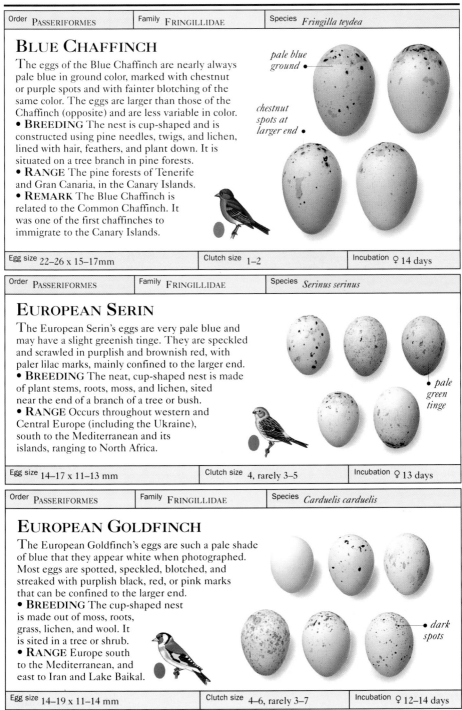

Order PASSERIFORMES	Family FRINGILLIDAE	Species *Carpodacus erythrinus*

COMMON ROSEFINCH

The Common Rosefinch's eggs are bright blue (fading in collections), sparingly dotted, streaked, or blotched around the larger end, with purplish black or pure black markings.
• **BREEDING** The nest is a loosely built structure of plant stems and grass, lined with roots and hair. It is sited in shrubs or low trees such as a juniper, hazel, alder, fir, or mountain redcurrant, at a variety of heights. Breeding takes place in swampy areas or close to water, often in woodland undergrowth, scrubby thickets, and farmland.
• **RANGE** Occurs from Finland, across to northern Siberia and the Bering Sea, and south to the Middle East, northern China, and India (in winter).

• *faded blue ground*

Egg size 16–22 x 13–16 mm	Clutch size 5, rarely 3–6	Incubation ♀ 12–14 days

Order PASSERIFORMES	Family FRINGILLIDAE	Species *Pinicola enucleator*

PINE GROSBEAK

The eggs of the Pine Grosbeak are greenish blue in ground color (difficult to capture photographically), with bold blackish or brownish spots and blotches.
• **BREEDING** The nest is said to be similar to that of the Bullfinch (below) but larger. It is a loose construction of interlaced twigs (usually birch or spruce) with an inner cup of roots, grass, and moss. The nest is situated fairly low in tree branches of coniferous or mixed forest.
• **RANGE** The Pine Grosbeak occurs widely throughout the Northern Hemisphere north to the timber line; Central Europe, central Russia, Manchuria, and the northern and western United States.

• *brown blotches*

Egg size 22–30 x 15–19 mm	Clutch size 4, rarely 3–5	Incubation ♀ 13–14 days

Order PASSERIFORMES	Family FRINGILLIDAE	Species *Pyrrhula pyrrhula*

COMMON BULLFINCH

The Common Bullfinch's eggs are pale blue, spotted, blotched, and scrawled with blackish purple or light brown with underlying marks of lilac, mostly around the larger end.
• **BREEDING** The nest is a loose structure of small twigs, moss, and lichen, and is lined with roots and hair. It is located in a bush or shrub, in woods with shrubby undergrowth, scrubland, gardens, and hedgerows.
• **RANGE** Occurs in Europe south to the Mediterranean, Iran, across northern Asia, and northern China.

• *purple-brown spots at larger end*

Egg size 17–23 x 12–16 mm	Clutch size 4–5, rarely 6–7	Incubation ♀ 12–14 days

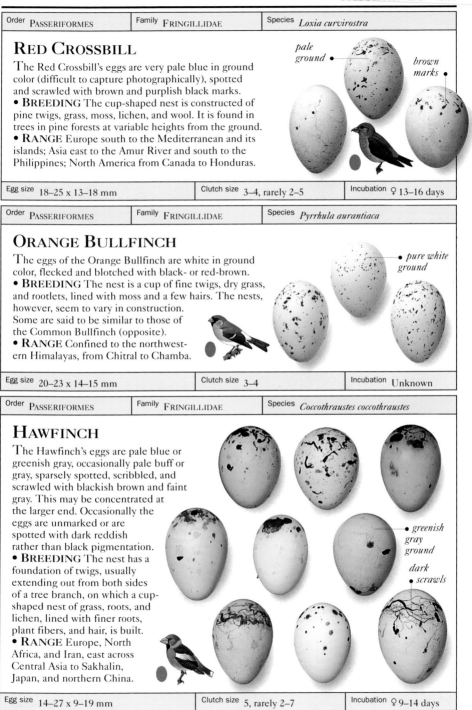

Order PASSERIFORMES	Family FRINGILLIDAE	Species *Loxia curvirostra*

RED CROSSBILL

The Red Crossbill's eggs are very pale blue in ground color (difficult to capture photographically), spotted and scrawled with brown and purplish black marks.
• **BREEDING** The cup-shaped nest is constructed of pine twigs, grass, moss, lichen, and wool. It is found in trees in pine forests at variable heights from the ground.
• **RANGE** Europe south to the Mediterranean and its islands; Asia east to the Amur River and south to the Philippines; North America from Canada to Honduras.

pale ground

brown marks

Egg size 18–25 x 13–18 mm	Clutch size 3–4, rarely 2–5	Incubation ♀ 13–16 days

Order PASSERIFORMES	Family FRINGILLIDAE	Species *Pyrrhula aurantiaca*

ORANGE BULLFINCH

The eggs of the Orange Bullfinch are white in ground color, flecked and blotched with black- or red-brown.
• **BREEDING** The nest is a cup of fine twigs, dry grass, and rootlets, lined with moss and a few hairs. The nests, however, seem to vary in construction. Some are said to be similar to those of the Common Bullfinch (opposite).
• **RANGE** Confined to the northwestern Himalayas, from Chitral to Chamba.

pure white ground

Egg size 20–23 x 14–15 mm	Clutch size 3–4	Incubation Unknown

Order PASSERIFORMES	Family FRINGILLIDAE	Species *Coccothraustes coccothraustes*

HAWFINCH

The Hawfinch's eggs are pale blue or greenish gray, occasionally pale buff or gray, sparsely spotted, scribbled, and scrawled with blackish brown and faint gray. This may be concentrated at the larger end. Occasionally the eggs are unmarked or are spotted with dark reddish rather than black pigmentation.
• **BREEDING** The nest has a foundation of twigs, usually extending out from both sides of a tree branch, on which a cup-shaped nest of grass, roots, and lichen, lined with finer roots, plant fibers, and hair, is built.
• **RANGE** Europe, North Africa, and Iran, east across Central Asia to Sakhalin, Japan, and northern China.

greenish gray ground

dark scrawls

Egg size 14–27 x 9–19 mm	Clutch size 5, rarely 2–7	Incubation ♀ 9–14 days

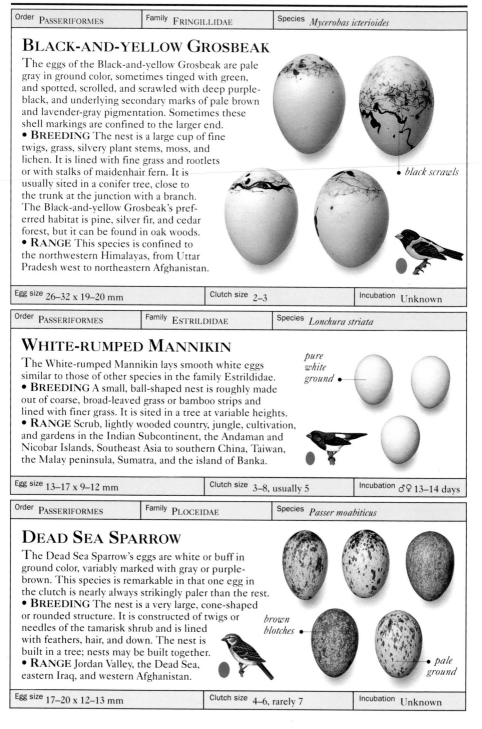

Order PASSERIFORMES	Family FRINGILLIDAE	Species *Mycerobas icterioides*

BLACK-AND-YELLOW GROSBEAK

The eggs of the Black-and-yellow Grosbeak are pale gray in ground color, sometimes tinged with green, and spotted, scrolled, and scrawled with deep purple-black, and underlying secondary marks of pale brown and lavender-gray pigmentation. Sometimes these shell markings are confined to the larger end.
• BREEDING The nest is a large cup of fine twigs, grass, silvery plant stems, moss, and lichen. It is lined with fine grass and rootlets or with stalks of maidenhair fern. It is usually sited in a conifer tree, close to the trunk at the junction with a branch. The Black-and-yellow Grosbeak's preferred habitat is pine, silver fir, and cedar forest, but it can be found in oak woods.
• RANGE This species is confined to the northwestern Himalayas, from Uttar Pradesh west to northeastern Afghanistan.

• *black scrawls*

Egg size 26–32 x 19–20 mm	Clutch size 2–3	Incubation Unknown

Order PASSERIFORMES	Family ESTRILDIDAE	Species *Lonchura striata*

WHITE-RUMPED MANNIKIN

The White-rumped Mannikin lays smooth white eggs similar to those of other species in the family Estrildidae.
• BREEDING A small, ball-shaped nest is roughly made out of coarse, broad-leaved grass or bamboo strips and lined with finer grass. It is sited in a tree at variable heights.
• RANGE Scrub, lightly wooded country, jungle, cultivation, and gardens in the Indian Subcontinent, the Andaman and Nicobar Islands, Southeast Asia to southern China, Taiwan, the Malay peninsula, Sumatra, and the island of Banka.

pure white ground •

Egg size 13–17 x 9–12 mm	Clutch size 3–8, usually 5	Incubation ♂♀ 13–14 days

Order PASSERIFORMES	Family PLOCEIDAE	Species *Passer moabiticus*

DEAD SEA SPARROW

The Dead Sea Sparrow's eggs are white or buff in ground color, variably marked with gray or purple-brown. This species is remarkable in that one egg in the clutch is nearly always strikingly paler than the rest.
• BREEDING The nest is a very large, cone-shaped or rounded structure. It is constructed of twigs or needles of the tamarisk shrub and is lined with feathers, hair, and down. The nest is built in a tree; nests may be built together.
• RANGE Jordan Valley, the Dead Sea, eastern Iraq, and western Afghanistan.

brown blotches •

• *pale ground*

Egg size 17–20 x 12–13 mm	Clutch size 4–6, rarely 7	Incubation Unknown

| Order PASSERIFORMES | Family PLOCEIDAE | Species *Passer domesticus* |

HOUSE SPARROW

The eggs laid by the House Sparrow are white in ground color. They can be tinged with grayish or greenish, and are variably speckled, spotted, or blotched with gray, blue-gray, greenish gray, purplish gray, brown, or black. Within a clutch, one egg often has paler markings or no marks.
• **BREEDING** The nest is constructed in a hole or crevice in a building, among vines growing on buildings, or more rarely among twigs in a tree. In the latter instance, a neat, rounded nest with a side entrance is built; in vines, however, the nest is less tidy.
• **RANGE** Native in Europe, North Africa, southwestern Asia to Iran, and India. Introduced to the Americas, South Africa, Australia, and New Zealand.

• gray spots

• plain white shell

| Egg size 16–26 x 13–17 mm | Clutch size 3–5, rarely up to 8 | Incubation ♀ 11–14 days |

| Order PASSERIFORMES | Family PLOCEIDAE | Species *Petronia brachydactyla* |

PALE ROCK-SPARROW

The Pale Rock-Sparrow's eggs are pure white, sparsely speckled and spotted over the shell with a few black marks.
• **BREEDING** The nest can be a crevice in rocks, buildings, or low bushes, but it varies with the locality. There are no confirmed reports of the materials used for the nest, but the bird will probably use whatever is available.
• **RANGE** Breeds in Armenia, Syria, and Palestine eastwards to eastern Iran, Turkestan, and Baluchistan.

scattering of black spots •

• pure white ground

| Egg size 19–23 x 13–15 mm | Clutch size 4–5 | Incubation Unknown |

| Order PASSERIFORMES | Family PLOCEIDAE | Species *Petronia xanthocollis* |

YELLOW-THROATED ROCK-SPARROW

The eggs of the Yellow-throated Rock-Sparrow are white or greenish white and blotched with brown, dark brown, and gray. The marks can be concentrated at the larger end and are similar to those of the House Sparrow (above) except that coloration is uniform within a clutch.
• **BREEDING** Hair, grass, stalks, and roots are used to build a nest in a tree hole or building, or an old nest hole of a woodpecker may be used.
• **RANGE** Savannah belt of North and East Africa south of the Sahara, through Iraq to India and Pakistan.

• gray-brown marks

| Egg size 16–21 x 12–15 mm | Clutch size 3–4 | Incubation Unknown |

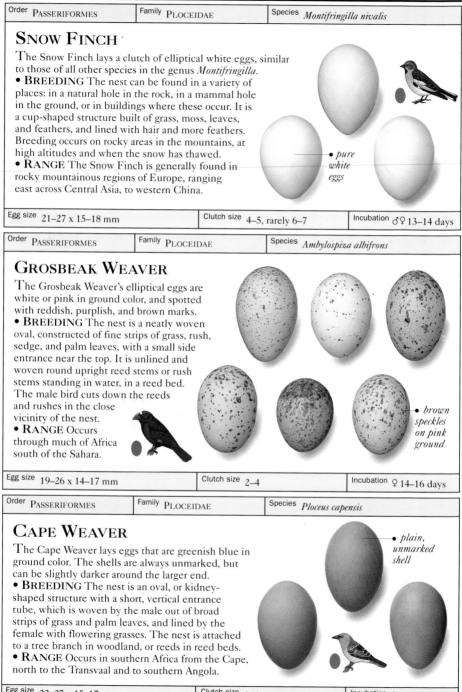

Order PASSERIFORMES	Family PLOCEIDAE	Species *Montifringilla nivalis*

SNOW FINCH

The Snow Finch lays a clutch of elliptical white eggs, similar to those of all other species in the genus *Montifringilla*.
• **BREEDING** The nest can be found in a variety of places: in a natural hole in the rock, in a mammal hole in the ground, or in buildings where these occur. It is a cup-shaped structure built of grass, moss, leaves, and feathers, and lined with hair and more feathers. Breeding occurs on rocky areas in the mountains, at high altitudes and when the snow has thawed.
• **RANGE** The Snow Finch is generally found in rocky mountainous regions of Europe, ranging east across Central Asia, to western China.

• *pure white eggs*

Egg size 21–27 x 15–18 mm	Clutch size 4–5, rarely 6–7	Incubation ♂♀ 13–14 days

Order PASSERIFORMES	Family PLOCEIDAE	Species *Ambylospiza albifrons*

GROSBEAK WEAVER

The Grosbeak Weaver's elliptical eggs are white or pink in ground color, and spotted with reddish, purplish, and brown marks.
• **BREEDING** The nest is a neatly woven oval, constructed of fine strips of grass, rush, sedge, and palm leaves, with a small side entrance near the top. It is unlined and woven round upright reed stems or rush stems standing in water, in a reed bed. The male bird cuts down the reeds and rushes in the close vicinity of the nest.
• **RANGE** Occurs through much of Africa south of the Sahara.

• *brown speckles on pink ground*

Egg size 19–26 x 14–17 mm	Clutch size 2–4	Incubation ♀ 14–16 days

Order PASSERIFORMES	Family PLOCEIDAE	Species *Ploceus capensis*

CAPE WEAVER

The Cape Weaver lays eggs that are greenish blue in ground color. The shells are always unmarked, but can be slightly darker around the larger end.
• **BREEDING** The nest is an oval, or kidney-shaped structure with a short, vertical entrance tube, which is woven by the male out of broad strips of grass and palm leaves, and lined by the female with flowering grasses. The nest is attached to a tree branch in woodland, or reeds in reed beds.
• **RANGE** Occurs in southern Africa from the Cape, north to the Transvaal and to southern Angola.

• *plain, unmarked shell*

Egg size 22–27 x 15–17 mm	Clutch size 2–4	Incubation ♀ 13–14 days

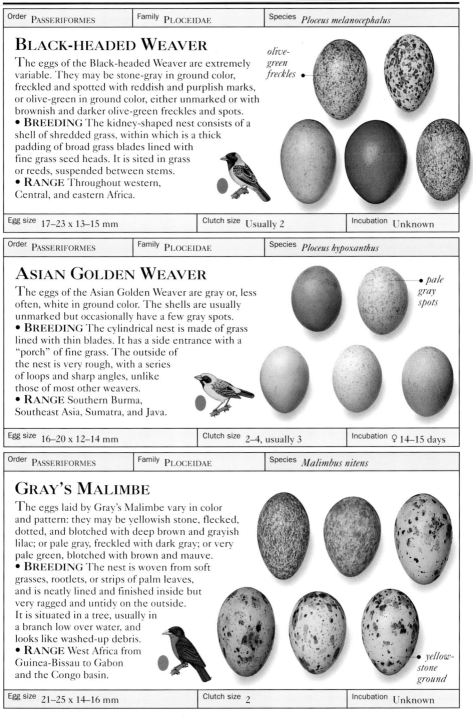

Order PASSERIFORMES	Family PLOCEIDAE	Species *Ploceus melanocephalus*

BLACK-HEADED WEAVER

olive-green freckles •

The eggs of the Black-headed Weaver are extremely variable. They may be stone-gray in ground color, freckled and spotted with reddish and purplish marks, or olive-green in ground color, either unmarked or with brownish and darker olive-green freckles and spots.
• **BREEDING** The kidney-shaped nest consists of a shell of shredded grass, within which is a thick padding of broad grass blades lined with fine grass seed heads. It is sited in grass or reeds, suspended between stems.
• **RANGE** Throughout western, Central, and eastern Africa.

Egg size 17–23 x 13–15 mm	Clutch size Usually 2	Incubation Unknown

Order PASSERIFORMES	Family PLOCEIDAE	Species *Ploceus hypoxanthus*

ASIAN GOLDEN WEAVER

• *pale gray spots*

The eggs of the Asian Golden Weaver are gray or, less often, white in ground color. The shells are usually unmarked but occasionally have a few gray spots.
• **BREEDING** The cylindrical nest is made of grass lined with thin blades. It has a side entrance with a "porch" of fine grass. The outside of the nest is very rough, with a series of loops and sharp angles, unlike those of most other weavers.
• **RANGE** Southern Burma, Southeast Asia, Sumatra, and Java.

Egg size 16–20 x 12–14 mm	Clutch size 2–4, usually 3	Incubation ♀ 14–15 days

Order PASSERIFORMES	Family PLOCEIDAE	Species *Malimbus nitens*

GRAY'S MALIMBE

The eggs laid by Gray's Malimbe vary in color and pattern: they may be yellowish stone, flecked, dotted, and blotched with deep brown and grayish lilac; or pale gray, freckled with dark gray; or very pale green, blotched with brown and mauve.
• **BREEDING** The nest is woven from soft grasses, rootlets, or strips of palm leaves, and is neatly lined and finished inside but very ragged and untidy on the outside. It is situated in a tree, usually in a branch low over water, and looks like washed-up debris.
• **RANGE** West Africa from Guinea-Bissau to Gabon and the Congo basin.

yellow-stone ground

Egg size 21–25 x 14–16 mm	Clutch size 2	Incubation Unknown

Order PASSERIFORMES	Family PLOCEIDAE	Species *Malimbus malimbicus*

CRESTED MALIMBE

The eggs of the Crested Malimbe are greenish gray in ground color, mottled with pale gray and dark brown.
• **BREEDING** The nest is a roughly woven structure with a short, uneven entrance tube pointing downwards. The nest is composed of strips of palm leaves. It is hung from the end of a drooping frond of a climbing palm, usually hanging over a brook or stream.
• **RANGE** Africa: from Sierra Leone to northern Angola, the Congo basin, and western Uganda.
• **REMARK** The bird's bright red crest is said to look similar to the brilliant red flowers that are sometimes seen on the tree trunks it inhabits.

greenish gray ground

dark brown blotches

Egg size 24–25 x 16–17 mm	Clutch size 2	Incubation Unknown

Order PASSERIFORMES	Family PLOCEIDAE	Species *Quelea quelea*

RED-BILLED QUELEA

The eggs of the Red-billed Quelea have a pale greenish blue ground color and are without shell markings.
• **BREEDING** The small nest is a ball-shaped structure with relatively thin walls and a large side entrance. It is simply constructed of fine strips of grass and lining material is rarely used. Usually the nests are built in thorny trees, but they can also be found in reed beds.
• **RANGE** Ranges widely over much of Africa south of the Sahara, reaching pest proportions in many regions.
• **REMARK** The Red-billed Quelea breeds in enormous colonies, often up to 500 in a single tree. The entire colony covers a large area in their search for food.

plain, pale ground

Egg size 17–21 x 11–15 mm	Clutch size 1–5, usually 2–4	Incubation ♂♀ 9–12 days

Order PASSERIFORMES	Family PLOCEIDAE	Species *Quelea cardinalis*

CARDINAL QUELEA

The eggs of the Cardinal Quelea are whitish, bluish, or greenish in ground color. Dark brown, reddish brown, and grayish mauve markings cover the shell or can be concentrated at the larger end.
• **BREEDING** The Cardinal Quelea builds an oval-shaped nest with a side entrance near the top. It is woven out of grass, lined with flowering grasses, and fastened to the upright stems of grasses or herbs.
• **RANGE** Eastern Africa from southeast Sudan and Ethiopia to Tanzania and northern Zambia.

dark brown spots

Egg size 15–18 x 11–13 mm	Clutch size 2–3	Incubation ♀ 12–14 days

Order PASSERIFORMES	Family PLOCEIDAE	Species *Euplectes hordeaceus*

RED-CROWNED BISHOP

The eggs of the Red-crowned Bishop are pale greenish blue, usually unmarked but sometimes spotted with brown or violet.
• **BREEDING** The nest is an upright, oval-shaped construction, made of strips of green grass, and either attached to the upright stems of grass or herbs or located in a bush. The bottom of the nest is often so thin that the eggs can be seen from below.
• **RANGE** Africa from Senegal to southern Sudan, south to Angola and Zimbabwe.

sparse brown dots

Egg size 15–20 x 12–14 mm	Clutch size 3, rarely 1–2	Incubation ♀ 12 days

Order PASSERIFORMES	Family STURNIDAE	Species *Aplonis panayensis*

GREATER GLOSSY STARLING

The Greater Glossy Starling's eggs are white or pale milky blue in ground color, speckled and blotched with reddish brown markings.
• **BREEDING** The nest is a cup of roots, grass, and leaves, but no more detailed information is available. The nest site is a natural hole or old woodpecker hole in a tree, preferably a coco-nut tree, but also in padouk and other trees, usually at a great height above the ground.
• **RANGE** Eastern India, Southeast Asia to Sulawesi, the Philippines, and south to Indonesia.

pale milky blue ground

chestnut-brown spots

Egg size 23–29 x 17–21 mm	Clutch size 2–4	Incubation Unknown

Order PASSERIFORMES	Family STURNIDAE	Species *Onychognathus morio*

RED-WINGED STARLING

The Red-winged Starling lays blue-green eggs, spotted with rust-colored markings.
• **BREEDING**
The nest is a bowl of mud and plant fibers lined with hair, pine needles, and roots. It is placed on a ledge or in a hole in a cave, cliff, building, or mine shaft, usually protected by an overhang. Occasionally, it can be situated at the base of a palm frond.
• **RANGE** Much of Africa south of the Sahara.

elliptical shape

rust-brown spots

blue-green ground

Egg size 29–37 x 20–25 mm	Clutch size 2–5, usually 3	Incubation ♀ 12–23 days

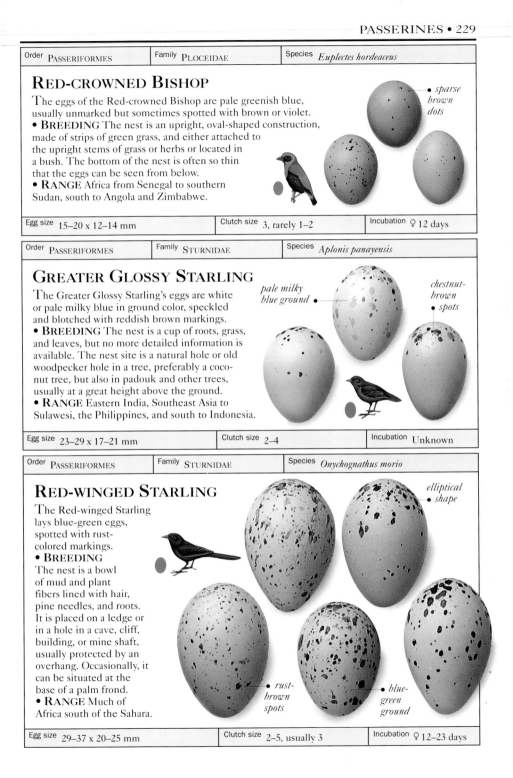

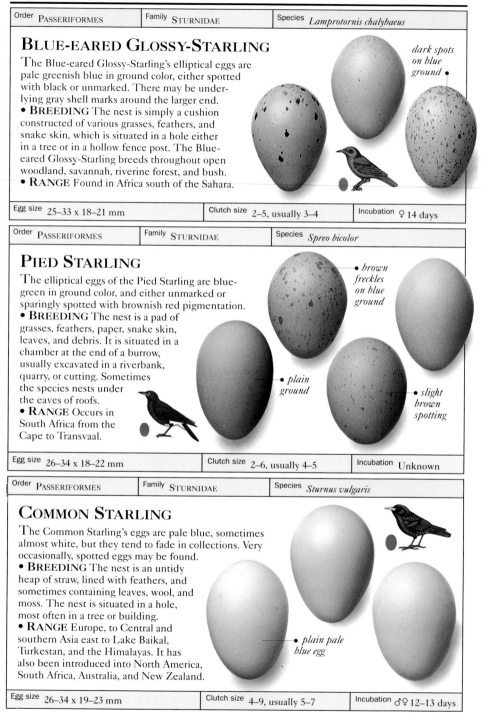

Order PASSERIFORMES	Family STURNIDAE	Species *Lamprotornis chalybaeus*

BLUE-EARED GLOSSY-STARLING

The Blue-eared Glossy-Starling's elliptical eggs are pale greenish blue in ground color, either spotted with black or unmarked. There may be underlying gray shell marks around the larger end.
• **BREEDING** The nest is simply a cushion constructed of various grasses, feathers, and snake skin, which is situated in a hole either in a tree or in a hollow fence post. The Blue-eared Glossy-Starling breeds throughout open woodland, savannah, riverine forest, and bush.
• **RANGE** Found in Africa south of the Sahara.

dark spots on blue ground •

Egg size 25–33 x 18–21 mm	Clutch size 2–5, usually 3–4	Incubation ♀ 14 days

Order PASSERIFORMES	Family STURNIDAE	Species *Spreo bicolor*

PIED STARLING

The elliptical eggs of the Pied Starling are blue-green in ground color, and either unmarked or sparingly spotted with brownish red pigmentation.
• **BREEDING** The nest is a pad of grasses, feathers, paper, snake skin, leaves, and debris. It is situated in a chamber at the end of a burrow, usually excavated in a riverbank, quarry, or cutting. Sometimes the species nests under the eaves of roofs.
• **RANGE** Occurs in South Africa from the Cape to Transvaal.

• brown freckles on blue ground

• plain ground

• slight brown spotting

Egg size 26–34 x 18–22 mm	Clutch size 2–6, usually 4–5	Incubation Unknown

Order PASSERIFORMES	Family STURNIDAE	Species *Sturnus vulgaris*

COMMON STARLING

The Common Starling's eggs are pale blue, sometimes almost white, but they tend to fade in collections. Very occasionally, spotted eggs may be found.
• **BREEDING** The nest is an untidy heap of straw, lined with feathers, and sometimes containing leaves, wool, and moss. The nest is situated in a hole, most often in a tree or building.
• **RANGE** Europe, to Central and southern Asia east to Lake Baikal, Turkestan, and the Himalayas. It has also been introduced into North America, South Africa, Australia, and New Zealand.

• plain pale blue egg

Egg size 26–34 x 19–23 mm	Clutch size 4–9, usually 5–7	Incubation ♂♀ 12–13 days

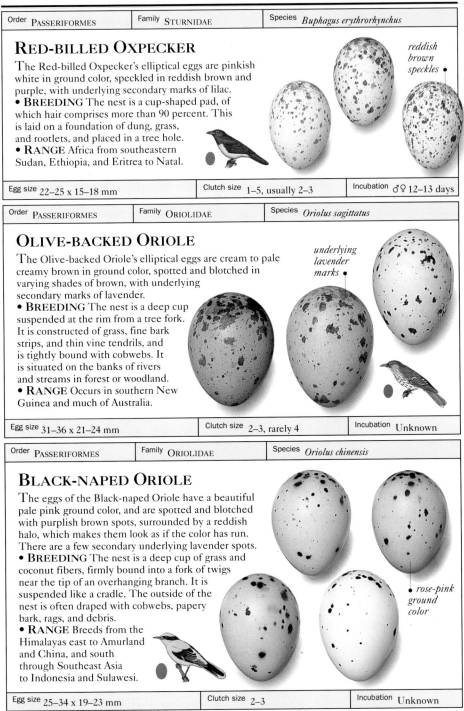

Order PASSERIFORMES	Family STURNIDAE	Species *Buphagus erythrorhynchus*

RED-BILLED OXPECKER

The Red-billed Oxpecker's elliptical eggs are pinkish white in ground color, speckled in reddish brown and purple, with underlying secondary marks of lilac.
• **BREEDING** The nest is a cup-shaped pad, of which hair comprises more than 90 percent. This is laid on a foundation of dung, grass, and rootlets, and placed in a tree hole.
• **RANGE** Africa from southeastern Sudan, Ethiopia, and Eritrea to Natal.

reddish brown speckles •

Egg size 22–25 x 15–18 mm	Clutch size 1–5, usually 2–3	Incubation ♂♀ 12–13 days

Order PASSERIFORMES	Family ORIOLIDAE	Species *Oriolus sagittatus*

OLIVE-BACKED ORIOLE

The Olive-backed Oriole's elliptical eggs are cream to pale creamy brown in ground color, spotted and blotched in varying shades of brown, with underlying secondary marks of lavender.
• **BREEDING** The nest is a deep cup suspended at the rim from a tree fork. It is constructed of grass, fine bark strips, and thin vine tendrils, and is tightly bound with cobwebs. It is situated on the banks of rivers and streams in forest or woodland.
• **RANGE** Occurs in southern New Guinea and much of Australia.

underlying lavender marks •

Egg size 31–36 x 21–24 mm	Clutch size 2–3, rarely 4	Incubation Unknown

Order PASSERIFORMES	Family ORIOLIDAE	Species *Oriolus chinensis*

BLACK-NAPED ORIOLE

The eggs of the Black-naped Oriole have a beautiful pale pink ground color, and are spotted and blotched with purplish brown spots, surrounded by a reddish halo, which makes them look as if the color has run. There are a few secondary underlying lavender spots.
• **BREEDING** The nest is a deep cup of grass and coconut fibers, firmly bound into a fork of twigs near the tip of an overhanging branch. It is suspended like a cradle. The outside of the nest is often draped with cobwebs, papery bark, rags, and debris.
• **RANGE** Breeds from the Himalayas east to Amurland and China, and south through Southeast Asia to Indonesia and Sulawesi.

• *rose-pink ground color*

Egg size 25–34 x 19–23 mm	Clutch size 2–3	Incubation Unknown

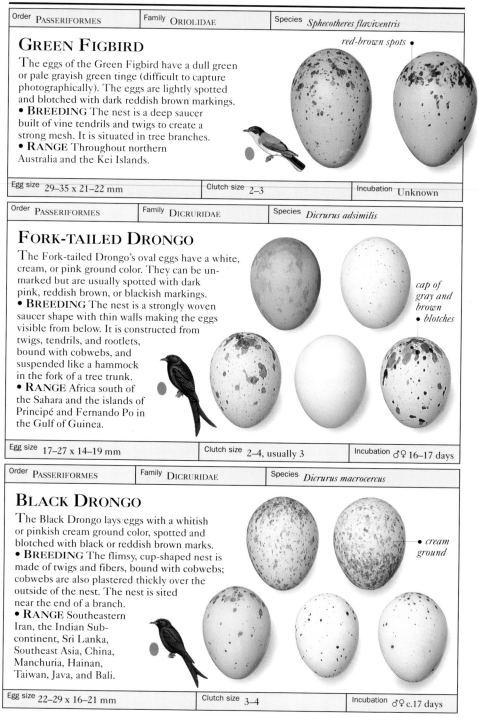

| Order PASSERIFORMES | Family ORIOLIDAE | Species *Sphecotheres flaviventris* |

GREEN FIGBIRD

red-brown spots •

The eggs of the Green Figbird have a dull green or pale grayish green tinge (difficult to capture photographically). The eggs are lightly spotted and blotched with dark reddish brown markings.
• **BREEDING** The nest is a deep saucer built of vine tendrils and twigs to create a strong mesh. It is situated in tree branches.
• **RANGE** Throughout northern Australia and the Kei Islands.

| Egg size 29–35 x 21–22 mm | Clutch size 2–3 | Incubation Unknown |

| Order PASSERIFORMES | Family DICRURIDAE | Species *Dicrurus adsimilis* |

FORK-TAILED DRONGO

The Fork-tailed Drongo's oval eggs have a white, cream, or pink ground color. They can be un-marked but are usually spotted with dark pink, reddish brown, or blackish markings.
• **BREEDING** The nest is a strongly woven saucer shape with thin walls making the eggs visible from below. It is constructed from twigs, tendrils, and rootlets, bound with cobwebs, and suspended like a hammock in the fork of a tree trunk.
• **RANGE** Africa south of the Sahara and the islands of Príncipe and Fernando Po in the Gulf of Guinea.

cap of gray and brown
• *blotches*

| Egg size 17–27 x 14–19 mm | Clutch size 2–4, usually 3 | Incubation ♂♀ 16–17 days |

| Order PASSERIFORMES | Family DICRURIDAE | Species *Dicrurus macrocercus* |

BLACK DRONGO

The Black Drongo lays eggs with a whitish or pinkish cream ground color, spotted and blotched with black or reddish brown marks.
• **BREEDING** The flimsy, cup-shaped nest is made of twigs and fibers, bound with cobwebs; cobwebs are also plastered thickly over the outside of the nest. The nest is sited near the end of a branch.
• **RANGE** Southeastern Iran, the Indian Sub-continent, Sri Lanka, Southeast Asia, China, Manchuria, Hainan, Taiwan, Java, and Bali.

• *cream ground*

| Egg size 22–29 x 16–21 mm | Clutch size 3–4 | Incubation ♂♀ c.17 days |

Order PASSERIFORMES	Family DICRURIDAE	Species *Dicrurus aeneas*

BRONZED DRONGO

The Bronzed Drongo's eggs are pinkish fawn or pale salmon-pink in ground color, with an irregular zone of cloudy reddish or purplish spots around the larger end.
• **BREEDING** The nest is a shallow cup-shape constructed out of fragments of tree bark, strips of banana leaves, and grasses. Cobwebs are plastered thickly over the outside. It is suspended like a hammock in a tree fork.
• **RANGE** Occurs throughout the Indian Subcontinent, to southern China, Hainan, Taiwan, Southeast Asia, Sumatra, and Borneo.

• *red marks*

• *fawn ground*

Egg size 19–26 x 15–20 mm	Clutch size 3–4	Incubation ♂♀ Unknown

Order PASSERIFORMES	Family DICRURIDAE	Species *Dicrurus hottentottus*

SPANGLED DRONGO

The elliptical eggs of the Spangled Drongo are cream to salmon-pink in ground color, and freckled with reddish and purplish markings.
• **BREEDING** The nest is a deep saucer built out of scraps of bark, grass, rootlets, creeper tendrils, and other material. Its very loose construction makes the eggs readily visible from below. The nest is built among twigs toward the end of a tree branch.
• **RANGE** Indian Subcontinent, China, Southeast Asia, Indonesia to the Philippines, New Guinea, Australia, and the Solomon Islands.

• *"ghost" markings on creamy white ground*

• *purple marks*

red • *freckles*

Egg size 25–34 x 19–22 mm	Clutch size 3–4	Incubation ♂♀ Unknown

Order PASSERIFORMES	Family CALLAEIDAE	Species *Creadion carunculatus*

SADDLEBACK

The Saddleback's eggs are pale brown or gray in ground color, blotched with dark brown marks.
• **BREEDING** The nest is composed of twigs, rootlets, flimsy fern stems, and palm fibers. It is situated in a tree hole or in the hollow stem of a dead tree fern, often just above the ground.
• **RANGE** Formerly occurred across New Zealand, but is now confined to Hen Island, and three small islets off the southwestern coast of Stewart Island.

pale ground •

cloudy gray shell marks

Egg size 28–32 x 20–23 mm	Clutch size 2–3	Incubation ♂♀ 20–21 days

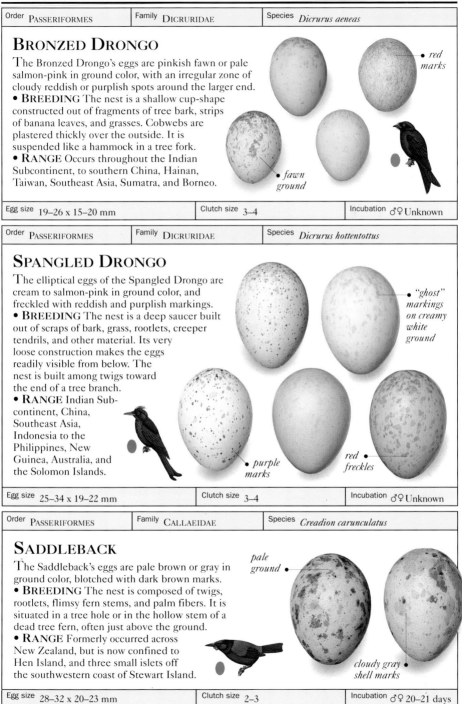

Order PASSERIFORMES	Family GRALLINIDAE	Species *Grallina cyanoleuca*

MAGPIE LARK

The Magpie Lark's eggs are dull white, pinkish, brownish, or grayish white in ground color. They are spotted and blotched with purplish red or brownish red and have secondary underlying marks of lavender-gray, concentrated at the larger end of the egg.
• **BREEDING** The nest is a mud bowl, bound together with dry grass and lined with grass and feathers. The chosen nest site can vary, from a tree branch or the crossarm of a utility pole, to a windmill or an old shed. The nest is smaller than that of the White-winged Chough (below) but similar in size to that of the Apostlebird (opposite), even though it tends to be rather more squat in shape.
• **RANGE** Almost any habitat except dense forest, usually by water. Occurs throughout the Australian continent.

• *cap of red-brown and gray speckles*

Egg size 24–31 x 19–22 mm	Clutch size 3–5, usually 4	Incubation Unknown

Order PASSERIFORMES	Family GRALLINIDAE	Species *Corcorax melanorhamphos*

WHITE-WINGED CHOUGH

The White-winged Chough's oval eggs are creamy white in ground color, with dark brown and black blotches and secondary underlying gray marks.
• **BREEDING** Like the Magpie Lark's (above), the nest is a bowl of mud held together with dry grass and lined with more grass and a few feathers. It is placed in a number of locations at any one of a variety of heights from the ground. The nest is much larger than that of the Magpie Lark.
• **RANGE** The White-winged Chough occurs in woodland and scrub, especially tall mallee, throughout eastern and southeastern Australia ranging from southern Queensland across to western Australia.

• *bold brown blotches*

Egg size 35–43 x 25–31 mm	Clutch size 3–5	Incubation Unknown

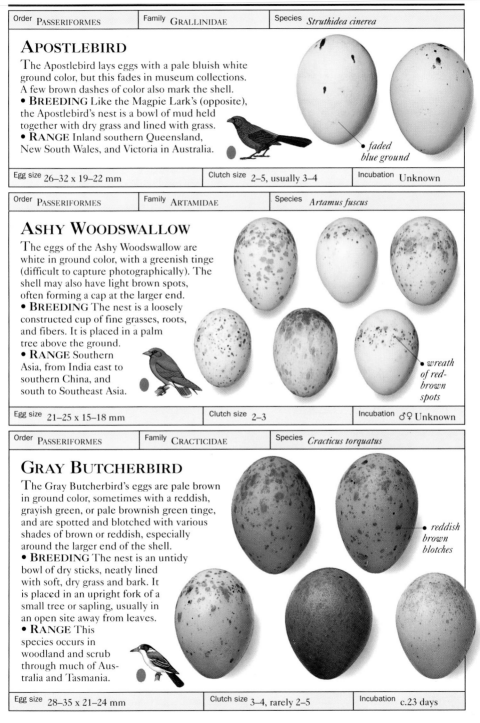

Order PASSERIFORMES	Family GRALLINIDAE	Species *Struthidea cinerea*

APOSTLEBIRD

The Apostlebird lays eggs with a pale bluish white
ground color, but this fades in museum collections.
A few brown dashes of color also mark the shell.
• **BREEDING** Like the Magpie Lark's (opposite),
the Apostlebird's nest is a bowl of mud held
together with dry grass and lined with grass.
• **RANGE** Inland southern Queensland,
New South Wales, and Victoria in Australia.

*• faded
blue ground*

Egg size 26–32 x 19–22 mm	Clutch size 2–5, usually 3–4	Incubation Unknown

Order PASSERIFORMES	Family ARTAMIDAE	Species *Artamus fuscus*

ASHY WOODSWALLOW

The eggs of the Ashy Woodswallow are
white in ground color, with a greenish tinge
(difficult to capture photographically). The
shell may also have light brown spots,
often forming a cap at the larger end.
• **BREEDING** The nest is a loosely
constructed cup of fine grasses, roots,
and fibers. It is placed in a palm
tree above the ground.
• **RANGE** Southern
Asia, from India east to
southern China, and
south to Southeast Asia.

*• wreath
of red-
brown
spots*

Egg size 21–25 x 15–18 mm	Clutch size 2–3	Incubation ♂♀ Unknown

Order PASSERIFORMES	Family CRACTICIDAE	Species *Cracticus torquatus*

GRAY BUTCHERBIRD

The Gray Butcherbird's eggs are pale brown
in ground color, sometimes with a reddish,
grayish green, or pale brownish green tinge,
and are spotted and blotched with various
shades of brown or reddish, especially
around the larger end of the shell.
• **BREEDING** The nest is an untidy
bowl of dry sticks, neatly lined
with soft, dry grass and bark. It
is placed in an upright fork of a
small tree or sapling, usually in
an open site away from leaves.
• **RANGE** This
species occurs in
woodland and scrub
through much of Aus-
tralia and Tasmania.

*• reddish
brown
blotches*

Egg size 28–35 x 21–24 mm	Clutch size 3–4, rarely 2–5	Incubation c.23 days

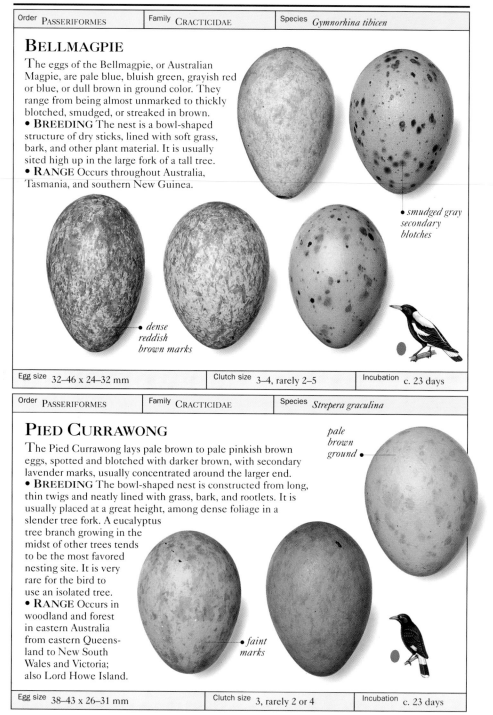

Order PASSERIFORMES	Family CRACTICIDAE	Species *Gymnorhina tibicen*

BELLMAGPIE

The eggs of the Bellmagpie, or Australian Magpie, are pale blue, bluish green, grayish red or blue, or dull brown in ground color. They range from being almost unmarked to thickly blotched, smudged, or streaked in brown.
• **BREEDING** The nest is a bowl-shaped structure of dry sticks, lined with soft grass, bark, and other plant material. It is usually sited high up in the large fork of a tall tree.
• **RANGE** Occurs throughout Australia, Tasmania, and southern New Guinea.

• smudged gray secondary blotches

• dense reddish brown marks

Egg size 32–46 x 24–32 mm	Clutch size 3–4, rarely 2–5	Incubation c. 23 days

Order PASSERIFORMES	Family CRACTICIDAE	Species *Strepera graculina*

PIED CURRAWONG

pale brown ground •

The Pied Currawong lays pale brown to pale pinkish brown eggs, spotted and blotched with darker brown, with secondary lavender marks, usually concentrated around the larger end.
• **BREEDING** The bowl-shaped nest is constructed from long, thin twigs and neatly lined with grass, bark, and rootlets. It is usually placed at a great height, among dense foliage in a slender tree fork. A eucalyptus tree branch growing in the midst of other trees tends to be the most favored nesting site. It is very rare for the bird to use an isolated tree.
• **RANGE** Occurs in woodland and forest in eastern Australia from eastern Queensland to New South Wales and Victoria; also Lord Howe Island.

• faint marks

Egg size 38–43 x 26–31 mm	Clutch size 3, rarely 2 or 4	Incubation c. 23 days

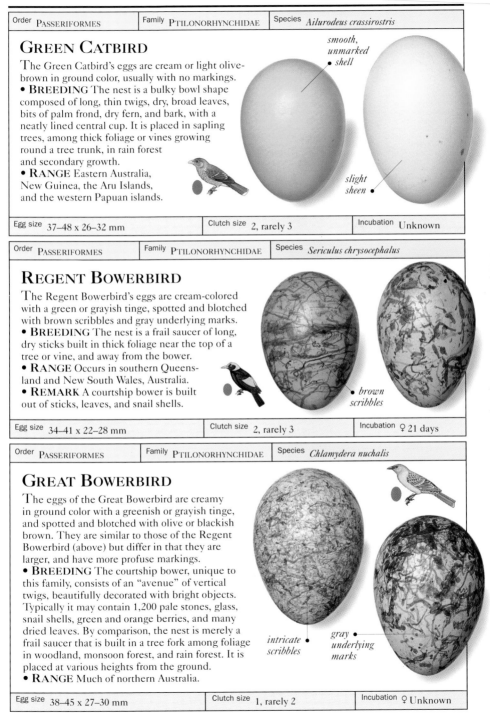

Order PASSERIFORMES	Family PTILONORHYNCHIDAE	Species *Ailurodeus crassirostris*

GREEN CATBIRD

The Green Catbird's eggs are cream or light olive-brown in ground color, usually with no markings.
• **BREEDING** The nest is a bulky bowl shape composed of long, thin twigs, dry, broad leaves, bits of palm frond, dry fern, and bark, with a neatly lined central cup. It is placed in sapling trees, among thick foliage or vines growing round a tree trunk, in rain forest and secondary growth.
• **RANGE** Eastern Australia, New Guinea, the Aru Islands, and the western Papuan islands.

smooth, unmarked shell

slight sheen

Egg size 37–48 x 26–32 mm	Clutch size 2, rarely 3	Incubation Unknown

Order PASSERIFORMES	Family PTILONORHYNCHIDAE	Species *Sericulus chrysocephalus*

REGENT BOWERBIRD

The Regent Bowerbird's eggs are cream-colored with a green or grayish tinge, spotted and blotched with brown scribbles and gray underlying marks.
• **BREEDING** The nest is a frail saucer of long, dry sticks built in thick foliage near the top of a tree or vine, and away from the bower.
• **RANGE** Occurs in southern Queensland and New South Wales, Australia.
• **REMARK** A courtship bower is built out of sticks, leaves, and snail shells.

brown scribbles

Egg size 34–41 x 22–28 mm	Clutch size 2, rarely 3	Incubation ♀ 21 days

Order PASSERIFORMES	Family PTILONORHYNCHIDAE	Species *Chlamydera nuchalis*

GREAT BOWERBIRD

The eggs of the Great Bowerbird are creamy in ground color with a greenish or grayish tinge, and spotted and blotched with olive or blackish brown. They are similar to those of the Regent Bowerbird (above) but differ in that they are larger, and have more profuse markings.
• **BREEDING** The courtship bower, unique to this family, consists of an "avenue" of vertical twigs, beautifully decorated with bright objects. Typically it may contain 1,200 pale stones, glass, snail shells, green and orange berries, and many dried leaves. By comparison, the nest is merely a frail saucer that is built in a tree fork among foliage in woodland, monsoon forest, and rain forest. It is placed at various heights from the ground.
• **RANGE** Much of northern Australia.

intricate scribbles

gray underlying marks

Egg size 38–45 x 27–30 mm	Clutch size 1, rarely 2	Incubation ♀ Unknown

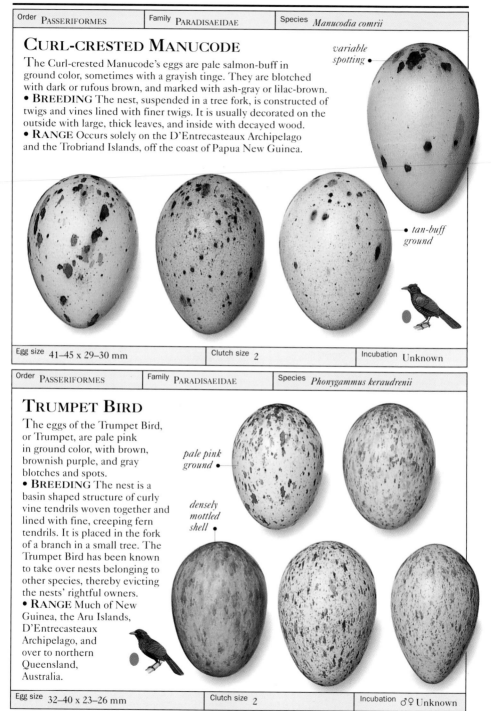

Order PASSERIFORMES	Family PARADISAEIDAE	Species *Manucodia comrii*

CURL-CRESTED MANUCODE

The Curl-crested Manucode's eggs are pale salmon-buff in ground color, sometimes with a grayish tinge. They are blotched with dark or rufous brown, and marked with ash-gray or lilac-brown.
• **BREEDING** The nest, suspended in a tree fork, is constructed of twigs and vines lined with finer twigs. It is usually decorated on the outside with large, thick leaves, and inside with decayed wood.
• **RANGE** Occurs solely on the D'Entrecasteaux Archipelago and the Trobriand Islands, off the coast of Papua New Guinea.

variable spotting •

• tan-buff ground

Egg size 41–45 x 29–30 mm	Clutch size 2	Incubation Unknown

Order PASSERIFORMES	Family PARADISAEIDAE	Species *Phonygammus keraudrenii*

TRUMPET BIRD

The eggs of the Trumpet Bird, or Trumpet, are pale pink in ground color, with brown, brownish purple, and gray blotches and spots.
• **BREEDING** The nest is a basin shaped structure of curly vine tendrils woven together and lined with fine, creeping fern tendrils. It is placed in the fork of a branch in a small tree. The Trumpet Bird has been known to take over nests belonging to other species, thereby evicting the nests' rightful owners.
• **RANGE** Much of New Guinea, the Aru Islands, D'Entrecasteaux Archipelago, and over to northern Queensland, Australia.

pale pink ground •

densely mottled shell •

Egg size 32–40 x 23–26 mm	Clutch size 2	Incubation ♂♀ Unknown

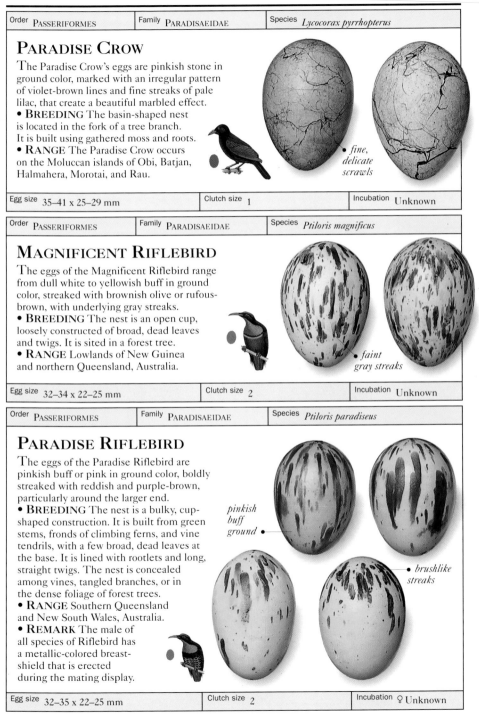

Order PASSERIFORMES	Family PARADISAEIDAE	Species *Lycocorax pyrrhopterus*

PARADISE CROW

The Paradise Crow's eggs are pinkish stone in ground color, marked with an irregular pattern of violet-brown lines and fine streaks of pale lilac, that create a beautiful marbled effect.
• **BREEDING** The basin-shaped nest is located in the fork of a tree branch. It is built using gathered moss and roots.
• **RANGE** The Paradise Crow occurs on the Moluccan islands of Obi, Batjan, Halmahera, Morotai, and Rau.

• *fine, delicate scrawls*

Egg size 35–41 x 25–29 mm	Clutch size 1	Incubation Unknown

Order PASSERIFORMES	Family PARADISAEIDAE	Species *Ptiloris magnificus*

MAGNIFICENT RIFLEBIRD

The eggs of the Magnificent Riflebird range from dull white to yellowish buff in ground color, streaked with brownish olive or rufous-brown, with underlying gray streaks.
• **BREEDING** The nest is an open cup, loosely constructed of broad, dead leaves and twigs. It is sited in a forest tree.
• **RANGE** Lowlands of New Guinea and northern Queensland, Australia.

• *faint gray streaks*

Egg size 32–34 x 22–25 mm	Clutch size 2	Incubation Unknown

Order PASSERIFORMES	Family PARADISAEIDAE	Species *Ptiloris paradiseus*

PARADISE RIFLEBIRD

The eggs of the Paradise Riflebird are pinkish buff or pink in ground color, boldly streaked with reddish and purple-brown, particularly around the larger end.
• **BREEDING** The nest is a bulky, cup-shaped construction. It is built from green stems, fronds of climbing ferns, and vine tendrils, with a few broad, dead leaves at the base. It is lined with rootlets and long, straight twigs. The nest is concealed among vines, tangled branches, or in the dense foliage of forest trees.
• **RANGE** Southern Queensland and New South Wales, Australia.
• **REMARK** The male of all species of Riflebird has a metallic-colored breast-shield that is erected during the mating display.

pinkish buff ground •

• *brushlike streaks*

Egg size 32–35 x 22–25 mm	Clutch size 2	Incubation ♀ Unknown

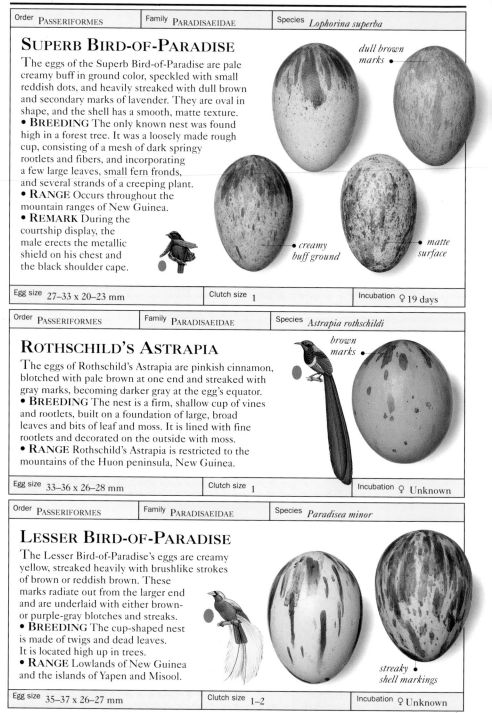

Order PASSERIFORMES	Family PARADISAEIDAE	Species *Lophorina superba*

SUPERB BIRD-OF-PARADISE

The eggs of the Superb Bird-of-Paradise are pale creamy buff in ground color, speckled with small reddish dots, and heavily streaked with dull brown and secondary marks of lavender. They are oval in shape, and the shell has a smooth, matte texture.
• **BREEDING** The only known nest was found high in a forest tree. It was a loosely made rough cup, consisting of a mesh of dark springy rootlets and fibers, and incorporating a few large leaves, small fern fronds, and several strands of a creeping plant.
• **RANGE** Occurs throughout the mountain ranges of New Guinea.
• **REMARK** During the courtship display, the male erects the metallic shield on his chest and the black shoulder cape.

dull brown marks •

• *creamy buff ground*

• *matte surface*

Egg size 27–33 x 20–23 mm	Clutch size 1	Incubation ♀ 19 days

Order PASSERIFORMES	Family PARADISAEIDAE	Species *Astrapia rothschildi*

ROTHSCHILD'S ASTRAPIA

brown marks •

The eggs of Rothschild's Astrapia are pinkish cinnamon, blotched with pale brown at one end and streaked with gray marks, becoming darker gray at the egg's equator.
• **BREEDING** The nest is a firm, shallow cup of vines and rootlets, built on a foundation of large, broad leaves and bits of leaf and moss. It is lined with fine rootlets and decorated on the outside with moss.
• **RANGE** Rothschild's Astrapia is restricted to the mountains of the Huon peninsula, New Guinea.

Egg size 33–36 x 26–28 mm	Clutch size 1	Incubation ♀ Unknown

Order PASSERIFORMES	Family PARADISAEIDAE	Species *Paradisea minor*

LESSER BIRD-OF-PARADISE

The Lesser Bird-of-Paradise's eggs are creamy yellow, streaked heavily with brushlike strokes of brown or reddish brown. These marks radiate out from the larger end and are underlaid with either brown- or purple-gray blotches and streaks.
• **BREEDING** The cup-shaped nest is made of twigs and dead leaves. It is located high up in trees.
• **RANGE** Lowlands of New Guinea and the islands of Yapen and Misool.

streaky shell markings •

Egg size 35–37 x 26–27 mm	Clutch size 1–2	Incubation ♀ Unknown

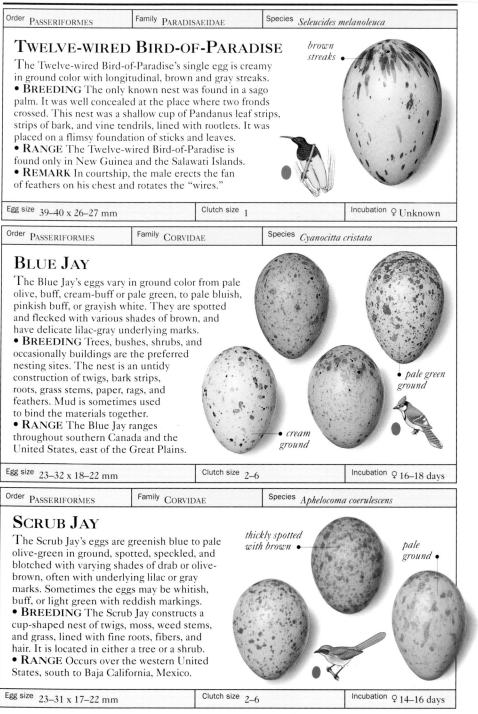

| Order PASSERIFORMES | Family PARADISAEIDAE | Species *Seleucides melanoleuca* |

TWELVE-WIRED BIRD-OF-PARADISE

brown streaks •

The Twelve-wired Bird-of-Paradise's single egg is creamy in ground color with longitudinal, brown and gray streaks.
• **BREEDING** The only known nest was found in a sago palm. It was well concealed at the place where two fronds crossed. This nest was a shallow cup of Pandanus leaf strips, strips of bark, and vine tendrils, lined with rootlets. It was placed on a flimsy foundation of sticks and leaves.
• **RANGE** The Twelve-wired Bird-of-Paradise is found only in New Guinea and the Salawati Islands.
• **REMARK** In courtship, the male erects the fan of feathers on his chest and rotates the "wires."

| Egg size 39–40 x 26–27 mm | Clutch size 1 | Incubation ♀ Unknown |

| Order PASSERIFORMES | Family CORVIDAE | Species *Cyanocitta cristata* |

BLUE JAY

The Blue Jay's eggs vary in ground color from pale olive, buff, cream-buff or pale green, to pale bluish, pinkish buff, or grayish white. They are spotted and flecked with various shades of brown, and have delicate lilac-gray underlying marks.
• **BREEDING** Trees, bushes, shrubs, and occasionally buildings are the preferred nesting sites. The nest is an untidy construction of twigs, bark strips, roots, grass stems, paper, rags, and feathers. Mud is sometimes used to bind the materials together.
• **RANGE** The Blue Jay ranges throughout southern Canada and the United States, east of the Great Plains.

• pale green ground

• cream ground

| Egg size 23–32 x 18–22 mm | Clutch size 2–6 | Incubation ♀ 16–18 days |

| Order PASSERIFORMES | Family CORVIDAE | Species *Aphelocoma coerulescens* |

SCRUB JAY

The Scrub Jay's eggs are greenish blue to pale olive-green in ground, spotted, speckled, and blotched with varying shades of drab or olive-brown, often with underlying lilac or gray marks. Sometimes the eggs may be whitish, buff, or light green with reddish markings.
• **BREEDING** The Scrub Jay constructs a cup-shaped nest of twigs, moss, weed stems, and grass, lined with fine roots, fibers, and hair. It is located in either a tree or a shrub.
• **RANGE** Occurs over the western United States, south to Baja California, Mexico.

thickly spotted with brown •

pale ground •

| Egg size 23–31 x 17–22 mm | Clutch size 2–6 | Incubation ♀ 14–16 days |

Order PASSERIFORMES	Family CORVIDAE	Species *Cissilopha sanblasiana*

SAN BLAS JAY

The oval to elliptical eggs of the San Blas Jay
are buffish pink or pale pink in ground color.
The shells have light and chestnut-brown
spots and blotches and underlying grayish
lavender marks. They have a slight sheen.
• **BREEDING** The nest is a simple structure
built of sticks and twigs, lined with coarse
plant fibers. This jay usually chooses to
nest in trees, shrubs, or among vines.
• **RANGE** Occurs in deciduous
and evergreen thickets bordering
palm groves, cleared fields, and
mangroves in southern Mexico,
Belize, and northeastern Guatemala. It is often seen in small groups.

*buffish pink
ground*

*chestnut
blotches*

smooth shell

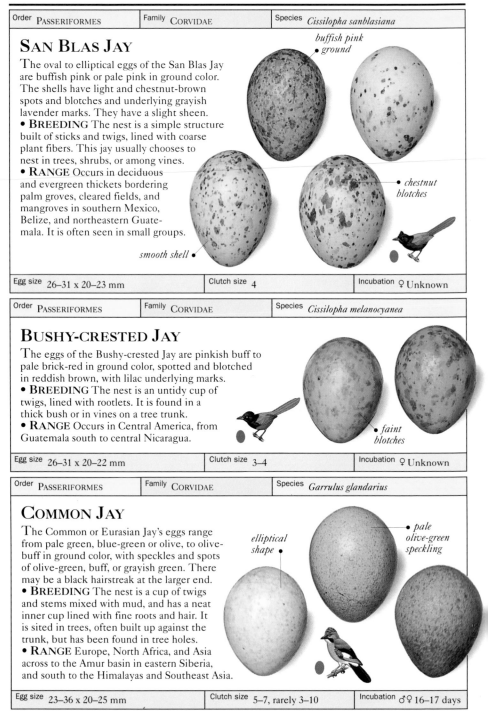

Egg size 26–31 x 20–23 mm	Clutch size 4	Incubation ♀ Unknown

Order PASSERIFORMES	Family CORVIDAE	Species *Cissilopha melanocyanea*

BUSHY-CRESTED JAY

The eggs of the Bushy-crested Jay are pinkish buff to
pale brick-red in ground color, spotted and blotched
in reddish brown, with lilac underlying marks.
• **BREEDING** The nest is an untidy cup of
twigs, lined with rootlets. It is found in a
thick bush or in vines on a tree trunk.
• **RANGE** Occurs in Central America, from
Guatemala south to central Nicaragua.

*faint
blotches*

Egg size 26–31 x 20–22 mm	Clutch size 3–4	Incubation ♀ Unknown

Order PASSERIFORMES	Family CORVIDAE	Species *Garrulus glandarius*

COMMON JAY

The Common or Eurasian Jay's eggs range
from pale green, blue-green or olive, to olive-
buff in ground color, with speckles and spots
of olive-green, buff, or grayish green. There
may be a black hairstreak at the larger end.
• **BREEDING** The nest is a cup of twigs
and stems mixed with mud, and has a neat
inner cup lined with fine roots and hair. It
is sited in trees, often built up against the
trunk, but has been found in tree holes.
• **RANGE** Europe, North Africa, and Asia
across to the Amur basin in eastern Siberia,
and south to the Himalayas and Southeast Asia.

*elliptical
shape*

*pale
olive-green
speckling*

Egg size 23–36 x 20–25 mm	Clutch size 5–7, rarely 3–10	Incubation ♂♀ 16–17 days

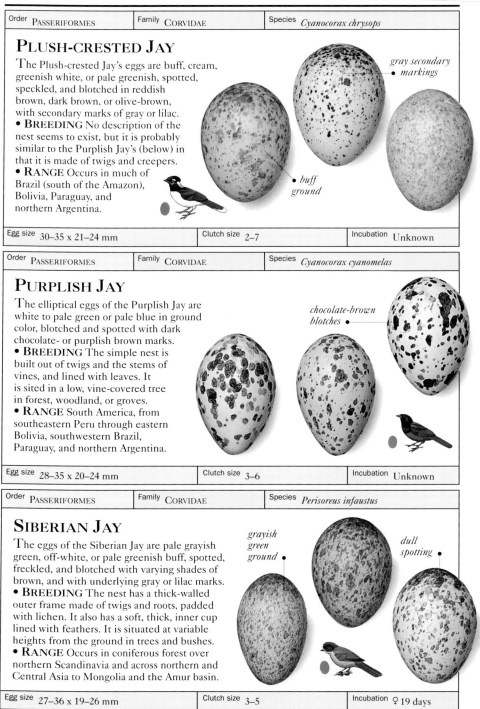

Order PASSERIFORMES	Family CORVIDAE	Species *Cyanocorax chrysops*

PLUSH-CRESTED JAY

The Plush-crested Jay's eggs are buff, cream, greenish white, or pale greenish, spotted, speckled, and blotched in reddish brown, dark brown, or olive-brown, with secondary marks of gray or lilac.
• **BREEDING** No description of the nest seems to exist, but it is probably similar to the Purplish Jay's (below) in that it is made of twigs and creepers.
• **RANGE** Occurs in much of Brazil (south of the Amazon), Bolivia, Paraguay, and northern Argentina.

gray secondary markings

buff ground

Egg size 30–35 x 21–24 mm	Clutch size 2–7	Incubation Unknown

Order PASSERIFORMES	Family CORVIDAE	Species *Cyanocorax cyanomelas*

PURPLISH JAY

The elliptical eggs of the Purplish Jay are white to pale green or pale blue in ground color, blotched and spotted with dark chocolate- or purplish brown marks.
• **BREEDING** The simple nest is built out of twigs and the stems of vines, and lined with leaves. It is sited in a low, vine-covered tree in forest, woodland, or groves.
• **RANGE** South America, from southeastern Peru through eastern Bolivia, southwestern Brazil, Paraguay, and northern Argentina.

chocolate-brown blotches

Egg size 28–35 x 20–24 mm	Clutch size 3–6	Incubation Unknown

Order PASSERIFORMES	Family CORVIDAE	Species *Perisoreus infaustus*

SIBERIAN JAY

The eggs of the Siberian Jay are pale grayish green, off-white, or pale greenish buff, spotted, freckled, and blotched with varying shades of brown, and with underlying gray or lilac marks.
• **BREEDING** The nest has a thick-walled outer frame made of twigs and roots, padded with lichen. It also has a soft, thick, inner cup lined with feathers. It is situated at variable heights from the ground in trees and bushes.
• **RANGE** Occurs in coniferous forest over northern Scandinavia and across northern and Central Asia to Mongolia and the Amur basin.

grayish green ground

dull spotting

Egg size 27–36 x 19–26 mm	Clutch size 3–5	Incubation ♀ 19 days

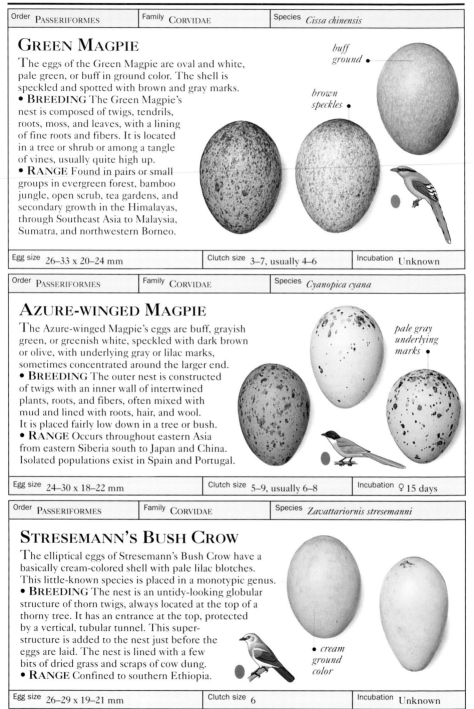

Order PASSERIFORMES	Family CORVIDAE	Species *Cissa chinensis*

GREEN MAGPIE

The eggs of the Green Magpie are oval and white, pale green, or buff in ground color. The shell is speckled and spotted with brown and gray marks.
• **BREEDING** The Green Magpie's nest is composed of twigs, tendrils, roots, moss, and leaves, with a lining of fine roots and fibers. It is located in a tree or shrub or among a tangle of vines, usually quite high up.
• **RANGE** Found in pairs or small groups in evergreen forest, bamboo jungle, open scrub, tea gardens, and secondary growth in the Himalayas, through Southeast Asia to Malaysia, Sumatra, and northwestern Borneo.

buff ground •

brown speckles •

Egg size 26–33 x 20–24 mm	Clutch size 3–7, usually 4–6	Incubation Unknown

Order PASSERIFORMES	Family CORVIDAE	Species *Cyanopica cyana*

AZURE-WINGED MAGPIE

The Azure-winged Magpie's eggs are buff, grayish green, or greenish white, speckled with dark brown or olive, with underlying gray or lilac marks, sometimes concentrated around the larger end.
• **BREEDING** The outer nest is constructed of twigs with an inner wall of intertwined plants, roots, and fibers, often mixed with mud and lined with roots, hair, and wool. It is placed fairly low down in a tree or bush.
• **RANGE** Occurs throughout eastern Asia from eastern Siberia south to Japan and China. Isolated populations exist in Spain and Portugal.

pale gray underlying marks •

Egg size 24–30 x 18–22 mm	Clutch size 5–9, usually 6–8	Incubation ♀ 15 days

Order PASSERIFORMES	Family CORVIDAE	Species *Zavattariornis stresemanni*

STRESEMANN'S BUSH CROW

The elliptical eggs of Stresemann's Bush Crow have a basically cream-colored shell with pale lilac blotches. This little-known species is placed in a monotypic genus.
• **BREEDING** The nest is an untidy-looking globular structure of thorn twigs, always located at the top of a thorny tree. It has an entrance at the top, protected by a vertical, tubular tunnel. This super-structure is added to the nest just before the eggs are laid. The nest is lined with a few bits of dried grass and scraps of cow dung.
• **RANGE** Confined to southern Ethiopia.

• *cream ground color*

Egg size 26–29 x 19–21 mm	Clutch size 6	Incubation Unknown

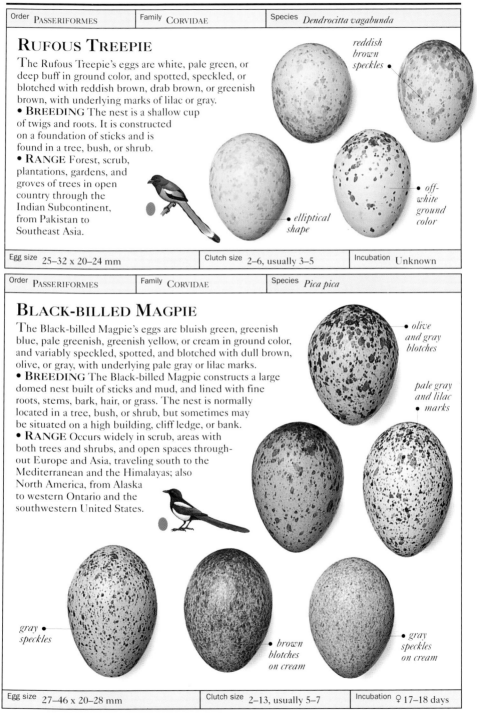

Order PASSERIFORMES	Family CORVIDAE	Species *Dendrocitta vagabunda*

RUFOUS TREEPIE

The Rufous Treepie's eggs are white, pale green, or deep buff in ground color, and spotted, speckled, or blotched with reddish brown, drab brown, or greenish brown, with underlying marks of lilac or gray.
• **BREEDING** The nest is a shallow cup of twigs and roots. It is constructed on a foundation of sticks and is found in a tree, bush, or shrub.
• **RANGE** Forest, scrub, plantations, gardens, and groves of trees in open country through the Indian Subcontinent, from Pakistan to Southeast Asia.

reddish brown speckles •

• off-white ground color

• elliptical shape

Egg size 25–32 x 20–24 mm	Clutch size 2–6, usually 3–5	Incubation Unknown

Order PASSERIFORMES	Family CORVIDAE	Species *Pica pica*

BLACK-BILLED MAGPIE

The Black-billed Magpie's eggs are bluish green, greenish blue, pale greenish, greenish yellow, or cream in ground color, and variably speckled, spotted, and blotched with dull brown, olive, or gray, with underlying pale gray or lilac marks.
• **BREEDING** The Black-billed Magpie constructs a large domed nest built of sticks and mud, and lined with fine roots, stems, bark, hair, or grass. The nest is normally located in a tree, bush, or shrub, but sometimes may be situated on a high building, cliff ledge, or bank.
• **RANGE** Occurs widely in scrub, areas with both trees and shrubs, and open spaces throughout Europe and Asia, traveling south to the Mediterranean and the Himalayas; also North America, from Alaska to western Ontario and the southwestern United States.

• olive and gray blotches

pale gray and lilac • marks

gray • speckles

• brown blotches on cream

• gray speckles on cream

Egg size 27–46 x 20–28 mm	Clutch size 2–13, usually 5–7	Incubation ♀ 17–18 days

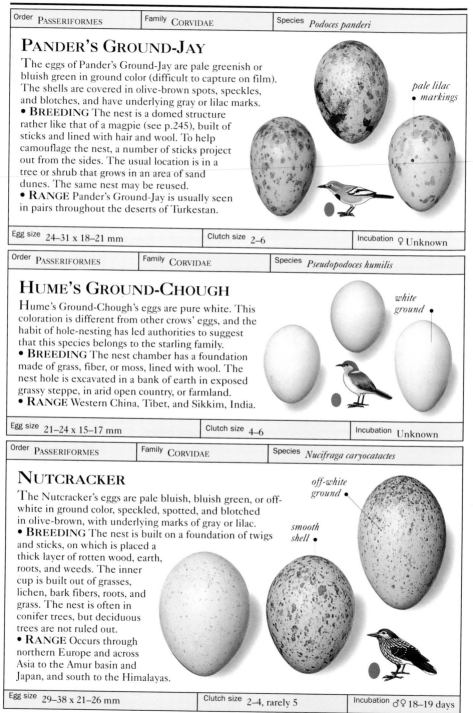

Order PASSERIFORMES	Family CORVIDAE	Species *Podoces panderi*

PANDER'S GROUND-JAY

The eggs of Pander's Ground-Jay are pale greenish or bluish green in ground color (difficult to capture on film). The shells are covered in olive-brown spots, speckles, and blotches, and have underlying gray or lilac marks.
• **BREEDING** The nest is a domed structure rather like that of a magpie (see p.245), built of sticks and lined with hair and wool. To help camouflage the nest, a number of sticks project out from the sides. The usual location is in a tree or shrub that grows in an area of sand dunes. The same nest may be reused.
• **RANGE** Pander's Ground-Jay is usually seen in pairs throughout the deserts of Turkestan.

pale lilac • markings

Egg size 24–31 x 18–21 mm	Clutch size 2–6	Incubation ♀ Unknown

Order PASSERIFORMES	Family CORVIDAE	Species *Pseudopodoces humilis*

HUME'S GROUND-CHOUGH

Hume's Ground-Chough's eggs are pure white. This coloration is different from other crows' eggs, and the habit of hole-nesting has led authorities to suggest that this species belongs to the starling family.
• **BREEDING** The nest chamber has a foundation made of grass, fiber, or moss, lined with wool. The nest hole is excavated in a bank of earth in exposed grassy steppe, in arid open country, or farmland.
• **RANGE** Western China, Tibet, and Sikkim, India.

white ground •

Egg size 21–24 x 15–17 mm	Clutch size 4–6	Incubation Unknown

Order PASSERIFORMES	Family CORVIDAE	Species *Nucifraga caryocatactes*

NUTCRACKER

The Nutcracker's eggs are pale bluish, bluish green, or off-white in ground color, speckled, spotted, and blotched in olive-brown, with underlying marks of gray or lilac.
• **BREEDING** The nest is built on a foundation of twigs and sticks, on which is placed a thick layer of rotten wood, earth, roots, and weeds. The inner cup is built out of grasses, lichen, bark fibers, roots, and grass. The nest is often in conifer trees, but deciduous trees are not ruled out.
• **RANGE** Occurs through northern Europe and across Asia to the Amur basin and Japan, and south to the Himalayas.

off-white ground •

smooth shell •

Egg size 29–38 x 21–26 mm	Clutch size 2–4, rarely 5	Incubation ♂♀ 18–19 days

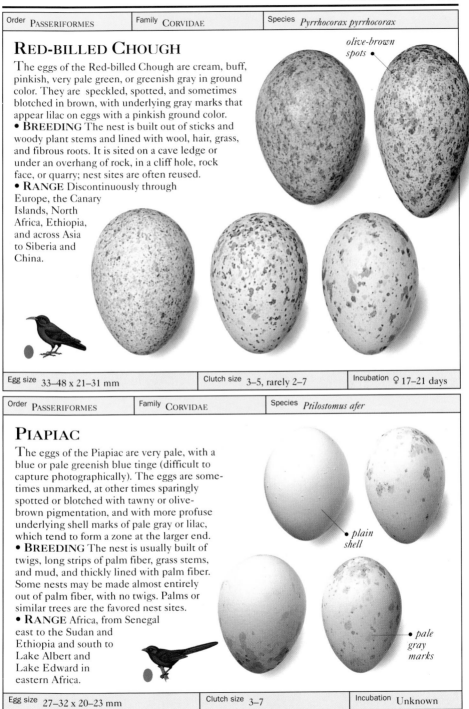

Order PASSERIFORMES	Family CORVIDAE	Species *Pyrrhocorax pyrrhocorax*

RED-BILLED CHOUGH

olive-brown spots •

The eggs of the Red-billed Chough are cream, buff, pinkish, very pale green, or greenish gray in ground color. They are speckled, spotted, and sometimes blotched in brown, with underlying gray marks that appear lilac on eggs with a pinkish ground color.
• **BREEDING** The nest is built out of sticks and woody plant stems and lined with wool, hair, grass, and fibrous roots. It is sited on a cave ledge or under an overhang of rock, in a cliff hole, rock face, or quarry; nest sites are often reused.
• **RANGE** Discontinuously through Europe, the Canary Islands, North Africa, Ethiopia, and across Asia to Siberia and China.

Egg size 33–48 x 21–31 mm	Clutch size 3–5, rarely 2–7	Incubation ♀ 17–21 days

Order PASSERIFORMES	Family CORVIDAE	Species *Ptilostomus afer*

PIAPIAC

The eggs of the Piapiac are very pale, with a blue or pale greenish blue tinge (difficult to capture photographically). The eggs are some-times unmarked, at other times sparingly spotted or blotched with tawny or olive-brown pigmentation, and with more profuse underlying shell marks of pale gray or lilac, which tend to form a zone at the larger end.
• **BREEDING** The nest is usually built of twigs, long strips of palm fiber, grass stems, and mud, and thickly lined with palm fiber. Some nests may be made almost entirely out of palm fiber, with no twigs. Palms or similar trees are the favored nest sites.
• **RANGE** Africa, from Senegal east to the Sudan and Ethiopia and south to Lake Albert and Lake Edward in eastern Africa.

• plain shell

• pale gray marks

Egg size 27–32 x 20–23 mm	Clutch size 3–7	Incubation Unknown

Order PASSERIFORMES	Family CORVIDAE	Species *Corvus monedula*

JACKDAW

The eggs of the Jackdaw have a pale ground with a hint of greenish blue or bluish white (difficult to capture photographically). They are spotted with blackish brown and gray marks.
• **BREEDING** The nest is composed of sticks and woody stems, mixed with mud and lined with fur, hair, wool, and rags. More soft materials are added to the lining throughout incubation. The nest is situated in a tree hole, cliff, or building, or less often, in a hole in the ground.
• **RANGE** The Jackdaw occurs in Europe, North Africa, Iran, Asia, Lake Baikal, and India.

blackish brown spots

brown blotches

Egg size 29–40 x 21–29 mm	Clutch size 4–5, rarely 3–7	Incubation ♀ 16–19 days

Order PASSERIFORMES	Family CORVIDAE	Species *Corvus capensis*

CAPE CROW

The Cape Crow's eggs are buff, buffish white, or pale pink in ground color, liberally blotched, speckled, and spotted with red or brown and with underlying marks of lavender. The eggs of this species are unusual in that they are similar to "erythristic" eggs that occur in other crow species.
• **BREEDING** The nest is a basket-shaped construction of dead twigs, open at both ends, within which is constructed a pad of grass stems and roots, with a lining of similar material. It is located high in a tree, sometimes in a shrub or bush.
• **RANGE** Occurs in northeastern and southern Africa, from Sudan and Ethiopia south to South Africa.

buffish white ground

reddish brown speckles

Egg size 38–53 x 26–34 mm	Clutch size 3–4	Incubation ♂♀ 18–19 days

Order PASSERIFORMES	Family CORVIDAE	Species *Corvus corax*

COMMON RAVEN

The elliptical eggs of the Common Raven have a large
variety of ground colors, ranging from light or greenish blue
to brownish green. The shells are speckled, spotted, and
blotched with various shades of olive and brown, and have
underlying secondary marks of gray or lilac pigment.
• **BREEDING** The nest is constructed on a base of sticks,
heather, and gorse, mixed with earth, moss, and grass.
Thinner sticks are used for the nest rim. The central area
in which the eggs are laid is composed of thin sticks, twigs,
lumps of earth, wool, and hair. The nest is sited on a ledge,
or in a crevice of a coastal or inland cliff, rarely in a tree.
• **RANGE** Open, mountainous, or coastal regions of the
Northern Hemisphere, south to Nicaragua in the Americas,
ranging east to the Mediterranean and northern India.

• *pale
blue-gray
ground*

• *brownish
green ground*

• *olive and
gray marks*

*underlying
marks* •

• *elliptical
shape*

Egg size 40–68 x 29–40 mm	Clutch size 3–6, rarely 7	Incubation ♀ 18–20 days

GLOSSARY

Although technical expressions have been avoided wherever possible, some are inevitable in a book of this nature. All those used are defined below. Terms that are explained elsewhere in the glossary are printed in bold type.

- **ABERRANT**
Unusual, either in shape or color.

- **ALTRICIAL**
Refers to birds whose chicks are hatched at a very early stage, usually naked and blind. Altricial chicks require extensive parental care. *See also* **Precocial**.

- **AMORPHOUS LAYER**
Chalky layer over the eggshell, often concealing its true color.

- **BRAKE**
Large-leaved undergrowth.

- **BROOD PATCH**
Patch of skin on the ventral area that loses most or all of its feathers throughout the breeding season, becoming, instead, engorged with blood vessels as a means of helping the parent to incubate the eggs.

- **CONSPECIFIC**
Considered to belong to the same **species**. It can include having enough differences to justify division into **subspecies**.

- **CRYPTIC**
Designed to be camouflaged against a certain background.

- **DUOTYPIC GENUS**
Genus consisting of two **species**.

- **EGG TOOTH**
False tooth on the bill of a baby bird used to help it break out of the egg. The egg tooth falls off after hatching.

- **EQUATOR**
Imaginary line around the middle of an egg, equidistant from either end.

- **ERYTHRISTIC**
Having an abnormal amount of red pigmentation. In birds' eggs it is usually due to lack or reduction of blue pigment.

- **EXTANT**
Still in existence (i.e. not extinct).

- **FERAL**
Living in a wild state, in an area to which a bird is not native but has been introduced.

- **FRASS**
Excrement of insect larvae.

- **GENUS**
Individual group within a family, containing one or more **species**.

- **GROUND COLOR**
Color of the ground or body of the egg surface, on which markings are superimposed.

- **GUANO**
Excrement of sea birds.

- **GUIANAS, THE**
Guyana, Surinam, and Cayenne, formerly known respectively as British, Dutch, and French Guiana.

- **HOST**
Bird species forced to raise the alien young of a **nest parasite** (such as a cuckoo or cowbird).

- **KAROO**
Raised South African plain where the soil is arid in the dry season.

- **LOWER ORDERS**
The orders of birds that are most primitive in evolutionary terms, such as the Podicipediformes.

- **MIMICRY**
Imitation of the shape, size, or markings of the egg of another species, with the purpose of deceiving the parent birds. Occurs among **nest parasites**, in order to introduce their eggs into the nest of a **host** species.

- **MONOTYPIC GENUS**
Genus consisting of one **species**.

- **NEST PARASITISM**
Practice of laying eggs in the nests of other birds, usually of a different **species**, thus forcing the **host** parents to raise the chick. *See also* **Mimicry**.

- **NON-PASSERINE**
Colloquial term used for any birds not of the order Passeriformes. *See also* **Passerine**.

- **OVIPAROUS**
Reproduction by means of egg-laying. *See also* **Viviparous**.

- **PASSERINE**
Commonly used to refer to any bird in the order Passeriformes, the perching birds. Birds of all other orders are referred to as **non-passerines**.

- **PELAGIC**
Refers to birds that live mainly at sea, rarely coming to land.

- **PRECOCIAL**
Refers to birds whose chicks are hatched at an almost independent stage, feathered and with eyes open. Such chicks often leave the nest soon after hatching.

- **RACE**
Subgroup of a **species**. *See also* **Subspecies**.

- **RANGE**
The areas of the world where a **species** occurs.

- **RUFOUS**
Reddish brown.

- **SAVANNAH**
Grassy but usually treeless land in tropical and subtropical regions.

- **SCRAPE**
Shallow depression in the ground, scraped out to use as a nest.

- **SCRUB**
Area of stunted trees and bushes, often arid, usually in tropical or subtropical areas.

- **SECONDARY MARKS**
See **Underlying marks**.

- **SPECIES**
Group within a **genus**, the members of which share similar characteristics and can breed successfully together.

- **STONE**
Literally the color of a stone i.e. pale gray or light brown.

- **STEPPE**
Flat grassland without trees, especially in Europe and Siberia.

- **SUBSPECIES**
Subgroup of a **species**, usually geographically separated. Often used synonymously with **race**.

- **THORNVELD**
Field of thorny bushes.

- **TIMBER LINE**
Upper limit of trees on a mountain.

- **TUNDRA**
Flat Arctic region where no trees grow due to frozen subsoil.

- **TUBE NOSES**
Birds with nostrils in the form of a tube. This is a general term for birds of the order Procellariiformes.

- **UNDERLYING MARKS**
Pale or "veiled" markings that occur in addition to normal spotting on an eggshell. They are caused by the pigment of the spot being below the surface of the shell, so that their full color is obscured by overlying layers. Also known as **secondary marks**.

- **VIVIPAROUS**
Bringing forth live young. *See also* **Oviparous**.

INDEX

ACKNOWLEDGMENTS

Dorling Kindersley would like to thank The
Natural History Museum at Tring, Hertfordshire,
UK, for their cooperation in the photographing of
their collection; Colin Harrison for his invaluable
advice and Mark Robbins for his expert
authentication of the text; Michael Allaby for
compiling the index; Mike Darton for proofreading;
Alastair Wardle for DTP management; Caroline
Church for the endpapers; Neal Cobourne for the
book jacket design; Julia Pashley for picture research;
Lesley Malkin for editorial assistance; Colin Walton,
Chris Legee, Ann Thompson, Murdo Culver, and
Lemon Graphics for design assistance.

All special photography (t=top, c=center,
b=bottom, l=left, r=right) by Harry Taylor, except
for 13r, 18l, by Peter Chadwick.

All bird illustrations by Steve Ling of Linden
Artists Ltd., except 10c, 15l, 16c by Stuart Lafford.

The publishers would also like to thank the
following for their permission to reproduce the
photographs listed below: Bridgeman Art Library 6c,
8tl (Fine Line, Fine Art); Mary Evans Picture
Library 7cr; The Natural History Museum, London
8tr; Bruce Coleman 8br, 11tr, 12bl, 14c, 15r, 16b,
17bl, 18br, 19cl, 19tr; Frank Lane Picture Agency
11bl; Oxford Scientific Films 19bl (David Cayles).

Note on bird classification and sizing

The classification system was based on that used in
Michael Walters, *The Complete Birds of the World*
(David and Charles, 1980). This in turn was based
(with modifications) on J.L. Peters, *Checklist of Birds
of the World* (Harvard University Press, vols 1–6;
Museum of Comparative Zoology, vols 7–15;
1930–1986). Egg sizes are all from Max Schönwetter,
Handbuch der Oologie (Akademie-Verlag, issued in
parts, 1960–1988).

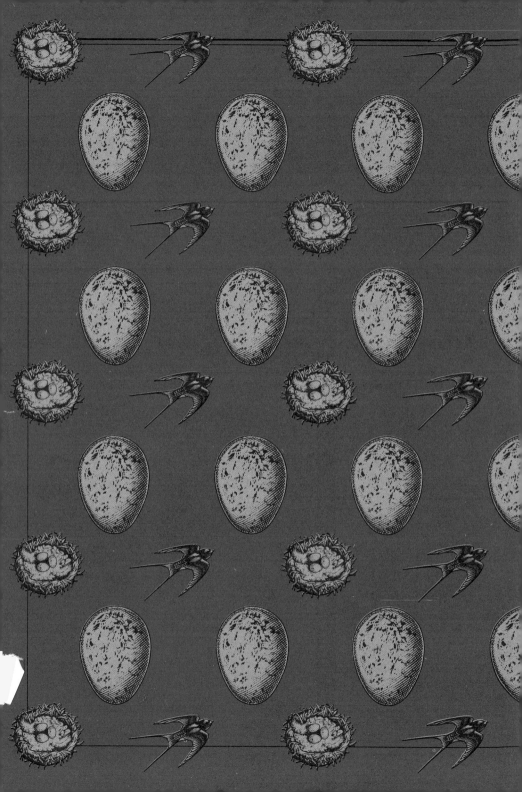